Y0-DNK-962

PUBLISHING POWER WITH VENTURA

The Complete Teaching Guide to Xerox Ventura Publisher

Martha Lubow and Jesse Berst

 New Riders Publishing
Thousand Oaks, California

PUBLISHING POWER WITH VENTURA
The Complete Teaching Guide to
Xerox Ventura Publisher

Martha Lubow and Jesse Berst

Published by:

New Riders Publishing
PO Box 4846
Thousand Oaks, CA 91360
U.S.A.

All rights reserved. No part of this book may be reproduced or transmitted in any form or by any means, electronic or mechanical, including photocopying, recording or by any information storage and retrieval system without written permission from the authors, except for the inclusion of brief quotations in a review.

Copyright © 1988 by Martha Lubow and Jesse Berst

First Edition 1988

Printed in the United States of America by Griffin Printing Company, Glendale California

Library of Congress Card Catalog Data

Lubow, Martha & Berst, Jesse
PUBLISHING POWER WITH VENTURA
The Complete Teaching Guide to Xerox Ventura Publisher
Library of Congress Card Catalog Number: 88-60084
ISBN 0-934035-19-9 Softcover

About the Authors

The writing team of Martha Lubow and Jesse Berst combines the experience of a leading technical educator with the expertise of a desktop publishing pioneer.

MARTHA LUBOW is one of the country's top trainers and author of the popular training guide *Working Out With AutoCAD*. She is Director of Educational Program Development for Lambda Systems, Blue Bell, PA, where she has established training programs in computer-aided design and publishing for Fortune 500 clients. A Stanford graduate, she has taught at the university level in association with Bucks County Community College and Temple University.

JESSE BERST was co-founder and Executive Editor of *MicroPublishing Report*, the nation's first desktop publishing newsletter. He has authored or co-authored seven books on desktop publishing and other computer topics, including the bestselling *Inside Xerox Ventura Publisher*. He has written hundreds of magazine articles for publications such as *PC World*, *Personal Publishing*, *Publishers Weekly*, *Small Press* and many others.

Martha and Jesse have produced thousands of pages — including books, manuals, brochures, newsletters, forms and many others — with Xerox Ventura Publisher.

Production

Director of Production: Carolyn Porter
Production Manager: Todd Meisler
Cover Design: Jill Casty
Page Design: Jesse Berst
Drawings and Illustrations: Martha Lubow, Todd Meisler, Melanie Powell
From a Concept by: Harbert Rice

Warning and Disclaimer

This book is designed to provide information about Xerox Ventura Publisher. Every effort has been made to make it as complete and as accurate as possible.

However, no warranty of suitability, purpose or fitness is made or implied. The authors and New Riders Publishing shall have neither liability nor responsibility to any person or entity with respect to loss or damages in connection with or arising from the information contained in this book.

If you do not agree with the above, you may return this book for a full refund.

Acknowledgments

The authors and New Riders Publishing wish to express their appreciation to those who helped with the creation of this book.

For review and comments: Michelle Polliard, John Meyer and Ventura Software, Ellen Brout, Oracle Corporation, Lainie Howard, Relational Technology, Richard Katz and the UCLA PC Users Group, Dorothy Kent, Lambda Systems, Ivy Strickler, Drexel University.

For software or hardware: Randi Doeker and Xerox Corporation, Annie Barfuss and Hill & Knowlton, AST Research, Autodesk, Inc., Digital Research, Executive Systems, Inc., MicroPro International, Microsoft Corporation, Sigma Designs, Symsoft, Verticom, ZSoft Corporation.

For permission to reprint the computer drawing from Chapter Five: Digital Research.

For their continued understanding and support: Lambda Systems, Blue Bell, PA: David B. Sharp, III, Janet Kiehart, Bill Stamp, Debra Neidig, Peter Huck, Jan Waldo, Sheryl DaCenzo, Pat Reis, Frank Lavin, Tim Lukens, Doug Schneider, Chip Willey and Steve Waldman.

Special thanks from Martha to Kathy Sharp and Jerry Waxler for their inspiration and support and to Oscar, Miriam and Nancy Lubow for their love and encouragement.

Special thanks from Jesse to Lori White for encouragement, assistance and understanding.

Trademarks

Ventura Publisher is a registered trademark of Ventura Software, Inc.
Xerox is a registered trademark of Xerox Corp.
IBM is a registered trademark of International Business Machines
Illustrator and PostScript are registered trademarks of Adobe Systems.
AutoCAD is a registered trademark of Autodesk, Inc.
WordStar is a registered trademark of MicroPro International Corp.
MS-DOS, Microsoft and Word are registered trademarks of Microsoft Corp.
LaserWriter is a registered trademark of Apple Computer, Inc.
Lotus 1-2-3 is a registered trademark of Lotus Development Corp.
PC Paintbrush is a registered trademark of Z-Soft, Inc.

Table of Contents

Chapter Five

An Advertising Flyer 5-1

Chapter Six

A Three-Column Newsletter 6-1

Becoming a Power Publisher

Please don't skip this introduction. Yes, we know that many authors use the introduction just to say hello. Many readers, therefore, skip to Chapter One so they can get right to business.

This particular introduction, however, has several crucial functions. First, it explains the most productive, efficient way to use *Publishing Power with Ventura*. Second, it explains how to prepare your computer system to work along with the sample projects. Third, it contains a key formula you will use over and over again. *The Ventura Formula explained at the end of this introduction is the foundation for the rest of the book.*

Goals and Objectives

Publishing Power with Ventura will help you tap the full potential of Xerox Ventura Publisher.

It's no secret that Ventura has more horsepower than ordinary page layout programs. Ventura can create virtually any type of document, from one-page ads to 500-page directories and anything in between. Yet with all that power, some users complain. They feel like beginning drivers who haven't learned to shift into high gear. They can get Ventura up and running, they can point it in the right general direction, but they can't seem to fine-tune its performance for maximum productivity.

This book will move you into the fast lane. Best of all, it will show you how to stay in control the whole time. You will know where to start and where to go next, no matter what kind of document you are preparing. In short, you will always be in the driver's seat.

How do we plan to accomplish these goals? First, we will put you behind the wheel right from the start. In every chapter, you will "test drive" Ventura by creating an actual business document. There's no better way to acquire skills than with hands-on practice. Second, you will start with simple documents before moving on to difficult ones. For example, Part One teaches fundamentals. You can follow along even if you're new to Ventura. Part Two, on the other hand, shows how to rev up your publishing with advanced techniques.

Don't be too impatient. Ventura Publisher is one of the most powerful applications ever written for the IBM PC. It will take some time before you reach expert status. To make the journey easier, we start each project with a roadmap: A before- and-after look at the document. As we proceed, we provide signposts to check your progress. Simply check your results against the sample screens and printouts. You'll always know if you're on the right track.

Why This Book Is Different

Publishing Power with Ventura differs from other books and tutorials. First, it is not just a beginner's session. It is a complete training course, from novice to advanced. Second, it takes you step-by-step through real-life applications. If you complete all the chapters, you will have a personal library of industrial-strength business documents and style sheets. You will also have the skills to modify those documents to fit the unique requirements of your business. Third, *Publishing Power* provides more than how-to skills. It also teaches you strategies, systems and formulas for working through design problems.

We believe that if you follow the examples in this book, you will be able to gain full control over Ventura's amazing capabilities. You will be able to create virtually any kind of document — books, ads, newsletters, manuals, reports — right on your desktop.

Now that's true publishing power.

How to Use This Book

Publishing Power with Ventura contains two sections. Part One, Getting Started, teaches basic skills. Part Two, Advanced Documents, teaches advanced techniques as they apply to specific business applications. We recommend that everyone complete Part One (Chapters One, Two and Three). Even experienced Ventura users should skim this first section, because it does more than clarify basic features. *Part One also provides a systematic plan for using Ventura.* The advanced chapters in Part Two assume that you understand the building blocks explained up front.

How to Use Part Two

Although Part One is essential, not everyone needs to go through all of Part Two. The method you use for the second half will depend on your needs. If you are an occasional user, produce only one type of document, or are short on time, select chapters that teach the skills you need right now. If you later expand to different documents, return to Part Two to learn more. A nearby table suggests an abbreviated curriculum based on the type of document you produce.

On the other hand, if you plan to use Ventura for many different documents, try to finish Part Two from start to finish. Completing all nine chapters guarantees that you will understand Ventura's full range of features.

Note to Instructors

If you are using *Publishing Power* for classroom instruction, you will want to know that each chapter has one or more suggested stopping points. If you have time for extended sessions, ignore them and proceed straight through. However, if you

An Abbreviated Curriculum

Document	Chapters to Study	Key Skills
Books	Part One	Basic skills
	Chapter Four — An Invoice	Box text
	Chapter Eight — A Book	Multi-chapter, footnotes, indexing, chapter templates
	Chapter Nine — A Technical Manual	Frames and anchoring, auto-numbering, figure numbering
Corporate Documents	Part One	Basic skills
Directories, Catalogs	Part One	Basic skills
	Chapter Four — An Invoice	Box text
	Chapter Seven — A Directory	Preformatting, databases and Ventura, chapter templates
	Chapter Eight — A Book	Multi-chapter, footnotes, indexing, chapter templates
	Chapter Nine — A Technical Manual	Frames and anchoring, auto-numbering, figure numbering
Marketing	Part One	Basic skills
	Chapter Four — An Invoice	Box text
	Chapter Five — An Advertising Flyer	Advanced graphics and typography
Newsletters, Magazines	Part One	Basic skills
	Chapter Four — An Invoice	Box text
	Chapter Five — An Advertising Flyer	Advanced graphics and typography
	Chapter Six — A Three-Column Newsletter	Advanced newsletter-style layout, captions
Tech Doc	Part One	Basic skills
	Chapter Four — An Invoice	Box text
	Chapter Eight — A Book	Multi-chapter, footnotes, indexing, chapter templates
	Chapter Nine — A Technical Manual	Frames and anchoring, auto-numbering, figure numbering

An abbreviated curriculum for those short on time. For best long-term results, study the entire book.

want to pause periodically, you will find clearly marked break points, with instructions on how to stop and how to resume.

Instructors may also want to assign advance reading before the classroom sessions. We suggest that students prepare by reading the theory section at the beginning and skimming the tips section at the end.

A final tip for instructors: If you want to focus on certain techniques, you can confine the classroom session to one portion of a chapter. Step through the project yourself up to the point at which you wish to begin. Save your work and distribute this partially completed chapter to students on floppy disks (or via network). Have the students load up the partially completed project at the beginning of the session. That way you and they can concentrate only on the specific skill you wish to present.

The Ground Rules

While we are explaining how to use this book, we should acquaint you with a few ground rules. The checklist that follows spells out five conditions. These are the assumptions that operate during the self-paced publishing projects. Before starting with Chapter One, make sure that your system matches all five.

WARNING: You may have difficulty recreating the examples if you do not meet the assumptions explained below.

1. You are using Ventura 1.1 or higher. The examples in this book use Ventura 1.1 features. The sample style sheets on the accompanying Publishing Power software disk will not work with version 1.0. Contact your local dealer or Xerox for upgrade information if you are working with the older version.

2. Ventura is located on disk C:. If you use a different letter for the hard disk containing Ventura, substitute that letter whenever you see C:. Consider, for example, an exercise that asks you to move to the C:\POWER subdirectory. If your hard disk was D:, you would type D:\POWER instead.

3. You have the original Ventura style sheets intact on the C:\TYPESET subdirectory. If you have moved these style sheets or if you have modified them in any way, copy the originals from disk #2 of the Ventura installation disks. The command "COPY A:&*.STY C:\TYPESET" will copy everything you will need for this book.

4. You have a Hercules-compatible graphics adapter. The sample screens in this book were created from a monitor in Hercules mode. If you have an EGA, a CGA or a big-screen monitor instead, your display may look slightly different than the illustrations. This should not affect your ability to follow along.

5. (Optional) You have installed PostScript as one of your printer choices. Although you can follow along without installing PostScript, a few of your dialog boxes will look slightly different from the examples. You may want to switch to PostScript during the on-screen exercises (use Set Printer Info from the options menu). You can quickly and easily install PostScript as a printer choice even if you do not own a PostScript printer and even if you have already installed Ventura 1.1. Simply reinstall the program. When it asks if this is the first time you are installing, answer No. Then add PostScript as one of your printer choices.

The Ventura Formula

One important task remains before we are ready for Chapter One: a brief explanation of the strategy that forms the foundation for this book. Every Ventura document, no matter how complex, is made up of just three parts: *text* (the words), a *style sheet* (the format), and *pictures* (the illustrations). Typically the text comes from word processing files and the pictures from graphics files, while the style sheets are created with Ventura Publisher. This formula helps explain how the software operates. It also becomes the perfect model for working with Ventura Publisher:

Text + Style + Pictures = Chapter

This formula illustrates not only the components, but also *the best order for building a document*. As we will show you, this simple idea is a powerful tool. It can serve as a blueprint for any document, long or short. The nearby illustration gives simplified look at the typical workflow.

TEXT	Load the text file(s)
+	
STYLE	Load a style sheet Apply it to the text file
+	
PICTURES	Create the frame(s) for the picture(s) Load the graphics file(s) into the frame(s)
=	
CHAPTER	Save the chapter Print the chapter

The Ventura Formula provides a blueprint for any document.

As Ventura authors and consultants, we've talked with hundreds of users. Most have similar troubles. When confronted with the complexities of page design and the power of Ventura, they don't know where to start. They flounder because they don't have a systematic approach. When they do get underway, they get lost among the menus. Or they forget key steps and have to redo the document. In short, they're often a bit confused.

It doesn't have to be that way. As you will see, the Ventura Formula can rescue you from confusion. No matter how complex the project, you can always use it as a guide. As you grow proficient, you may decide to modify the Formula or abandon it entirely. As you are learning, however, it should be the foundation for everything you do. We have used it throughout this book.

Rather than belabor the theory, let's see it in practice by using the Formula to prepare a business report. Turn to Chapter One for your first hands-on Ventura project.

Part One

Getting Started

Chapter One
Skills Checklist

Theory

✓ How Ventura manages files

✓ Renaming and relocating files

Text

✓ Loading and placing text

Style

✓ Easy rules for faster formatting

✓ The secret of the "Big Three" dialog boxes

✓ Why you should always start with body text

✓ A standard spacing unit

Picture

✓ Loading and placing a picture

Chapter

✓ Saving and printing

✓ The right way to back up Ventura chapters

A Single-Column Report

Ready to start putting Ventura through its paces? This first chapter provides a solid grounding in Ventura fundamentals. It also demonstrates how the Formula guides you step-by-step through a work session. The checklist to the left summarizes some of the skills you will acquire. You'll find a similar list in every chapter.

Before You Start

A few preliminaries before we begin. All the projects in this book start with a before-and-after look at the document. They also include a few remarks about its intended audience. In other words, we start by showing you *where* you are going and *why*. Then it's on to the sample project. In most cases, you can produce the results just by imitating the screens on the page. For instance, when you see an explanation followed by an illustration, simply make your dialog box match the one in the book.

That's all there is to it. Merely by following along, you will learn to handle Ventura like a pro.

Theory

We know you are eager to get started. Before you get behind the controls, however, you need to understand a few fundamentals. The hands-on practice will make more sense if you understand how Ventura manages files.

The Parts of a Chapter

Most other programs do all their work in one large file. By contrast, Ventura works with many different files. A master file, called the *chapter file*, stores *pointers* to other files, plus instructions on how to assemble these files onto the page. When you format on screen or print on paper, the chapter uses its pointers to find the files it needs, and then uses its instructions to put the document together.

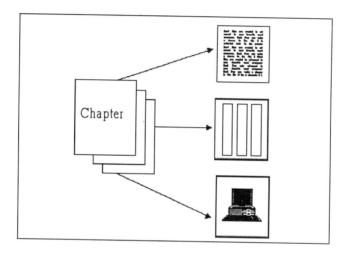

What kinds of files go into a document? The Ventura Formula provides the answer:

Text + Style + Pictures = Chapter

As Ventura builds a document, it creates additional files on its own if it needs them. For instance, if you put captions on the page, Ventura creates a separate caption file. If you use the drawing tools, Ventura opens a graphics file. When it opens these files, Ventura uses the same name as the chapter, but with a different extension. Thus, if the chapter is called SAMPLE.CHP, the caption file becomes SAMPLE.CAP and the graphics file SAMPLE.VGR. The nearby table gives a more in-depth look at the components of a typical Ventura chapter.

Renaming and Relocating Files

One more bit of theory about Ventura's file management and

FILE TYPE	TYPICAL NAME(S)	CONTENTS OF THE FILE
Text	TEXT.TXT	Text file created with word processor and imported into Ventura (can be more than one)
	SAMPLE.CAP	Caption file created and named by Ventura to match the chapter name
Style	SAMPLE.STY	Style sheet. Can be named anything you want as long as it has the .STY extension
Picture	PICTURE.IMG	Picture file created with outside graphics program and imported into Ventura (can be more than one)
	SAMPLE.VGR	Graphics file created and named by Ventura to match the chapter name
Chapter (Program)	SAMPLE.CHP	Chapter File containing pointers to all the other files
	SAMPLE.CIF	Special program file containing information about the status of the document. Created and named by Ventura to match the chapter name

A chapter called SAMPLE.CHP might have file names and extensions like these. Some files are created and named by the user. Others are generated and named automatically by Ventura.

you will be ready to start the project. Ventura permits you to rename and/or relocate most of the files that make up a chapter. Ventura doesn't care where you store those files, as long as you tell it where to find them.

In Ventura's eyes, the location of a file is part of its name. The four files below *are completely different* as far as Ventura is concerned:

```
A:SAMPLE.TXT
C:SAMPLE.TXT
C:\TEMP\SAMPLE.TXT
C:\POWER\SAMPLE.TXT
```

Renaming and relocating are accomplished in the same fashion (in fact, we use the word rename to mean either function). Although the procedure is slightly different for different files, the principle is the same. By entering a new name and/or a new location in a dialog box, you tell Ventura where to find it in the future.

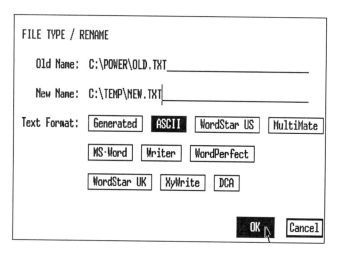

When you rename/relocate a file inside Ventura, you accomplish two things:

- You make a copy of the file under the new name at the new location (you will have to delete the old one if you don't want it anymore)

- You change the pointers in the chapter file. From then on, Ventura looks for that file under the new name in the new location

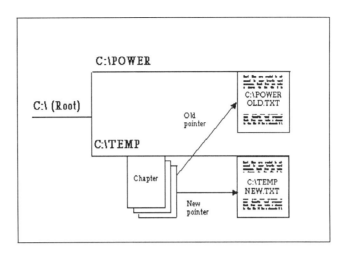

WARNING: Do not use standard DOS functions to move Ventura chapters. Use Ventura's Multi-Chapter function instead, as taught at the end of this chapter.

DOS copies files, but it does not change the pointers inside the chapter file. If you reopen the chapter at the new location, Ventura will be unable to reassemble the document. It will look for the files in their old locations, because the pointers were never changed.

By contrast, Ventura's built-in copying function not only moves the files, but changes the pointers as well. In addition, it moves all the files at once. By telling Ventura to copy a chapter, you are telling it to copy not only the chapter file, but also every other file associated with that chapter. You do not have to specify the individual files. Ventura remembers them for you, finds them on the disk and copies them to their new location. At the same time, it changes the pointers to these new locations. This copying function is located in the Multi-Chapter dialog box.

➡ *TIP: Even though the name Multi-Chapter implies that it is intended only for multiple chapters, you can also use Multi-Chapter to copy a single chapter. You will have several opportunities for hands-on practice with Multi-Chapter in both Part One and Part Two.*

So much for your first exposure to the principles behind Ventura Publisher. You will need to learn additional theory before you're ready to strike out on your own. In the meantime, however, we suggest concentrating on the project that follows without worrying too much about the wherefores and whys. We will present more fundamentals in Chapters Two and Three.

Before

Report on Installation and Implementation of Ventura Publisher

Executive Summary

XYZ Corporation has embarked on a program to implement Ventura Publisher software on existing IBM AT-compatible computers as needed throughout the company. The Marketing Communications department will oversee and supervise this project. Marketing Communications makes the following recommendations:

* Use of Ventura in every department for all publishing/communications tasks
* Designation of an in-house desktop publishing specialist with responsibility for training, maintenance and standards
* A company-wide training program to teach basic Ventura skills
* Advanced workshops as needed to teach specialized skills

Use of Ventura Company-Wide

The three-month pilot program undertaken by Marketing Communications has determined that Ventura Publisher can be used for every type of document currently produced by the company. Company-wide use of Ventura will reduce publishing/printing costs by 35% over the next two years (see chart next page). It will reduce the confusion and duplication of effort now in evidence, whereby every department had developed different (and often incompatible) solutions to publishing problems. It will also permit the company to establish and enforce appearance and image standards. Since Ventura Publisher uses style sheets to store formatting information, the company can create a library of approved designs and code them into style sheets. Every document produced with these style sheets will automatically meet minimum standards for graphic design and quality; and all documents seen by the public will reinforce the same image.

We have indentified potential uses in five departments; more will be developed as users become more proficient with Ventura and discover new applications.

After

Report on Installation and Implementation of Ventura Publisher

Executive Summary

XYZ Corporation has embarked on a program to implement Ventura Publisher software on existing IBM AT-compatible computers as needed throughout the company. The Marketing Communications department will oversee and supervise this project. Marketing Communications makes the following recommendations:

- Use of Ventura in every department for all publishing/communications tasks
- Designation of an in-house desktop publishing specialist with responsibility for training, maintenance and standards
- A company-wide training program to teach basic Ventura skills
- Advanced workshops as needed to teach specialized skills

Use of Ventura Company-Wide

The three-month pilot program undertaken by Marketing Communications has determined that Ventura Publisher can be used for every type of document currently produced by the company. Company-wide use of Ventura will reduce publishing/printing costs by 35% over the next two years (see chart next page). It will reduce the confusion and duplication of effort now in evidence, whereby every department had developed different (and often incompatible) solutions to publishing problems. It will also permit the company to estab-

Planning a Single-Column Report

The first step in producing a business document is to consider its purpose and audience. Your goal is two-fold: (1) to make the appearance appropriate to the readership and (2) to make the document easier and more efficient to use. Ventura's vast array of capabilities can help you achieve both goals.

Our first project is a business report. We use the word "report" to refer to a simple, straightforward document, usually intended for internal use (as opposed to proposals and annual reports, which often go outside the company). Target readers are other members of the same company, usually at your own level or higher. Since reports often summarize difficult or dull information, they must use page design to make that information easily accessible. They should include charts, graphs and other illustrations when possible, to help get the message across.

Because a report is an internal document, it does not demand high-end, cutting-edge graphic effects. At the same time, since most reports go up the ladder to management, they need a professional image: clean, simple and uncluttered without being loud or flashy. Look at the *before* example nearby. It is a typical report from the days before desktop publishing. Here are a few ways to enhance its effectiveness and appearance:

- An easy-to-read line length
- Bullets to make lists stand out
- A header and page numbers to help readers find their way around
- Prominent headlines and subheads
- Spacing based on a uniform, standard unit
- Additional white space for an open look

Let's implement these ideas. You will begin by preparing for work.

Before You Start

We assume that you are sitting in front of your computer with Ventura Publisher on the screen. If you are using the optional Power disk, you should have previously copied its files to a subdirectory called \POWER (as explained in the instructions with the disk and in Appendix C).

➡ NOTE: If you do not have the optional disk, you may order it by mail or phone from the card at the back of the book. Rush delivery is available.

Choose New from the File menu if there is a previous document active. Don't worry about what shows in the title bar at first. We will be changing the title bar anyway, by loading a new style sheet and renaming the chapter. Your screen should look similar to the illustration below. If it does not, go to the View menu and select Reduced View. If you are new to Ventura, take a moment to familiarize yourself with the key features of the Ventura interface as shown in the following illustration.

Title Bar

Function
Selector

Addition
Button

Assignment
List

Current
Selection Box

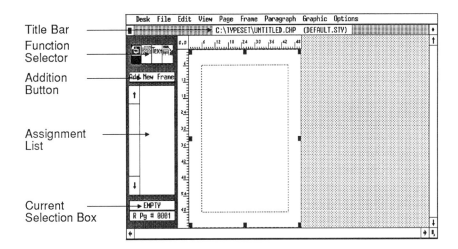

Our Starting Configuration

Ventura Publisher is easier to work with if you use the Options menu to make the selections shown in the adjacent table. There's nothing that says you can't configure Ventura dif-

OPTION	SETTING	WHAT IT DOES
Set Preferences	Generated Tags: Shown	Displays tags created by Ventura at the bottom of the assignment list
	Text to Greek: 6	Speeds screen redraw by showing un-readably small text as blocks
	On-Screen Kerning: None	Speeds screen redraw by eliminating screen kerning
	Auto-Adjust Styles: No	Does not adjust inter-line spacing when you change the font
Set Printer Info	Device Name: PostScript	(Optional) Can be used even if you don't have a PostScript printer so font dialog boxes match those in the book. PostScript printer must be installed
Set Ruler	Horizontal and Vertical Units: Picas	Displays ruler in same units this book uses for its other measurements
Show Rulers		Displays rulers on top and left side of page
Show Column Guides		Displays lines to show the boundaries of the columns. Makes it easier to line up new frames
Show Tabs & Returns		Visible marks in the text denoting tabs, returns, line breaks, footnotes, etc. Makes text editing easier
Turn Column Snap On	Set toggle so column snap is on	Aligns frames with the edges of the column
Turn Line Snap On	Set toggle so line snap is on	Aligns frames vertically with the line spacing of body text

You may find it easier to follow along if you use the Options menu to match these settings

ferently. However, our experience has shown that these settings make page design easier and more accurate. If you cannot duplicate the results in the exercises, check to see that you
are configured as shown here.

Step One — File Maintenance

If you don't tell Ventura where to put a file, it defaults to the
location used last. The original default location is the
C:\TYPESET subdirectory. Many beginners continue to store
all their files in that one single directory. It soon becomes too
crowded.

If you installed the optional Power disk for this book, you
created a subdirectory called C:\POWER. This subdirectory
stores sample documents and style sheets. As part of this first
project, you will create a subdirectory to store the results of
your work. From now on, you will always place your documents into this new subdirectory. Although you can create
subdirectories in DOS, you can also do so within Ventura. Let's
try it right now. Follow the step-by-step instructions below at
your computer to create a subdirectory called C:\TEMP.

■ Select DOS File Ops from the File menu.

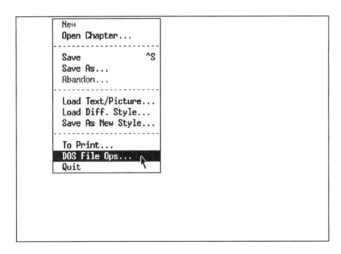

■ Move to the File Spec line and press Esc to clear the line.
  Then type: **C:\TEMP**

■ Choose Make Subdirectory and Done.

```
┌──────────────────────────────────────────────────────────┐
│ DOS FILE OPERATIONS                                        │
│                                                            │
│ File Spec:  C:\TEMP│_____       │
│                                                            │
│ Operation:  ┌──────────────────────────────────────┐      │
│             │ Select Different File Specification  │      │
│             └──────────────────────────────────────┘      │
│             ┌──────────────┐ ┌──────────────────┐         │
│             │ Make Directory│ │ Remove Directory │        │
│             └──────────────┘ └──────────────────┘         │
│             ┌─────────────────────────┐                   │
│             │ Delete Matching File(s) │                   │
│             └─────────────────────────┘                   │
│                                                            │
│                                                            │
│                                                            │
│                                          ┌──────┐          │
│                                          │ Done │          │
│                                          └──────┘          │
└──────────────────────────────────────────────────────────┘
```

If you already have a C:\TEMP subdirectory, choose another
name. In future chapters, substitute that name whenever you
see C:\TEMP.

➥ *TIP: The best way to organize the hard disk is to create a
separate subdirectory for each project, and use it to store all
the files for that project — text, style, picture and chapter.*

Advanced users take this organizational idea one step further
and create multiple subdirectories to manage large projects.

Ventura Prep

File management is one of the most difficult aspects of desktop
publishing. Novice users sometimes encounter problems:

- They can't find files when it comes time to load them into
  Ventura

- They use DOS copy improperly and cannot get the chapter
  to load

- They destroy new versions by copying the old one on top

- They forget to save and thereby lose their work

To avoid such problems, you will start every project with a
Ventura Prep section. You will load, rename, relocate, and save

all the files for the exercise *before* you begin working. Although this file maintenance may seem a bit confusing at first, we hope it will soon become a habit.

By taking these steps at the beginning of every document, you can avoid losing work. In addition, you can easily take a break. Since all the files you will need are already loaded and renamed, all you have to do is save the chapter and quit. When you are ready to resume, load Ventura, open the chapter and start where you left off.

WARNING: Renaming and relocating files does not take effect until you save the chapter. If you quit without saving you lose the benefit of the Ventura Prep process.

We will step through the prep section in the same order as the Ventura Formula: text, style, pictures, chapter. If you are used to working with DOS, it may take you a few times through before you are comfortable with Ventura's methods. Although you can often type in paths and file names, as in DOS, it is usually faster to navigate with the mouse.

We will walk you through the Ventura Prep process the first few times until it becomes second nature. It may seem lengthy at first, but with experience you can perform the entire process in a few moments.

Load a Text File

When you load text, Ventura retrieves the original word processing file. It does not make a separate copy. It temporarily hyphenates this file, then makes it a permanent part of the chapter by storing a pointer. This pointer tells Ventura where to find the file in the future.

Follow the steps outlined below to load, place and rename a text file called 1RPRT.TXT. This text file is provided on the optional Power disk. If you did not purchase the disk, skip to the section below titled "If You Do Not have the Power Disk."

■ Select Load Text/Picture from the File menu.

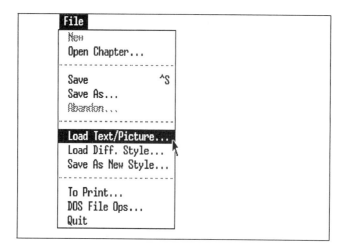

■ Choose Type of File: Text, Text Format: ASCII, # of Files: One and OK.

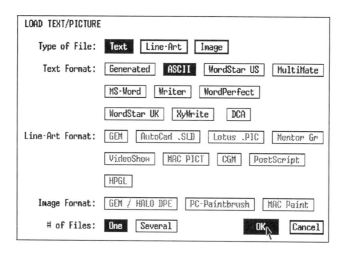

The Item Selector dialog box appears. Its listing shows both file names and subdirectories. Subdirectories are distinguished by a diamond in front of the name.

In the next section, you will begin to learn to move around the hard disk with the mouse. To move "backward," you click on the backup button. To move "forward" to a given subdirectory, click on the diamond that precedes its name.

Directory Line ———→

Backup Button ———→

Subdirectory
Name

File Name ———→

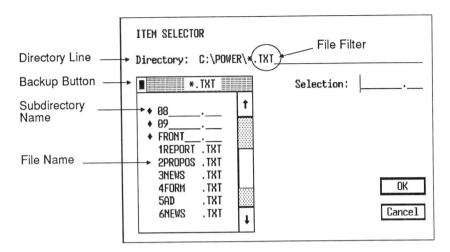

To move to a new subdirectory, click on its name:

■ Click on the backup button and diamonds until the
C:\POWER subdirectory is displayed on the Directory line.

■ Scroll through the list until you see 1RPRT.TXT.

Click on the scroll arrows to move a few lines at a time. Click
on the gray area to move one screen at a time. To move a distance you select, drag the scroll box in the direction you want
to move.

■ Select the file 1RPRT.TXT by double-clicking on the name,
or by clicking once on 1RPRT.TXT and once on OK.

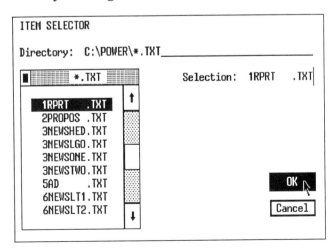

➡*NOTE: Once you click on a file, the name appears on the
Selection line. You can also select a text file by typing the name
directly onto the Selection line and clicking OK.*

Ventura loads the file and the name 1RPRT.TXT appears on
the Assignment list. (It may or may not appear on the Underlying Page.)

If You Do Not Have the Power Disk

Exit Ventura and load a word processor. Type the text
1RPRT.TXT from Appendix A and save it under the name and
location C:\POWER\1RPRT.TXT. Return to Ventura and follow the steps above for loading the text file.

Place the Text File

After you load a text file you must place it — that is, tell Ventura where you want it to appear. You can place text onto the
underlying page, or into separate frames that reside on top of
the page. For this business report, you will place the text onto
the underlying page.

Select the Underlying Page

- Click on the Frame button in the function selector.

- Place the cursor anywhere on the workspace and click once.

Notice the eight black handles around the border of the page.
They show you what has been selected and where Ventura is
going to place the text.

- Click once on 1RPRT.TXT in the Assignment List to place
  the file onto the page.

The text fills the underlying page.

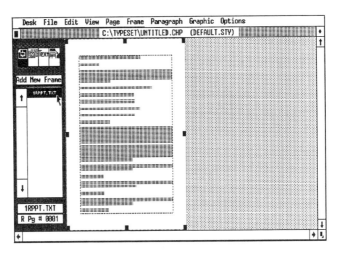

Don't worry if your screen differs slightly from the example shown here. You may have started the exercise with something other than the DEFAULT.STY style sheet. That other style sheet may have different margins and columns. You will soon load a different style sheet.

➡ *NOTE: Ventura may have already put the file on the page without your intervention. If you select an empty frame or a page before loading a single file, Ventura assumes that you want the file in that location, and places it without being asked.*

Because you placed the file on an underlying page, Ventura continues to make new pages until the entire file is placed. If you were to press the PgDn key to move ahead in the document, you would find the additional pages already created.

➡ *NOTE: Chapter Three gives further details about frames and the underlying page.*

Rename the Text File

Once the file is on the underlying page you can change its name and/or its location. When you make changes to text they are reflected back to the original file. If you do not want the original to be permanently modified, you must rename it before you save the chapter.

■ In frame setting mode, click on the underlying page.

The current text file name is displayed in the Current Selection Box.

■ Select File Type/Rename from the Edit menu.

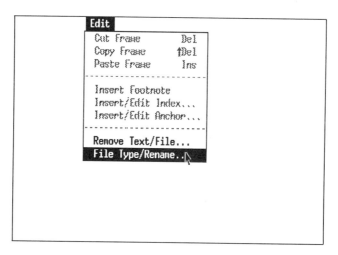

■ Move to the New Name line and press Esc to clear the line. Then type in the new location and name: **C:\TEMP\1REPORT.TXT**

■ Click on ASCII and OK.

If you prefer, you can save the file in your favorite word processing format instead. Follow the steps above and click on the format you want rather than ASCII.

Load a Style Sheet

To continue Ventura Prep, you will load one of the original style sheets included with the Ventura software package.

WARNING: If you have moved or changed the style sheets in any way since buying Ventura, reload the originals as explained in the Introduction to this book.

■ Select Load Diff. Style from the File menu.

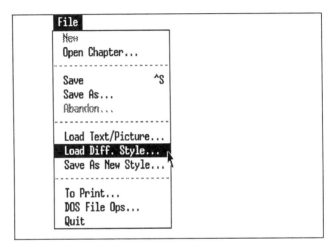

■ Move to the C:\TYPESET subdirectory. Select the style sheet &PRPT-P1.STY.

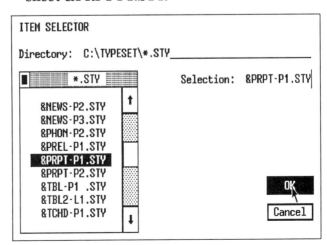

If you cannot find the style sheet, check that you are in the correct subdirectory. Scroll down the listing until &PRPT-P1.STY appears.

➥*REMEMBER: You can move from subdirectory to subdirectory either by clicking on the backup button and the diamonds, or by typing the destination onto the directory line and clicking OK.*

Rename the Style Sheet

If you save a chapter without renaming the style sheet, you will permanently change the original. It's better to leave the original intact for future use, and rename the new version.

■ Select Save as New Style from the File menu.

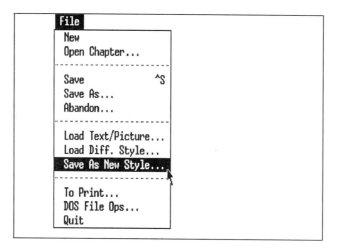

```
File
 New
 Open Chapter...
 ......................
 Save              ^S
 Save As...
 Abandon...
 ......................
 Load Text/Picture...
 Load Diff. Style...
 Save As New Style...
 ......................
 To Print...
 DOS File Ops...
 Quit
```

■ Move to the Directory line, press Esc and type: **C:\TEMP*.STY** and press Enter.

The Item Selector searches the new subdirectory for files with the .STY extension. Since you haven't put any here yet, the list is blank.

■ Move to the Selection line and type: **1REPORT** and Click OK. Ventura stores the style sheet as C:\TEMP\1REPORT.STY.

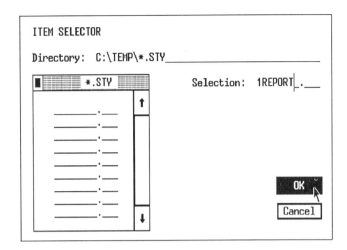

➡ *TIP: Ventura automatically assigns a .STY extension to style sheets and .CHP extensions to chapter files. You do not need to type them in.*

Load a Picture File

Loading pictures is very similar to loading text. In fact, you use the same option from the File menu: Load Text/Picture. As with text, you first load the file onto the Assignment List and then place it where you want it.

■ Select "Load Text/Picture" from the File menu.

■ Select Line Art, GEM, One, and OK.

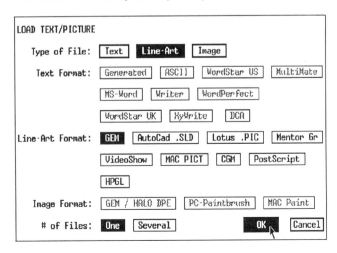

Ventura displays the Item Selector, which you will use to choose a picture file to load.

- Click the backup button until the C:\TYPESET subdirectory shows on the list (preceded by a diamond). Click once on the diamond to move to that subdirectory.

- Click the down arrow or scroll bar until you see NOZZLE.GEM.

- Select NOZZLE.GEM.

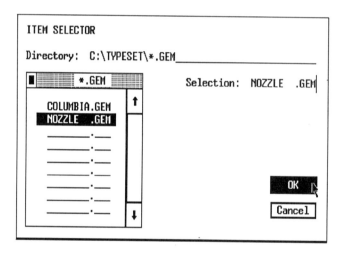

Ventura loads the file. The name NOZZLE.GEM appears on the Assignment List. Do not place the picture for the moment. Later in this chapter you will draw a frame and place this picture inside it.

➡NOTE: Although you can rename text files and style sheets with Ventura, you cannot rename picture files.

Save the Chapter

When you save a chapter for the first time, use Save As from the File menu to specify the new name and location.

■ Select Save As from the File menu.

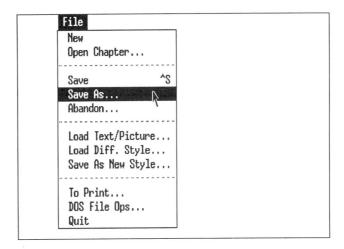

■ Move the cursor to the Directory line and press Esc. Type in the new location: **C:\TEMP*.CHP**

■ Move to the selection line and type in the name: **1REPORT** and click OK.

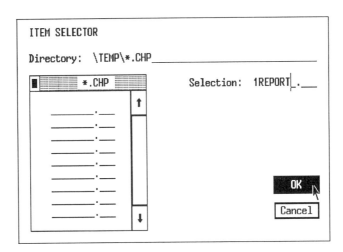

➥*NOTE: If you lose a chapter through a computer malfunction, you may be able to restore it from the back up files.*

Ventura maintains backups of all key files, provided you choose Keep Backup Files: Yes from the Set Preferences dialog box. Ventura renames all the files with a $ extension. Thus the backup for SAMPLE.CHP is SAMPLE.$HP and so on.

The backups represent the files as they were the last time you saved the chapter. To restore the backups, you must return to DOS. Delete all the original files. Then rename the backups to their original names. Thus, you would rename SAMPLE.$HP to SAMPLE.CHP. SAMPLE.$TY would become SAMPLE.STY, etc. Be sure to include any and all chapter files, including .CHP, .STY, .VGR, .CAP and .CIF files.

In the next section, you will have a chance to stop and shut down the computer if you do not have time to continue. To restart, load Ventura and open the sample chapter, C:\TEMP\1REPORT.CHP.

If you have the time, you should simply go straight to the next section without stopping.

STOPPING POINT

You have reached the first of our recommended breaking points for Chapter One. Before you do anything else, save what you have done so far.

■ Press Ctrl-S (or select Save from the File menu).

Even if you plan to continue on without stopping, we recommend that you save your work to prevent loss in the event of a power surge or computer malfunction.

What to Do if You Make a Mistake

If you've never made a mistake and don't ever plan to, you can skip this next section. Otherwise, you may want to know what to do in the event of a major error. If you goof and can't recover, you can always choose Abandon from the File menu. Abandon reverts to the previous version — that is, it goes back to where you were the last time you saved the file.

For this reason, you may want to save fairly often. If you make a serious mistake, it may be simpler just to go back to the previous version with the Abandon option.

Text

Even though you haven't yet started to work on the actual document, you have already acquired a collection of valuable Ventura skills. Most Ventura users learn about file maintenance the hard way — by accidentally destroying or losing some of their work. The Ventura Prep section you just completed is the key to avoiding such disasters.

Now we are going to step through the construction of the sample document. In case you don't have time to finish the entire project in one session, we will suggest a stopping point about halfway through.

The normal progression through a Ventura document follows the Formula: Text + Style + Pictures = Chapter. You already have a head start on the text portion, since you loaded and placed a text file during Ventura Prep. Normally you would do some text editing at this stage. However, to prevent this first project from dragging on too long, we will postpone teaching you about text editing until the next chapter. Instead, you will take a quick look at moving around and viewing the page.

Moving Around the Document

Before proceeding to the style section of this sample project, take a moment to practice getting around. To move a few lines at a time, click on the arrows at the ends of the scroll bars at the far right of the screen. To move one screen at a time, click on the gray area. To move a distance you determine, drag the scroll bar (click and move while holding the mouse button down).

To move to the next page, use PgDn (on the numeric keypad). Use PgUp to move to the previous page. Press Home to move to the first page of a chapter and End to move to the last.

Viewing the Document

Ventura provides four views of the page. You will experiment with three of them in this exercise.

- Use the View Menu to cycle between Enlarged, Normal and Reduced views.

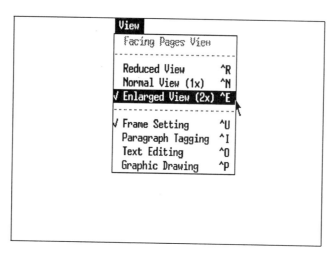

You can also use keyboard shortcuts to cycle between different views. Press Ctrl-E, Ctrl-N, and Ctrl-R to change from enlarged to normal to reduced view.

Style

In accordance with the Formula (Text + Style + Pictures = Chapter), the next section is concerned with style. More specifically, you will load an existing style sheet and modify some of its tags.

A style sheet contains formatting rules. Some apply to the overall page — margins, columns, vertical rules, and so forth. Others, called tags, apply to individual text elements. Style sheets are the key to Ventura's power. In fact, they are so powerful and so sophisticated they can intimidate a beginning user. Ventura has so many options you may have trouble knowing where to begin or remembering where you've been already. Fortunately, there several easy ways to make sense of style sheets.

Rules of Thumb

Three rules of thumb can help keep you from becoming disorganized and forgetting important steps.

➡ *TIP: Concentrate on three key menus during the style phase: Page, Frame and Paragraph.*

➡ *TIP: Format the overall page before the individual text paragraphs.*

➡ *TIP: Work from left to right and from top to bottom in the menus.*

These three suggestions are guidelines only. You will find occasional exceptions. Nevertheless, they work well together. Most overall (global) formatting occurs in the Page and Frame menus. Most of the individual text formatting occurs in the Paragraph menu. Thus, if you move from left to right (Page, frame, and paragraph), you automatically perform global functions first.

When we say to work from top to bottom, we do not mean that you must open each and every dialog box. In the very beginning you may indeed want to do so, as a way of learning your way around. As you grow more accomplished, you'll soon know which options to ignore. But even if you skip options along the way, it's best to work from top to bottom. If you work randomly you're likely to overlook something important.

You will follow these rules of thumb while in the style section of this first document. You will concentrate on the Page, Frame and Paragraph menus. You will start with the global layout, the design choices that affect the entire chapter — margins, columns, headers, footers and so on. These layout decisions are applied to the underlying page and therefore to all the pages of the chapter.

Begin with the first option in the Page menu.

Open the Page Layout Dialog Box

- Select Page Layout from the Page menu.
- Choose Portrait, Letter, Single Sides, Start On: Right Side, and Kerning: Globally On. Click OK to close the dialog box.

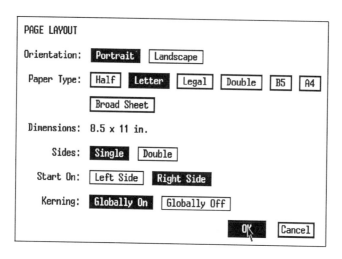

Page Layout contains several options that affect the size of the underlying page and how pages are printed. The illustration below summarizes the effects of some of these choices.

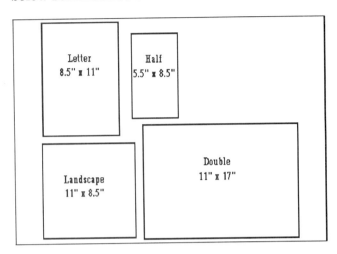

Single Sides applies to document that are printed on only one side. Later in the book you will work with double-sided documents, where print appears on both sides and such things as headers and footers and margins may be different for the left and right versions of the page.

Create a Header with Page Numbers

Our rule of thumb says that you should work from top to bottom in the Page menu. In this document, you will not be concerned with Widows & Orphans, or with any of the counting options. You can, therefore, move down to the Headers & Footers option.

Although we are using a header as an example, most of the concepts you are learning apply equally to footers. You can achieve similar effects in footers instead of headers, or you can combine both headers and footers on one page. For example, you could place the description in the header and the page numbers in the footer.

In this example, however, you will place both a descriptive title and a page number in the header.

■ Select Headers & Footers.

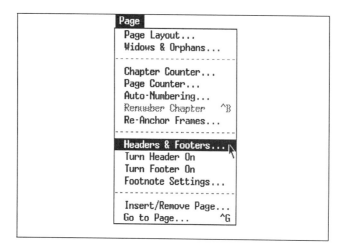

■ Select Right Page Header, Usage: On.

■ Move the text cursor to the Left line and type:

`Ventura Implementation`

This action positions the report title (Ventura Implementation) on the left side of the page.

■ Place the text cursor on the line labeled "Right:" and type:
Page followed by a blank space.

■ Choose the Page symbol [Page #] from the bottom of the dialog box. Then click OK.

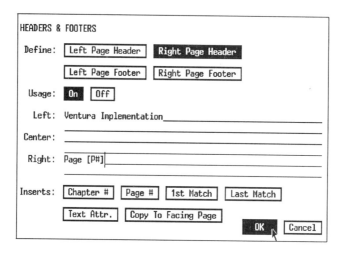

By choosing the page number symbol [P#], you tell Ventura to display the current number of each page in the header. Note that choosing the button caused the page numbering code ([P#]) to appear on the line. If you prefer, you can also enter such codes into dialog boxes by typing them directly. Most people, however, prefer to use the buttons, thereby eliminating the need to memorize codes.

As soon as you close the dialog box, the header you specified appears at the top of the page. (Since you are working with an existing style sheet, the format of the header has already been specified.) However, most reports do not include headers and footers on the first page. Let's turn the header off for the first page only while permitting it to remain on the following pages. Move further down the Page menu.

■ Select Turn Header Off.

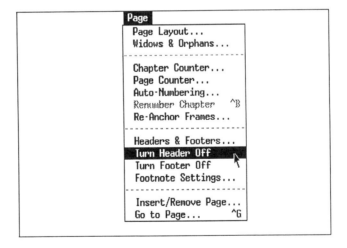

Only the first page will be affected by this command. To turn a header (or footer) off for an individual page, move to that page and then select that option from the Page menu. To turn it back on, you would return to the Page menu. You would see that the option now reads "Turn Header On."

Change the Margins

Since you are finished with the Page menu, the next rule of thumb says you should now move right to the Frame menu. Proceeding top to bottom, you come first to Margins & Columns. You will use this option to change the margins from their original setting.

■ Enable frame setting mode and select the underlying page.

■ Select Margins & Columns from the Frame menu.

■ Leave the Top and Bottom margins at 06,00 picas. Make the Left 09,00 picas and the Right 09,00 picas.

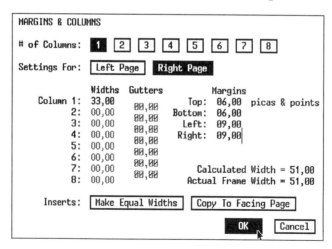

If the dialog box shows measurements in units other than picas & points, place the mouse cursor anywhere on top of the unit (e.g. inches or centimeters) and click until "picas & points" appears. If you are unfamiliar with picas and points, simply enter the settings for the time being. We will explain this measurement system in Chapter Two.

Ventura sets the margins of the header equal to the margins of the underlying page. Because you built the headers before you changed the margins, the header margins remain at the old value. In actual practice, you might want to vary from the left-to-right rule of thumb and change the margins *before* creating the header.

Modifying Tags

That's all the global formatting you will do for this first document. You are ready to proceed to the formatting of individual paragraphs. You have finished with the Frame menu. Now move right to the Paragraph menu.

For the most part, the formatting of individual paragraphs occurs in (surprise!) the Paragraph menu. We've got some bad news and some good news. The bad news: the Paragraph menu gives some users headaches because it packs so much power into so little space. The good news: we have a suggestion to make it simpler.

➡ *TIP: Roughly 75% of all paragraph formatting is done in the first three dialog boxes: Font, Alignment and Spacing.*

If you follow our previous suggestion to work from top to bottom, you'll soon make a discovery. By the time you finish with Font, Alignment and Spacing, you've probably accomplished most of what you needed to do. In the beginning, concentrate your efforts on the "Big Three" and you'll soon gain a sense of control.

Let's pause for a moment to remind ourselves where we've been and where we're headed. You've completed the text portion of the report and now you're working on style. You've made the global changes and you're ready to start on the individual paragraphs.

As you proceed through the rest of the style section, you will be assigning tags from the pre-existing style sheet you loaded at the beginning of the project. Assigning a tag begins by selecting a paragraph from the text. Then, while the paragraph is still highlighted, you tell Ventura which tag you want it to become by clicking on a tag name in the Assignment List. After assigning tags, you will also modify them to change their appearance on the page.

Your next question might be *Which paragraph should I work on first?* Here's a guideline that applies to all documents:

➡ *TIP: When you are ready to start working on individual paragraphs, format the body text first.*

As you will discover later in this chapter, the choices you make for body text affect the rest of the document.

Change the Body Text Font

- Enable paragraph tagging mode.

- Select the first body text paragraph ("XYZ Corporation has embarked...")

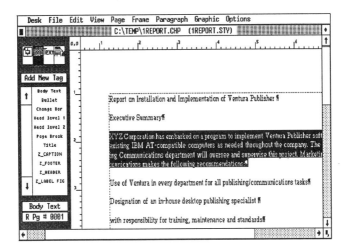

- Select Font from the Paragraph menu.

- Select Face: Helvetica, Style: Normal, Color: Black and Size: 012 points. Click OK to close the dialog box.

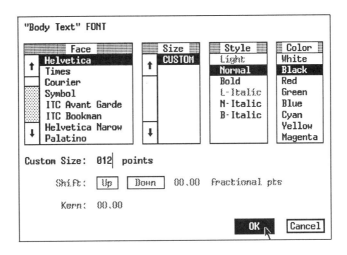

If You Do Not Have a PostScript Printer

Your Font dialog box may differ slightly from the one shown here if you did not choose PostScript as your printer. Do not worry about the slight variation.

All of the documents in the first section are constructed with the two basic fonts: Times and Helvetica. If you have a non-PostScript printer, you know these fonts as Dutch and Swiss.

As you may recall, we recommend that you install PostScript as one of your printer options even if you do not have a PostScript printer. Then you can switch to PostScript with the Set Printer Info dialog box during the exercises so your screens will match the ones in the book (you would switch back to print). However, if you prefer not to install or use Post-Script, you can use another printer. When you see instructions to use PostScript fonts, substitute your own font names instead. When you see Times, substitute Dutch. When you see Helvetica, substitute Swiss. (As an aid to remember which is which, it may help to recall that Helvetica is another name for Switzerland.)

Here's how the dialog box would look for the example above for a non-PostScript printer.

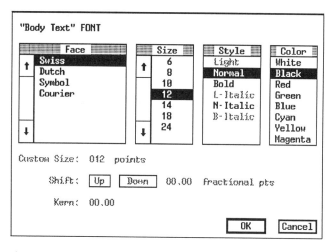

As you can see, there are only two differences. One is that you substitute Swiss for Helvetica. The second is that you choose the point size from a list rather than entering it on a line.

➡ *TIP: If you do not have a PostScript printer, substitute Dutch whenever you see Times Roman; substitute Swiss whenever you see Helvetica.*

Change the Body Text Alignment

■ With the body text still highlighted, select Alignment from the Paragraph menu.

■ Choose Justified and click OK.

```
┌────────────────────────────────────────────────────────────┐
│ "Body Text" ALIGNMENT                                        │
│                                                              │
│      Alignment:  [ Left ]  [ Center ]  [ Right ]  [Justified]│
│                                                              │
│    Hyphenation:  [ Off ]  [USENGLSH]  [ USENGLSH ]           │
│                                                              │
│ Successive Hyphens:  [ 1 ]  [ 2 ]  [ 3 ]  [ 4 ]  [ 5 ]  [ Unlimited ]│
│                                                              │
│   Overall Width:  [Column-Wide]  [ Frame-Wide ]             │
│                                                              │
│     First Line:  [ Indent ]  [ Outdent ]                    │
│                                                              │
│ In/Outdent Width:   00,00│  picas & points                  │
│                                                              │
│ In/Outdent Height:   001   lines                            │
│                                                              │
│ Relative Indent:  [ None ]  [ Length of Previous Line ]     │
│                                                              │
│                                   [ OK ]⟍  [ Cancel ]       │
└────────────────────────────────────────────────────────────┘
```

As you can see from the example above, most dialog boxes have multiple choices. We do not have the time to discuss every choice for every dialog box the first time we encounter it. For the moment, make the choices we suggest and leave the others unchanged. Rest assured that almost every choice in every dialog box is covered somewhere in the nine chapters of *Publishing Power with Ventura*.

Change the Body Text Spacing

The Spacing dialog box is one of the most complex, so take a deep breath. We need to spend a few paragraphs to get you started in the right direction. If you bear with us for a few minutes, you will have an easier time from now on.

The Spacing dialog box controls both vertical and horizontal spacing. Vertical is handled in the top half (Above, Below, etc.), horizontal in the bottom half (In From Left, In From Right).

About Vertical Spacing

Vertical spacing is confusing because it has four variations: Above, Below, Inter-Line and Inter-Paragraph. Most tags require only two of these.

➥ *TIP: Use Inter-Line for all tags. Use Above if you need addition-*

al white space. Do not use Below unless you cannot get what you want with Above and Inter-Line. Use Inter-Paragraph only as a last resort.

In other words, if you needed additional white space between two paragraphs, you would create it with Above spacing applied to the lower paragraph.

Limiting spacing to Above and Inter-Line has advantages. Above spacing can be automatically eliminated at the top of a column (notice the button labeled When Not at Column Top). What's more, to resolve conflicts between tags, Ventura uses Below from the uppermost tag. If you set Below to zero, you don't have to worry about one tag overriding another.

It is important to be consistent when working with Ventura. If you follow the tip above you will minimize the confusion some beginners experience with the Spacing dialog box. Nevertheless, there are occasional exceptions to this rule. We'll explain the exceptions as you get to them. In general, however, you can get the look you want about 80% of the time using just Above and Inter-Line.

Let's put this rule of thumb into practice.

■ Select Spacing from the Paragraph menu. Click on the unit of measurement until it reads fractional pts.

■ Move the cursor to Above, press Esc to clear the line, and type: **14**

There is no need to type the .00. Ventura treats blanks as zeros. Thus, 14.00 and 14._ are the same.

■ Move the cursor to Below. Press Esc to clear the line. Leave it blank.

Since Ventura treats blanks as zero, leaving the line blank is equivalent to entering 00.00.

■ Move the cursor to Inter-Line. Press Esc and type: **14**

■ Move to Inter-Paragraph. Press Esc to clear the line. Leave it blank. Click OK.

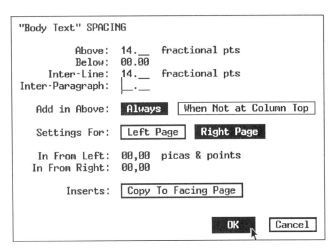

```
"Body Text" SPACING

          Above:  14.__   fractional pts
          Below:  00.00
     Inter-Line:  14.__   fractional pts
Inter-Paragraph:  |__.__

   Add in Above:   Always    When Not at Column Top

   Settings For:   Left Page    Right Page

  In From Left:   00,00   picas & points
  In From Right:  00,00

       Inserts:   Copy To Facing Page

                                 OK     Cancel
```

WARNING: As you enter values, Ventura may change the number slightly. This adjustment is due to Ventura's method of converting between measurement systems.

For instance, if you enter 00.25 points, you may see Ventura convert that value to 00.24 points when you move the cursor to a new field. Likewise, if you enter 14,00 points, Ventura may convert it to 13.98. Do not be concerned about these minor discrepancies. They will not affect the look of your documents.

Here's a second tip on vertical spacing:

➥ *TIP: Spacing values should have an integer relationship to the inter-line spacing of the body text.*

You create a more pleasing page design by using standard spacing, including spacing above subtitles and padding around pictures. That unit should be equal to the line spacing of the body text. For instance, a standard spacing unit allows text to align across columns.

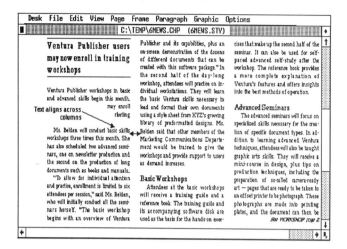

In the example above, Inter-Line was 14.00 points, and we chose 14.00 points for Above. Other good choices might have been 07.00 points, 28.00 points, 42.00 points or other multiples of 14.00. If the inter-line spacing had been 12.00, then 06.00, 24.00 and 36.00 would have been valid options.

About Horizontal Spacing

Hang in there. You're halfway home. You've covered vertical spacing. Stick with it for a few more paragraphs as we explain horizontal spacing.

➡ *TIP: Treat In From Left and In From Right as "extra" margins when the original margins set in the Frame menu are not enough.*

In certain cases, you want an overall margin for most of the document, but different, smaller margins for certain text elements. In such a case, use the Spacing dialog box to create secondary margins with In From Left and In From Right.

Create a Secondary Margin for Body Text

Try creating a secondary margin for the body text tag with In From Left. Shortening the line length will make the text easier to read.

■ Select Spacing from the Paragraph menu. If necessary, change the unit measurement next to In From Left to picas

& points. (Put the mouse cursor on top of the measurement units and click until picas & points shows.)

■ Make In From Left spacing 06,00 picas. Click OK.

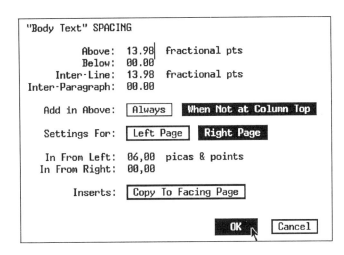

```
"Body Text" SPACING

          Above:  13.98|  fractional pts
          Below:  00.00
     Inter-Line:  13.98   fractional pts
Inter-Paragraph:  00.00

   Add in Above:  [ Always ]  When Not at Column Top

   Settings For:  [ Left Page ]  Right Page

   In From Left:  06,00  picas & points
  In From Right:  00,00

        Inserts:  [ Copy To Facing Page ]

                              OK    Cancel
```

In From Left is measured from the edge of the margin *not* from the edge of the paper.

When you return to the document, the body text now starts six picas in from the original left margin.

We suggested starting with body text and proceeding in order down the Paragraph menu. You have already used the Big Three: the Font, Alignment and Spacing options. Since there is nothing more that needs to be done to body text, you are ready to move to another text paragraph.

➡ *NOTE: Thanks to Ventura's style sheet approach, the changes you made to the first body text paragraph are automatically reflected in each and every body text paragraph throughout the document. There is no need to format each one individually. Any format change to one affects them all.*

Stopping Point

You have reached another recommended stopping point. If your time is limited, save your work and exit Ventura. Return to complete the project when your schedule permits.

Since you already renamed the chapter in the Ventura Prep section, you can save simply by pressing the keyboard shortcut Ctrl-S (or by choosing Save from the File menu.) Even if you plan to continue on without stopping, we recommend that you save your work now.

Change the Title Tag

If you are restarting after leaving Ventura, use Open Chapter from the File menu to open C:\TEMP\1REPORT.CHP. Ventura automatically loads the files for that chapter, (including the picture file which you have not yet put into place).

If body text should always be the first tag you modify, what should be the second? We recommend that you start at the top of a document and march through in order. Using this concept, the next paragraph encountered is the title.

In the next few steps, you will apply the Title tag. Then you will modify the Title tag by changing its font, alignment and spacing.

■ Select the paragraph "Report on Installation and Implementation of Ventura Publisher."

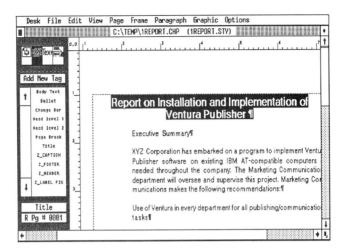

■ Select Title from the Assignment List.

■ Select Font from the Paragraph menu.

■ Make the point size 024 points and click OK.

Change the Title Alignment

■ Select Alignment from the Paragraph menu.

■ Choose Left and Hyphenation Off. Leave the remaining settings unchanged. Click OK.

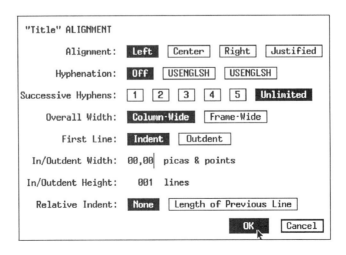

The title appears flush against the left margin.

Notice that you turned off hyphenation. Titles and display type should generally not be hyphenated.

Adjust the Title Spacing

■ Select Spacing from the Paragraph menu. Verify that the units of measurement are displayed as fractional points.

■ Move to Above, press Esc to clear the line and type: **42**

■ Move to Below and press Esc to clear the line. Leave it blank. Move to Inter-Line spacing, press Esc and type: **28**

■ Move to Add in Above and choose Always. Move to In From Left and press Esc to clear the line. Click OK.

As you can see, the settings adhere to the rule of thumb. Since the body text inter-line spacing is 14.00 points, you used a multiple of 14 for the spacing above and below the title.

WARNING: As you proceed through the additional tags, your results may not match the book unless you select Auto-Adjust Styles: No from Set Preferences in the Options menu.

```
SET PREFERENCES

     Generated Tags:  [ Hidden ]  [ Shown ]

      Text to Greek:  [ None ]  [ 2 ]  [ 4 ]  [ 6 ]  [ 8 ]  [ 10 ]  [ All ]

   Keep Backup Files:  [ Yes ]  [ No ]

  Double Click Speed:  [ Slow ]  [ 2 ]  [ 3 ]  [ 4 ]  [ Fast ]

    Decimal Tab Char:  046|  (ASCII)

   On-Screen Kerning:  [ None ]  [ 36 ]  [ 24 ]  [ 18 ]  [ 14 ]  [ 10 ]  [ All ]

  Auto-Adjust Styles:  [ Yes ]  [ No ]


                                            [ OK ]  [ Cancel ]
```

Auto-Adjust Styles refers to the Spacing dialog box. If it is set to On, Ventura will automatically adjust inter-line spacing each time you change the font. If you increase the font size by 20%, Ventura will increase the inter-line spacing by the same percentage.

This automatic adjustment may seem like a convenience. In practice, however, it usually results in hard-to-use fractional spacing. We recommend spacing related to the standard unit of the body text. Auto-Adjust Styles throws off this standardization. For these reasons, we recommend working with it off. Instead, you will manually adjust spacing as necessary.

In addition, as you get further along, we will not tell you each and every choice to make in each and every dialog box. Instead, we will mention only the changes. You will leave everything else unchanged. If you have Auto-Adjust Styles set to On, Inter-Line may differ from what we expect you to have.

The Head Level 1 Tag

Now that we are finished with the Title tag, we are ready to move on to the next paragraph down the page. Tag it as Head level 1 and then change the way it looks.

■ Select the first paragraph ("Executive Summary").

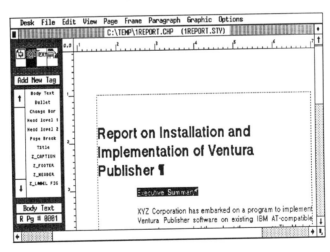

■ Select Head level 1 from the Assignment List.

Change the Head Level 1 Font

Now that you have assigned the tag, you can go through the "Big Three" — Font, Alignment and Spacing — to change its appearance.

To speed the process, we will use a shorter method to note changes. For example:

■ Font   Size: 018 points

This abbreviated form means that you should open the Font dialog box, change the the point size to 018 points, *leave everything else unchanged* and click OK to close the dialog box.

➡*REMEMBER: Make only the changes indicated. Leave anything not listed the way you found it when you opened the dialog box. After making the indicated changes, click OK to close the dialog box.*

Change the Head Level 1 Spacing

Use Above to add extra white space between Head level 1 and the Title tag.

■ Spacing   Above: 42.00 points
                          Below: 00.00 points
                          Inter- Line: 28 points
                          Inter-Paragraph: 00.00 points
                          Add in Above: When Not at Column Top
                          In From Left: 00.00 picas

The Bullet Tag

■ Select the paragraph "Use of Ventura in every department..." and tag it as Bullet (select Bullet from the Assignment List).

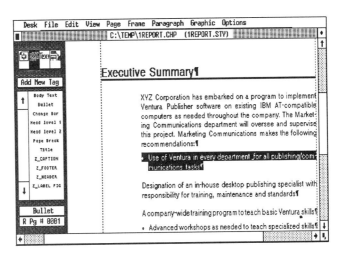

To change the tag, step through Font, Alignment and Spacing. Since you have already encountered these dialog boxes several times, we will list the changes in abbreviated form.

■ Font   Face: Helvetica
                Size: 012 points

■ Alignment   Justified

■ Spacing   Above: 07.00 points
                Below: 00.00 points
                Inter-Line: 14.00 points
                Add in Above: When Not at Column Top
                In From Left: 06,00 picas (72.00 points)

Create Additional Bullet Paragraphs

Next, you will tag three more paragraphs as Bullet using the Shift-Click technique. Shift-Click lets you tag several paragraphs at one time. Click on the first paragraph as you would normally. Then hold down the shift key while clicking on the additional paragraph. All the paragraphs are high-lighted simultaneously and the Current Selection Box shows the word Multiple.

➡ *TIP: Use Shift-Click whenever possible to give several paragraphs the same tag name.*

■ Select the paragraph "Designation of an in-house..." *While holding down the Shift key,* click again on the paragraph "A company wide..." *Without releasing the Shift key*, click a third time on the paragraph "Advanced workshops...."

■ When all three paragraphs are selected, release the Shift key. Move the cursor to the Assignment List and select the Bullet Tag.

When you have finished, your document should look like this:

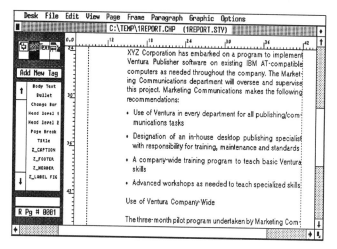

Now finish the page by assigning the Head level 1 tag to the paragraph immediately below the bullets.

■ Select the paragraph "Use of Ventura Company- Wide" and tag it as Head level 1.

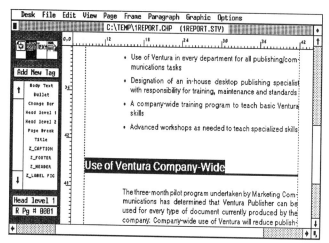

The Head level 2 Tag

Next go to page two where you will assign the Head level 2 tag and change its attributes.

■ Press the PgDn key to go to page two.

■ Select the paragraph "Accounting Department:" and tag it as Head level 2.

With the paragraph still highlighted, make the changes shown below in abbreviated form.

■ Font   Face: Helvetica
      Size: 014 points

■ Spacing Above: 28.00 points
      Below: 00.00 points
      Add in Above: When Not at Column Top
      In From Left: 06,00 picas

■ Assign the Head level 2 tag to the following paragraphs: "Advertising Department," "Market Communications," "Internal Publications" and "Engineering."

Complete the Tags

You have made all the changes to tags. All that remains in the style section is to assign these tags to a few more paragraphs.

■ Select the paragraph "Company-Wide Basic Training for Ventura" and tag it as Head level 1.

■ Press the PgDn key to go to page three.

■ Select the two paragraphs "It Will Explain" and "It Will Teach" and tag them as Bullet.

■ Select the paragraph "Advance Workshops" and tag it as Head level 1.

Pictures

Congratulations. You have finished the style portion of this document. By now you should already be seeing some improvement in the appearance of the report.

Before you finish this first project, add a picture by drawing a frame on the page and placing a picture file inside.

Add a Frame

Before placing a picture, you must add a frame to contain it. Move to the second page.

■ Press PgDn.

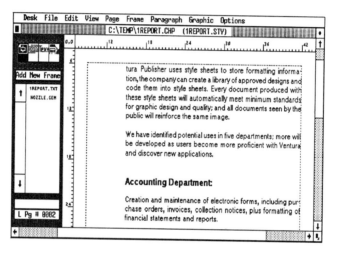

■ Enable frame setting mode.

■ Click on the addition button which displays the words Add New Frame.

■ Place the cursor where you want the upper left corner of the frame to appear. Use the ruler to position the cursor so it lines up with the left margin of body text and the top of the column guide. (Perfect accuracy is not important for this first attempt.)

■ Press and hold the mouse button. When the cursor changes to a pointing finger icon, drag the lower right corner of the frame downwards. Release the mouse button when you reach position 21 on the vertical ruler.

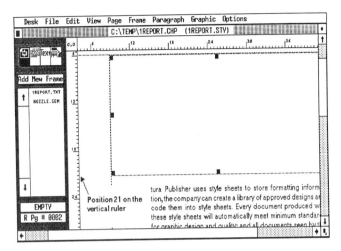

Ventura's column snap and line snap force the new frame to line up properly. If you make a mistake, press the Del key to delete the highlighted frame and try again.

After you set the location of the frame, you should add some *padding* — extra breathing space that keeps surrounding text from touching the border of the frame. In the following example, you will set vertical padding to 14.00 points — the standard spacing unit derived from body text.

The vertical padding option places a white space buffer both above and below the frame. Thus, in the example above, the frame will have 14.00 points of padding at the top and 14.00 points at the bottom. Text will not be allowed to come within 14.00 points at top or bottom.

■ Select Sizing & Scaling from the Frame menu.

■ Choose fractional points as the unit of measurement.

■ Move to the Vert. Padding line, press Esc to clear the line and type: **14.00**

The frame now has a 14-point cushion of white space aabove and below it.

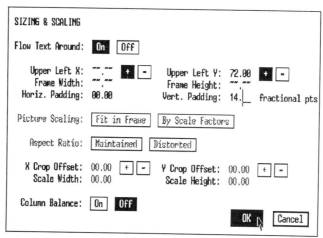

Place the Picture

■ With the new frame still selected, select the picture file NOZZLE.GEM from the Assignment List.

The drawing appears inside the frame.

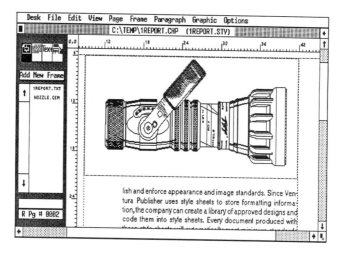

Chapter

With text, style and picture finished, you need only complete the chapter portion of the report.

Print the Chapter

The only real test of a document is how it looks on paper. In the chapter section of this project, you will print the report you just created. Then we will show you how to back it up on a floppy disk using Ventura's Multi-Chapter function.

■ Press Ctrl-S to save the chapter.

■ Select To Print from the File menu.

■ Choose Which Pages: All, Collated Copies: Off, Printing Order: Last to 1st. Leave Configuration at its current setting, which should match the default printer you selected when you installed Ventura. Click OK to print a single copy of your three-page report.

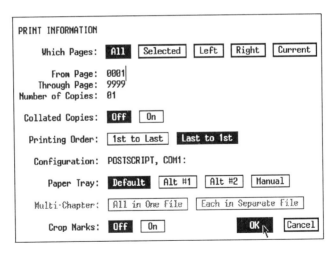

Ventura displays a message that it is printing. If you need to cancel the printing command, press Esc. Ventura will then give you the choice of stopping or continuing.

➥ *WARNING: If you installed the PostScript width tables for the purposes of this exercise but you do not have a PostScript printer, use Set Printer Info to switch back to your original printer.*

Chapter Three contains a detailed explanation of the Set Printer Info dialog box.

Back Up a Chapter

As explained earlier, Ventura uses pointers to keep track of the files in a chapter. If you use DOS COPY to back up a chapter, you will move all the files to a new location *but the pointers will still be set to the old location.* The chapter will load from the new location, but when it looks for the text, style and picture file it needs it will be unable to locate them. It will still be looking for them at the old location.

To solve this dilemma, use Multi-Chapter from the Options menu to back up chapters. This utility not only copies the files *it automatically changes the pointers to correspond to the new locations.*

Ventura permits you to create a *publication*, which can be a collection of many chapters. You can then copy or print all of the chapters in the publication with a single command. You will practice this skill in Chapter Three. But you don't have to create a publication just to copy a single chapter. Here's how it works:

■ Place a formatted floppy disk in the A: drive.

■ Select Multi-Chapter from the Options menu.

The Multi-Chapter dialog box appears.

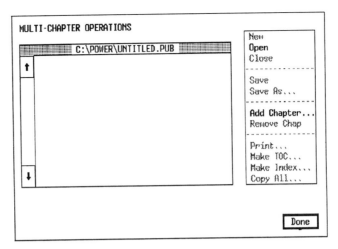

■ Select Add Chapter.

Ventura displays the item selector, with which you can choose the chapter you wish to copy to the floppy disk.

■ With the backup button, locate the C:\TEMP subdirectory and scroll through the listing until you find 1REPORT.CHP. Select the chapter.

Ventura returns to the Multi-Chapter dialog box. Notice that the chapter now appears on the list.

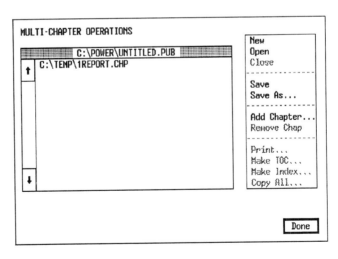

■ Select Copy All.

A new dialog box appears.

```
COPY ALL

                         SOURCE (from this file)

   PUB or CHP:  C:\TEMP\1REPORT.CHP_____


                    DESTINATION (to these directories)

   PUB & CHPs:  A:|_____
   STYs & WIDs: A:_____
   Text Files:  A:_____
Graphic Files:  A:_____
  Image Files:  A:_____

      Command:  [ Make All Directories the Same As the First ]
```

The name of the chapter is displayed at the top of the dialog
box. The destination lines show the disk drive and subdirectory to which each file will be copied. When you first select
Copy All, Ventura will "guess" where you want to copy the
files. You will change this guess to the actual destination (the
A: drive).

■ Move the cursor to the line PUB & CHPS. Press Esc to clear
  the line and type: **A:**

As you can see, you have the option to copy different kinds of
files to different subdirectories. In this case, however, you will
copy all the chapter files to the A: drive. Luckily, Ventura has
a feature that makes it unnecessary to type A: on each line.

■ Choose Make All Directories the Same As the First. Click
  OK.

Ventura copies all the files to the A: drive. When the copy function is complete, you return to the Multi- Chapter dialog box.

■ Choose Done to close the Multi-Chapter dialog box.

When Ventura asks you if you want to abandon or save changes made to the publication, click on Abandon to return to the
work area.

Once you have completed printing and backing up the chapter,
you can go onto the next project or exit from Ventura. To exit:

■ Select Quit from the File menu.

If you haven't saved recently, Ventura will ask you if you want to Save or Abandon. Choose Save.

You made it. You created a business document with Ventura. Although some of the new concepts and theory may have been tough going for beginners, you have already learned many of the basics — basics you will reuse again and again. Along the way, you made a big improvement in the appearance and efficiency of the sample report.

And you can do even more to enhance basic business documents. Turn to Chapter Two for more ideas and techniques for power publishing with Ventura.

Tips

Text Tips

- ❏ Use File Type/Rename from the Edit menu to relocate text files (copy them to a new subdirectory) or to convert them to a different word processing format.

- ❏ Do as much editing, changing, adding and spell checking as possible in the word processor before bringing the file into Ventura. Text editing in Ventura is less efficient.

Style Tips

- ❏ Always rename the style sheet at the beginning of the work session to avoid corrupting the original.

- ❏ To avoid confusion, many users give the style sheet the same name as the chapter (for instance, SAMPLE.CHP and SAMPLE.STY).

- ❏ Perform overall document formatting first, then move to individual paragraph formatting.

- ❏ You will feel less confused if you concentrate on the Page, Frame and Paragraph menus during the style phase of a document.

❏ Work from left-to-right and from top-to-bottom in Ventura's menus to avoid overlooking important operations.

❏ When working in the Paragraph menu, focus on the Font, Alignment and Spacing menus.

❏ If you change the margins of the document, you can make the margins of the header (or footer) match by turning the header off and then on again. Use Headers & Footers to turn the header off for the entire document. Your settings are retained even though the header is no longer active. Now go back to the same dialog box and turn the header back on (don't forget to turn on both left and right pages). When you return to the workspace you will discover that the headers have been reset to match the current page margins.

❏ Use Inter-Line spacing for every tag. Use Above spacing if necessary to provide additional separation from the preceding paragraph. Avoid Below spacing unless you cannot get the effect you want with Inter-Line and Above. Use Inter-Paragraph only as a last resort.

❏ If possible, make all spacing a unit of the line spacing of the body text. This applies to spacing above and below headlines, subheads and bullets, as well as to frame sizes and frame padding (white space around pictures).

❏ For faster tagging, use Shift-Click to select several paragraphs at once.

Chapter Tips

❏ Use Save As to rename (and/or relocate) the chapter at the beginning of every work session. Once you have renamed the chapter you can save it as you go along simply by pressing Ctrl-S.

❏ Create a separate subdirectory for each project. If the document is very large, subdivide the hard disk even further.

❏ Never use DOS copy to move chapters and associated files. Use Multi-Chapter so the internal pointers are changed to match the new location. Exception: You can use DOS to move files between two identically configured computers.

For instance, you could move SAMPLE.CHP from the C:\TEMP subdirectory of one computer and put it on the C:\TEMP subdirectory of a second computer. As long as each and every file is found in the same location on both computers, the chapter will load properly on the new computer.

❏ You can type the new location on the Selection line and move to it by pressing Enter (or clicking OK). However, the easiest way to navigate around the hard disk is with the mouse and the backup button.

Chapter Two
Skills Checklist

Theory

✓ Understanding printer's measure

✓ Preformatting text in your word processor

✓ Preparing spreadsheet files to import in Ventura

Text

✓ Editing text in Ventura

✓ Using text mode to add text attributes

Style

✓ The benefit of two-column page formats

✓ Creating a page break tag

✓ Using horizontal tabs to make a table

Pictures

✓ Placing text inside a frame

✓ Adding captions to illustrations

Chapter

✓ Printing the current page

A Two-Column Proposal

Although you may not realize it yet, you have already acquired a solid grounding in Ventura fundamentals just by completing the first chapter. Chapter Two reinforces these basics while teaching the new skills summarized in the checklist to the left.

Why You Should Not Get Discouraged

This may be a good time to reassure novice users. If Ventura seems a bit intimidating during the first few weeks, remember that you are really tackling two things at once. First, you must learn the software — not a trivial task considering that Ventura is one of the most powerful packages ever written for a personal computer. At the same time, you must learn about layout and design, a separate (and complex) discipline of its own.

This dual struggle frustrates some beginners. The best solution is to worry less and practice more. Mastery of Ventura is a matter of hands-on experience. The more documents you work on, the sooner you'll reach true proficiency. If you continue to follow along with the exercises, things will soon fall into place.

Theory

In this section we will introduce you to the measuring system the professionals use when working with Ventura. The second half of the theory section discusses how to preformat text with your word processor to save production time in Ventura.

Picas and Points

Most Americans are comfortable with inches. But for desktop publishing, the method called *printer's measure* or *the point system* is superior. Since type sizes are always specified in points, it makes sense to use printer's measure for everything on the page so you don't waste time converting back and forth. In addition, the point system has units that are much smaller than inches, so it is rarely necessary to complicate things with fractional units. By contrast, using inches requires you to make many fractional computations.

For these reasons, printer's measure is the easiest way to talk to a page layout program. (Most programs let the user choose between inches, centimeters or printer's measure.) The two most important units in printer's measure are *points* and *picas.*

Points are a very small unit, about 1/72 inch. They are used to measure type sizes and rules. The point size of a typeface is roughly the measurement from the highest ascender (the top of a "b" for instance) to the lowest descender (the bottom of a "g"). This is only an approximation, since point sizes originate from the metal body used to carry type in the days before phototypesetting. The best way to get familiar with point sizes is by example. You'll soon develop an eye for the most common sizes.

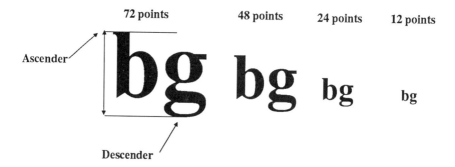

Picas are a larger unit. Don't confuse them with the typewriter style of the same name. They are equal to 12 points (about 1/6 inch). Printers and typographers use picas to measure lines, margins and columns. The following figure shows a page from this chapter's sample project with the measurements expressed in picas and points. (The measurements refer to the full-sized page.)

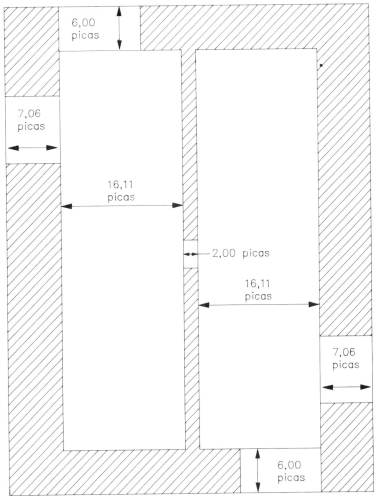

Trim size 51 x 66 picas
(8.5 x 11 inches)
Right page

The following table will help you convert common sizes from one system to the other.

Inches	Picas	Points
1/4 inch	1,06 picas	18 points
1/3 inch	2,00 picas	24 points
1/2 inch	3,00 picas	36 points
1 inch	6,00 picas	72 points
5 1/2 inches	33,00 picas	
8 1/2 inches	51,00 picas	
11 inches	66,00 picas	

Preparing Text for Ventura

You can make life with Ventura a lot easier if you learn how to prepare text files for Ventura in advance. All the sample files that you use for the publishing projects are already prepared for you. Since preformatting text can save you time in Ventura, we want you to understand the theory so you can use it for files you create on your own.

You've probably heard the expression "less is more." When creating text files for Ventura, however, less is *less* when it comes to inserting global formats such as indents, centering, page numbering and so forth. The less you format with the word processor — the less formatting, the less extra spaces, the less extra carriage returns — the less work you'll have when you bring the file into Ventura. At best, global formatting from a word processor is ignored by Ventura. At worst, it creates extra spaces, tabs or characters that must be manually removed.

➥ *TIP: Do as little global formatting as possible with the word processor. Perform global formatting in Ventura instead.*

The table nearby lists some of the things you should *not* do with the word processor.

WHAT NOT TO DO WITH A WORD PROCESSOR

Do not:

- center text

- justify text

- indent the first line of a paragraph

- create temporary margins

- put more than one space after a period, colon or question mark

- put more than one carriage return between paragraphs

- put more than one tab stop between columns

The table recommends only one carriage return betwee paragraphs. Although this reduces the time spent deleting e: traneous returns in Ventura, it does make the file hard to rea in the word processor. Luckily, Ventura has a built-in featur‹ to handle this problem: the @PARAFILTR ON = code.

When you insert the @PARAFILTR ON = code in the wor processing file, it instructs Ventura to filter out extra carriag returns between paragraphs. The paragraph filter code mu‹ be inserted as the very first line the the document and it mu‹ be typed correctly, or Ventura will ignore it. Make sure yo place a space before and after ON and a space *before and aft* the equals sign.

```
@PARAFILTR ON = ▢
Consulting Proposal to ABC Company¶
¶
XYZ Corporation¶
¶
September 1, 1988¶
¶
Consulting Proposal to ABC Company¶
¶
Project Description¶
¶
XYZ Corporation proposes to advise ABC Company on all
aspects of desktop ¶
publishing systems, including needs analysis, product and
market surveys, specifications ¶
and purchase, and system implementation.¶
¶
The initial short-term goal is to computerize the production
of ABC's ¶
```

We said that "less is less" for global formatting. When it comes to formatting individual paragraphs, however, we could say the opposite: more is more. The more individual formatting you do in the text file the more efficient you'll be.

Individual Formatting in Text Files

Individual formatting falls into two categories. The first is text attributes: boldface, italics, underlines, etc., when applied to a few words within a paragraph. The word *italics* in this sentence is an example of individual formatting (if the entire paragraph was in italics, it would be considered global formatting). The second category is typographic characters. Ventura Publisher provides the capability to insert true typographic characters, including characters that don't appear on the computer keyboard, such as the em dash (—), the copyright symbol (©) and so on.

➥ *TIP: You can enter text attributes and typographic characters with Ventura, but it's faster with a word processor.*

One advantage a word processor has over Ventura's current version is its search and replace function. For instance, you could use search and replace to remove all extra spaces after periods. Likewise, if you make a text change throughout a document — for example, substituting one name for another — do it with search and replace before starting Ventura.

Bracket Codes

Some people use search and replace to insert bracket codes for true typographic characters. After typing the text file, they replace incorrect characters with a code. Ventura interprets this code and substitutes the correct typographic character.

Other people prefer to use keyboard macros for the same task. They program the keyboard to insert the proper bracket codes as they go along. Thus, they might program the key combination Alt-C to insert the code <189>. When Ventura sees this bracket code, it inserts the copyright symbol, ©, onto the page. The illustrations below show a coded paragraph from a word processor and the same paragraph in Ventura.

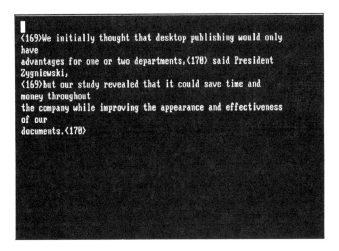

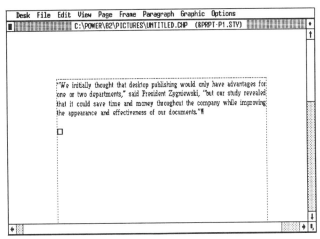

The nearby table provides the proper substitutions and codes for the most common typographic characters not available from the keyboard. You can use this table as a reference whether you use the search and replace method or the keyboard macro method.

Character	Symbol	Code
open quote	"	169
close quote	"	170
em dash	—	197
en dash	–	196
copyright	©	189
registered	®	190
trademark	™	191
bullet	•	195
cents symbol	¢	155
pounds symbol	£	156
yen symbol	¥	157
franc symbol	f	159
section sign	§	185
paragraph	¶	188
ellipsis	…	193
degree symbol	°	198

Before

Consulting Proposal to ABC Company

XYZ Corporation

September 1, 1988

Consulting Proposal to ABC Company

Project Description

XYZ Corporation proposes to advise ABC Company on all aspects of desktop publishing systems, including needs analysis, product and market surveys, specifications and purchase, and system implementation.

The initial short-term goal is to computerize the production of ABC's internal and external publications using personal computers and desktop publishing software. This short-term goal must be substantially completed before the end of ABC's fiscal year six months from now. The long-range objective is to integrate all of ABC's publications into a company-wide system with common procedures, databases and shared output devices.

Statement of Work

XYZ proposes to accomplish and complete this project in five phases, as described in more detail:

Phase One
Market Research. XYZ will analyze commercially available products for suitability. Phase One will culminate in an in-depth report outlining alternatives and recommendations.

Phase Two
Evaluate Needs. XYZ will gain an in-depth knowledge of ABC's computerization needs through on-site and telephone interviews. We will consider such areas as:

- Word processing and editorial requirements
- Graphics requirements
- Laser printer requirements
- Ease of learning and use
- Speed and throughput requirements

Phase Three
Installation. Once ABC makes it purchase decision, XYZ will oversee installation, setup and conversion. This will include integration of hardware, software and peripherals, plus the initial setup. Setup will include the creation of electronic formats, style sheets and document templates for reuse by ABC personnel.

Phase Four

After

Consulting Proposal to ABC Company

Project Description

XYZ Corporation proposes to advise ABC Company on all aspects of desktop publishing systems, including needs analysis, product and market surveys, specifications and purchase, and system implementation.

The initial short-term goal is to computerize the production of ABC's internal and external publications using personal computers and desktop publishing software. This short-term goal must be substantially completed before the end of ABC's fiscal year six months from now. The long-range objective is to integrate all of ABC's publications into a company-wide system with common procedures, databases and shared output devices.

Statement of Work

XYZ proposes to accomplish and complete this project in five phases, as described in more detail:

Phase One
Market Research. XYZ will analyze commercially available products for suitability. Phase One will culminate in an in-depth report outlining alternatives and recommendations.

Phase Two
Evaluate Needs. XYZ will gain an in-depth knowledge of ABC's computerization needs through on-site and telephone interviews. We will consider such areas as:

- Word processing and editorial requirements
- Graphics requirements
- Laser printer requirements
- Ease of learning and use
- Speed and throughput requirements

Phase Three
Installation. Once ABC makes it purchase decision, XYZ will oversee installation, setup and conversion. This will include integration of hardware, software and peripherals, plus the initial setup. Setup will include the creation of electronic formats, style sheets and document templates for reuse by ABC personnel.

Phase Four
Data Conversion. Once the system is installed, XYZ will supervise the conversion of current databases and publications to an electronic form. This will include the use of optical character recognition whenever possible to minimize the time and cost of

data entry. Where it is not possible to optically read existing information, XYZ will supervise data entry personnel who will rekey the data into the computers. XYZ will design and implement custom keyboard macro programs to facilitate data entry.

Phase Five
Training and Implementation. With the system up and running and data converted to electronic form, XYZ will train ABC personnel in proper computer procedures, use of the software and interfacing to typesetters, databases and other existing systems. This will include training ABC personnel in all aspects of the word processing/page layout interface, including computer basics, word processing basics, desktop publishing basics, and backup procedures.

XYZ will be available to support the system as needed, whether to (1) troubleshoot problems, (2) explore ways to gain further value from existing hardware and software, (3) more fully integrate the system with other hardware and software or (4) expand the system.

Project Costs

The spreadsheet below illustrates XYZ's best estimate of the costs required to complete the project within a three month period.

	JANUARY	FEBRUARY	MARCH
Phase One	6000.00	2750.00	1225.00
Phase Two	2600.00	1175.00	895.00
Phase Three	1600.00	1600.00	0.0
Phase Four	1500.00	1500.00	3750.00
Phase Five	2500.00	2500.00	2500.00
TOTALS	$13100.00	$9525.00	$8370.00

Project Costs for Desktop Publishing Implementation

Planning the Proposal

In the first chapter you prepared an in-house document, a report for distribution within the company. Now you will work on a document that you might send to a prospective customer outside your company.

The typical proposal serves as a sales document. Sometimes it goes to another department in the same company, or to upper management. Often, however, it is sent to customers. Since a proposal may go to the outside world, it must represent your company in the best light. The graphic design should work together with the words to reinforce the image your company wishes to project.

Although we kept our example short to conserve time and disk space, a real-life proposal may be many pages long. It may also incorporate graphics and/or financial tables. The document needs headers or footers for easy reference, plus captions to help readers correlate the visuals with the text.

Take a look at the "before" and "after" pictures of the proposal. Here are some of the effects you will work on in this chapter to improve its appearance:

- A separate title page

- A banner headline

- A two-column format to get more information on the page while enhancing readability

- A spreadsheet file integrated with the text

Ventura Prep

If You Have the Publishing Power Disk

For the purposes of this publishing project, we will assume that you have prepared a text file (2PROPOS.TXT) and a spreadsheet file (LOTUS.TXT) in accordance with the preformatting tips given in the theory section. (In actual fact, the sample text files on the Publishing Power disk have been preformatted for you.) Now they are ready to be loaded into the Assignment List.

In Chapter One you learned how to load one file at a time. Now we will show you how to load several files at once.

- Select Load Text/Picture from the File menu.

- Select Type of File: Text, Text Format: ASCII, # of Files: Several, and OK.

- Locate the C:\POWER subdirectory and scroll through the listing until you find the file 2PROPOS.TXT. Select the file and load it into the Assignment List.

After the first file is loaded, the Item Selector reappears and you can continue to load the next file.

- Scroll through the file listing again to locate the text file, LOTUS.TXT. Select the file name and choose OK to return to the document.

➡ *NOTE: From this point on, when we ask you to select an item, use whichever selection method you prefer — typing the name on the selection line, double clicking or clicking on the name and then OK.*

Normally, when you load one text file at a time, Ventura immediately places it on the underlying page. However, when you load several files at once, Ventura can't judge which file should be placed first. When you're ready to place a file, you must select the underlying page, then select the text file from the Assignment List.

Renaming the Document Files

We want you to get in the habit of renaming text files, style sheets and chapters immediately to avoid making permanent changes to the the originals. Start by renaming the text files.

To rename the text files, place them one at a time onto the underlying page. Once they are placed, use File Type/Rename to rename them and relocate them to a different subdirectory.

- Select the underlying page. When the eight frame handles are visible select the text file name, LOTUS.TXT from the Assignment List.

Ventura places the text on the page. Now rename and relocate the file.

- Select File Type/Rename from the Page menu.

- Move to the New Name: line and type: **C:\TEMP\TABLE.TXT** then choose ASCII and OK.

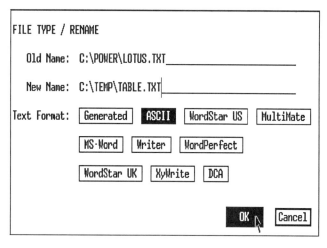

```
FILE TYPE / RENAME

   Old Name:  C:\POWER\LOTUS.TXT_____

   New Name:  C:\TEMP\TABLE.TXT|_____

Text Format:  [ Generated ]  [ ASCII ]  [ WordStar US ]  [ MultiMate ]

              [ MS-Word ]  [ Writer ]  [ WordPerfect ]

              [ WordStar UK ]  [ XyWrite ]  [ DCA ]

                                        [ OK ]  [ Cancel ]
```

To rename the second text file, place it on the underlying page.

With the underlying page still selected, choose Remove Text/File from the Edit menu.

Ventura displays the file name, TABLE.TXT in the dialog box.

- Choose Remove From: Frame and click OK.

The new file name, TABLE.TXT appears in the Assignment List.

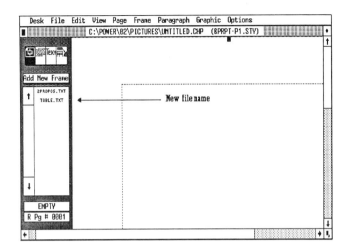

> ➡ *TIP: You can remove the existing text file from the underlying page by selecting another file from the Assignment List. Ventura automatically replaces one text file with another.*

Now place the proposal text on the underlying page.

- Select the underlying page. Then select the file name 2PROPOS.TXT from the Assignment List.

Rename the second text file.

- Select File Type/Rename from the Edit menu.

- Move to the New Name: line and type:
  C:\TEMP\PROPOSAL.TXT

- Choose ASCII and OK.

> ➡ *NOTE: File Type/Rename works for text files only. Use DOS to rename picture files.*

Load and Rename a Style Sheet

After renaming the two text files, load the style sheet.

- Select Load Different Style from the File menu. Locate the style sheet &PRPT-P1.STY in the C:\TYPESET subdirectory and load it into the document.

Now save the style sheet with a new name.

- Select Save as New Style from the File menu. Locate the

original C:\TEMP subdirectory with the Item Selector. Move to the Selection line and type: **2PROPOS**

```
┌─────────────────────────────────────────────────────┐
│  ITEM SELECTOR                                        │
│                                                       │
│  Directory:  C:\TEMP\*.STY_____     │
│  ┌───────────────────────┐                            │
│  │█ ▓▓▓▓▓ *.STY ▓▓▓▓▓    │      Selection:  2PROPOS . │ │
│  ├──────────────────────┬┤                            │
│  │ ─────·──             │↑│                            │
│  │ ─────·──             │ │                            │
│  │ ─────·──             │ │                            │
│  │ ─────·──             │ │                            │
│  │ ─────·──             │ │          ┌────────┐        │
│  │ ─────·──             │ │          │   OK ↖ │        │
│  │ ─────·──             │ │          └────────┘        │
│  │ ─────·──             │↓│          │ Cancel │        │
│  └──────────────────────┴─┘          └────────┘        │
│                                                       │
└─────────────────────────────────────────────────────┘
```

➥ *Ventura automatically assigns the .STY extension to the file.*

Rename and Save the Chapter

Now save the new chapter with the new text and style sheet.

■ Select Save As ... from the File menu.

■ Move to the C:\TEMP subdirectory. Move to the Selection line and type: 2PROPOS.CHP. Click OK.

If You Do Not Have the Publishing Power Disk

■ Use your favorite word processor to type in the two text files PROPOSAL.TXT and TABLE.TXT from Appendix A. Save them (or copy them) in the C:\TEMP subdirectory. Then follow the steps explained above to load the text files, and load and rename the style sheet and chapter files.

Now that you've organized the chapter files, you're ready to begin. Where to start? As we know from the previous chapter, the Ventura Formula (Text + Style + Pictures = Chapter) helps with that question. As always, therefore, we will begin with text.

Text

Ventura's Editing Tools

Although it is usually easier to edit large sections of text with a word processor, Ventura provides a text editing toolkit for last minute changes. You can cut, copy, and paste text or change the attributes of selected words within a paragraph.

Change Text Attributes

■ Select the Text Function button to enable text mode.

When you enable text mode, Ventura displays attributes — Bold, Italic, Normal, Small, and so forth — in the Assignment List and the words Set Font in the Addition Box.

In Chapter One you changed the font using paragraph mode. But as you can see, Ventura also allows you to change text attributes in text mode. What's the difference?

➥ *TIP: Use text editing mode to change one or two words within a paragraph. Use a paragraph tag to change the text attributes of an entire paragraph.*

Let's use Ventura's text editing tools to italicize several key words in the proposal. The italics will add emphasis and set them off from the rest of the paragraph. To italicize the text, first select the text then select the attribute.

■ Move the cursor in front of the "M" in the word "Market Research". Press and hold the mouse button as you drag the cursor to the end of the word "Research". Release the mouse button.

Now that the text is highlighted, italicize it.

■ Select Italic from the Assignment List.

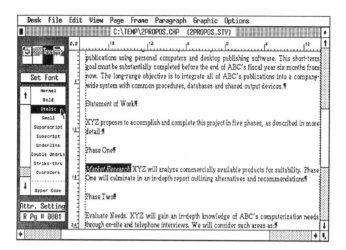

The action you just took placed markers into the text file to turn the italics on and off. If you were to return now to the text file, these markers would be visible as bracket codes:

```
Phase One

<MI>Market Research<D>. XYZ will analyze commercially
available products
for suitability. Phase One will culminate in an in-depth
report outlining
alternatives and recommendations.

Phase Two

Evaluate Needs.XYZ will gain an in-depth knowledge of ABC's
computerization
needs through on-site and telephone interviews. We will
consider such
areas as:

Word processing and editorial requirements
```

In Ventura, however, the markers are invisible on the screen. Nevertheless, you can locate them using the arrow keys and the Current Selection Box at the bottom of the Sidebar.

■ Place the cursor between the "M" and the "a" in Market Research. Press the left arrow key several times until the words "Attr. Setting" appear in the Current Selection Box. This shows the location of the hidden marker.

➡ *TIP: To remove text attributes, select the text then select Normal from the Assignment List.*

Dragging the mouse is one way to select text. However, there is a more accurate way called the "Shift-Click" method.

■ Place your text cursor before the "E" of "Evaluate Needs" and click once. Move the text cursor to the end of the phrase (after the "s") and click again *while holding down the Shift key.*

■ With "Evaluate Needs" highlighted, select Italic from the Assignment List.

➡ *NOTE: You can change the amount of text selected by moving the cursor to another position and clicking again while holding down the Shift key.*

■ Press PgDn to go to the next page.

■ Select the three following phrases and make them italic as explained above: "Installation," "Data Conversion," and "Training and Implementation."

When you are finished applying text attributes, your screen should look like this:

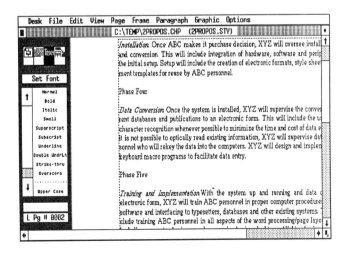

Edit Text

Now use Ventura's cut and paste tools to rearrange the copy in our proposal. First select the text you want (by dragging or by using the Shift-Click method). With the text highlighted, select Cut Text or Copy Text from the Edit menu.

After you cut or copy text, Ventura stores it in temporary memory. To insert text from temporary memory onto the page, select Paste Text from the Edit menu.

➠ *TIP: Use keyboard shortcuts to speed text editing. Press Del to cut, press Shift-Del to copy and press Ins to paste.*

■ Go back to page one. Select the paragraph starting with "Market Research" as shown below. Make sure you include the end of paragraph mark (¶) in the text selection .

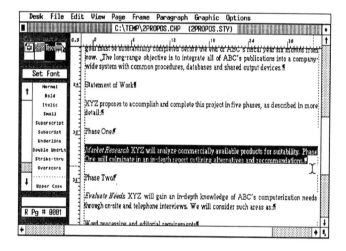

■ Press the Del key.

The text is cut from the document and placed in temporary memory. Now you can paste it into a new location:

■ Place the cursor before "Evaluate." Click the text cursor once.

■ Press the Ins key.

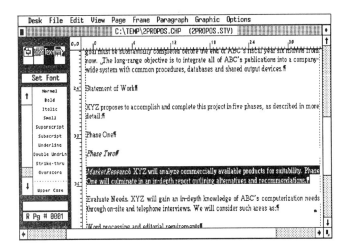

➦ *NOTE: Text remains in temporary memory until something else is cut or copied.*

■ Select the text starting with "Evaluate Needs" and ending with "Speed and throughput requirements" as shown below. (Be sure to include the end of paragraph mark in your selection.)

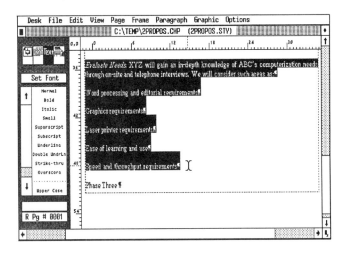

■ Press the Del key.

Now paste the text back into the document below the paragraph "Phase One."

■ Place the cursor in front of the "P" of "Phase Two" and press Ins.

After you rearrange the text, your screen should look like this:

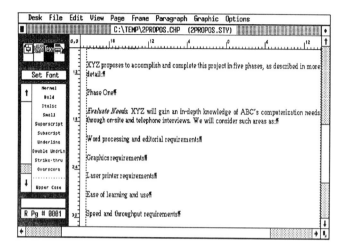

➥ *NOTE: Do not be concerned if you have to adjust a text attribute or two to get your screen to match ours. Sometimes, when you move text in a document, you can move a text attribute.*

Nice work. With just a little practice, you've learned the basics of text editing.

Style

Begin the style portion of this project by completing the global (overall) page layout. Then we will show you how to add tags to a style sheet and how to use a special tag named Page Break to isolate text on a page. These tips may save you some of the mistakes and confusion we experienced as first-time Ventura users.

Page Layout Strategy

Let's take a moment to review the formatting strategy we introduced in Chapter One, a strategy that helps you stay on course when working on the style of a document. First make the global changes to the page. Then tag individual paragraphs, starting with body text. As you make changes, step through the menus from left to right and from top to bottom.

Change the Page Layout

■ Select Page Layout from the Page menu. Select Sides: Single and Start On: Right Page.

Build the Footer

Next, build a footer that includes the name of the proposal and the page number.

■ Select Headers & Footers from the Page menu.

■ Select Right Page Footer, Usage On. Move to the Left line and type: **ABC Proposal**

■ Move to the Right line and type: **Page** followed by a space. Then choose the Page # button. Click OK to close the dialog box.

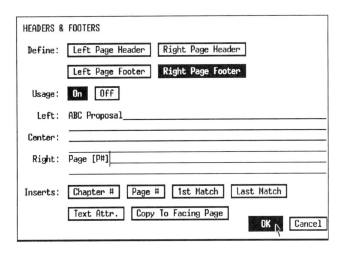

Turn the footer off for the first page only.

■ Verify that you are on page one. If not, press Home.

■ Select Turn Footer Off from the Page menu.

Change to Two-Column Format

After making the footer, you're ready to change the page margins and columns. As we explained earlier, a two column page layout lets you fit more text on a page and enhance its readability. When you change from one to two-column format, watch how easily Ventura reflows the text.

■ Enable Frame mode.

■ Select Margins & Columns from the Frame menu. Choose # of Columns: 2. Make the top and bottom margins 6,00 picas and the left and right margins 7,06 picas.

After setting the page margins enter column and gutter margins. To make the columns equal widths, enter the first column size, then enter the gutter size (the space between columns), then choose Make Equal Widths. Use this selection order to ensure that Ventura accurately calculates the columns.

■ Move to the Column 1 line, press Esc to clear the line, and type: **16,11**

■ Move to the first line of the Gutters column, press Esc and type: **0200**

■ Choose Make Equal Widths.

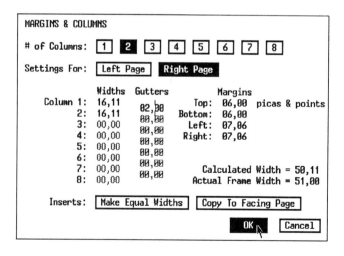

Turn Column Balance On

To balance the text in adjacent columns, turn Column Balance On in the Sizing & Scaling dialog box. Without column balance on, Ventura fills the first column with text before starting the second. With Column Balance on, Ventura fills both columns equally.

■ Select the underlying page. Select Sizing & Scaling from the Frame menu. Choose Column Balance On.

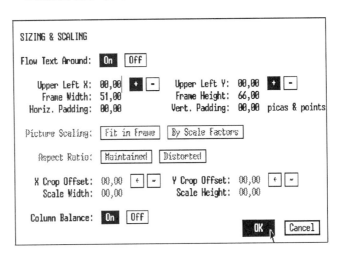

Modifying Individual Tags

Since there are no more overall changes to make, you can begin to tag individual paragraphs. Start with body text, since its inter-line spacing is the basis for all other tags. Once you complete body text, proceed systematically through the document from top to bottom. You can achieve most of the effects you want with the Font, Alignment, and Spacing options in the Paragraph menu. In this section, you will build up your tagging repertoire by learning about the different options in the Breaks menu. But first let's modify the body text tag.

Change the Body Text Tag

Proceed through the "Big Three" (Font, Alignment and Spacing) to change the body text.

■ Select the paragraph that begins "XYZ Corporation proposes to advise...".

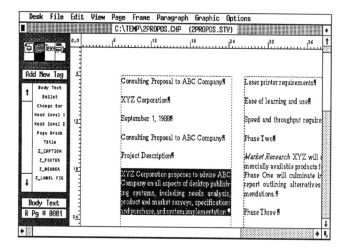

The tag name Body Text appears in the Current Selection Box.

- Font   Face: Times
                          Style: Normal
                          Size: 012 points

- Alignment   Justified
                          Overall Width: Column-Wide
                          First Line: Indent
                          In/Outdent Width: 01,00 pica

Ventura measures indents from the left margin of the column.

- Spacing   Inter-Line: 14.00 points

Change the Title Page Tags

Now that you've finished changing the body text tag, apply and modify the other tags on the title page of the proposal.

- Select the paragraph "Consulting Proposal to ABC Company" and tag it as Title.

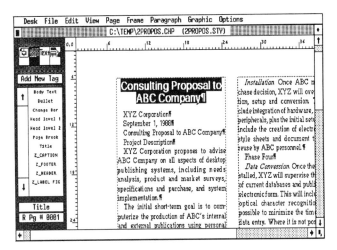

The current format is part of the original style sheet you loaded at the beginning of this project. Now you will modify its design to better suit the new page design. Make the Title tag stand out on the page by centering it frame-wide, enlarging its type size, and adding extra space above and below.

- Font

  Face: Times
  Style: Bold
  Size: 024 points

- Alignment

  Center
  Overall Width: Frame-Wide

- Spacing

  Above: 96.00 points
  Below: 28.00 points
  Inter-Line: 36.00 points
  Add in Above: Always

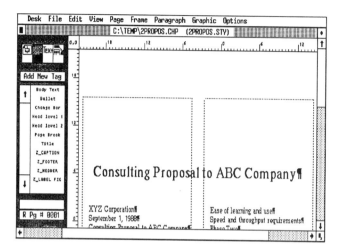

A note about spacing: In Chapter One we said that (1) you should never use Inter-Paragraph spacing and (2) you can do without Below spacing about 75% of the time. The Title tag, however, is an exception to the rule. Because it is a banner headline — a headline that stretches across two or more columns, it usually requires space below to separate it from the following text.

After defining the Title tag, apply it to the next paragraph.

■ Select the paragraph "XYZ Corporation" and tag it as Title.

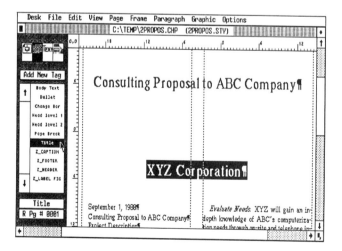

Add a New Tag

The next paragraph to tag is the date. To make it better match the Title tag, you will center it frame-wide and make it 12-point Times Bold. Since there are currently no tags in the Assignment List with these attributes, you will add a new tag.

To make a new tag, Ventura copies the attributes from an existing tag to the new one. Then you add or subtract attributes to the new tag name until you get the right effect. Here are the steps to add a new tag.

- Enable paragraph tagging mode

- Select a paragraph with attributes similar to the tag you want to add

- Select Add New Tag from the Sidebar

- Type in the name of the new tag

- Go through the Paragraph menus and add or subtract attributes to achieve the right effect

Don't worry if this sounds confusing at first. You will see the light as soon as you add a tag or two. So let's get started. Create a tag named "Center" and apply it the date paragraph.

■ Select the paragraph "September 1, 1988."

■ Select Add New Tag from the Sidebar.

■ Move to the Tag Name to Add line and type: `Center`

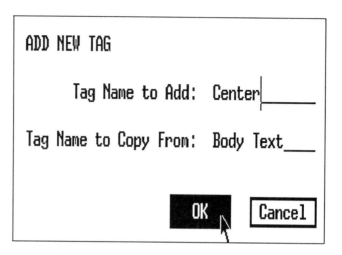

Ventura copies the attributes of Body Text — its Font, its Alignment, its Spacing, etc. — to the new tag.

Modify the New Tag

Now that you've added a new tag, begin to change its attributes. Work through the Paragraph menu from top to bottom until you achieve the right effect.

- ■ Font
  Face: Times
  Style: Bold
  Size: 012 points

- ■ Alignment
  Center
  Overall Width: Frame-Wide
  First Line: Indent
  In/Outdent Width: 00,00 picas

- ■ Spacing
  Above: 28.00 points
  Inter-Line: 14.00 points
  Add in Above: When Not at Column Top

Add a Page Break

With the first three three paragraphs tagged the title page is complete. Now you must separate the title page text from the rest of the document. To do this you use a special Page Break tag. The Page Break tag includes a *Page Break: After* which forces everything after it to appear on a new page. The Page

Break tag was already defined in the style sheet using the Breaks options from the Paragraph menu.

Here's how to use the Page Break tag to create a separate title page.

Make sure that Show Tabs & Returns is On from the Options menu. This allows you to see an on-screen display of the symbols that mark an empty paragraph.

- Enable text editing mode. Place the text cursor after the last "8" in the word "1988." Then press the Enter key once to create an empty paragraph.

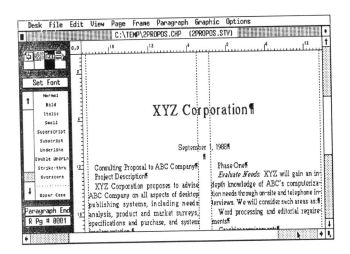

Now tag the empty paragraph as Page Break, just as you would tag any other paragraph.

➥ *TIP: You can apply tags to empty paragraphs as well as to text.*

- Enable paragraph tagging mode.
- Select the empty paragraph (highlight the "¶" symbol) and tag it as Page Break.

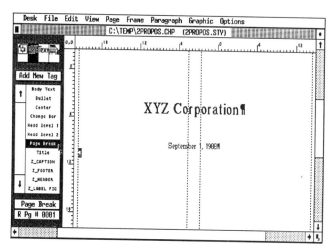

The remaining text is pushed on to the second page.

To understand this effect, leave the empty paragraph high-lighted and select Breaks from the Paragraph menu. There you see that the Page Break: After option was specified.

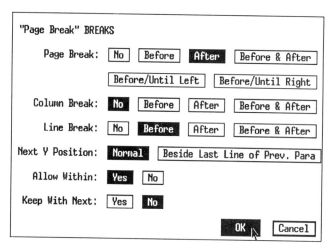

The page break effect is an important one. Use the page break tag whenever you want to start text on a new page. Try to avoid the common mistake of entering a string of carriage returns to force text to another page.

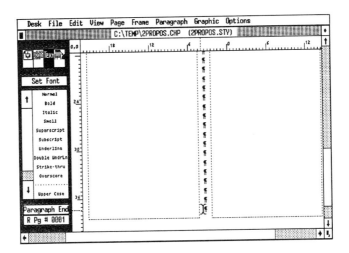

This is *not* the right way to make a page break. If you later add text, or change of attributes of a tag, some of the extra carriage returns will "float" onto the next page causing everything in the document to be pushed out of place. Remember to use the a Page Break tag instead.

Stopping Point

You have finished the tagging on page one and reached a stopping point for Chapter Two. Continue on immediately to page two if time permits. If not, you may wish to save the chapter, then print it out. Compare it with the example below:

Consulting Proposal to ABC Company

XYZ Corporation

September 1, 1988

Apply a Tag to Multiple Paragraphs

If you are beginning fresh, open the chapter C:\TEMP\2PROPOS.CHP and start from where you left off.

Go to page two to continue tagging.

■ Press PgDn to go to page two.

- Tag the paragraph "Consulting Proposal to ABC Company" as Title.

Next you'll change the Head level 1 tag. Since there are several Head level 1 tags on the same page, you can use the "Shift-Click" selection method to tag multiple paragraphs at one time.

- Select the paragraph "Project Description."

- While holding down the Shift key, select the paragraph "Statement of Work." Tag both paragraphs as Head level 1.

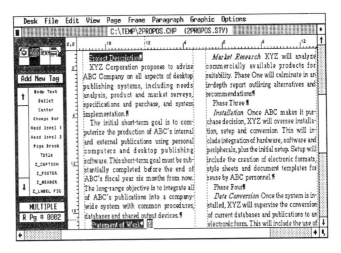

➡ *NOTE: Even if the selected tag is out of view, its attributes will be changed.*

Change the Head Level 1 Tag

With the two paragraphs still highlighted, modify the tag. First remove the ruling line below, then change the Font, Alignment, Spacing, and Breaks.

- Select Ruling Line Below from the Paragraph menu. Choose None.

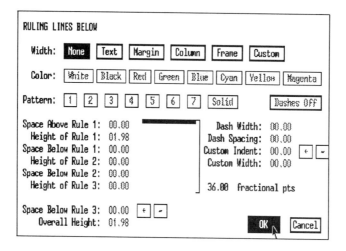

- ■ Font   Face: Times
                 Style: Bold
                 Size: 018 points

- ■ Alignment   Center
                 Overall Width: Column-Wide

- ■ Spacing   Above: 28.00
                 Inter-Line: 28.00
                 Add in Above: When Not at Column Top

When you are finished, the tag should look like this:

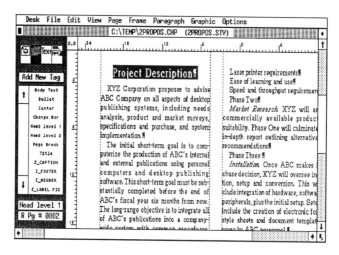

To keep Head level 1 from becoming isolated at the bottom of a column or page use the Breaks option Keep With Next. Keep

With Next guarantees that a tag stays next to the text that follows it.

■ Select Breaks from the Paragraph menu. Choose Keep With Next: Yes.

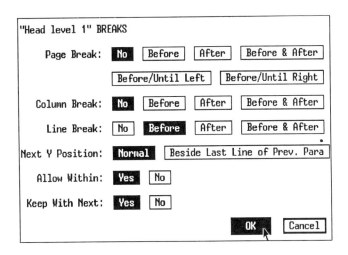

➥ *TIP: Headlines, headings and subheads should have Keep With Next set to Yes to keep them from becoming isolated at the bottom of a page or column.*

The Head Level 2 Tag

Now tag each paragraph that begins with the word "Phase" as Head level 2.

■ Select the first paragraph "Phase One." Then use Shift-Click to select the paragraphs, "Phase Two," "Phase Three," and "Phase Four." Tag them as Head level 2.

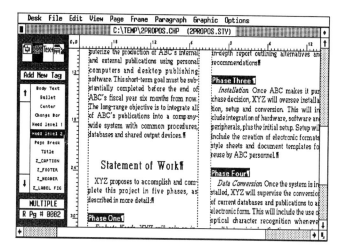

Change Head Level 2

Now change the attributes of the Head level 2 tag.

- Font
  Face: Times
  Style: Bold
  Size: 012 points

- Alignment
  Left
  Overall Width: Column-Wide

- Spacing
  Above: 14.00 points
  Inter-Line: 14.00 points
  Add in Above: When Not at Column Top

Like Head level 1, Head level 2 includes a Break: Keep With Next to prevent it from becoming isolated at the bottom of a page or a column.

- Breaks
  Keep with Next: Yes

Check that the tag you just completed looks like this:

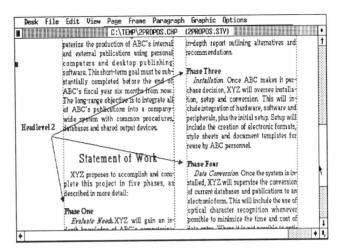

The Bullet Tag

The next tag you encounter is the Bullet tag. In addition to making the bullet size larger, you will reduce the Above Spacing and the In From Left Spacing.

■ Select the following five bullet paragraphs using the Shift-Click method and tag them as Bullet.

"Word processing and editorial requirements"

"Graphic requirements"

"Laser printer requirements"

"Ease of learning and use"

"Speed and throughput requirements"

➡ *NOTE: As long as you keep the Shift key depressed, you can scroll up and down the page to select multiple paragraphs. Select the first bullet at the bottom of the first column, hold down the Shift key, then scroll to the top of the second column and select the rest of the bullets.*

Change the Bullet Tag

Now change the attributes.

■ Spacing   Inter-Line: 14.00 points
                 Add in Above: When Not at Column Top
                 In From Left: 1,00 pica

➡️ *NOTE: If you tend to confuse Spacing/In From Left with Align-
ment/Indent, remember this rule of thumb: Alignment/Indent affects only the first few lines of a paragraph. Spacing/In From
Left affects every line.*

■ Breaks   Keep With Next: No

Setting Keep With Next to No allows Ventura to split a list of
bullets across a column or a page. Otherwise, if the list is too
long, Ventura pushes all the bullets to the next column or page
leaving a big, empty gap in the document.

Increase the Bullet Size

To change the size of the bullet itself, use the Special Effects
dialog box in the Paragraph menu.

■ Select Special Effects from the Paragraph menu. Choose
Set Font Properties.

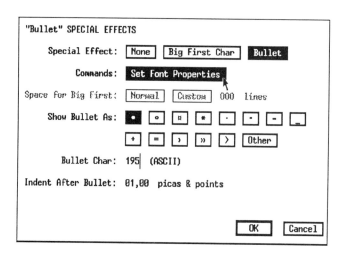

The Set Font Properties dialog box looks familiar, doesn't it?
It's the same Font dialog box you've seen before. You simply
got here a new way. The changes you make in this dialog box
will affect *only* the bullet, not the rest of the paragraph.

■ Select Times, Normal, Black and 014 points. Then click OK to return to the Special Effects dialog box. Click OK again to complete the effect and return to the document.

Change the Footer Tag

Footers are among the special tags that Ventura creates on its own called "generated" tags. These tags are given names that begin with the letter Z (Z_HEADER for the header, Z_FOOTER, for the footer, and so on) to distinguish them from others in the Assignment List. Like all tags, you can change the attributes of a generated tag simply by working through the options in the Paragraph menu. Let's change the font of the Z_FOOTER tag so it matches the rest of the proposal.

■ Select the footer on page two and change its attributes.

■ Font   Face: Times
                     Style: Normal
                     Size: 010 points

When you are finished, the footer should look like this:

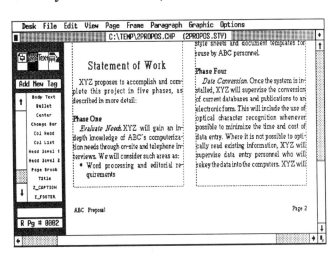

Finish Tagging the Document

After you change the footer, finish tagging the remaining paragraphs in the document.

■ Press the End key to go to the last page of the document.

- Verify that paragraph "Phase Five" is tagged as Head level 2.

- Select the paragraph "Project Costs" and tag it as Head level 1.

Pictures

Now that you've completed the Text and Style sections of this document, let's continue with pictures.

As you learned from Chapter One, to add a picture to a document you load a graphics file and place it in a frame. You can make a frame any size or shape to fit with the page design and the artwork.

In Chapter One you added a frame to hold a picture. However, frames can also contain text. One common example is a spreadsheet file. Instead of retyping a worksheet from scratch, you can load it into Ventura and place it in a frame. Once you have it in the frame, you can format it into a table. In the pictures section, you will learn how to place and format a simple spreadsheet file.

Preparing Spreadsheet Files for Ventura

If you regularly work with spreadsheet files, we recommend that you read through the next section, which explains the steps for creating text from a spreadsheet program.

Before loading a spreadsheet file, you must convert it to ASCII format and replace spaces between columns with single tab characters. Ventura requires one and only one tab between columns. Otherwise, the columns will not align properly.

To convert to ASCII format, you can either use the built-in ASCII option of the spreadsheet program or print the worksheet to a disk file. Once the file is converted to ASCII, you must strip out the spaces between the columns and replace those spaces with tab characters. You can accomplish this task in several ways. One is to load the file into a word processor and use its search and replace feature. Another is to use a utility program such as CONVERTD (a MicroSoft Word utility) or VPTABS from Laser Edge. Or, if you prefer, you can load the file into Ventura and make the substitution manually. For the purposes of this project, you'll place and format the TABLE.TXT file that was already prepared using one of the methods described above.

Create the Frame

Before you place the text file, you must add a frame to contain it.

➡ *NOTE: Placing text files in frames allows you to place several different text files on the same page.*

To make frame placement easier, make sure Column and Line Snap are turned on (Options menu). These snap-to functions ensure that frames align with the margins and with the line spacing of the body text tag.

■ Switch to Reduced View (press Ctrl-R).

■ Enable frame mode.

■ Select Add New Frame from the Sidebar.

■ Starting at position 29 on the vertical ruler, place the upper left corner of the frame cursor next to the left margin.

■ Drag the lower right corner of the frame downwards and to the right. When the frame aligns with the right margin of the page (at about 50,00 picas), release the mouse button.

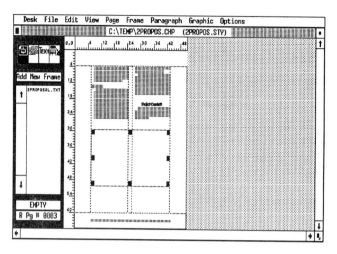

Resize the Frame

The Sizing & Scaling dialog box allows you to precisely control the placement and size of frames on the page. You can enter an exact X,Y value for the upper left corner of the frame and a precise width and height.

- Select Sizing & Scaling from the Frame menu. Make the Upper Left X: 7,06 picas (if this is not the current value, press Esc to clear the line and type in 7,06 picas). Make the Upper Left Y: 29,03 picas. Make the frame width 36,00 picas and the frame height 21,00 picas.

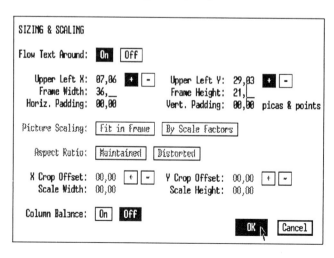

Place the Spreadsheet File

After you position and size the frame, place the sample spreadsheet file.

■ Switch to Normal View (press Ctrl-N).

■ With the frame still highlighted, select the text file name TABLE.TXT and place it in the frame.

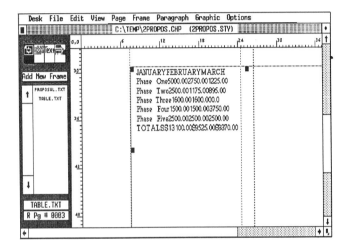

Add Margins to the Frame

To center the spreadsheet text within the frame, add margins to the frame. These margins will affect only the selected frame. *They will not affect the underlying page.*

➡ *NOTE: Frames that you place on top of the underlying page can have their own margins and columns, independent of the underlying page.*

■ Margins &   Top Margin: 2,00 picas
  Columns   Bottom Margin: 2,00 picas
                     Left Margin: 2,00 picas
                     Right Margin: 2,00 picas

Place a Box Around the Frame

Next separate the frame from the surrounding text by placing a ruling box around the frame.

■ Select Ruling Box Around from the Frame menu.

■ Choose Frame. Give Rule 1 a height of 00.50 points.

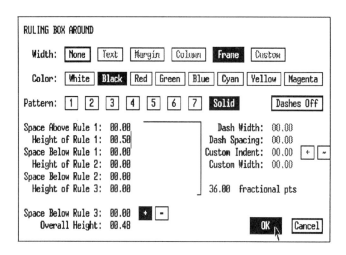

When you are satisfied with the appearance of the frame, continue to format the table.

Format the Table

There are several ways to format tabular material, but the easiest and simplest way is to use horizontal tabs.

➡ *TIP: Use horizontal tabs for tables that do not exceed one line per entry, and vertical tabs (explained in Chapter Nine), for more complex tables.*

Ventura allows up to sixteen tab positions per paragraph, with left, right, decimal or center alignment. The sample table uses both right aligned and decimal tabs. To format the table properly you need to create two new tags — one for the table headings and one for the table listings.

Format the Table Headings

Before you add the tag settings, you must add a new tag for the table heading and modify its Font, Alignment, and Spacing.

■ Enable paragraph tagging mode and select the paragraph "JANUARY, FEBRUARY, MARCH...."

■ Select Add New Tag. Move to the Tag Name to Add line: and type: **Col Head**

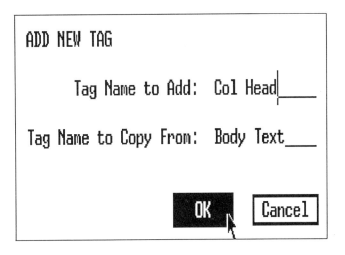

ADD NEW TAG

Tag Name to Add: Col Head___

Tag Name to Copy From: Body Text___

OK   [Cancel]

■ Font
    Face: Helvetica
    Style: Bold
    Size: 010 points

■ Alignment
    Left
    In/Outdent Width: 00,00 picas

Set the First Tab Stop

Place the columns at 15,03, 23,03 and 29,03 picas from the left margin of the frame. Take the tab stops one at a time. First enter the tab alignment and then the tab location.

➡ *NOTE: The tab location is always measured from the left margin. Since the left margin of this new frame is 2,00 picas in from the frame edge, Ventura measures each tab location starting two picas in from the edge of the frame.*

■ Select Tab Settings from the Paragraph menu.

Tab number "1" is already highlighted.

■ Choose Tab Type: Right, Tab Display: Shown as Open Space. Move to the Tab Location line and type: **15,03**

■ *Do not* choose OK yet, since we still have more tabs to set.

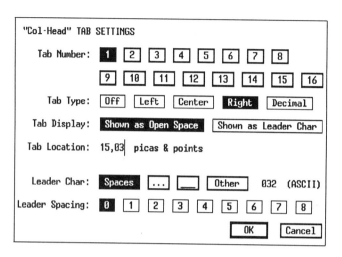

Set the Second Tab Stop

■ Choose Tab Number: 2, Tab Type: Right, Tab Display: Shown as Open Space. Move to the Tab Location line and type: **23,03**

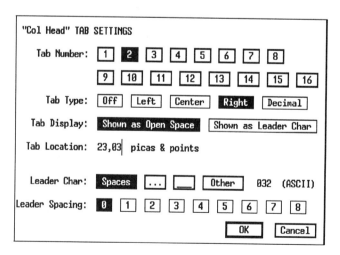

Set the Third Tab Stop

■ Choose Tab Number: 3, Tab Type: Right, Tab Display:

Shown as Open Space. Move to the Tab Location line and type: **29,03**

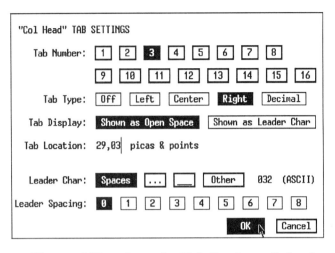

■ Choose OK to close the Tab Settings dialog box.

Format the Listings

If tab settings seem confusing at first, don't worry. The more tables you format, the easier tabs will become. You'll get more practice with tabs right away by formatting the table listings.

■ Select the paragraph "Phase One ..." and tag it as Col Head.

■ Select Add New Tag from the sidebar. Move to Tag Name to Add and type: **Col List**

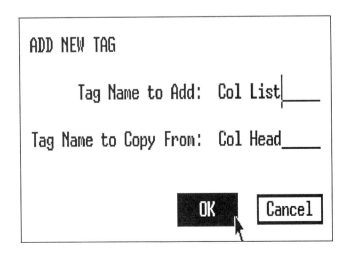

When creating a new tag, Ventura starts by copying the attributes of an old one. It makes sense, therefore, to copy from the tag that is most similar to the new effect you want. In this case, Col Head is nearest to the final format.

➡ *TIP: When adding a new tag, always copy from the tag that is nearest in appearance and format.*

Since you copied from Col Head, the listing tag should be pretty close to the correct style. To finish the tag, change the font style to Normal and change the above spacing.

■ Font
    Face: Helvetica
    Style: Normal

■ Spacing
    Above: 14.00 points
    Add in Above: Always

Set the Tab Stops

Since the font, alignment and spacing are already correct, you need only modify the tab settings to get the new Col List tag to look the way you want. When you choose tab settings this time, use decimal tabs to line up the numbers with the decimal character in each column of the table.

■ Tab Settings
    Tab number: 1
    Tab Type: Decimal
    Display: Shown as Open Space
    Tab Location: 14,00 picas

    Tab Number: 2
    Tab Type: Decimal
    Tab Display: Shown as Open Space
    Tab Location: 22,00 picas

    Tab Number: 3
    Tab Type: Decimal
    Tab Display: Shown as Open Space
    Tab Location: 28,00 picas

Now check the appearance of your tag with the illustration below.

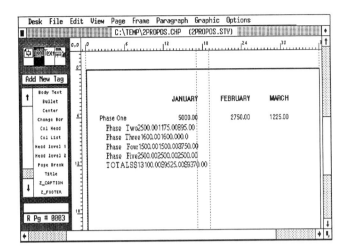

Apply Col List to the Other Paragraphs

Now that you've completed the attribute and tab settings for the new tag, apply it to the remaining paragraphs in the table. Remember, you can select multiple paragraphs using the Shift-Click method.

■ Select the five paragraphs shown in the next illustration and tag them as Col List.

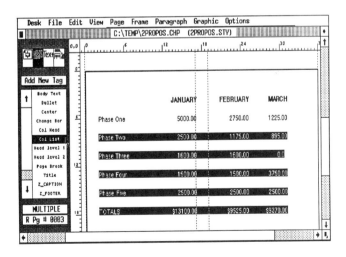

Add a Caption

To put the final touch on the spreadsheet, attach a caption and label to the frame.

■ Enable frame setting mode and select the frame that contains the spreadsheet.

■ Select Anchors & Captions from the Frame menu.

■ Choose Below and OK.

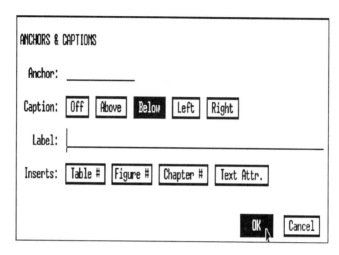

A blank caption frame appears below the existing frame.

Enlarge the Caption Frame

■ Enable frame mode. Click anywhere in the caption frame so that eight "handles" appear around its borders.

■ Place the cursor on any handle at the bottom of the frame. Press and hold down the mouse cursor until the pointing hand icon appears. Drag the frame downwards about 3 lines and release the cursor. You should see an end of paragraph marker in the middle of the frame. If the marker is not visible, enlarge the caption frame a few lines.

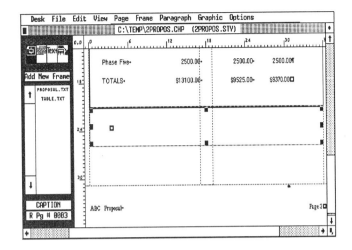

Add the Caption Text

■ Enable text mode. Place the cursor in front of the end of paragraph marker. Type: **Project Costs for Desktop Publishing Implementation**

Format the Caption Text

You've just created your first caption text. Now you can change its format just as you would change any other tag. Notice that the paragraph is another of Ventura's *generated* tags, as signaled by a name beginning with Z_ — in this case, Z_Caption.

■ Enable paragraph tagging mode. Select the caption paragraph: "Project Costs for Desktop Publishing Implementation."

■ Font   Face: Helvetica
                      Style: Bold
                      Size: 012 points

■ Alignment   Centered
                      Overall Width: Frame-Wide
                      In/Outdent Width: 00,00 picas

■ Spacing   Inter-Line: 14.00 points
                      Add in Above: Always.

Your caption should look like the following illustration.

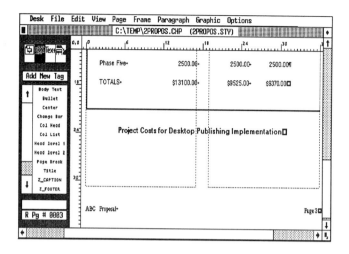

➥*NOTE: If the caption text disappears from view, simply make the caption frame bigger.*

Chapter

Now that you've completed text, style and picture, it's time to complete the chapter part of our proposal. But first take a breather and save your work.

■ Select Save from the File menu (or press Ctrl-S).

Print the Current Page

To evaluate the editorial and stylistic changes you've made on screen, and to determine if you've achieved a more pleasing page design time, print out the proposal. This time we will show you how to print the current page of a chapter.

■ Select To Print from the File menu.

■ Choose Which Pages: Current and OK.

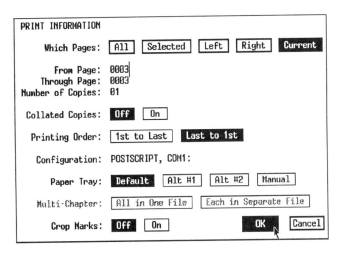

Ventura prints out the current page.

In the first two chapters you have learned how to build a report and a proposal using basic Ventura techniques. In the next chapter, you will polish off the remaining fundamentals while learning how to construct a new and important type of document — the newsletter.

Tips

Text Tips

❏ Use a word processor to globally search and replace double spaces before loading a text file into Ventura.

❏ When you prepare text for Ventura follow these guidelines. Do not: Center or justify text; Indent the first line of a paragraph; Create temporary margins; Put more than one space after a period, colon, or question mark; Put more than one carriage return between paragraphs; Put more than one tab stop between columns

❏ Use the @PARAFILTR code to filter out extra carriage returns in a text file. It must be inserted as the very first item in the document and it must be typed accurately or Ventura will ignore it.

❑ If you want to load a single file into Ventura without it automatically being placed on the underlying page, select Load Text/Picture from the File menu while you are in paragraph tagging, text editing or graphic mode.

❑ Rename text, style sheet, and chapter files before you make any changes to the document. Renaming files eliminates the possibility of permanently changing the originals.

❑ Use a word processor to make changes to large sections of text. Use Ventura's text editing tools to make small, last minute changes to text. You can cut, copy or paste text or change text attributes of selected words within a paragraph.

❑ Use text editing mode to change one or two words within a paragraph. Use a paragraph tag to change the attributes of an entire paragraph.

❑ Keyboard shortcuts can be used to speed up text editing in Ventura. Press Del to cut text, Shift-Del to copy text, and Ins to paste text.

❑ When you cut or copy text, it remains in temporary memory until something else is cut or copied. This features allows you to insert text from one chapter to another. Simply copy or cut the text, close the current chapter, then open another chapter. Press Ins to insert the text into the new chapter.

Style Tips

❑ To make equal column widths, enter the value of the first column size, then the first gutter width, then choose Make Equal Widths from the bottom of the Margins & Columns dialog box. Use this selection order to ensure that Ventura accurately calculates the column widths.

❑ Turning Column Balance On from the Sizing & Scaling dialog box tells Ventura to fill all columns on the page equally. Without column balance on, Ventura fills the first column before starting the next.

❑ Ventura measures the In/Outdent width from the left margin of the column.

❑ When you create a new tag, always copy from the tag that is nearest in appearance and format to the effect you want.

❑ To isolate text on a page, use a page break tag instead of a string of carriage returns. If you change a tag or add extra text, the carriage returns will "float" to the next page and push everything in the document out of place.

❑ You can use the Shift-Click method to tag multiple paragraphs.

❑ Headlines, headings and subheads should include a Breaks: Keep With Next: Yes to keep them from becoming isolated at the bottom of a page or a column.

❑ Headers, footers, and captions are tags that are automatically generated by Ventura. Like all tags their attributes can be changed by working through the paragraph menu options. Generated tags have names that begin with a Z to distinguish them from other tags in the Assignment List.

Picture Tips

❑ The Sizing & Scaling dialog box allows you to precisely control the position and size of a frame.

❑ Use horizontal tabs to format a table that does not exceed one line per entry. Use vertical tabs (see Chapter Nine) to format more complex tables.

❑ The tab location is always measured from the left margin.

❑ The caption labels you create with Anchors & Captions can only be edited through this dialog box. For longer captions, type text directly into the caption frame.

Chapter Three
Skills Checklist

Theory

✓ Frames versus the underlying page

Text

✓ Creating a text file directly in Ventura

✓ Faster tagging with function keys in text mode

Style

✓ Renaming and removing tags

✓ How to create leader dots

✓ More tricks with ruling lines

Pictures

✓ Sizing and scaling an image

✓ Creating caption labels

Chapter

✓ Archiving several chapters with Multi-Chapter

✓ Switching printers properly

A Two-Column Newsletter

Now that you've gained some momentum with Ventura, are you ready to step up the pace? In Chapter Three you will create a newsletter, a document with different design requirements than business reports and proposals. This project will introduce you to some of Ventura's most powerful features. The checklist on the left lists some of the techniques you will learn.

Theory

By the time you've finished with Chapter Three, you'll have been exposed to all of Ventura's fundamental skills. You'll be equipped with the basic tools to construct virtually any type of document. You are not ready to graduate, however, until you understand the difference between frames and the underlying page, and how to use this difference to build newsletter-style layouts.

Understanding Frames

Ventura uses frames to enclose text and pictures. You can draw frames anywhere on the page.

To work on a frame — to change its size or to place something inside — you must first select it. To select a frame, click once anywhere inside the boundary. Black handles appear around the edges.

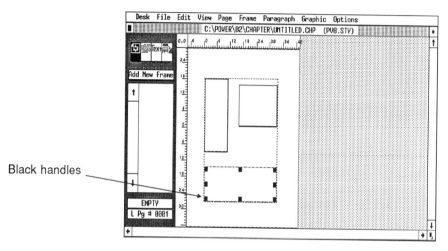

Black handles

You can use these handles to change the size of the frame. Place the cursor on top of a handle and press the mouse button until the pointing finger appears. Now *drag* the mouse — that is, move the mouse while holding the button down. When the frame is the proper size, release the button.

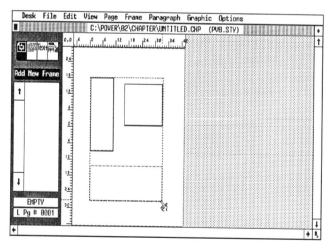

You can also move frames with ease. Place the mouse cursor anywhere inside the frame. Press and hold the button until the four-way arrow appears. Then drag the frame to the new location (move the mouse while holding the button down).

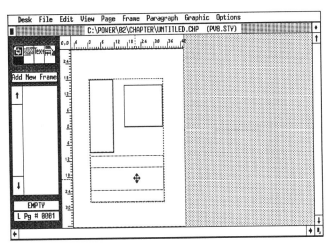

You can copy a frame into temporary memory and then paste as many copies as you want onto the page. Initially, the copy is invisible because it appears on top of the original. When you move the copy away, you will see the original underneath. You can also overlap frames.

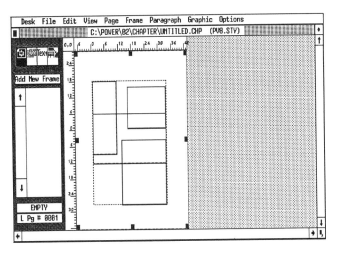

All frames have a boundary. That boundary can be invisible. Or, if you prefer, you can put a ruling line above, below or around the frame. The thickness of the line is up to you.

As you can see in the next illustration, the boundary acts as a container. You can place text or pictures inside.

No rules

Rule Above and Below

Ruling Box Around

Double Rules

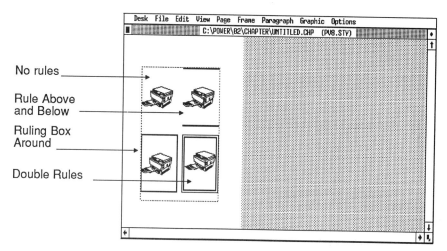

Suppose, however, that you pour a long text file into a small frame. In that case, Ventura fits as much of the text inside as it can, then waits for you to tell it what to do with the remainder. If you like, you can draw additional frames for the rest of the text file.

Frames can have margins and columns inside their boundaries. For instance, you might place a margin inside a frame to keep a picture from butting up against the boundary. Or you might create two columns within a single frame.

Frame can have their own margins

Frames can have their own columns

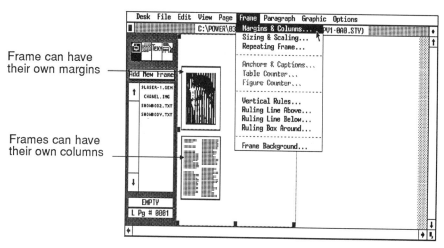

If you place a frame on top of the underlying page, the margins of the frame will override the margins of the page. For instance, in the illustration below, a three-column frame has been placed on top of a two-column page.

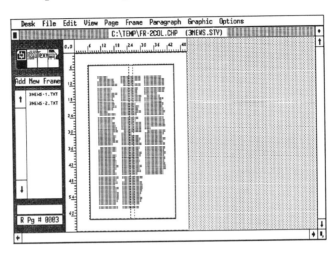

You can also create a caption for any frame. This caption is itself a separate, smaller frame attached to the original. If you move the original frame, the caption moves with it. The text of the caption is contained within the caption frame.

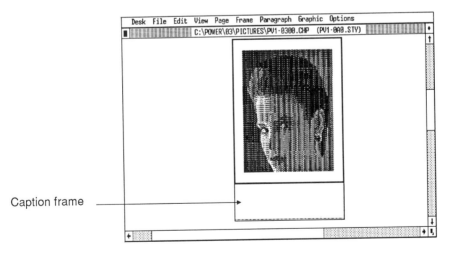

Caption frame

Understanding the Underlying Page

When you first start learning Ventura, it is easy to become confused by Ventura's *underlying page*. Think of the underlying page as a large frame. The boundaries of this frame equal the edges of the page (for instance, 8.5 x 11 inches for standard letter-size paper). Even though you can't see the boundaries, they are there, just as for smaller frames.

In most respects, the underlying page acts like any other frame. For instance, you can change its size with the Sizing & Scaling dialog box. And you can give it margins and columns just like a frame.

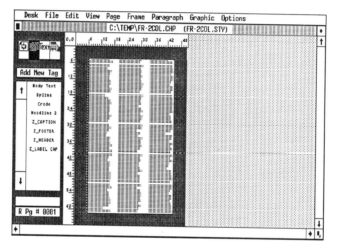

But the underlying page differs in one key aspect. When you place a text file into a frame, Ventura fits as much as possible, then waits for you to tell it where to put the rest. When you put text onto the underlying page, on the other hand, Ventura fits as much as possible onto the first page, *then automatically creates as many pages as necessary to accommodate the rest of the file.*

Frames Versus Pages

You have placed text on the underlying page in the previous two chapters. It is the method of choice when most of the chapter is made up of a single text file.

But some documents contain many different text files. Newsletters are a prime example. Theoretically, you could combine all the copy for a newsletter into one large file, and then format that file on the underlying page. In practice, however, it is much easier to keep each article as a separate text file.

But how do you keep the articles separate when you bring them into Ventura? Simple: you draw frames on top of the underlying page. Then you place the articles into those frames.

By the way, you can combine both frames and pages in the same document, as we did in Chapter Two. The bulk of the proposal was in a single text file on the underlying page. The worksheet, however, was a separate file that resided inside a frame. That frame had been drawn on top of the underlying page.

Newsletter-Style Layout

Let's summarize what we've learned and then apply it to the construction of a newsletter. Frames create boundaries that separate files. For example, you could use frames to place one text file into the left column of page 1 and a second, separate file into the right column of the same page.

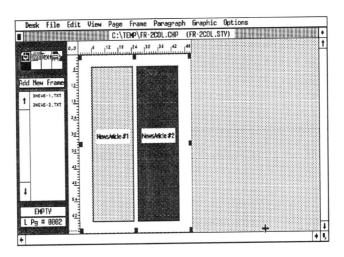

Both pages and frames can contain text, but they have a fundamental difference. When you place text on the underlying page, it flows to the end of the page. If there is text left over, Ventura creates as many new pages as needed.

When you put text into a frame, it flows to the end of that frame. But even if there is text left over, *Ventura does not create additional frames.* Instead, it remembers where it left off, and waits for you to tell it where to put the remainder. For instance, you can put part of a file into column one on the page 1, and continue the rest of it onto page 2. Ventura remembers this path. As you make editing changes, the text automatically flows back and forth between page 1 and page 2. In addition, articles can "leap frog" one another.

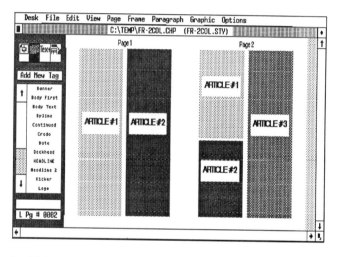

➡ *TIP: When building newsletter-style documents composed of several different text files, put the text into frames, not onto the underlying page.*

How do you know where to position the frames? Simple: format the underlying page with the correct margins and columns. Then use the underlying page as a guideline. Thanks to Ventura's snap-to features, your frames will automatically align with the columns on the page.

➡ *TIP: Use the underlying page to create a snap-to grid for positioning frames for newsletter-style layout.*

There is one more crucial principle you need to know before you are ready to start building a newsletter: *Ventura can only flow text in a "forward" direction.*

We put quotes around the word forward, because it means different things to Ventura than it does ordinarily. On a page-by-page basis, the meaning is straightforward. Ventura cannot flow text backwards to a previous page.

The "forward-only" restriction also applies on a single page with several frames. On a single page, however, the flowing order depends on which frame was drawn first. Ventura can flow text from the first frame to the second frame, but it cannot flow "backward" from the second frame to the first.

The position on the page makes no difference. Ventura determines text flow strictly on the basis of the order the frames were placed on the page. For instance, in the picture below, Ventura can flow text from frame #1 to frame #2 — not the reverse.

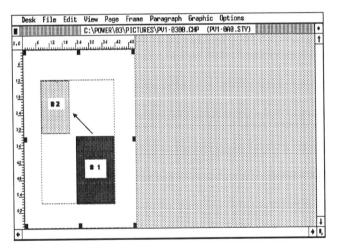

Likewise, in the following picture Ventura can flow text from frame #1 to frame #2 (not from frame #2 to frame #1).

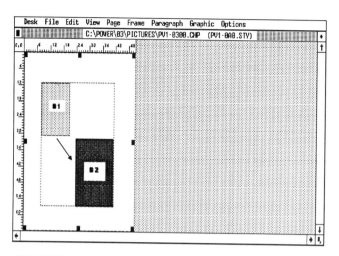

WARNING: The sample project in this chapter uses numbered frames. Draw these frames in the order shown. If you draw them in a different sequence you may be unable to flow the text.

Fortunately, Ventura provides a simple method for changing the order of frames. To make a frame the "last" one, simply select the frame, delete it and reinsert it again. In Ventura's eyes, it is now the last frame on the page. If you accidentally draw frames out of order, use this method to correct the problem.

You will use the principles explained above to construct the newsletter in this chapter. First you will format the underlying page. Then you will draw frames on top, using the margins and columns of the page as your guide. Finally, you will put text into the frames.

Before

After

Planning the Newsletter

The goal of a newsletter is to provide timely information to a specialized audience. This chapter's example is a corporate newsletter, an in-house organ for the fictitious XYZ Corporation.

Most newsletters are 8.5 x 11 inches. The simplest design consists of two pages stapled together or printed on both sides. Even the most complex newsletters rarely exceed 24 pages or so. Overall design should be informal and relaxed to help convey a sense of timeliness. The best design is simple, open and uncluttered.

Look at the "before" example nearby. Below we list some of the methods you will use to enhance its appearance and effectiveness.

- Large type for a logo
- Rules to separate and define different sections
- A kicker and a banner headline
- A table of contents
- Two-column format
- Uniform spacing to align text across columns

Ventura Prep

As you did in the previous two chapters, you will start the project by loading and renaming the text, style, picture and chapter files.

Load Text Files

For this project you will load four files at once. Later in the chapter, you will place them into frames — one for the logo, one for the headline, and two for articles. The text files are provided on the Publishing Power disk and should have previously been copied to the C:\POWER subdirectory according to the directions with the disk. These files have been preformatted with tag names and non-keyboard character codes. (Refer to Chapters Two and Seven for more on preformatting.)

➡ *NOTE: If you did not purchase the Power Disk, skip to the section below entitled "If You Do Not Have the Power Disk."*

■ Select Load Text/Picture from the File menu.

■ Choose Type of File: Text, Text Format: ASCII, # of Files: Several, and OK.

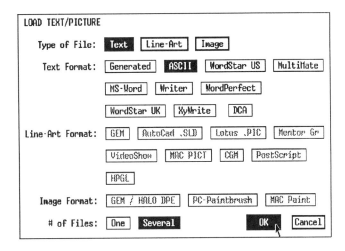

■ Find the C:\POWER subdirectory and scroll through the list until you find the file 3NEWSHED.TXT. Select the file.

After you select the first file, Ventura loads it, then redisplays the Item Selector so you can load more files.

■ Load the files 3NEWSLGO.TXT, 3NEWSONE.TXT and 3NEWSTWO.TXT. When you are finished, choose Cancel to close the dialog box.

Rename the Text Files

In frame setting mode, place each of the text files on the underlying page in turn. Using File Type/Rename from the Edit menu, rename the files as shown below:

Load from C:\POWER	Save to C:\TEMP
3NEWSHED.TXT	3HEAD.TXT
3NEWSONE.TXT	3NEWS-1.TXT
3NEWSTWO.TXT	3NEWS-2.TXT
3NEWSLGO.TXT	3LOGO.TXT

- If necessary, use Text/File Remove to remove text files from the underlying page. Remove them from the frame but not from the list of files.

Load and Rename a Style Sheet

As before, you will be modifying one of the style sheets provided with the Ventura program disks.

- Select Load Diff. Style Sheet from the File menu.

- Go to the C:\TYPESET subdirectory. Load the style sheet named &NEWS-P2.STY.

- Select Save as New Style from the File menu.

- Go to the C:\TEMP subdirectory and type in the new file name, 3NEWS. Then click OK.

Load a Picture

- Select Load Text/Picture from the File menu. Choose Type of File: Image, Image Format: Gem/Halo DPE, # of Files: One, and OK.

- Move to the C:\TYPESET subdirectory and load CHANEL.IMG.

If the picture is placed on the page, use Text/File Remove to remove it from the frame (not the Assignment List).

➥*NOTE: CHANEL.IMG was copied to the \TYPESET subdirectory during Ventura installation. If you have deleted or moved this file, use DOS to copy it back from disk #11 of your original Ventura software disks.*

Rename the Chapter

When you have finished loading and renaming the text and style sheet files, save the chapter with a new name.

■ Select Save As from the File menu. Go to the C:\TEMP subdirectory and type in the new chapter name, 3NEWS, and click OK.

If You Do Not Have the Power Disk

Exit from Ventura. Use your word processor to type in the text files 3HEAD.TXT, 3NEWS-1.TXT, 3NEWS-2.TXT and 3LOGO.TXT from Appendix A. Place them in the C:\TEMP subdirectory. Then return to Ventura and proceed through the rest of Ventura Prep.

Text

Normally you would place the text files at this point. However, since you will be putting those files into frames, and not onto the underlying page, you must deviate slightly from the Ventura Formula. The only change is to delay placing the text files until you build frames to contain them. To build these frames, proceed to the Style section.

Style

Your goal is to create frames of the right size and position to hold the text files. To make this job easier, first construct the underlying page. Then you can use the underlying page as a guideline for placing frames.

➡ *NOTE: Remember our rule of thumb: format the overall document before the individual text paragraphs. This rule is even more important when using newsletter-style layout.*

Change to Double Sides

The in-house newsletter will be printed on both sides of the paper, so you must switch to double-sided page layout. Ventura then makes a mirror image of headers, margins, etc., from the right to the left page. For instance, the page number on the right side of a right-page header will be copied to the left side of the left-page header.

■ Select Page Layout from the Page menu. Choose Sides: Double and Start On: Right Page.

Change the Margins

Now increase the size of the page margins and the gutter margin. You are altering the original style sheet to make the columns shorter and to add more white space.

■ Select Margins & Columns from the Frame menu. Make the top and bottom margins 04,06 picas, the left and right margins 06,00 picas. Make the Column 1 width 18,06 picas and the first gutter 02,00 picas. Make Column 2 width 18,06 picas and choose Copy to Facing Page. (The Copy to Facing Page button does not stay highlighted.)

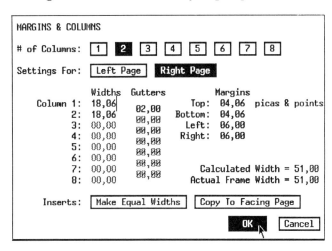

➥*NOTE: If you selected Make Equal Widths, Ventura would make each column widths 18,05 picas. The overall width of the columns and gutters would be 50,11 picas instead of 51,00 picas.*

Create a Vertical Rule

The Vertical Rule option creates a ruling line between columns *on the underlying page.* The rule is always the same height as the columns. A vertical rule visually separates columns and makes left-justified text easier to read.

■ Select Vertical Rules from the Frame menu.

■ Change to fractional points.

■ Select Settings For: Right Page, Inter-Col. Rules: On, Width: 00.25 fractional points. Click on Copy to Facing Page to mirror these settings to the opposite page. Click OK to close the dialog box.

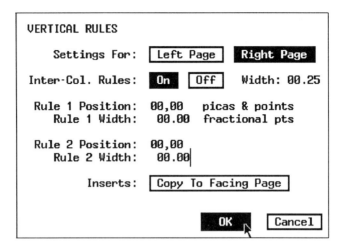

Add a Header

To complete the overall page layout, add a header that includes the newsletter's name, the page and the month of the issue.

■ Select Headers & Footers from the Page menu.

■ Choose Right Page Header, Usage: On. Then type in the text you wish to appear on the appropriate lines.

Left: **The Newsletter**

Center: **Page [#]**

Right: **Fall/Winter 1988**

■ Click on Copy to Facing Pages to mirror these settings to the left page.

```
┌─────────────────────────────────────────────────────────┐
│ HEADERS & FOOTERS                                         │
│                                                           │
│  Define:  [ Left Page Header ]  [ Right Page Header ]     │
│                                                           │
│           [ Left Page Footer ]  [ Right Page Footer ]     │
│                                                           │
│   Usage:  [ On ] [ Off ]                                  │
│                                                           │
│    Left:  The Newsletter_____     │
│                                                           │
│  Center:  Page [P#]_____     │
│                                                           │
│   Right:  Fall/Winter 1988_____     │
│                          _____     │
│                                                           │
│ Inserts:  [ Chapter # ]  [ Page # ]  [ 1st Match ]  [ Last Match ] │
│           [ Text Attr. ]  [ Copy To Facing Page ]         │
│                                        [ OK ] [ Cancel ]  │
└─────────────────────────────────────────────────────────┘
```

Now turn the header off for the first page only.

■ Select Turn Header Off from the Page menu.

Before you continue, take a moment to save your work.

➥ *TIP: Save every 15 to 30 minutes to reduce the risk of losing work due to a computer glitch, software crash or power outage.*

From now on, we will not remind you to save. We will assume that you are regularly hitting Ctrl-S as you progress through the chapter.

Add Frames

Now that you have completed the overall page layout, you can draw frames on the underlying page.

Before you start, go to the Options menu and confirm that Line Snap and Column Snap are On (when Column and Line Snap are On, the Options menu displays Column Snap Off and Line Snap Off). These features help line up frames properly. Thanks to Column Snap, the frames you draw will automatically be the right width, since they will snap to the column guides on the underlying page. Use the ruler to gauge the approximate height.

■ Enable frame mode. Select Add New Frame from the Sidebar. Place the the frame cursor at the upper left corner of the dotted column guides on the underlying page.

■ Press and hold the mouse button. Drag the lower right corner of the frame downwards.

■ Release the button when the frame reaches position 16,06 on the vertical ruler.

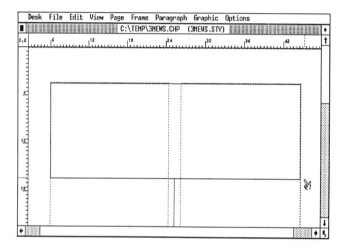

■ Repeat the step above to place all the frames on the page. Use the following illustration as an approximate guide before you fine-tune the frame size as explained in the next step.

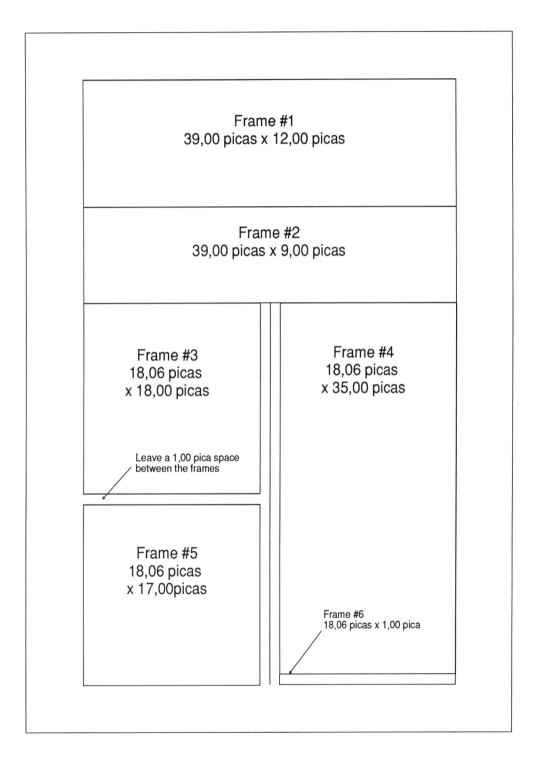

Frame #1
39,00 picas x 12,00 picas

Frame #2
39,00 picas x 9,00 picas

Frame #3
18,06 picas
x 18,00 picas

Frame #4
18,06 picas
x 35,00 picas

Leave a 1,00 pica space
between the frames

Frame #5
18,06 picas
x 17,00picas

Frame #6
18,06 picas x 1,00 pica

➥*TIP: Some users prefer to make the initial placement in reduced view, before switching to normal view for fine-tuning.*

After placing the frames free-hand, use the Sizing & Scaling dialog box to make sure they match the values shown in the illustration.

■ Select each frame in turn.

■ Select Sizing & Scaling from the Frame menu. If necessary, change the frame height, width or X,Y position.

For instance, the illustration below shows the correct Sizing & Scaling settings for frame #1.

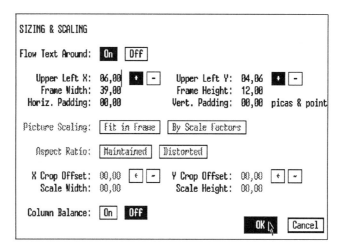

➥*NOTE: Don't be concerned if the small "jump text" at the bottom of the page overlaps the frame above it. Later when you change the body text line-spacing, you will be able to fine-tune the frame so it lines up with the bottom column guide. (Remember: Line Snap is set to the inter-line spacing of body text.)*

Add a Ruling Box Around

Before you place the text, add a Ruling Box Around the frame reserved for the Table of Contents (frame #5). This line will visually separate the TOC from the adjacent articles.

■ Ruling Box Around

Height of Rule 1: 00.25 points.

Place the Text Files

With the frames in place and correctly sized, you are ready to place the text files. Since they were pretagged, they will be partially formatted as soon as they are placed. However, the files include some tag names that are not in the current style sheet. Ventura displays these undefined tags as body text.

■ Select frame #1, then place the file 3LOGO.TXT (select its name from the Assignment List).

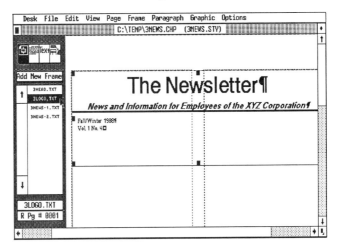

■ Select frame #2 and place 3HEAD.TXT inside.

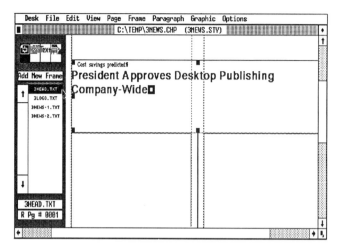

- Select frame #3 and place 3NEWS-1.TXT inside.

Ventura fits as much of 3NEWS-1.TXT into the frame as it can and then stops. To continue placing the text file, select another frame and click again on the file name in the Assignment List.

- Select frame #4 and select 3NEWS-1.TXT from the Assignment List again.

Ventura picks up where it left off and flows more of the file into frame #4. It stops again when the frame is filled. Later you will place the remainder of the article on page two.

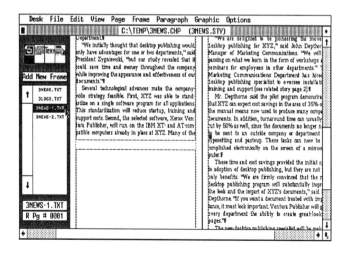

Create a Table of Contents

To create a table of contents you will type text directly into a frame. The text you enter will be treated as a separate file when you save the chapter.

➡ *NOTE: Text typed into a separate frame is saved as part of the caption file unless you rename it as shown below.*

■ Enable text mode. Click anywhere inside frame #5.

The end of file marker appears at the top left corner of the frame.

■ Place the text cursor in front of the marker and type: **Table of Contents [Enter]**

Now type the TOC entries, line by line. Press the tab key once between each entry and the page number.

President   approves   desktop   publishing[Tab]1[Enter]

XYZ hires specialist[Tab]2[Enter]

New plant comes on-line[Tab]3[Enter]

People on the move[Tab]5[Enter]

Letters to the Editor[Tab]6[Enter]

Calendar[Tab]8[Enter]

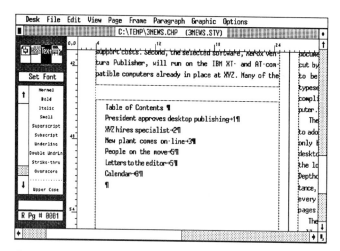

Once you type text into a frame, you can give it a name and save it in the text format of your choice as shown below.

- Enable Frame mode. Select the table of contents frame (frame #5).

The default file name, "Frame Text" appears in the Item Selection Box.

- Select File Type/Rename from the Edit menu.

- Move to the New Name line. Press Esc to clear the line and type: `C:\TEMP\3NEWSTOC.TXT`

- Choose ASCII and click OK to close the dialog box.

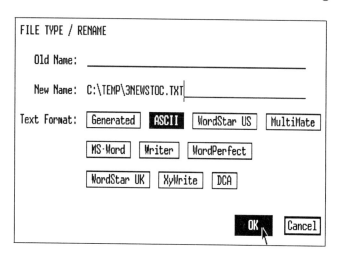

This saves the Table of Contents text as the file 3NEWSTOC.TXT in the C:\TEMP subdirectory.

There's one thing left on the first page: the so-called *jump* text at the bottom of the page ("Continued on page 2"). You will create it just as you created the TOC text: by typing directly into the frame. This time, however, you will not give it a new file name. Because you are not renaming the file, the text you type will be stored in the caption file.

■ Enable Text Editing and click anywhere inside frame #6. Then Type: **Continued on page 2**

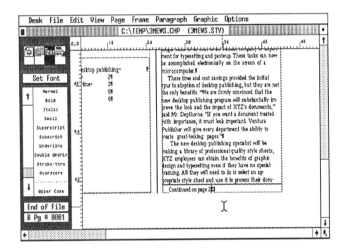

Stopping Point

Are you keeping up with the pace? Take a moment to catch your breath and review what you've done and what remains to be completed in the style section. First you made global changes to the document. Then you laid out page one by adding frames and placing text inside.

Now you are ready to tackle page two. Once the layout is complete, you can begin to format the text by working systematically through each paragraph in each frame.

If you must stop now, save your work by pressing Ctrl-S, then select Quit from the File menu. Return to this spot in the text when you are ready to resume the project. Otherwise, move on to the next section now.

Insert a Page

If you are starting up again, load Ventura and open the chapter C:\TEMP\3NEWS.CHP to begin where you left off. Once you are on page one of the document, you are ready to follow the instructions that follow.

When you place text in frames (as opposed to putting it on the underlying page), Ventura does not create new pages automatically. Therefore, you must manually insert a new page.

■ Select Insert/Remove page. Choose Operation: Insert New Page After Current Page.

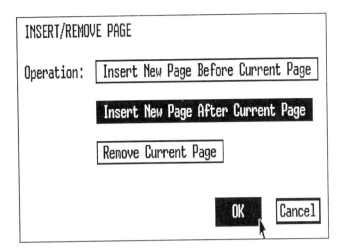

Ventura inserts the new page and moves to it.

At this point, you can add frames to this new blank page as you did earlier on page one. Use the diagram below to gauge the approximate positions and sizes.

You can use several strategies for placing frames on the page. One idea is to draw the frames in approximate position, then return to each frame one by one to check its position with the Sizing & Scaling dialog box (as explained below). In that case, we recommend that you press and hold the Shift key as you click on the Add Frame button. As long as the Shift key is depressed, Ventura will let you continue to draw frames without the need to click the Add Frame button each time.

If you prefer, you can draw and position each frame as you go. First draw the frame as closely as you can. Then, with the frame still highlighted, choose Sizing & Scaling from the Frame menu. Once you've chosen Sizing & Scaling, you can return to this dialog box for the next frame by pressing Ctrl-X, a keyboard shortcut that tells Ventura to bring up the last dialog box again.

Finally, you can also create frames by drawing the first one, then copying it to memory. Create new frames by pressing Ins to put a copy on the page. Move the copy into position and change its size.

Frame #7
18,06 picas x 2,00 picas

Frame #8
18,06 picas
x 16,00 picas

Frame #10
18,06 picas
x 34,00 picas

Frame #9
18,06 picas
x 39,00 picas

Space between frames
(for caption frame):
18,06 picas x 2,00 pica

Frame #11
18,06 picas
x 21,00 picas

Size and Scale the Frames

After adding the frames, check the dimensions one by one with Sizing & Scaling from the Frame menu. Use the illustration above as your guide.

Place the Text

Finish placing the text files by selecting the frame, then choosing a file name from the Assignment List. At this stage, don't worry whether or not the text fits perfectly inside the frame.

■ Select frame #6 and place the remainder of text file 3NEWS-1.TXT inside.

■ Select frame #7 and place 3NEWS-2.TXT inside.

■ Select frame #8 and place 3NEWS-2.TXT inside.

When you have finished, change to reduced view to check that your screen looks similar to this:

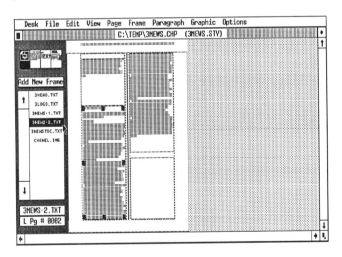

Add Jump Text on Page Two

■ Enable text editing.

■ Place the text cursor anywhere in the small frame at the top of the left column. Type: **Continued from page 1**

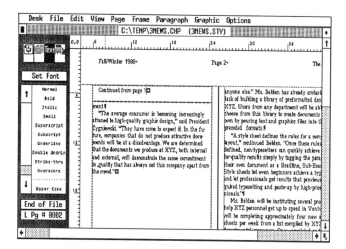

Mission accomplished. Since frame #4 is reserved for a picture file (to be added later) you have finished the basic layout. Now you can start tagging. As always, you should start with body text and then step through the document from beginning to end.

Format the Body Text

- Press the Home key to return to the first page of the document.

- Select the paragraph that begins "We initially thought..."

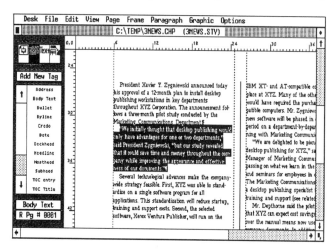

■ Font   Face: Times
                    Size: 010 points

■ Alignment   Left
                    Overall Width: Column-Wide
                    First Line: Indent
                    Indent/Outdent Width: 01,00 pica

■ Spacing   Inter-Line: 12.00 points

➡ *NOTE: From this point on, any spacing values not specified should be set to 0. In the example above, for instance, you would set Above, Below, Inter-Paragraph, In From Left and In From Right to 00.00.*

Format the Logo

A newsletter's name, or *logo* should be the dominant element on the page. It should be easy to read and large enough so it doesn't vie for attention with the credo or the headlines.

■ Enable paragraph tagging mode. Select the paragraph "The Newsletter."

■ Font   Face: Helvetica
                    Style: Bold
                    Size: 072 points

➡ *NOTE: Your printer may not be capable of 72-point type.*

You have two choices if your printer cannot produce 72-point type. First, you can use the Set Printer Info dialog box to switch to PostScript just for the on-screen examples. Switch back before printing. When you switch back, Ventura will make an attempt to substitute font and font sizes.

Second, you can simply use your original printer, and substitute the largest font available in place of 72-point type. Keep the line spacing and other selections the same so your screen will match the book's as closely as possible. Your example will not look quite as good at printout time, but you should be able to follow along for learning purposes without any problems.

Don't worry yet about the way the logo looks. In a moment you will adjust it to fit. First work through the Paragraph menu and change the Alignment and Spacing.

- Alignment   Centered
                   Overall Width: Frame-Wide

- Spacing   Inter-Line: 48.00 points
                   Below: 24.00 points
                   Add In Space Above: Always

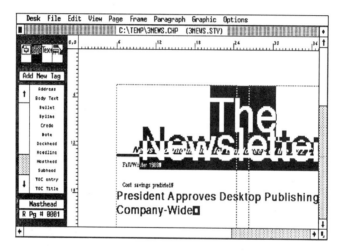

The logo is too large for the current frame. We could reduce the font size, but that would diminish the impact of the logo. Instead, you can one of Ventura's typographic functions to tighten up the spacing between characters. This technique, called tracking, has two benefits: It fits the word into the frame and it enhances its readability.

- Select Typographic Controls from the Paragraph menu.

- Choose Automatic Kerning: On, Letter Spacing: Off. Move to Tracking. Choose Tighter. Press ESC to clear the line and type **0.048**

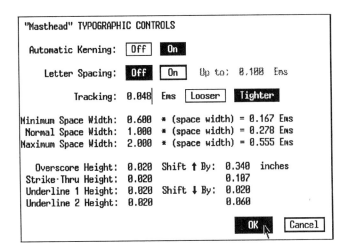

There's a lot of power in the Typographic Controls dialog box. For now, we'll talk about tracking and leave the other features for later. Tracking controls the space between letters. It is measured in ems. An em space is equal to the point size of the type. For 10-point type, an em space is 10 points, for 18-point type it is 18 points, and so on.

➥ *TIP: Standard spacing is generally too wide for display type larger than 24 points. To make your pages look more professional, use tracking to tighten display type.*

Once you adjust the tracking, the logo should fit neatly into the frame on one line. If not, tighten it further.

Format the Credo Tag

The next tag you should format is the credo. You will change the font and increase the width of its ruling line.

■ Select the paragraph starting with "News and Information...."

■ Font   Face: Times
                      Size: 014 points

■ Alignment   Centered
                      Overall Width: Frame-Wide

■ Spacing   Inter-Line: 18.00 points
                      Add in Above: Always

When you widen the rule, you will also add extra space above it. The extra white space helps to visually separate the rule from the text.

■ Select Ruling Line Below from the Paragraph menu. Choose Frame, Black, and Solid. Make Space Above Rule 1: 12.00 points and give Rule 1 a height of 10.00 points.

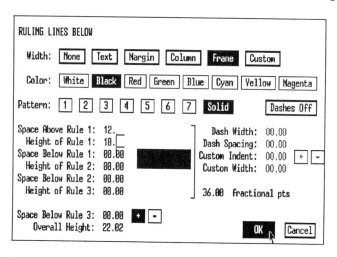

Create a Dateline

Next you will create a dateline that puts two different tags — Date and Volume — on the same line.

■ Select the paragraph "Fall/Winter 1988."

Since this paragraph was already pretagged, the tag name (Date) appears in the Current Selection Box. However, since the format for this tag doesn't yet exist in the style sheet, Ventura displays it as body text. You will adjust its font, alignment, and spacing and add a rule below.

■ Font   Face: Times
                           Size: 008 points

■ Alignment   Left
                           Overall Width: Column-Wide

■ Spacing   Inter-Line: 12.00 points
                           Add Space Above: Always

■ Select Breaks from the Paragraph menu. Confirm that Line Break is set to Before.

Now add a frame-wide rule below the tag.

■ Select Ruling Line Below. Choose Frame, Black, and Solid. Enter 06.00 points of Space Above Rule 1, and a Height of 00.25 points.

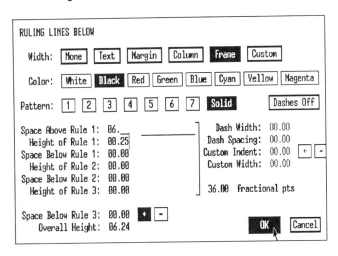

Change the Volume Tag

Now select the paragraph pre-tagged as Volume. To allow it to reside on the same line as the Date, make it right-justified and set the Line Break *after* the tag instead of before.

■ Select the paragraph "Vol.1.No.4."

■ Font   Face: Times
                          Size: 008 points

■ Alignment   Right
                          Overall Width: Column- Wide
                          In/Outdent: 00.00

■ Breaks   Line Break: After

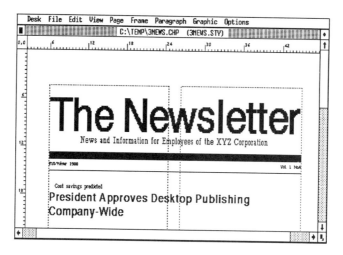

You've just learned a valuable skill: How to make two different tags reside on the same line. As you saw, the trick is to give the first tag a line break *before* and the second tag a line break *after*.

You have to be careful when putting two paragraphs on the same line or the text will overlap. In the example above, you kept them separate by making one flush left and the other flush right. You could also have used In From Left and In From Right spacing to separate the two.

Add the Kicker Tag

A kicker is a lead-in heading that introduces a headline. Since the tag name does not exist in the current style sheet, you will add a new tag.

■ Select the paragraph "Cost savings predicted."

■ Select Add New Tag from the Sidebar.

■ When the dialog box appears, move to Tag Name to Add and type: **Kicker**

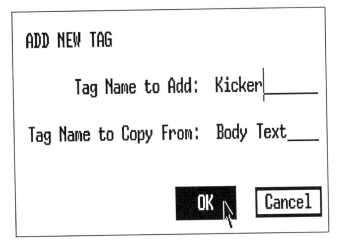

Format the Kicker Tag

■ Font

Face: Helvetica
Style: N-Italic
Size: 012 points

■ Alignment

Left
Overall Width:Frame-Wide
In/Outdent: 00.00 points

■ Spacing

Above: 24.00 points
Inter-Line: 24.00 points
Add in Space Above: When Not at Column Top

Now add a ruling line below the kicker to separate it from the headline.

■ Select Ruling Line Below. Choose Text, Black, and Solid. Give Rule 1 a Height of 06.00 points.

By selecting Text in the Ruling Line dialog box, you are telling Ventura to make the line exactly as long as the text. If you write a longer kicker, the rule will automatically be lengthened. For a shorter kicker, the line will be shortened.

Change the Headline Tag

To make the headline easier to read, increase its size and its inter-line spacing.

■ Select the paragraph,"President Approves Desktop Publishing Company-Wide."

■ Font   Face: Helvetica
                            Style: Bold
                            Size: 030 points

■ Alignment   Left
                            Overall Width: Frame-Wide

■ Spacing   Inter-Line: 30.00 points
                            Add in Above: When Not at Column Top

Are you beginning to notice improvements? By enlarging the logo and the headline and adding rules you have made the front page easier to read and less cluttered.

We realize you are working very hard in this chapter. We are asking you to duplicate the steps you must go through in real life to construct a professional-looking newsletter. Although taking the "real-life" approach means spending a few extra minutes, it pays off. By the end of this chapter, you will be familiar with all of Ventura's basic functions. Stick with it.

Add a Body First Tag

To distinguish the lead-in paragraph from body text, create a tag called Body First. The tag will be aligned flush left with no first line indent.

■ Select the paragraph that begins "President Xavier Y. Zygniewski announced...."

■ Add New Tag   Tag Name to Add: Body First

■ Alignment   Left
                            Overall Width: Column-Wide
                            In/Outdent: 00.00.

■ Spacing   Inter-Line: 12.00 points
                            Add Space Above: Always

The last frame on the page includes the text for the table of contents. To format the TOC, first tag the text, then change the tag attributes.

Change the TOC Title

■ Select the paragraph "Table of Contents" and tag it as TOC Title.

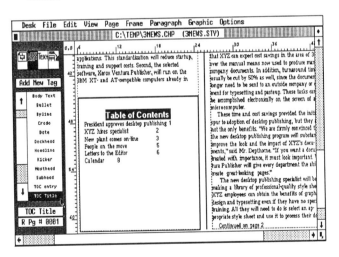

■ Font

Face: Times
Style: Bold
Size: 014 points

- Alignment   Left
  Overall Width: Column-Wide

Use the In From Left spacing option to move the TOC Title in from the left margin of the frame.

- Spacing   Above: 12.00 points
  Inter-Line: 12.00 points
  In From Left: 12.00 points

- Ruling Line   Width: Text
  Below   Height of Rule 1: 05.00 points
  Space Below Rule 1: 30.00 points

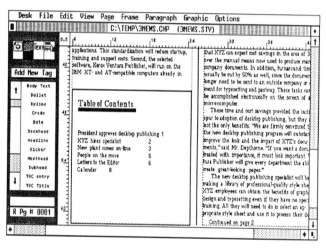

Modify the TOC Entry Tag

- Select the paragraph "President Approves Desktop Publishing ..." and tag it as TOC Entry.

- Font   Face: Times
  Style: Bold
  Size: 010 points

- Alignment   Left
  Overall Width: Column-Wide

■ Spacing   Above: 18.00 points
                   Inter-Line: 06.00 points
                   Add Space Above: Always
                   In From Left: 12.00 points
                   In From Right: 12.00 points

Use Tab Settings to create leader dots. As the name implies, these dots help lead the eye across the page. They are useful for indices, tables of contents, and other lists.

■ Select Tab Settings from the Paragraph menu. Choose Tab 1, Tab Type: Right, Tab Display: Shown as Leader Character, Tab Location: 17,00 picas. Then Choose Leader Char: (...) and Leader Spacing: 1.

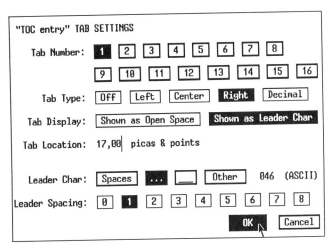

Tag the remaining paragraphs in the table of contents as TOC entry. (Hint: use the Shift-Click method to tag them all at once.)

The finished TOC should look like this:

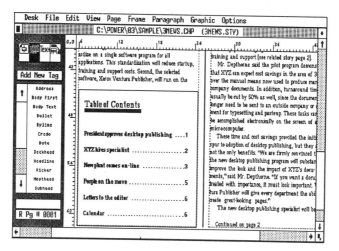

Add the Continued Tag

There's only one more paragraph to tag on page one: the jump text.

- Select the paragraph "Continued on page 2."

- Add New Tag: Tag Name to Add: Continued

- Font   Face: Times
                              Style: N-Italic
                              Size: 010 points

- Alignment   Left
                              Overall Width: Column-Wide
                              In/Outdent Width: 00.00
                              Inter-Line: 12.00 points

After you finish making these changes, your screen should look similar to the illustration on the following page.

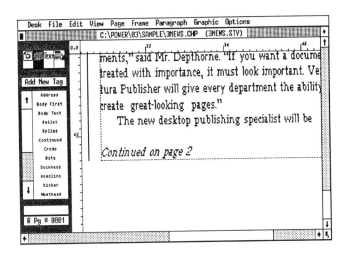

Stopping Point

With only a page to go, take a break and admire your handiwork. (Hint: Save what you've done so far before you start patting yourself on the back.) Your efforts have paid off: The newsletter is really shaping up. If you must pause, you can quit now and resume at a later time. Otherwise, continue on to the next section.

Assigning Function Keys

If you are starting up anew, load Ventura and open the chapter C:\TEMP\3NEWS.CHP. Before you go to page two, we want to introduce another time-saving Ventura feature that speeds up tagging.

Until now you have always tagged text with the mouse while in paragraph tagging mode. You can decrease formatting time by using the Assign Function Keys option. By assigning key tags to each of the 10 function keys, you can edit and tag simultaneously, without switching back and forth between text and paragraph modes. Here's how:

■ PresS Ctrl-K (or select Assign Function Keys from the Paragraph menu).

■ Move to the F2 line and type: **Body First**

Now complete the dialog box as shown below. Click OK when you are finished.

Notice that we have listed the tags in the same alphabetical order as they are found on the assignment list. Alphabetical order may make it easier to remember which tags are assigned to which function keys. However, feel free to use any order that makes sense to you. For instance, you might choose to assign Head1 to F1, Head2 to F2 and so on. Many people reserve the F10 key for body text, to follow the convention established with the style sheets that come with Ventura.

```
ASSIGN FUNCTION KEYS

F1:  Address_____    F2:  Body First___
F3:  Bullet_____     F4:  Byline_____
F5:  Continued___     F6:  Credo_____
F7:  Date_____     F8:  Deckhead____
F9:  Headline____     F10: Body Text___


                        [   OK   ]   [ Cancel ]
```

➡ *TIP: It is generally best to assign tag names to function keys in the same alphabetical order as they appear in the assignment list.*

Now go to page two and try out the new function key assignments.

■ Press End to go to the last page of the document.

■ Go to frame #9. Enable text editing. Place the text cursor anywhere within the paragraph "By Joe Smith." Press the F4 key to tag it as Byline.

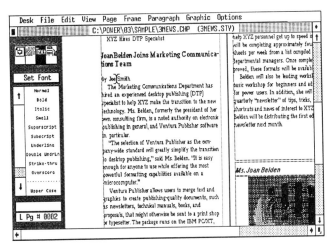

Use the function keys again to tag the first paragraph of the article as Body First.

➥ *TIP: If you forget which tags are assigned to which function keys, press Ctrl-K to bring up the dialog box again. When you are finished reviewing the assignments, press Enter to close the dialog box.*

■ Place the text cursor anywhere in the paragraph "The Marketing Communications Department...". Press F2.

■ Go to small frame (frame #7) at the top of the page. Move the text cursor to the paragraph "Continued from page 1." Press F5.

➥ *NOTE: You can use function keys to apply tags, but you must switch to paragraph tagging mode to change tags or add tags.*

Change the Z_Header Tag

Continue formatting page two. Add a ruling line below the header text. As you will see, you can change the appearance of the header just as you can change any other paragraph on the page. The difference, however, is that any changes apply to all the headers throughout the document.

■ Enable paragraph tagging. Select the header.

■ Alignment   Width: Frame-Wide
                          In/Outdent Width: 00.00 points

■ Ruling Line   Width: Frame
   Below   Space Above Rule 1: 02.00 points
                       Height of Rule 1: 10.00 points

Add a Headline 2 Tag

Since the original style sheet contained only one tag for headlines, you must add a second one. The new Headline 2 tag includes a rule with a custom width.

■ Select the paragraph "XYZ Hires DTP Specialist" in frame #9. Select Add New Tag and type in the new tag name: **Headline 2**

■ Font
Face: Helvetica
Style: Bold
Size: 024 points

■ Alignment
Left
Overall Width: Frame-Wide
In/Outdent: 00.00

■ Spacing
Above: 24.00 points
Inter-Line: 24.00 points
Add In Above: When Not At Column Top

■ Select Ruling Line Above. Choose Width: Custom, Pattern: Black. Make the Height of Rule 1: 06.00 points and the Space Below Rule 1: 03.00 points. Now switch from fractional points to picas & points by clicking on top of the measurement units several times. Next move to Custom Width, press Esc to clear the line and type: **14,00**

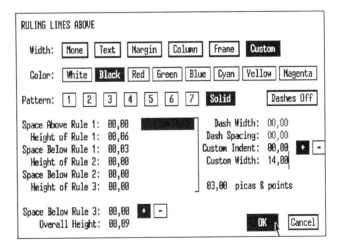

Change the Deckhead Tag

Only two more tags to change. Then we will show you how to rename and remove tags and you will be ready to move on to the picture section.

■ Select the paragraph "Joan Belden Joins Marketing Communications..." in frame #9.

■ Font
Face: Helvetica
Style: B-Italic

■ Spacing   Above: 12.00 points
                     Inter-Line: 12.00 points
                     Add Space Above: Always

The finished tag looks like this:

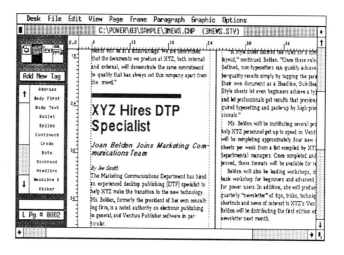

Change the Byline Tag

■ Select the Byline paragraph "By Joe Smith."

■ Font   Face: Times
                     Style: N-Italic

■ Spacing   Above: 12.00 points
                     Inter-Line: 12.00 points
                     Add In Above: When Not At Column Top

Rename a Tag

After tagging the text, take a moment to clean up the Assignment List. Remove tags you don't need, and rename tags with unclear names. For instance, rename the tag "Masthead" to "Logo."

■ Go to page one. Select the paragraph "The Newsletter" in frame #1.

■ Select Rename Tag from the Paragraph menu. Confirm that the Old Tag Name is Masthead. Move to New Tag Name and type: **Logo**

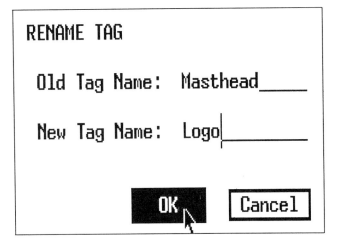

Remove a Tag

- Select Remove Tag from the Paragraph menu.
- Move to Tag Name To Remove and type: **Address**

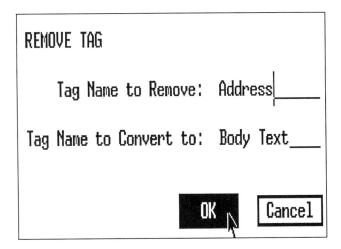

➡ NOTE: When you remove a tag, Ventura converts all occurrences of this tag to body text unless you tell it otherwise.

Pictures

Give yourself another pat on the back. You've completed the style portion of this document. With text and style complete, you're ready to add a picture to your newsletter. In this section you will load and place a picture, and then add a caption.

- Go to page two.

- Enable frame setting mode. Click anywhere on the empty frame (frame #11).

- Select CHANEL.IMG from the Assignment List.

The picture is placed into the frame. Now size the picture to fill the frame.

➡*NOTE: If the picture is not visible, select Show Pictures from the Options menu.*

- Select Sizing & Scaling from the Frame menu.

- Choose Fit in Frame and Aspect Ratio: Maintained.

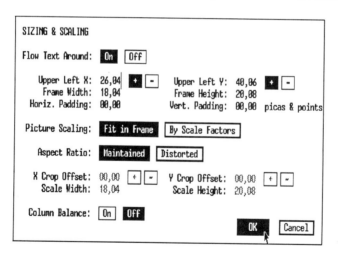

This fits the picture in the frame while maintaining the same horizontal and vertical proportions.

Once the picture has been placed, add a caption to the frame. In the previous chapter, you created a caption by typing directly into the caption frame. This method allows you to create long captions and edit them in text editing mode.

This time you will create a *caption label*. Caption labels are entered and edited in the Anchors & Captions dialog box. *They cannot be entered or changed in text editing mode.* Chapter Nine explains how to use caption labels for automatic numbering. Right now, however, you will simply use this feature to add a short, unnumbered label.

■ Select Anchors & Captions from the Frame menu.

■ Choose Above. Move to the Label line. Type: **Ms. Joan Belden**

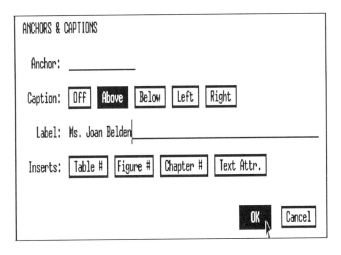

At this point you can change the attributes of the label you just created.

■ Enable paragraph tagging mode. Select the paragraph "Ms. Joan Belden."

Notice that the Current Selection Box displays a generated tag name: Z_Label Cap. Ventura automatically assigned this tag to the label when you typed it into the Anchors & Captions dialog box. You can change this tag in paragraph tagging mode as you would any other.

■ Font   Face: Helvetica
                          Style: B-Italic
                          Size: 010 points

■ Spacing   Inter-Line: 10.00 points

After you change the attributes, shorten the caption frame one line length.

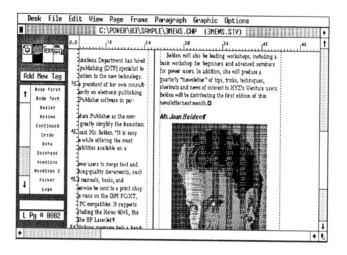

Chapter

Print Selected Pages

Having added a picture, you are ready to print the newsletter to see the results of your changes. The Print option lets you specify which pages to print and the order in which to print them.

■ Save the chapter (press Ctrl-S).

■ Select To Print from the File menu.

■ Choose Which Pages: Selected. Move to From Page, press Esc to clear the line, and type: **0001**

■ Move to Through Page, press Esc and type: **0002**

■ Choose Printing Order: Last to 1st.

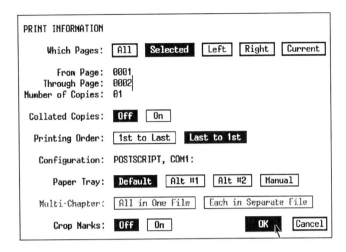

Ventura prints out the newsletter back to front.

Understanding Set Printer Info

This is a good point to introduce you to the Set Printer Info dialog box. This selection from the Options menu allows you to change printers. Take a moment to glance through the sample dialog box shown below.

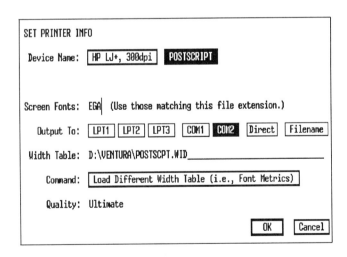

Let's consider each line and its function. At the top is Device Name. As you can see from the example above, this line permits you to choose between different printers.

➡ *TIP: To add a new printer after installing Ventura, insert Ventura Disk #1 into the A: drive and type* **VPPREP***, just as you did when originally installing the program. Answer No when VPPREP asks you if you are installing for the first time so you will not have to redo the entire installation.*

Switching printers is not as simple as making a choice from the Device Name line. You must also confirm that the width table matches the printer. The width table is a separate file that tells Ventura how much space to allow for each character. The last line in the dialog box, Quality, signals whether or not the width table matches the printer. If Quality says "Ultimate," then you have a correct match. If Quality reads "Draft," you have a mismatch.

Suppose you choose a new device name and notice that Quality says "Draft." To switch to the correct width table, click on the Load Different Width Table button. Ventura will display an item selector. Width tables are clearly labeled with names similar to printer names. Pick the one that matches your printer, then click OK. When you return to the Set Printer Info dialog box, the Quality line will read "Ultimate."

➡ *TIP: Use Draft quality to mimic one printer with another. For instance, you could use a LaserJet Plus to imitate a PostScript typesetter for proofing purposes. Select the LaserJet device, but use the PostScript width table. Although the output will not be very attractive, the line endings will be accurate.*

The Screen Fonts line enables you to add screen fonts that more closely mimic printed fonts. Adding screen fonts is outside the scope of this project. The Output To line lets you change the printer port. For example, if you switch your printer from COM1 to COM2, there is no need to reinstall Ventura. Just make the correct selection on this line. From then on, Ventura will send its output to the COM2 serial port instead.

The Width Table line enables you to confirm which width table is in use. It is originally set for the default width table, called OUTPUT.WID. Under most circumstances, OUTPUT.WID is the best choice for the documents you create. Ventura saves the name of the width table with the style sheet. As long as a style sheet specifies the default OUTPUT.WID, it can be used on another system, even if that system has a different printer. OUTPUT.WID automatically matches the printer in use on that particular computer.

Back Up a Publication

You have already encountered Multi-Chapter, which you use to back up individual chapters. You can also combine chapters into what Ventura calls a *publication*. Publications can be copied or printed as a group.

Create a Publication

You will use Multi-Chapter to create a publication called PART_ONE. You will use this publication to back up all three of the chapters you created in the first section of this book.

■ Place a formatted floppy disk in the A: drive.

■ Select Multi-Chapter from the Options menu. If you haven't saved recently, Ventura asks you to Save or abandon your changes. Choose Save.

The Multi-Chapter dialog box appears and the current chapter, C:\TEMP\3NEWS.CHP appears at the top of the list.

■ Choose Add Chapter.

Ventura displays the Item Selection box.

■ With the backup button, locate the C:\TEMP subdirectory and scroll through the listing until you find the 1REPORT.CHP chapter. Select the chapter.

Ventura returns you to the Multi-Chapter Operations Box. Use the same Add Chapter function to add 2PROPOS.CHP to the publication list.

■ Choose Add Chapter. Select the chapter 2PROPOS.CHP.

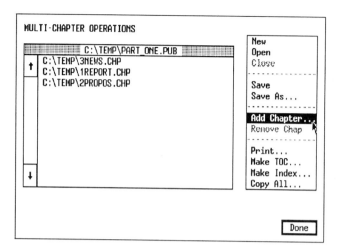

Save the Publication

■ While still in the Multi-Chapter dialog box, select Save As.

■ Find the C:\TEMP subdirectory and enter the name PART_ONE (notice the underline character between the "T" and the "O").

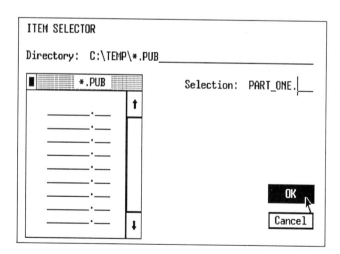

Copy the Publication

■ Make sure that none of the chapters is highlighted.

If a chapter is highlighted, you will copy just the chapter instead of the publication. To de-select a chapter, click anywhere inside the dialog box.

■ Select Copy All.

The name of the publication is displayed at the top of the dialog box. The destination lines show the disk drive and sub-directory to which each file will be copied. Tell Ventura which disk and subdirectory you want to use.

■ Move your cursor to next to the PUB & CHPs: line, press Esc to clear the line and type: **A:**

■ Choose Make All Directories the Same As the First.

```
COPY ALL

                         SOURCE (from this file)

      PUB or CHP:  C:\TEMP\PART_ONE.PUB_____

                    DESTINATION (to these directories)

     PUB & CHPs:  A:_____
     STYs & WIDs: A:_____
     Text Files:  A:_____
  Graphic Files:  A:_____
    Image Files:  A:_____

        Command:  [Make All Directories the Same As the First]

                                        [  OK  ]  [Cancel]
```

Ventura copies all the files for all three chapters to the A:drive. When the copy function is complete, you return to the Multi-Chapter dialog box.

■ Choose Done. When Ventura asks you if you want to abandon or save changes made to the publication, click on Abandon to return to the workspace.

Congratulations — you made it through Ventura boot camp. Getting started from scratch is always the hardest part. Now that you've completed basic training you're in shape for almost any assignment. You've got the know-how to make documents more professional, more pleasing and more effective.

In the next section of this book, you will use this fundamental knowledge as the jumping off point. Part II will teach you to put Ventura through its paces by creating a series of specialized, high-performance documents.

Tips

Frame Tips

❏ To select a frame, click once anywhere inside its boundary while in frame setting mode.

❏ To resize a frame, place the cursor on a handle and drag with the mouse to the new size.

❏ To move a frame, place the mouse cursor anywhere inside the frame. Use the mouse to drag it to new location.

❏ Once you copy a frame into temporary memory, it stays there until you replace it with a new frame (or until you exit Ventura).

❏ You can copy several frames into memory at once. Use Shift-Click to select the frames, then delete them or copy them to temporary memory.

❏ You can move frames and their contents from one chapter to another using temporary memory. Open the first chapter. Place the frames you want to move onto one page, then put them into temporary memory. Now open the second chapter. (Abandon the changes to the first chapter so it will revert to its original form.) When you press Ins, the frames will appear inside the new chapter.

❏ If you will be drawing many frames with similar attributes (frame backgrounds, ruling lines, etc.), use temporary memory to speed the process. Draw one frame and change its attributes. Copy it to memory. Now paste copies for the succeeding frames. This is faster than changing line and background attributes one by one for each frame as you draw it.

❏ Ventura can flow a long text file from one frame to another. Select the first frame and click on the file name in the Assignment list. Now select the second frame and click on the file name again. If you make additions or deletions to the text, it will flow back and forth between the frames.

❏ Ventura cannot flow text "backwards." It cannot flow text to a previous page. In addition, it cannot flow text to a previous frame (one that was drawn on the page first).

❏ Use Sizing & Scaling from the Frame menu to fine-tune the size and position of frames.

❏ Think of the underlying page as a page-sized frame that automatically repeats itself if necessary to accommodate large text files.

❏ You can change the size of the underlying page with Sizing & Scaling just as if it were an ordinary frame.

❏ For documents with several text files, such as newsletters, place text into frames rather than placing it on the underlying page.

❏ When creating a newsletter-style document with frames, format the underlying page and use it as an invisible snap-to grid for drawing frames.

Text Tips

❏ You can type text directly into frames while in Ventura.

❏ Text typed in frames is stored in the caption file unless you specify otherwise. To save to a different file, select the frame, then use File Type/Rename from the Edit menu to specify the file name you want instead.

❏ Use the function keys to tag paragraphs while in text editing mode. First assign tag names to different function keys using Assign Function Keys from the Paragraph menu. Then you can retag any paragraph in text mode just by pressing a function key while the cursor is anywhere within that paragraph.

❏ Assign function keys alphabetically, or in any fashion that makes the assignments easy to remember (for example, F1 for Head1, F2 for Head2, etc.)

❏ If you cannot remember which tags are assigned to which

function keys, press ^K for a quick reminder. Press Enter to close the dialog box.

Style Tips

❑ To place two tags on the same line, give the first tag a line break before. Give the second tag a line break after.

❑ There are two ways to keep two tags on the same line from overlapping. First, you can align one flush left and the other flush right. This method is satisfactory as long as the text is short enough that the tags will not meet in the middle and overlap each other. Second you can use In From Left and In From Right (Spacing, Paragraph menu) to confine each tag to a specific area.

❑ Create leader dots with the Tab Settings dialog box. Instead of showing the tab as an open space, show it as leader dots. The dialog box also lets you vary the spacing between the dots.

Picture Tips

❑ Use Ventura's caption label function for brief captions, or captions that must be numbered (for example, "Figure 1-1"). Use the Anchors & Captions dialog box to type them in or to edit them. Longer captions are typed directly into the caption frame in text editing mode.

❑ Caption labels are automatically tagged by Ventura and can be modified in paragraph tagging mode like any other paragraph.

Chapter Tips

❑ Use the Last to First print option if your printer produces pages face up. If it puts out pages face down, use the First to Last option.

❑ You can install additional printers by reusing the VPPREP installation program. You will not have to go through the entire process. Ventura will only copy over the new fonts and drivers you need.

❑ Use Set Printer Info from the Options menu to switch from

one printer to another. Be sure to change width tables at the same time.

❏ You can mimic one printer with another by using a different width table. The most common use of this capability is to use a non-PostScript laser printer to preview pages that will ultimately be sent to a PostScript typesetter.

❏ To copy or print several chapters at once, place them into a publication using Multi-Chapter from the Options menu. Then copy or print the entire publication.

Part Two

Advanced Documents

Chapter Four
Skills Checklist

Theory

✓ Understanding graphics drawing mode

✓ Easy drawing with snap-to grid

✓ When to use box text (and when not to)

Text

✓ Editing box text

Style

✓ Special style formats in headers

✓ Fold line effects using tab settings

✓ Variations of the box text tag

Pictures

✓ Dressing up shapes with line types and screen tints

Chapter

✓ Printing multiple copies

An Invoice

Welcome to Chapter Four, where you will learn a simple but highly effective strategy for creating a standard business form. In this first advanced chapter, we will be showing you a lot of new techniques and features. The checklist on the left lists some of the skills you will learn.

Like all of the advanced section, Chapter Four assumes that you understand the basics from Part One. We will move faster than we did before and we will assume you can handle standard functions such as loading and placing files, adding and changing tags, etc., with a minimum of instructions. We will save step-by-step explanations for techniques you haven't seen before.

Theory

Most of this chapter's sample document is built using Ventura's graphics drawing mode. You will find it easier to follow along if you understand these three important concepts:

- How graphics mode works
- The snap-to grid
- Box text

Graphics Drawing Mode

Ventura has tools for building lines, circles, rectangles, and box text (text within a rectangle). You can use these shapes to draw simple artwork, create tables, add crop marks, annotate illustrations from other programs or to build forms. Once you've learned to operate these tools, you'll find important uses for them in many kinds of documents. Nevertheless, we recommend using a specialized, standalone graphics program to create complex illustrations, just as we recommend using a standalone word processor to create more than a page or so of text.

How Graphics Mode Works

The six key points explained below will help you understand how the graphics function operates. We use the term *shape(s)* to refer to lines, boxes or circles created with graphics mode.

➡ *Key Point #1: Every shape is attached to a "parent," which can be a frame or a page.*

If you move, copy or delete the parent, the graphics are moved, copied or deleted as well.

➡ *Key Point #2: The parent is the frame that was active when graphics mode was selected.*

The parent can be the underlying page itself, or a frame on top of the underlying page. Anything you draw is attached to that parent. In frame setting mode, look for the black handles that indicate which frame is active. In graphics mode, Ventura displays the handles in gray as a reminder that this frame (or page) is the parent.

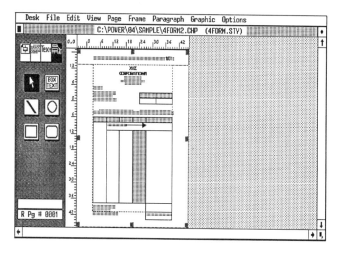

➥ *Key Point #3: Shapes do not have to be near the parent frame as long as they are on the same page.*

There is no restriction on the placement of graphics. They can be inside the parent frame; touching the parent frame; or completely removed from the parent frame, *as long as they are on the same page.* For instance, you could place a tiny frame in the upper left corner of the page, and then draw a shape in the lower right corner. That shape would still be tied to the parent, even though the two are nowhere near each other on the page.

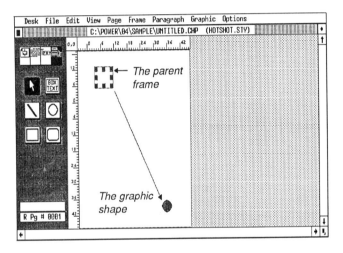

➥ *Key Point #4: You cannot edit shapes unless you select the parent first.*

After you create a shape, you may later want to return to graphics mode to change it. To work on a shape, you must select the parent in frame mode *before* switching to graphics mode. If you fail to select the correct parent, you will be unable to work on the shape.

➥ *Key Point #5: Different shapes can have different parents even if they are on the same page.*

To choose a new parent frame, switch out of graphics drawing mode to frame setting mode. Select a new frame. Now switch back to graphics mode. The new frame will be the parent to any shapes you draw from now on.

➡*Key Point #6: If the underlying page is the parent, the shape repeats on every page.*

If a frame is the parent, the shape appears on one page only. Move the parent frame to another page and the shape moves with it. But if the underlying page is the parent, the shape is duplicated in the exact same position on every page of the document.

The six points above are the major factors to consider when using graphics drawing mode. There are additional tips at the end of the chapter. If you have never used graphics mode before, you may want to read through the tips now. Then after you've had some practice drawing shapes you can review the list again.

The Snap-To Grid

The most important part of graphics drawing is getting shapes the right size and position. Ventura's Column Snap and Line Snap functions do not work in graphics mode. Fortunately, graphics mode has its own snap-to grid function.

The snap-to grid is the secret to working painlessly and productively in graphics mode. If you know how to set up a good grid, Ventura does the hard work for you. The grid settings feature is found in the graphics menu. It allows you to turn the grid snap on and off, and to set the horizontal and vertical grid spacing.

The invisible grid starts from the upper left edge of the page and divides it into horizontal and vertical units.

Take a look at the next illustration, which shows how a typical grid would appear if its lines were visible.

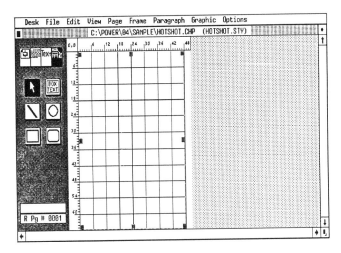

This example has both horizontal and vertical units set to six picas. The tick marks on the ruler show that the first grid lines begin six picas from the left edge of the paper and six picas from the top edge of the paper, and continue in six-pica increments.

The grid acts like a magnetic field. Any shape you place on the page snaps automatically to the nearest line. You cannot misalign a shape; Ventura won't let you. With the grid shown above, for example, you can draw a box that is six picas on each side; or 12 picas on one side and 6 on another; or 18 picas on each side — or any shape with measurements in units of six. You cannot, however, draw a 10-pica box. To do that, you would have to change the grid settings to 2, 5, or 10.

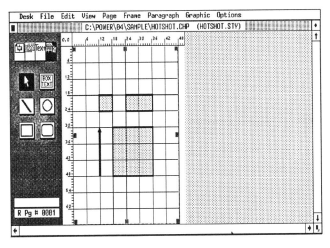

Planning the Grid

Once you understand that the grid is measured from the upper left corner of the page or frame *no matter what the margin settings are*, then you can plan the grid settings to coordinate with the overall page design.

First you must consider the size of the grid setting. With a large grid setting it is harder to make mistakes. If you want to draw six-pica boxes and you set the grid at six picas, it will be hard to go wrong.

Next consider the margin settings. For instance, if you wanted to draw a row of six-pica boxes across the page, you might set your page margins *and* your grid settings to six picas. The grid would let you line up the shapes with the margin. But if you were drawing those same boxes on a page with four-pica margins, the boxes would not line up with the margin. The grid would force the shapes six picas from the edge of the paper, or 12 picas, or 18 picas — but not four picas.

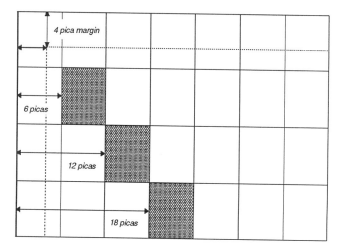

To line up boxes with the margins, set the grid *to the common denominator of the shapes and the margins*. For instance, you might choose two picas for the grid setting in the example above. Two picas is the lowest common denominator between the six-pica boxes and the four-pica margins. You could, in fact, turn the grid off and align the boxes by eye. However, you will never be as accurate manually as Ventura's automatic grid.

In some cases, you might want to change the grid as you go along. For instance, you might select six picas to draw six-pica boxes, then switch to two picas to draw narrower boxes. Be careful, though. If you change the size of the boxes you have already drawn, they will automatically snap to the current grid settings.

You will learn more about how to use the snap-to grid by following along with this chapter's project.

Box Text

Box text is the third and final concept you should be sure to understand before tackling the invoice. Box text is a special type of graphic shape. It is drawn, placed and sized just like an ordinary rectangle. But when you release the mouse key, the phrase *Box Text* appears inside the rectangle. You replace this phrase with your own text.

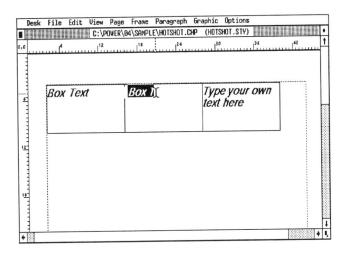

The name *box text* leads some users to believe that the text must always appear inside a visible rectangle. In fact, you can make the rectangle "invisible" so the text is the only thing that shows. This is a convenient way to stick a word or two anywhere on the page without regard to the margin or frame boundaries. Box text, like all shapes, can appear anywhere on the same page as the parent frame.

You can vary the lines and the background shading of box text to create a variety of effects. When combined with Ventura's line drawing function, box text is a handy way to create callouts — labels that point to a particular feature of an illustration.

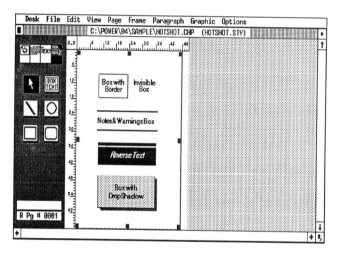

WARNING: Not all of the effects shown in the illustration above are available with all printers.

You may have to test your printer to see just how well it performs at overlapping one graphic shape with another. With many PostScript printers, for example, you cannot place box text with a white background over a frame with a pattern background. The box text will show on screen, but it will not print out. Here's how to trick most PostScript printers into printing overlapping graphics: First draw a solid white rectangle shape over the frame background. Then place a white, hollow, transparent box text shape on top of the rectangle. This double overlap effect allows you to print out box text shapes on patterned backgrounds.

Box Text Versus Frame Text

In some ways, box text resembles text in small frames. Indeed, there are many situations when you can create the same effect with frame text as with box text. Perhaps the easiest way to distinguish between them is to say that frame text can be a separate file (if you want it to be). Box text, by contrast, must always be typed by the user directly into the chapter, where it is stored in the caption file.

As a general rule, you should use frames to place more than two dozen words or so. Use box text to place smaller amounts of text. At the end of the chapter we give you more tips on when to use frames and when to use box text.

Box Text Versus Rectangles

A final point about box text: Sometimes you should use it instead of the standard rectangle drawing tool. If you simply want a box without any words inside, the rectangle tool is fine. But if you think that you might want to place text inside at any time, use the box text tool instead. Simply delete the box text phrase and do not type anything in its place. You will now have the same empty rectangle, but you will be able to type text into this rectangle at a later time.

For example, when creating the form in this chapter, we used box text to build all the empty boxes and columns. Because of this, an operator could fill in the form on-screen.

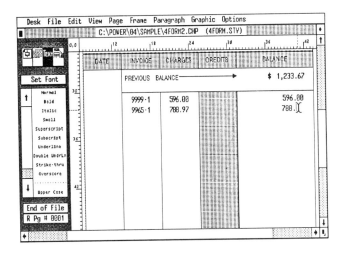

The Z_BoxText Tag

Now that you understand the graphic capabilities of box text, let's take a closer look at the "text" part of box text. Box text, like headers, footers, and captions, is a generated tag (Z_Box-Text). You can format it with the attributes in the Paragraph menu, rename it to another tag, or remove it from the Assignment List. In this chapter's invoice, for example, all the text is created via box text, then formatted with different tags from the style sheet.

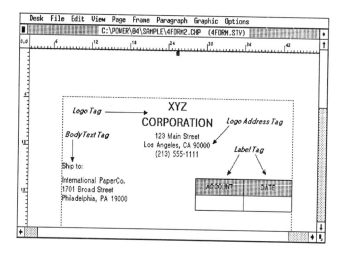

After reading the theory behind graphics drawing, you're ready to put the theory into practice. While you work on the invoice, you may find it helpful to refer back to this theory section or refer ahead to the tips at the end of the chapter.

Before

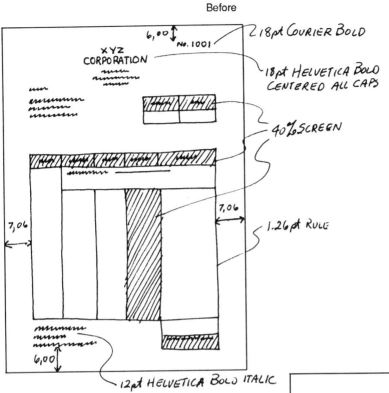

∠18pt COURIER BOLD

18pt HELVETICA BOLD
CENTERED ALL CAPS

40% SCREEN

1.26pt RULE

12pt HELVETICA BOLD ITALIC
LEFT JUSTIFIED

After

No. 1001

XYZ
CORPORATION
123 Main Street
Los Angeles, CA 90000
(213) 555-1111

Ship to:
International Paper Co.
1701 Broad Street
Philadelphia, PA 19000

ACCOUNT	DATE

Please Return Top Portion With Payment   Amount of Payment $ _____

DATE	INVOICE NO.	CHARGES	CREDITS	CREDITS
PREVIOUS BALANCE				

XYZ CORPORATION
123 Main Street
Los Angeles, CA 90000

PLEASE PAY THIS AMOUNT

Planning the Invoice

An invoice is a standard business form for billing information. Its goal is to present separate categories of information in an orderly fashion while making the most important numbers stand out. For example, you want it to be very easy for your customers to spot how much they owe you. Our example uses boxes, lines and shading to differentiate and clarify information.

There are other design considerations. For instance, many invoices are divided into two parts so customers can return one portion with their payments. The design should include a place for the company address on both halves of the form, so customers know where to write or call even if they have already sent off the other half. In addition, the customer's mailing address should be positioned to show through a standard-size window envelope.

The method of fill-in must also be part of your planning. If the form will be filled out with a typewriter, make the (body text) line spacing in increments of one pica so it matches the standard line spacing of typewriters. If it will be filled out by hand, make sure the blanks and boxes are large enough for easy writing.

A Thumbnail Sketch

It is easier to work with Ventura if you draw a simple thumbnail sketch before starting. In the first three chapters, the "after" versions of the sample documents have served this role. As you begin creating documents of your own, spend a few moments planning the design with pencil and paper before loading Ventura. Creating a thumbnail sketch forces you to do some hard thinking and decision-making up front.

"Start with a thumbnail sketch" is probably found in more books on page design than any other piece of advice. Certainly, advance planning can speed the process of producing pages in Ventura. Here are a few of the elements to consider as you draw the sketch:

- Margins

- Columns

- Gutters

- Size of frames or box text

- X,Y position of frames or box text

Do as much of the math as possible while preparing the sketch. Jot down dimensions and positions of key page elements. While you're at it, figure out the horizontal and vertical grid units by finding a common denominator between the margins and the size of the shapes. It is much easier to do calculations on paper than in your head while staring at a dialog box.

Look at our thumbnail sketch and the final version of the invoice on the nearby page. Here are some of the techniques you will use to achieve these effects:

- Snap-to grid

- Black type on a patterned background

- Lines and line attributes

- Box text, rectangles and tint screens (fill patterns)

- Automatic invoice numbering in the header

Ventura Prep

As always, set up the desktop environment by loading and renaming files to their proper location.

Start a New Chapter

If you are continuing directly from Chapter Three, use the File menu to start a new chapter. This removes the current chapter from your screen but retains the current style sheet.

■ Select New Chapter from the File menu.

You can only use the New option after you have opened an existing chapter. It is not available when you start Ventura for the first time. If you are starting from the DOS prompt, Ventura begins with an untitled chapter and you do not need to select New from the File menu.

Load a Style Sheet

■ Load the style sheet, 4FORM.STY from the C:\POWER and save it as C:\TEMP\4INVOICE.STY.

Rename the Chapter

While you are at it, save and rename the chapter so you can safely save your progress under the correct name just by pressing ^S.

■ Select Save As and save the chapter as C:\TEMP\4IN-VOICE.CHP

➡ *NOTE: Save As ... makes a copy of the chapter file. It does not make a copy of the text or picture files linked to the chapter.*

If You Do Not Have the Power Disk

You will find it a bit more difficult to follow along without the Publishing Power disk in the advanced section. The Power disk includes sample style sheets, text files and (in a few cases) sample chapters with most of the basic work done already. You need only work on advanced techniques and skills to complete the document.

Nevertheless, with just a bit more work on your part it is possible to complete all the sample documents without the disk. In general, you must take these four steps:

• Type in the text file for that chapter from Appendix A using a word processor. Then load it into the C:\TEMP subdirectory.

• Load one of the style sheets that come with Ventura instead of the style sheet from the Power disk. In each chapter, we give you brief suggestions on which style sheets to use and what modifications to make.

- Modify the columns and margins as necessary to match the Power style sheet using the illustrations provided.

- Add or modify tags as you go along to match the tags you see on the sample screens and sample documents.

Load a Style Sheet

For this chapter, we recommend starting with the &INV-P1.STY sheet from the C:\TYPESET subdirectory. (If you cannot find it, then copy the style sheet from the original Ventura Examples Disk #2.) Load it into the new chapter and then save it under the new name C:\TEMP\4INVOICE.STY. Change the margins and columns to match the following diagram.

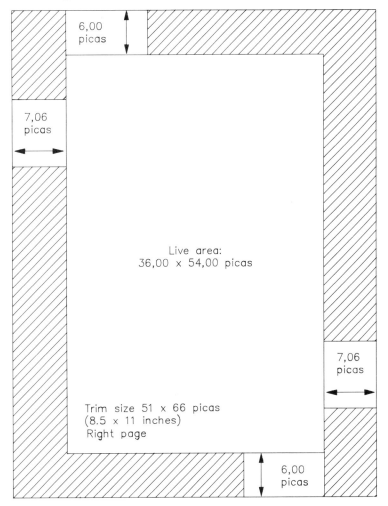

6,00 picas

7,06 picas

Live area:
36,00 x 54,00 picas

7,06 picas

Trim size 51 x 66 picas
(8.5 x 11 inches)
Right page

6,00 picas

Since all the text for this document is created with box text shapes, you do not need to type in a separate text file for this chapter.

Rename the Chapter

After loading and renaming the style sheet, save and rename the chapter file.

■ Select Save As from the File menu and save the chapter as C:\TEMP\4INVOICE.CHP.

Text

The Ventura Formula provides a solid strategy for completing most documents, but you must vary it slightly for documents where you place text in frames and boxes. In Chapter Three, for example, you placed text files *after* building frames to contain them. Similarly, to create this chapter's invoice you will add text *after* building boxes. Here's the order to follow:

• Format the underlying page

• Build a snap-to grid

• Draw the box text shapes

• Add your own text to the boxes

After you enter the text to the boxes you can proceed with the rest of the Ventura Formula.

➡NOTE: The Ventura Formula is a handy rule of thumb to get you started. As you become more proficient, you will carve out your own pathways and discover new strategies to fit your personal style.

Style

Now that you've finished the groundwork, you're ready to lay out the page.

Complete the Global Layout

Whether you loaded the style sheet from the Power disk or recreated it on your own, you should have the correct values for the paper size, starting page, and margins and columns. To complete the global layout you only need to enter the header text. Header text is not stored in the style sheet (although the header *format* is).

Build the Header

Since you learned how to create basic headers in Part One, we are now going to show you some advanced techniques.

You already know that you can change the attributes of the header text using the Paragraph menu. In this example, you will learn how to make similar format changes using text attribute codes in the Headers & Footers dialog box. By using the dialog box, you can make part of the header display in one format (which you set in the dialog box) while another part displays a different format (which you set with the Paragraph menu).

If you refer back to the "After" example on page 13, you will notice that the "Invoice No." portion of the header displays in 14-point Times Roman, but the "1001" portion is in 18-point Courier Bold. Now we will show you how to achieve this effect.

Change Text Attributes in the Dialog Box

In the instructions that follow, you make use of the buttons at the bottom of the dialog box to enter a generic code. After you choose a button, you must then erase part of the code and put in the information you want to use. For instance, choosing the Text Attr. button inserts the code <D>. Since <D> is the code to turn off attributes, you must substitute another code inside the brackets to turn on the attributes you want. For instance, you could substitute the letter B inside the brackets to specify bold. Keep in mind that all the buttons in the dialog box merely serve as a shortcut. You could just have easily typed <B> right from the start. However, most people find that it is faster to use the buttons, since they eliminate the need to memorize the correct codes.

➡ *NOTE: The buttons at the bottom of the dialog box are for con-venience only. If you prefer, you can type in the settings without using the buttons.*

■ Select Headers & Footers. Choose Define: Right Page Header, Usage: On. Move to the Right line and type: `No.[space]`

■ Choose Text Attr. and delete the letter "D" (do not delete the right and left brackets). Then type the following codes in-side the brackets: `BF1P18`

You have just inserted the codes for three text attributes. Let's look at each one in turn.

• B tells Ventura to make the following text bold.

• F1 tells Ventura to switch to font #1, which is Courier. (Ven-tura assigns numbers to fonts. Appendix D in the Ventura manual lists which numbers apply to which fonts.)

• P18 tells Ventura to change the point size to 18 points.

Now tell Ventura to display the current page number after the word "N." As you will see, Ventura's page counter will then automatically number the invoices in sequence.

■ Move the cursor after the right bracket and choose [Page #].

To complete the header dialog box, add another text attribute at the end of the line. The last <D> symbol tells Ventura to reset the font back to normal.

■ Choose Text. Attr.

Check to make sure the dialog box looks like this:

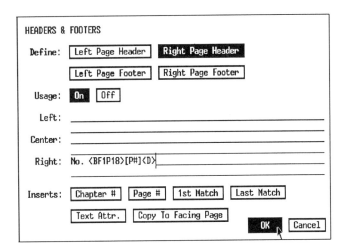

After you complete the dialog box, the header appears at the top of the page.

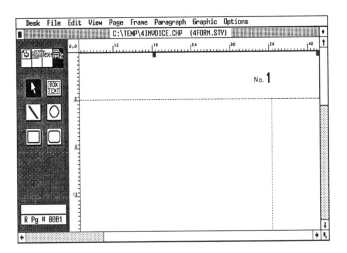

Change the Page Number

Right now the header displays the number 1. With Ventura's page counter, you can make a document begin at any number. For example, let's make the first page start at 1001.

■ Select Page Counter from the Page menu. Choose Restart Counting: Yes, With Number: 1001, Number Format: 1,2.

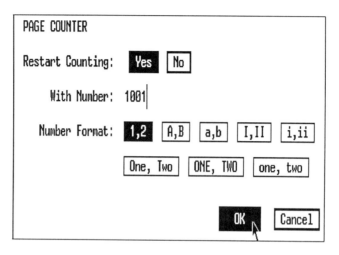

Since the invoice number is based on the current page number, it will change as soon as you click OK and return to the page.

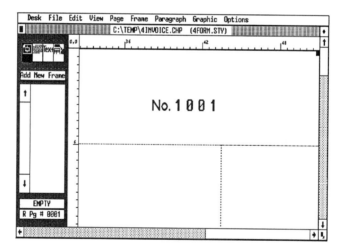

Once you finish the header, the global layout is complete. Now you can begin to add the boxes. Start with the lower half of the form and then continue with the top half. The dimensions in the following illustration will help you gauge the size of the shapes.

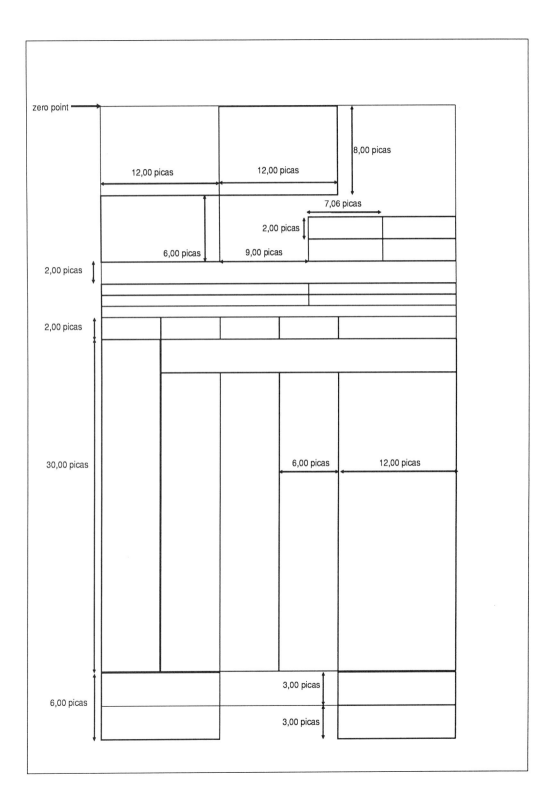

Select the Parent Frame

- Enable frame mode. Click anywhere on the page to select the underlying page as the parent.

- Select graphics drawing mode.

By selecting the underlying page and then selecting graphics drawing, you have made the underlying page the parent to everything you draw.

➡ *NOTE: Because the underlying page is the parent, the graphics will appear on every page of the document. You will be able to create a duplicate invoice by inserting a new page into the document.*

Select Grid Settings

To help you accurately line up graphic shapes, select grid settings from the graphic menu. Set the horizontal and vertical units to the largest common measurement. In this example, we recommend that you set the horizontal spacing to 01,06 picas and the vertical spacing to 03,00 picas.

- Select Grid Settings from the graphic menu.

- Choose Grid Snap: On. Make the Horizontal Spacing: 01,06 picas and Vertical Spacing: 03,00.

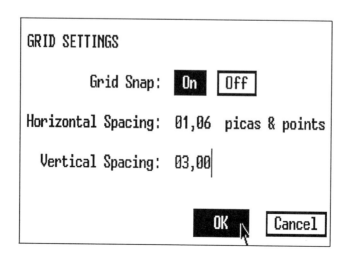

Reset the Zero Point

Another technique that makes it easier to draw and measure the invoice shapes is to reset the zero point of the ruler so it lines up with the upper left corner of the column margin. Here's how to reset the zero point:

- Change to Reduced View (press ^R).

- Place the cursor on the zero point in the ruler. Press and hold the mouse button until the four-way arrow appears. Drag it downwards until the horizontal and vertical crosshairs line up with the upper left corner of the column margin. Then release the mouse button.

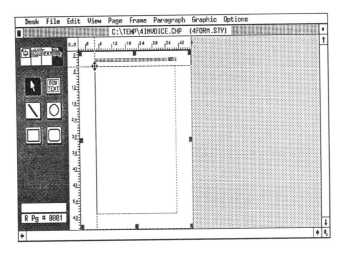

Draw Box Text

After you reset the zero point, you are ready to draw.

- Select the box text icon in the Sidebar.

- Place the upper left corner of the box 21 picas down from 0,0 so it lines up with the left page margin.

- Drag the box downwards and to the right until it snaps to position 51 on the vertical ruler and 6 on the horizontal ruler. Release the mouse button.

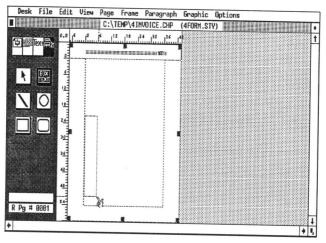

The word "Box Text" appears inside the shape.

If you need to change the dimensions of a shape after it is drawn you can re-size it with the cursor. Place the cursor on one of the black handles around the outside of the shape. Then press and hold the mouse button until the pointing hand icon appears. Stretch the shape to the new size and release the mouse button.

If you want to delete a shape, simply click on it and press the Del key (or select Cut Graphic from the Edit menu).

Change Line Attributes

When you are satisfied with the size of the first box text, set then save the line and fill attributes so they will automatically apply to the other box text shapes you draw.

■ Select Line Attributes from the Graphic menu (or press Ctrl-L).

■ Choose Thickness: 2 and Color: Black. Make both End Styles: Square (as shown below). Choose Save To.

➥*NOTE: The Save To ... button does not stay highlighted after you choose it in the dialog box.*

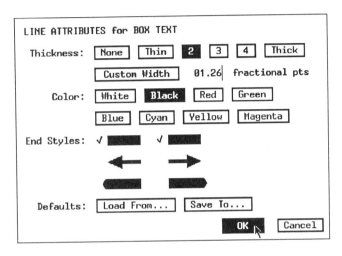

Save to... stores these line attributes as default values. Ventura remembers your choices the next time you draw a box text.

Let's take a moment to explain Ventura's application of end styles which can be confusing. Ventura doesn't care which end is left or right. It only cares which end was drawn first.

Look again at the Line Attributes dialog box above. The End Styles on the left apply to the *starting* point. The End Styles on the right apply to the *ending* point. This holds true whether you draw from left to right, from right to left, from top to bottom, or from bottom to top.

Change Fill Attributes

■ With the box text still selected, select Fill Attributes from the Graphic menu (or press ^F). Choose White, Hollow, Transparent, and Save To.

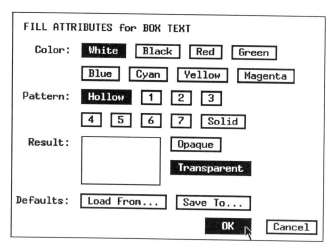

Copy the Box Text

Now that you've made one box text, we will show you a shortcut for the next four. Instead of using the box text tool to draw each shape, use the copy and paste commands to reproduce four copies of the original.

- With the first box text still selected, press Shift-Del (or select Copy Graphic from the graphic menu).

You have just copied the box text into temporary memory.

➡ *NOTE: Ventura uses the same copy and paste procedures for graphics, text editing and frame mode. Since Ventura treats all three independently, you can copy or delete to three separate temporary memories at the same time.*

Paste the Box Text

- Press the Ins key or select Paste Graphic from the graphic menu.

You will see the screen redraw itself, which is your sign that Ventura has indeed pasted a new box text onto the page. Otherwise you might not know for sure, since Ventura always pastes the copy directly on top of the original.

Once you paste the copy, you can move it to a new position.

Move the Copy

■ Press and hold the cursor anywhere in the middle of the box text until the four-way arrow appears. With the mouse button still depressed move the box text into place.

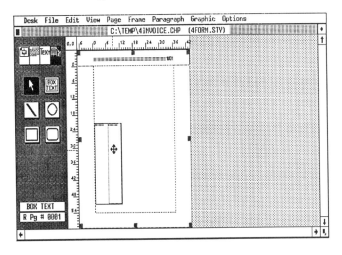

Paste and move three more box text shapes into place as illustrated in the next figure. The snap-to grid should make alignment easy.

➡ *NOTE: Once you copy a shape into temporary memory, it remains there until replaced by something else. To insert another copy, simply press the Ins key again. You do not need to repeat the copy command.*

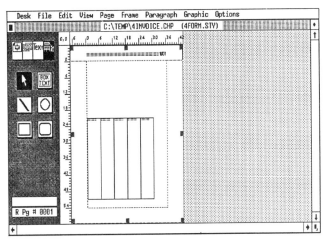

Stretch the Last Box Text

When you are finished placing copies, stretch the last box text so it lines up with the right edge of the column margin.

- Select the last box text drawn.

- Place the cursor on any black handle on the right side. Press and hold the mouse button until the pointing hand icon appears.

- Stretch the box text until it lines up with the right page margin. Release the mouse button.

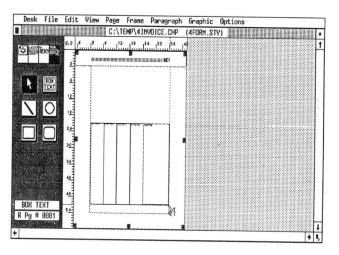

Re-Size Box Text

Make four of the box text shapes shorter to make room above for the next box text shape. Select the four shapes.

- Click on one of the box text shapes. Then as you hold down the Shift key click on the other three.

➡ *NOTE: If you accidentally click on the wrong graphic shape, simply click on it again to "deselect" it. Then choose another shape.*

After all four shapes are selected, re-size them together.

- Place the cursor on the black handle at the upper right corner of the rightmost box text. Press and hold down the mouse button until the hand icon appears and drag the boxes downwards one snap grid.

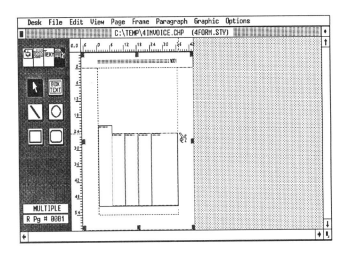

See how quick and easy it is to draw when you use a grid? Now that you've shortened the four boxes, you're ready to draw the next box text shape.

Draw Box Text

■ Select the box text icon from the sidebar.

➡ *NOTE: You can draw several shapes, one after another, by holding down the Shift key while you draw. The cursor stays in the current shape drawing mode (box text, rectangle, line, or ellipse) and you can draw a second shape without re-selecting a graphic icon from the Sidebar.*

■ Line up the cursor with the upper right corner of the first rectangle. Stretch it down one grid snap and over to the right so it lines up with the right column margin.

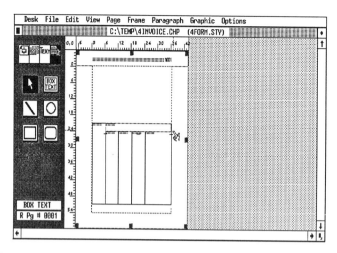

Draw More Shapes

Now that you have the basics of graphics drawing under your belt, draw the graphic shapes at the bottom of the form.

■ Select box text.

■ Align cursor with bottom left corner of rightmost box. Stretch box down one grid unit and over to right margin.

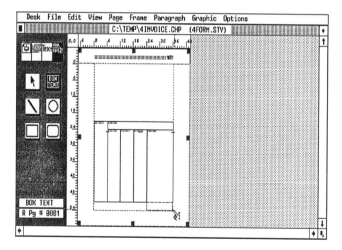

Add another box text shape immediately below.

■ Select box text.

■ Align the cursor with the lower left corner of the box text just drawn. Stretch the shape down one grid unit and over to the right column margin. (The bottom of the shape extends below the column guide.)

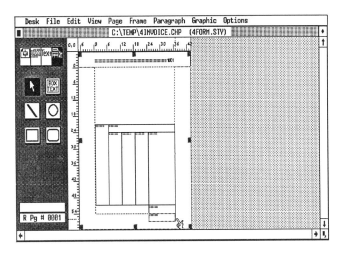

➡ *NOTE: You could also use copy and paste graphic to create the second shape.*

Draw the Final Shape

Only one more shape and you are finished with the lower half of the form.

■ Select the box text icon.

■ Align the cursor with the lower left corner of the form. Stretch the shape down two snap units (06,00 picas) and over two columns to the right.

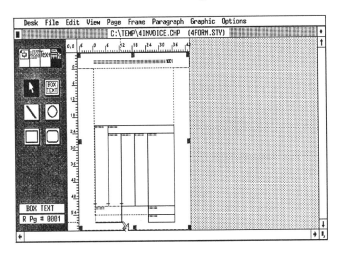

Stopping Point

Good work. You've already completed more than half of the invoice. Now that you've learned how to draw and re-size shapes, the second part of the invoice should be a cinch. Take a moment to evaluate your progress. Check to make sure your screen matches the following illustration:

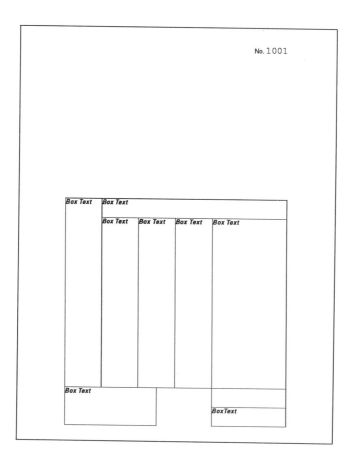

This is a good point in the exercise to take a break and save your work (press ^S to save). If you're short on time, quit now and start again later. If your schedule permits, continue on to the next section without stopping. If you're in a real rush, you can simply read through the next few pages without actually drawing in the rest of the box text, and skip to the section titled "ReCap," where we show you how to edit box text. However, we highly recommend that you complete the entire project if you possibly can. The more time you devote to practice now, the easier it will be to do your own projects later. And drawing the last shapes should only take a few more minutes.

If You Are Starting Again After a Break

If you are starting fresh, reload Ventura and open the chapter C:\TEMP\4INVOICE.CHP. Go to the next section where you will complete drawing the invoice.

Change Grid Settings

To make the narrower boxes in the top portion of the form make the vertical spacing smaller (the horizontal spacing stays the same).

■ Grid Settings   Grid Snap: On
                      Horizontal Spacing: 01,00
                      Vertical Spacing: 01,06

Draw Box Text

Draw the next five box shapes that will contain the words Date, Invoice No., Charges, Credits and Balance. Use the same shortcut you did to create the first set of boxes — draw one shape, then copy and paste it to make four more.

➡ NOTE: Depending on your display screen, you may find it easier to draw these smaller shapes if you change to Normal (^N) or Enlarged (^E) view.

■ Select box text.

■ Starting at position 19 on the vertical ruler, draw a box text shape that is 2,00 picas high and 6,00 picas wide. (Since the vertical setting is 01,00 pica and the horizontal is 01,06 picas, the box is two snap units high and four snap units wide).

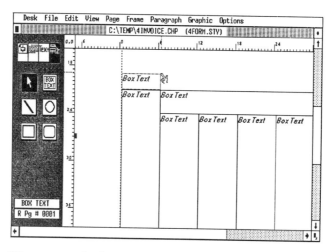

Now copy the box text to the clipboard and paste it back onto the page.

■ With the first box text still selected, press Shift-Del to place a copy into temporary memory.

Paste and Place the Copies

■ Press the Ins key to paste a copy back onto the page.

Once the copy has been pasted onto the page, move it to the right of the original. Insert three more box text shapes and move them so they line up side-by-side as shown below. Then stretch the last box text so it snaps to the right page margin. After you make the copies, the invoice should look like this:

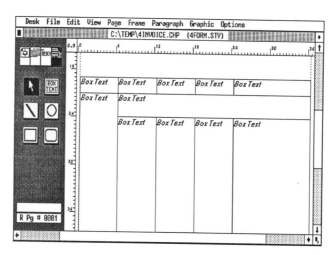

Add Box Text for the Tear Off Line

Add another box text above the five just drawn. You will use it later to contain the dotted tear off line. (The dotted line itself will be created with the Tab Settings option from the Paragraph menu.)

- Select box text.

- Starting at position 17 on the vertical ruler, stretch the box text shape so it measures 2,00 picas high and one column wide.

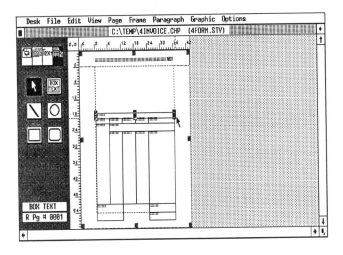

Add Two Box Texts

Add two more box text shapes to contain the text "Please Return Top Portion With Payment" and "Amount of Payment $." Initially these shapes will overlap the box text shapes below them by one pica. However, later, when you change the line and fill attributes, the overlapping boxes will become "invisible."

- Select box text.

- Starting at position 16 on the vertical ruler, draw a box text shape that measures 2,00 picas high and 21,00 picas wide. Draw a second shape adjacent to the first and make it 2,00 picas high and 15,00 picas wide (it automatically snaps to the right column margin).

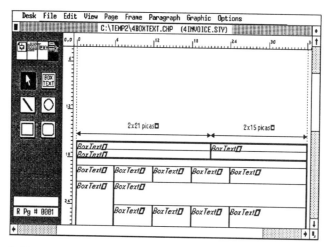

Draw the Final Shapes

Only six more shapes to go. Now that you've had some practice, you're ready to step out on your own. For the last part of the layout refer to the following illustration for placing and drawing the final shapes.

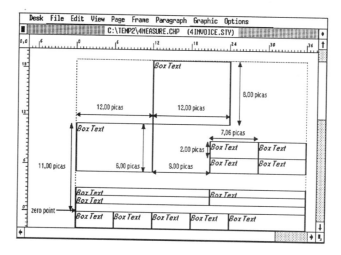

Here are a couple of tips to help you get started:

➡ *TIP: Reset the zero point to line up with the upper left corner of the box text that will contain the word "DATE."*

➡ *TIP: Use the rulers to align and measure shapes.*

When you finish, your screen should look like this:

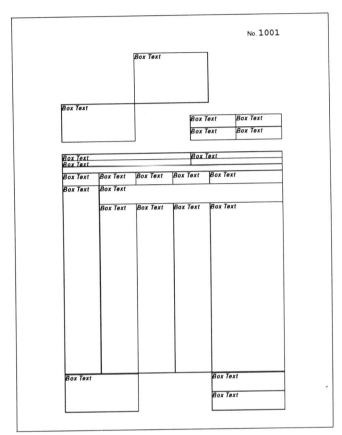

A Recap

At this point you have finished the global formatting. You built a header and you added box text. Now you are ready to add your own text. As we explained earlier, you will type this text directly onto the page. You will use text editing mode to delete the phrase "Box Text" and substitute your own words. You may want to change to an enlarged view to better see the text you typed.

Add the Logo Text

Start at the top of the page and work downwards. Do not be concerned yet with appearance of the text, which you will later reformat with tags.

- Enable text editing mode.

- Place the cursor in front of the square end of file mark in the topmost shape.

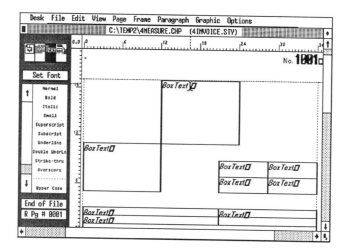

- Press the Backspace key to erase the words "Box Text" and type:

```
XYZ [Ctrl-Enter]
CORPORATION [Enter]
```

The line break (hold down the Ctrl key and press Enter) tells Ventura to treat the first two sentences as the same paragraph even though they are on separate lines. The line break appears on the screen as a backward arrow. Line breaks are useful when you want information on separate lines, but you don't want to bother retagging each line.

Add the Logo Address

- Type:

```
123 Main Street [Ctrl-Enter]
Los Angeles, CA 90000 [Ctrl-Enter]
(213) 555-1111
```

Add the Shipping Address

When typing the shipping address, make a line break after each sentence so Ventura treats all the lines as one paragraph.

■ Place the cursor in front of the square end of file mark in the shipping address box. Delete the words Box Text and type:

```
Ship to: [Ctrl-Enter]
International Paper Co. [Ctrl-Enter]
1701 Broad Street [Ctrl-Enter]
Philadelphia, PA 19000
```

Add the Amount of Payment

Now place the text cursor in the Amount of Payment box. Delete the words Box Text and type: `Amount of Payment $ [tab]`

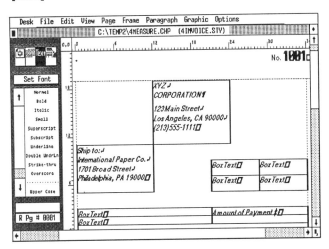

Add the Remaining Text

To add the rest of the text, remain in text editing mode and reposition the text cursor from box to box. Erase the phrase "box text" and add the new text, or leave it blank as shown in the illustration below. When you come to the box text reserved for the perforated line, delete the words "Box Text" and enter only a tab (by pressing the tab key once) without any text. When you begin tagging, you will create the tear off line using tab settings.

When you are finished adding text, your invoice should look like this.

No. **1001**

XYZ
CORPORATION

123 Main Street
Los Angeles, CA 90000
(213) 555-1111

Ship to:
International Paper Co.
1701 Broad Street
Philadelphia, PA 19000

ACCOUNT	DATE

Please Return Top Portion With Payment	Amount of Payment $

DATE	INVOICE	CHARGES	CREDITS	BALANCE
	PREVIOUS BALANCE			

XYZ CORPORATION
123 Main Street
Los Angeles, CA 9000

PLEASE PAY THIS
AMOUNT

Tagging the Text

The style sheet loaded at the beginning of the chapter already includes pre-defined tags. This will make formatting go fairly fast — all you need to do is apply the right tag to the right text. Once you apply the pre-defined tags, we will show you how to create the tear off line with a new tag. Otherwise, the tags we provide in the style sheet will create the effects you need without modification. (If you did not purchase the Publishing Power disk, you must build the tags on your own.)

Apply the First Tags

Start at the top of the document and work down. Although box text starts as a generated tag, you can retag it as any other tag name.

- Enable paragraph tagging mode. Select the paragraph "XYZ CORPORATION" and tag it as Logo.

- Select the company address paragraph and tag it as Logo Address.

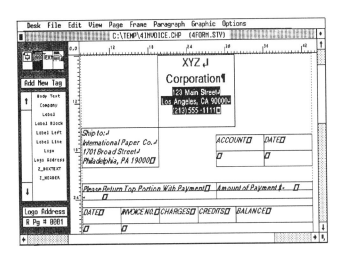

- Select the ship to address paragraph and tag it as Body Text.

- Use Shift-Click to select the next three paragraphs, "AC-COUNT," "DATE," and "Please Return Top Portion With Payment," and tag them as Label.

■ Select the paragraph "Amount of Payment $" and tag it as Label Line.

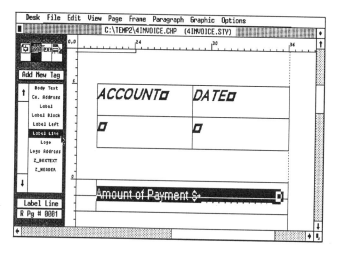

Creating an Underscore

Let's pause for a minute to show you how we got the underscore effect in the Label Line tag above. Open the Tab Settings dialog box so you can see what we did.

■ With the paragraph still selected, select Tab Settings from the Paragraph menu.

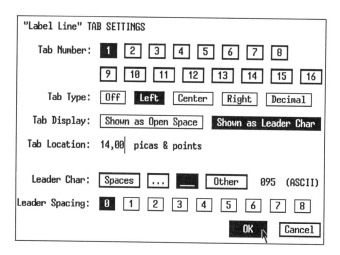

To make an underscore, we created a tab setting with a leader character. The position of the tab is the point at which we wanted the line to end – in this case, 14,00 picas from the left margin of the box (*not* from the left margin of the page). Notice that the leader character is a straight line (___) with no spacing. In other words, the single solid line you see was actually created by placing small underline characters side-by-side with no space between.

Create the Tear Off Line

You will use the Tab Settings technique described above to construct the dotted line in the next box text shape. First you will add a tag named Tab, then you create a tab setting with a leader character. In this case, however, the leader character will be a dotted line instead of a solid line.

■ Select the tab symbol and the end of paragraph mark (¶) just as you would select any other paragraph you wanted to tag.

➡ *TIP: If you don't see the tab symbol, make sure that Show Tabs & Returns is On in the options menu.*

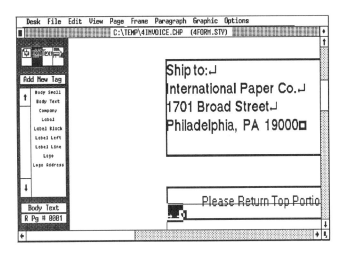

■ Add New Tag   Tag Name to Add: Tab

To create the dotted line effect add a tab setting to the new tag.

■ Select Tab Settings from the Paragraph menu. Choose Tab Number: 1, Tab Type: Left, and Tab Display: Shown as Leader Character. Then make the tab location 36,00 picas &

points and the Leader Character (...) with 0 Leader Spacing.

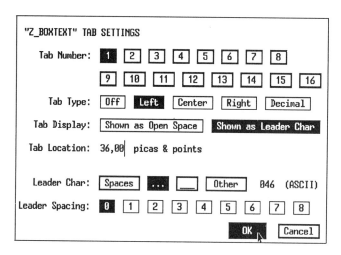

Tag the Remaining Text

Now finish tagging the invoice using the pre-defined tag names from the Assignment List. Change views as necessary.

- Select the paragraphs "DATE," "INVOICE NO.," "CHARGES," "CREDITS," and "BALANCE" and tag them as Label.

- Select the paragraph "PREVIOUS BALANCE" and tag it as Label Left.

- Select the paragraph "PLEASE PAY THIS AMOUNT" at the bottom of the page and tag it as Label Black.

- Select the paragraph at the bottom of the page that begins "XYZ CORPORATION, 123 Main Street..." and tag it as Co. Address.

Before you continue to the pictures section, check your progress against the following illustration.

No. 1001

XYZ CORPORATION

123 Main Street
Los Angeles, CA 90000
(213) 555-1111

Ship to:

International Paper Co.
1701 Broad Street
Philadelphia, PA 19000

ACCOUNT	DATE

Please Return Top Portion With Payment	Amount of Payment $ _____

DATE	INVOICE NO.	CHARGES	CREDITS	BALANCE
	PREVIOUS BALANCE			

XYZ CORPORATION
123 Main Street
Los Angeles, CA 90000

PLEASE PAY THIS AMOUNT

Pictures

With Text and Style behind you, you can look ahead to the next part of the formula: Pictures. Now that you've placed and positioned the shapes, you can modify the line and fill attributes to create new effects. In this section you will create a gray pattern (tint screen) effect and make the border lines around selected box text invisible.

Change Fill Attributes

Start by selecting the shapes you want to fill with a pattern.

■ Enable frame mode then enable graphics drawing mode.

■ Use Shift-Click to select the boxes that will be shaded. Use the following illustration as your guide.

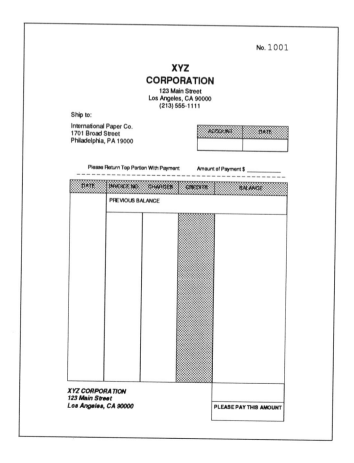

➡️*NOTE: If you mistakenly click on the wrong box, simply click on it again and it is immediately "de-selected." Then select another shape.*

■ Select Fill Attributes. Choose Black, 2, and Transparent.

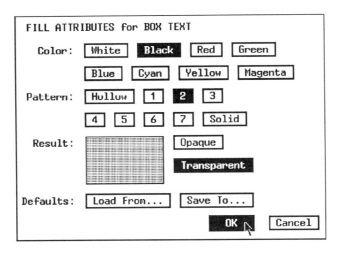

All the selected shapes are filled in with a gray pattern.

Change Line Attributes

Now remove the lines around selected box text shapes.

■ Use Shift-Click to select the box text shapes shown in the following illustration.

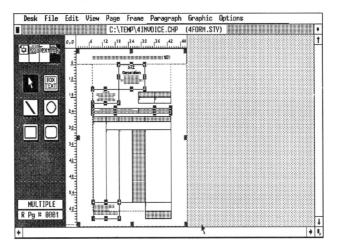

■ Select Line Attributes. Choose None to make the borders invisible.

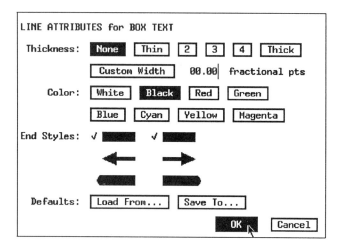

If any of the borders are still visible after a multiple selection,
simply re-select an individual box and change its line attributes to none.

Check that the invoice looks like the following illustration.

No. 1001

XYZ CORPORATION

123 Main Street
Los Angeles, CA 90000
(213) 555-1111

Ship to:

International Paper Co.
1701 Broad Street
Philadelphia, PA 19000

ACCOUNT	DATE

Please Return Top Portion With Payment   Amount of Payment $ _____

- -

DATE	INVOICE NO	CHARGES	CREDITS	CREDITS
	PREVIOUS BALANCE ——————————→			

XYZ CORPORATION
123 Main Street
Los Angeles, CA 90000

PLEASE PAY THIS AMOUNT

Add Line and Arrow

To add the finishing touches to the form, add a line with an arrow end after the words "Previous Balance."

■ Select the line icon from the Sidebar. When the pencil icon appears, place its "point" after the e in the word Balance.

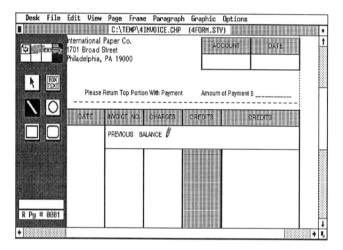

■ Drag the line to the right until it lines up with the B in the word BALANCE above.

Use the Line Attributes dialog box to put an arrow at one end of the line.

■ Select Line Attributes. Choose Thin, Black and the arrow in the right column of End Styles.

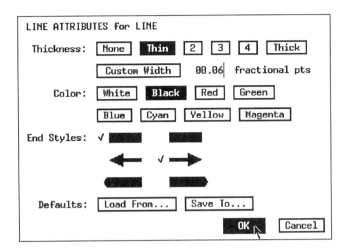

Chapter

Now that you've seen the invoice on the screen, let's see how it looks printed out. Ventura's print option allows you to print multiple copies of a document. When you print this time, tell Ventura to make three copies of the form.

■ To Print   Which Pages: Current
                    No. of Copies: 3

Ventura spins out three copies of the invoice. In fact, once a laser printer has processed one copy of a single page, it takes little extra time to make additional copies.

In this chapter, you learned how to create a graphics-intensive document using Ventura's graphic toolkit. In the next chapter, you will learn how to create another document that relies heavily on graphics to convey a message: an advertising flyer.

Tips

When to Use Box Text

Use box text to contain text if you want to:

❏ Quickly place less than two dozen words. For longer selections, consider using a frame so the text can be placed into a separate file if desired.

❑ Attach the text to something else. If, for example, you wish to create callouts for an illustration, you want the text to be tied to that frame. When you move the frame, the box text automatically moves with it.

❑ Move box text shapes as a group. Box text can be grouped by attaching them all to the same parent frame. When you move the parent you automatically move all the box text. Frames, on the other hand, cannot be permanently linked (although you can temporarily group them using shift-click to select several at a time).

When to Use Frames

Use a frame to contain text if you want to:

❑ Import a file. You cannot load a file into box text. You must always type box text directly onto the page.

❑ Rename the text to a separate file. Even if you originally type the text into the chapter, you may sometimes want to rename text into a separate file. A standalone text file can be easily edited or updated with a word processor.

❑ Create more than one column inside the rectangle. You can create multiple columns inside a frame, but not inside box text.

❑ Flow text around the rectangle. Text can flow automatically around a frame. By contrast, box text coexists with whatever else is in the same space.

❑ Put more than one ruling line around the rectangle. Box text can have only a single ruling line around. Frames can have up to three.

More Graphic Drawing Tips

❑ Align text rectangles along a grid. The snap-to grid available in graphics mode is more versatile than the column- and line-snap available in frame mode.

❑ Select the correct frame before entering graphics drawing

mode. This frame is the parent. Select a frame if you want the shape to appear on one page only. Select the underlying page if you want the shape to repeat on every page of the document.

❑ When selecting the parent, make logical groupings so all related shapes can be moved as one by moving the parent. For instance, if you were constructing a two-part form using frames instead of the underlying page, you could attach all the shapes on the top half to one parent, and all the shapes on the bottom half to a different frame. That way the two halves could be adjusted independently. (This tip does not apply to shapes that appear on every page of the document. Those shapes must always be tied to the underlying page.)

❑ Locating the parent can be difficult if you return to edit shapes, especially if there are many frames on the page. If you are having trouble locating the parent, simply select a frame then press the Ctrl and the Q keys simultaneously. Do this for every frame on the page until handles appear around the shape(s) you want.

❑ Ctrl-Q is the keyboard shortcut for Select All from the graphics menu. This graphics command operates even in frame mode. (It is the only one that works. To use any other graphic commands, you must switch to graphics drawing mode.)

❑ Establish grid settings before you start to draw. There may be a few exceptions where you wish to turn grid settings off for complete freedom in placing a shape. In most cases, your drawings will be more accurate and attractive if you establish a snap-to grid in advance.

❑ Set the grid as large as possible. The larger the units of the grid setting, the smaller the possibility for error.

❑ Consider the margin when setting the grid. If possible, give the grid units an integer relationship with the margin settings so the shapes snap to the margin.

❑ To move a very small shape, attach it to a larger frame. (The frame can be "invisible" if you do not want it to print.) Then move the frame. The shape moves with it.

❏ To draw several shapes at once, hold the shift key down while dragging the mouse. The cursor stays in shape drawing mode and you can draw a second shape immediately.

❏ To speed the creation of identical shapes, use the Save to button in the Line Attributes and Fill Attributes dialog boxes. This saves the attributes you have just chosen. From then on, every shape you draw is identical to the previous one.

❏ To select several shapes at once, use the same Shift-Click method that operates in paragraph tagging mode. Once you have selected more than one shape, you can move, resize or change the attributes of these shapes as a group.

❏ To select a shape that is underneath another, hold down the Ctrl key while clicking on the shape with the mouse. Each time you Ctrl-Click, Ventura selects the next lowest "layer," no matter how many shapes are piled one on top of the other.

Chapter Five
Skills Checklist

Text

✓ Improving headlines with kerning

✓ Entering non-keyboard characters

Style

✓ Mixing two formats in one document

✓ Fixing display type with tracking and manual kerning

Pictures

✓ Importing Postcript files

✓ Cropping an image

✓ Running text around irregular shapes

✓ Creating a drop shadow

Chapter

✓ Printing to a disk file

✓ Creating Encapsulated PostScript files

An Advertising Flyer

Advertisements and flyers are invaluable promotional tools. In Chapter Five, you will learn how to create a self-mailing ad. Although we constructed this project as a direct mail piece, many of the techniques apply equally well to print advertisements. In essence, we will show you the basics of creating an ad *plus* the added techniques to turn that ad into a self-mailing flyer. The checklist on the left lists some of the special skills you will learn.

Theory

In Chapter Four, you learned how to use Ventura's built-in graphics to create simple box, line, and rectangle shapes. These basic shapes are useful for forms, annotations, and simple artwork. But for the sophisticated graphics required of an advertisement, you need dedicated, standalone graphics programs. Programs like AutoCAD, Adobe Illustrator, and PC Paintbrush provide specialized drawing and painting tools for creating high-quality images. Fortunately, Ventura makes it easy to import these complex images into a document.

The advertising project you will complete in this chapter depends heavily on graphics effects. You will find it easier to follow along if you understand these three key concepts:

• How Ventura manages picture files

• The two kinds of pictures

• How to change the size of pictures inside the frame

How Ventura Manages Pictures

After you create a picture, you load and place it in a frame or on the underlying page just as you would a text file. However, the similarity ends there. Ventura treats picture files differently than text files. The chapter doesn't store the image itself, but rather stores *a pointer* to the picture file with information about how to display it. Picture files cannot be changed inside Ventura.

Two Kinds of Pictures

Ventura accepts two kinds of picture files: images and line art. Paint programs, scanners, and screen capture utilities create bit-mapped images. These images are a collection of thousands of individual dots (or bits). As you draw, the computer makes a map of the screen and figures out which dots to turn on and off.

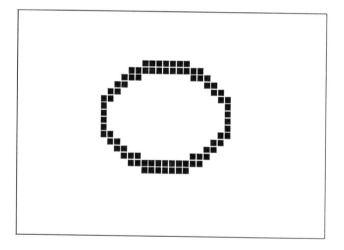

Since an image is a map of the screen, the final picture is only as good as the screen's resolution. Few screens can match the 300 dots-per-inch resolution of a laser printer. At print time, bit-map curves and diagonals appear jagged. Despite this tradeoff in quality, a paint package can provide subtle, painterly effects and shades and shadows that are difficult with line art.

By contrast, line art programs such as AutoCAD, MacDraw, and GEM Draw do not use bit-maps. They combine basic shapes to build up picture. Shades, surfaces and planes are reduced to lines, arcs, circles and other basic geometric objects. Hence the term "object-oriented" graphics.

These objects are stored by the computer as mathematical expressions. A circle is described as a center point and a radius; a line is described as a starting and ending point, an arc as three consecutive points and so forth. This format has several advantages. For instance, when you print an object-oriented picture, the computer sends the descriptions to the printer. The picture is then printed at whatever resolution the printer or phototypesetter is capable of — 300, 600, 1200 or 2500 dots per inch. As a result, lines and curves appear smooth.

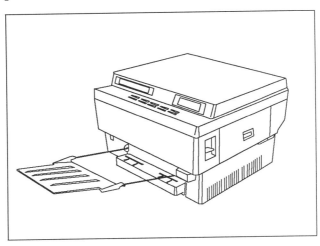

Line art has another advantage. You can enlarge or reduce it without losing picture quality. You don't have to worry about creating it at the same size as the final version.

Encapsulated Postscript Files

If you have a PostScript printer you can also use a special kind of line art. With the Encapsulated PostScript (EPS) format you can create facsimile pages and insert them into a document. For instance, we used the EPS format to produce the "after" pictures near the beginning of each chapter. When you place a PostScript file, the picture is not displayed on screen.

Instead, it appears as a large X. However, the picture is visible when you print. You will have a chance to use Encapsulated PostScript to build the sample advertisement in this chapter.

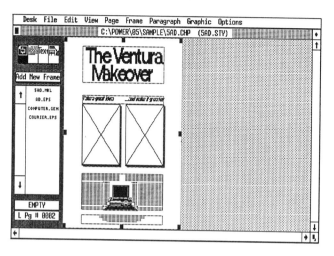

Sizing and Scaling Pictures

Both line art and images can be scaled and cropped through the Sizing & Scaling dialog box.

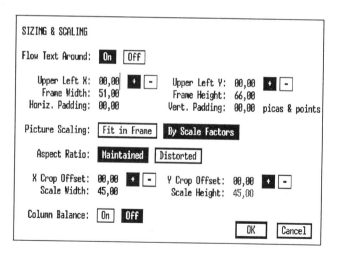

For many beginners, Sizing & Scaling is one of the most difficult Ventura techniques to grasp. We will present you with basic concepts here in the theory section, but don't be too surprised if you don't understand all the ins and outs until you've had some hands-on practice.

Sizing & Scaling gives you two options: Fit in Frame and By Scale Factors. Fit in Frame enlarges the picture until it fills the entire frame. (If you've set margins, Ventura will fill the frame up to the frame margins.)

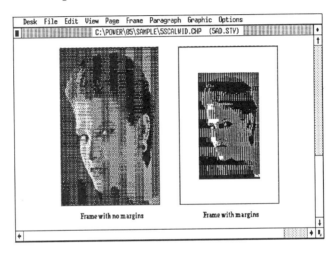

When you fit into a frame, you can instruct Ventura whether to maintain or ignore the original aspect ratio. Aspect Ratio: Maintain enlarges the picture as much as it can without changing the horizontal and vertical proportions. This may leave some extra white space around the image.

Aspect Ratio: Distorted stretches the picture as necessary to fill the frame even if it has to distend the proportions.

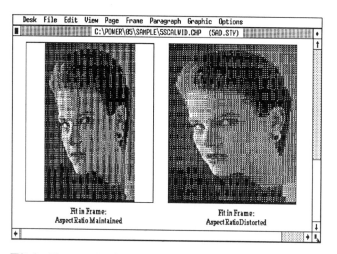

Fit in Frame is the first option. By Scale Factors is the second. When you choose the By Scale Factors button, Ventura displays the original size of the picture. To change the size, enter a new width or height (or both). For instance, suppose you start with a picture six picas wide by eight picas tall. To double the picture's width, you would choose By Scale Factors and then enter 12,00 picas as the new value.

As with Fit in Frame, you can choose whether or not to keep the original proportions. Aspect Ratio: Maintain calculates the height for you to maintain the same proportions. In the example above, Ventura would double the height to 16,00 picas. Aspect Ratio: Distorted lets you choose any combination of widths and heights you wish.

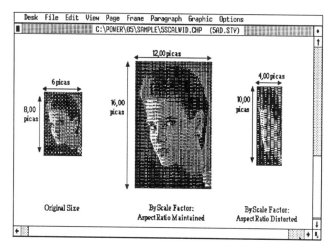

➡️ *IMPORTANT: When working with scale factors, remember that the height and width displayed in the Sizing & Scaling dialog box represent the current size of the picture. Enter the new size to change the dimensions.*

Cropping Pictures

While scaling enlarges or reduces a picture, cropping moves it up, down, right, or left within the frame to display selected portions of the picture.

With a bit-map image you can crop freehand by moving the picture with the mouse cursor. Here's how: In frame setting mode, select the frame containing the picture to crop, and place the cursor in the middle. Then hold down the mouse button while pressing the Alt key. A small "hand" icon will appear. Keep the mouse button down and move the hand to move the image.

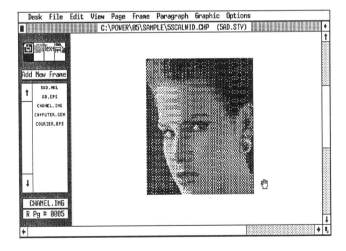

With line art you can not crop interactively. Instead, you enter a positive or negative X or Y offset. The "offset" is the distance you move the picture from its starting position. When you place a picture in its frame, Ventura positions the upper left corner of the picture at the upper left corner of the frame. This is the starting position. Therefore, all offset distances are measured from the upper left corner of the frame.

Imagine a horizontal and vertical axis starting at the upper left corner. You can slide the picture along the horizontal (X) axis or the vertical (Y) axis. A positive X offset moves the picture left; a negative X offset moves it right. A positive Y offset moves the picture up; a negative Y offset moves it down.

Practice cropping by changing one variable at a time: enter a positive X offset only, then a positive Y offset and so forth. Then try combining a positive X and a positive Y offset; a negative X and a Y. The more you practice, the better you'll be able to anticipate the position of the picture in the frame. The following sequence illustrates the various combinations of X and Y offsets.

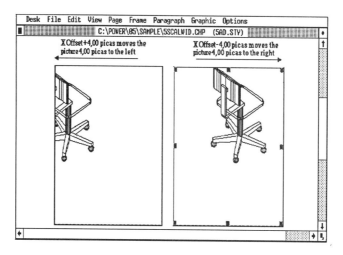

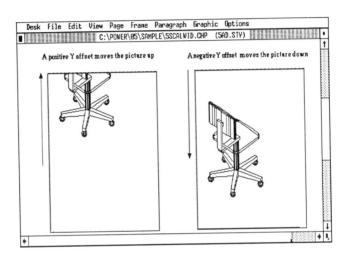

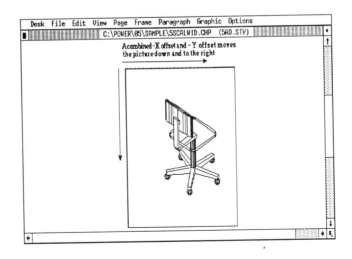

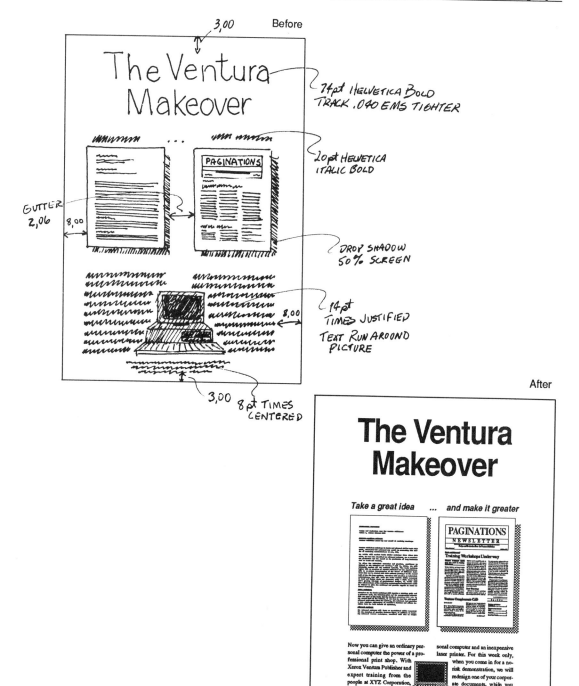

Before

3,00

The Ventura Makeover

74pt HELVETICA BOLD
TRACK .040 EMS TIGHTER

20pt HELVETICA
ITALIC BOLD

GUTTER
2,06   8,00

DROP SHADOW
50% SCREEN

PAGINATIONS

8,00

14pt
TIMES JUSTIFIED

TEXT RUN AROUND
PICTURE

3,00   8 pt TIMES
CENTERED

After

The Ventura Makeover

Take a great idea ... *and make it greater*

PAGINATIONS
NEWSLETTER

Now you can give an ordinary personal computer the power of a professional print shop. With Xerox Ventura Publisher and expert training from the people at XYZ Corporation, you can learn to create professional-quality documents using a personal computer and an inexpensive laser printer. For this week only, when you come in for a no-risk demonstration, we will redesign one of your corporate documents, while you watch! But hurry—our offer is limited. Call (213)555-1111 today.

Planning the Flyer

Consider the thousands of advertisements you see each year. How many do you remember? In a small amount of space an advertisement must provoke, lure, entice (or annoy) the prospect into reading the copy and (hopefully) buying the product. And advertisements carry another responsibility: They project the company name and image to the outside world. For these reasons, good design is crucial to the success of an advertisement. Some documents — reports, proposals, memos — can get by with an "adequate" page design. But "adequate" is not good enough for an ad. The public is bombarded by hundreds of advertisements each day. Sales materials that are merely average will be ignored.

The design of an advertisement carries several burdens. First, it must attract attention. Second, it must lead the eye into the copy and keep it moving. And third, it must reinforce the underlying theme and message of the words. Meeting these goals requires attention to all the details that make up good design — the layout, the typography, the white space, the graphics, and so on. Fortunately, Ventura Publisher provides the tools to fine-tune your pages until they stand out from the crowd.

This chapter's sample advertisement is a self-mailer — it can be folded in thirds, stapled and mailed. The first page is the mailer. It has been divided into three panels as illustrated in the figure below. The top panel (#1) is the inner flap, which will be tucked inside when the flyer is folded and stapled for mailing. The center panel (#2) is the back flap. Both the inner and the back flap contain "teaser copy," designed to entice the reader into opening the mailer and reading further. The bottom panel (#3) is for the address. It will appear on top when the flyer is folded and will contain the return address, mailing label and stamp.

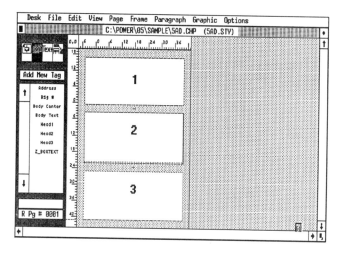

The second page of this document is the advertisement itself. It will be printed on the opposite side from the mailer. When the reader opens the flyer, he or she will be able to read the ad as a single, full-page unit.

➡ *NOTE: If your company does not prepare mailers, you can skip page one and produce only the ad on page two. The principles and theories taught for page two apply equally to print advertisements.*

The nearby thumbnail sketch of the advertisement shows you some of the techniques you will use to create these effects:

• Frames on the underlying page

• Box text

• Text runaround

• Kerned headlines

• Drop shadows

• Special non-keyboard characters for a trademark symbol, ellipses, and em dash

• Typographic controls to fine-tune the headlines and body copy

Ventura Prep

If You Have the Power Disk

- Load the ASCII format text file 5AD.TXT from the C:\POWER subdirectory. Use File Type/Rename to rename it as C:\TEMP\5MAILER.TXT.

When you load a single file while frame setting mode is enabled, Ventura automatically places it on the underlying page (when you load several files, Ventura will not attempt to place any of them them on the page). However, because you will be placing text inside of frames, you must remove the text from the underlying page before adding frames.

- Select Remove Text/File from the Edit menu. Move to the File Name line and enter: `5MAILER.TXT` and choose Remove from: Frame.

➡ *NOTE: As we explained earlier in Chapter Two, Ventura will not allow you to rename a text file until it has been placed on the underlying page.*

- Load the style sheet 5AD.STY from C:\POWER and save it as C:\TEMP\5MAILER.STY.

Now load the two PostScript pictures.

- Select Load Text/Pictures and choose Type of File: Line-Art, Line-Art Format: PostScript, and # of Files: Several. Load the two files, 5AD.EPS and 5COURIER.EPS in turn from the C:\POWER subdirectory.

Next, load the line-art picture.

- Press Ctrl-X to redisplay the Load/Text Picture dialog box. Choose Type of File: Line-Art, Line-Art Format: GEM. Load the file COMPUTER.GEM from the C:\POWER subdirectory.

➡ *TIP: You can use Ctrl-X whenever you want to redisplay the last dialog box.*

If Ventura places a picture file on the underlying page, use Remove Text/File to remove it from the frame (not from the List of Files).

■ Save the chapter as C:\TEMP\5MAILER.CHP.

If You Do Not Have the Power Disk

■ Using your favorite word processor, type the text file from Appendix A and save it as C:\TEMP\5MAILER.TXT.

■ Load the original Ventura style sheet &PREL-P1.STY from the C:\TYPESET subdirectory. Change the margins and columns to match the illustration below. Rename it as C:\TEMP\5MAILER.STY.

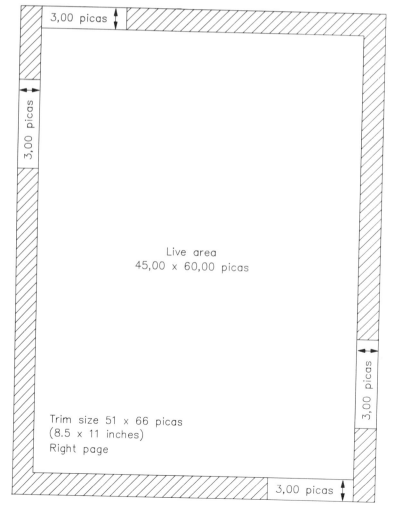

3,00 picas

3,00 picas

Live area
45,00 x 60,00 picas

3,00 picas

Trim size 51 x 66 picas
(8.5 x 11 inches)
Right page

3,00 picas

■ Load three Ventura sample line-art picture into the Assignment List. If you don't have any line-art pictures of your own, load the Ventura sample picture COLUMBIA.GEM from the C:\TYPESET subdirectory.

■ Save the chapter as C:\TEMP\5MAILER.CHP.

Text

In this project, you will use three techniques to place text. You will load an external file into a frame; you will type text directly into a frame; and you will use box text. This is a good opportunity to apply what you've already learned to a design that requires a combination of different skills. Like the newsletter and form in Chapters Three and Four, this sample document relies heavily on text in frames and box text. Therefore, you will vary slightly from the Ventura Formula and delay placing text until you build frames and boxes to contain it.

Style

Your first task is to size and position frames and box text. If you start by laying out margins and columns on the underlying page, you can use them as a guide.

➡ *TIP: Even when creating a freeform, graphics-intensive document like an advertisement, start by formatting the underlying page so it can provide guidelines.*

Select the Page Format

Since this piece is a self-mailer, it will be printed on both sides — the mailer on the outside and the ad on the inside. As you know from Chapter Three, a double-sided format allows you to mirror identical headers, footers, margins, etc. on right and left pages. For this advertisement, however, you will create left and right pages that have completely different values.

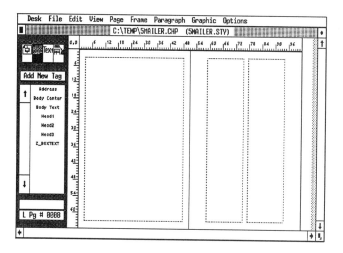

■ Select Page Layout from the page menu. Choose Sides: Double, Start On: Right Page, and Kerning: Globally On.

Layout Page One

The style sheet you loaded (or created) contains the column and margin settings for the first page. This one-column format lets you easily place and size frames for the mailing panels. Continue on to add frames and box text to the page.

■ Verify that Line Snap and Column Snap are On from the Options menu.

■ Reset the zero point to the upper left corner of the live area.

Draw Three Frames on Page One

Draw three frames on the page. Draw frame #1 starting at position 0,0 on the ruler. Draw frame #2 starting at position 21 on the vertical ruler and frame #3 starting at position 42 on the vertical ruler. Use the horizontal and vertical crosshairs and ruler, and the Sizing & Scaling dialog box to position and size the frames on the page. The following illustration will help you gauge the frame dimensions.

➡ *TIP: For more accuracy, you may want to change to normal or enlarged view when placing frames. In enlarged view, place the upper left corner in position and stretch the frame as large as possible. Then switch back to reduced view and enter the width and height of the frame through the Sizing & Scaling dialog box.*

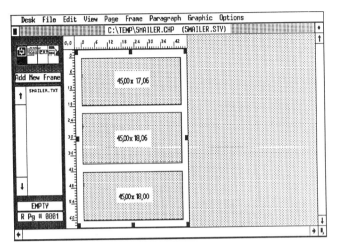

You will notice that the frames are not of equal size; nor are they spaced equally. Rather, they have been sized so that the smaller inner flap can fold up comfortably beneath the address flap.

Draw Box Text Shapes in the Bottom Frame (Frame #3)

Now that you have placed the three frames, add the box text shapes that show the position of the return address, mailing label and stamp in the bottom frame. Start by setting a snap-to grid.

■ Enable frame setting mode. Select the bottom frame (frame #3) then enable graphics mode.

■ Select Grid Settings. Choose Grid Snap On. Make both the Horizontal and the Vertical Spacing 01,00 picas.

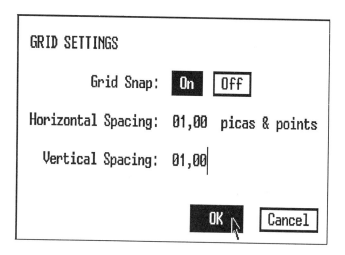

Draw the Return Address Box Text

Draw the return address using a box text.

- Reset the zero point of the ruler to align with the upper left corner of the bottom frame.

- Select the box text icon from the Sidebar. Starting at position 1 on the vertical ruler and position 1 on the horizontal ruler, draw a box 5 picas high and 12,00 picas wide.

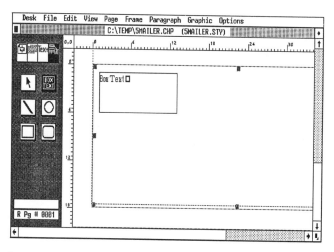

➥ *TIP: You can check the size of a box text or rectangle by placing the zero point of the ruler on one corner of the shape.*

Change the Line Attributes for the Box Text

- ■ Line
  Attributes
  Thickness: Thin
  End Styles (Beginning and End): Square
  Defaults: Save To

- ■ Fill
  Attributes
  Color: White
  Pattern: Hollow, Transparent
  Defaults: Save To

Draw the Mailing Label

Change the snap-to grid before you draw the next shape.

- ■ Grid Setting
  Horizontal Spacing: 06,00 picas
  Vertical Spacing: 06,00 picas

Use box text to draw a mailing label 6 picas high and 24 picas long (1 inch by 4 inches, a standard label size) in frame #3.

- ■ Select the box text icon. Starting from position 8,00 on the vertical ruler and 13,00 on the horizontal ruler, draw the box one snap unit down and 4 snap units to the right.

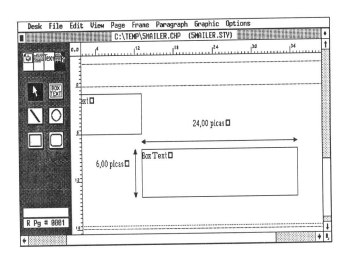

Ventura remembers the line and fill attributes from the last box text.

Draw the Stamp

Last but not least, draw the "stamp" with a rectangle.

■ Grid Settings   Horizontal Spacing: 00,06 picas
                  Vertical Spacing: 00,06 picas

■ Select the rectangle icon. Draw a rectangle 3 picas high and
  4,06 picas wide in the upper right corner of the frame.

If necessary, move the rectangle into position afterwards.

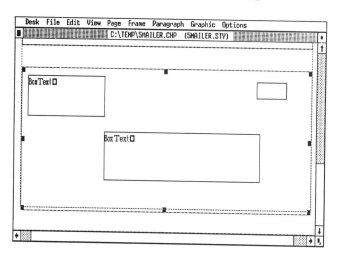

➥ *NOTE: Judge the position as best you can from previous illustrations. Accuracy is not essential.*

Change the Rectangle's Attributes

■ Line   Thickness: Thin
  Attributes   End Style (Beginning and End)s: Square
                Defaults: Save To...

■ Fill   Color: White
  Attributes   Pattern: Hollow, Transparent
                Defaults: Save To...

Layout Page Two

You have completed the overall layout for page one. Before you
continue, reset the zero point back to its original position at
the upper left corner of the column margin. As you saw earlier,
when you place text in frames (instead of on the underlying
page), Ventura doesn't automatically create new pages. Therefore, add one manually.

- Select Insert/Remove Page to insert a new page after the current one.

On the second page, you will create a two-column format with different margins and columns than the first page. This will make it easier to size and place the frames for the desired layout.

- Select frame setting mode. Select the underlying page.

- Select Margins & Columns from the Frame menu. Choose # of Columns. Make the top and bottom margins 03,00 picas and the left and right margins 08,00 picas. Make column one 16,03 picas then make the first gutter margin 02,06 picas. Last, make the second column width 16,03 picas.

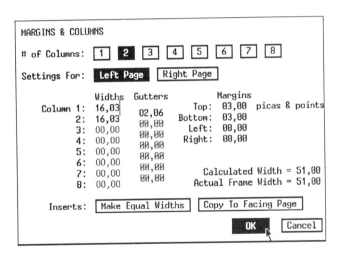

➡ *TIP: As a general rule, always enter the top, bottom, left and right margins before you enter the column widths. To enter the column and gutter widths follow this sequence: enter the first column value, the first gutter value, and then the second column value.*

Add Frames to Page Two

Once you set the margins and columns for page two, you are ready to add the frames. Use the ruler plus Line and Column Snap to accurately position the frames as shown in the following illustration. Use the Sizing & Scaling dialog box to verify the position and size of the frames.

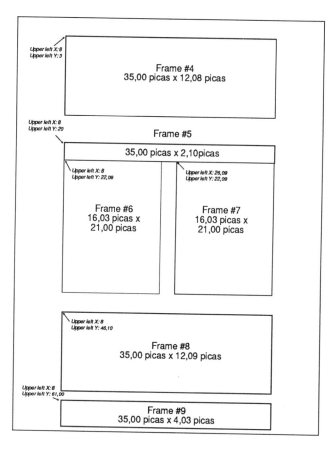

➡ *NOTE: The bottommost frame (frame #9) intentionally extends below the bottom column guide.*

Add a Ruling Box Around the Center Frames

To make the two center frames (frame #6 and #7) stand out on the page, and to enclose the pictures that will be placed inside, add a Ruling Box Around.

- Select the left frame (frame #6).

- Select Ruling Box Around. Give Rule 1 a height of 00.24 points.

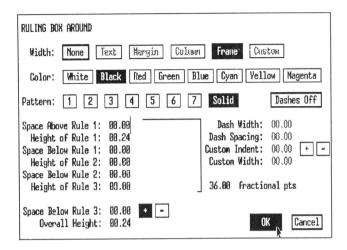

Repeat for the right picture frame (frame #7). When you are finished the frames should look like this:

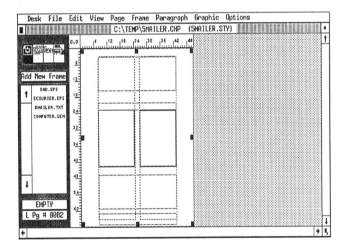

Change the Number of Columns in One Frame

When you place a frame on the underlying page, Ventura gives it a single column and sets the margins to 0. With Margins & Columns you can change these values.

■ Select the frame reserved for the body copy (frame #8).

■ Select Margins & Columns. Choose 2 columns. Notice that Ventura remembers the two-column column and gutter settings from the underlying page. Leave the column and gutter settings as they are and keep the margins at 00,00 picas.

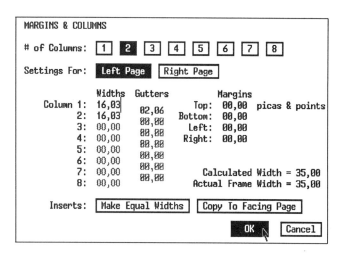

This frame now has the same column and gutter settings as the underlying page.

Adding Text to Page One

With the frames in their proper place you can place text on the page. Start on page one and work frame-by-frame until you have placed all the text.

■ Press PgUp to go to page one.

■ Enable text editing mode and click the text cursor anywhere inside the top frame (frame #1).

➡ *NOTE: You may want to change to normal or enlarged view to better view the typed-in text.*

Type the First Teaser

Use a non-keyboard character to create the ellipsis at the end of the first teaser headline. At this point do not worry about the appearance of the text. You will format it later.

■ Type:

Introducing a cure for the common document

Now make the ellipsis:

■ Hold down the Alt key and use the numeric keyboard to type: **193**

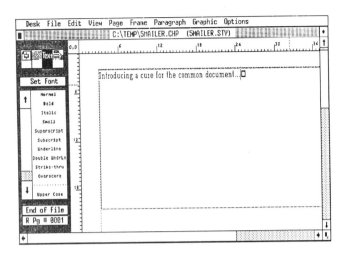

Type the Second Teaser

Now enter the second headline, which includes another non-keyboard character — the em dash in frame #2.

■ Place the text cursor anywhere in the middle frame (frame #2), and type the text shown in the following illustration:

(To make the em dash, hold down the Alt key and type: **197** on the numeric keypad).

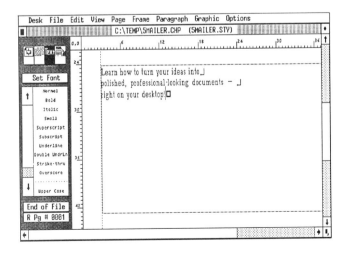

Type the Return Address

Now move to the bottom frame (frame#3).

■ Use the text cursor to delete the words "Box Text" and type the text shown below. Place line breaks at the end of each line. (Press Ctrl-enter.)

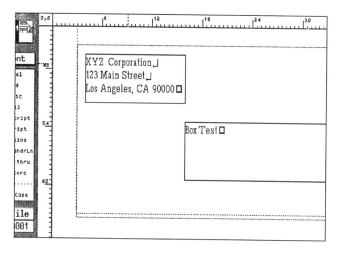

Type the Mailing Address

In a real life application, you might leave the area for the mailing address blank so you could use stick-on labels. However, we have used box text to "imitate" a mailing label.

■ Delete the words "Box Text" and type in the text shown below:

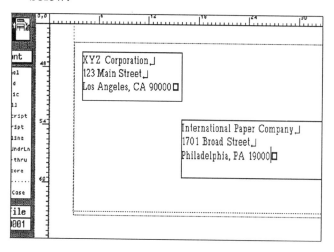

Add Text to page Two

Continue to page two and finish adding text.

■ Press PgDn to go to page two.

■ Place the cursor inside the top frame (frame #4) and type:

The Ventura (Ctrl-Enter)
Makeover

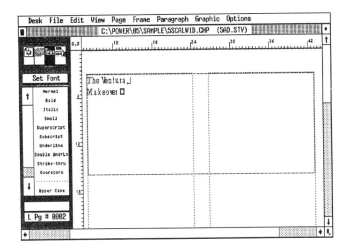

■ Now place the text cursor in the second frame (frame #5) and type:

Take a great idea [tab][Alt-193][tab] and make
it greater

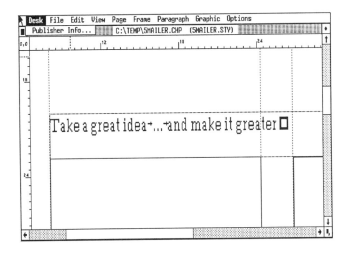

Place a Text File on Page Two

The two frames in the middle of the page are reserved for graphics. Skip them for now and move to the frame second from the bottom (frame #8) which will contain the body copy you loaded at the beginning of the project.

■ Enable frame setting mode and select the frame.

■ Select the file, 5MAILER.TXT from the Assignment List.

Ventura flows the text into the frame and stops. Do not be concerned that the text doesn't fill the frame. When you get to the picture section, you will place a picture between the text columns. This will reflow the text to the end of the frame.

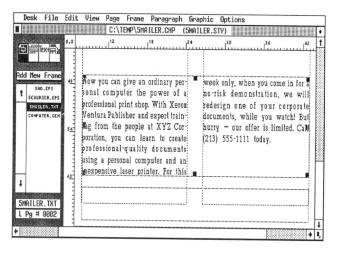

Type the Remaining Text on Page Two

Finish placing text in the bottommost frame (frame #9). Use a non-keyboard character to create the registered sign after the word Xerox.

■ Enable text mode.

■ Place the text cursor in the bottommost frame (frame #9) and type:

```
Contact your nearest XYZ representative for
further information. [Ctrl-Enter]
XYZ Corporation, 123 Main Street, Los Angeles,
CA 90000 [Ctrl-Enter]
```

```
Xerox [Alt-190] is a trademark of Xerox Cor-
poration
```

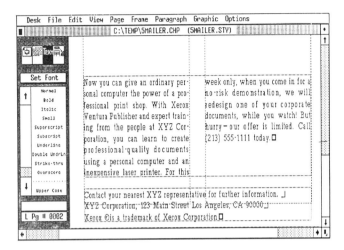

Apply Tags to Page One

Because the tags have been predefined, just choose the right paragraph and apply the proper tag. Start on page one and apply the first two headline tags. If you have questions about any tags, take a few moments to examine the pertinent dialog boxes from the Paragraph menu.

➡ *NOTE: If you are not using the pre-defined style sheet from the Publishing Power disk, you must create the tags as you go along, using the sample screens and printouts as your guide.*

■ Press PgUp to go to page one.

■ Enable paragraph tagging mode.

■ Select the two teaser headlines and tag them as Head3.

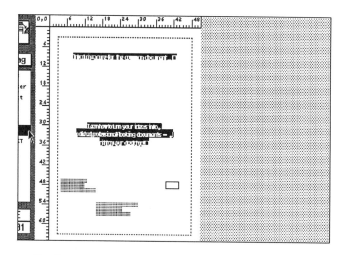

■ In frame #3 select XYZ's return address and tag it as Address.

■ Select the mailing address and tag it as Body Center.

Your screen should look like this:

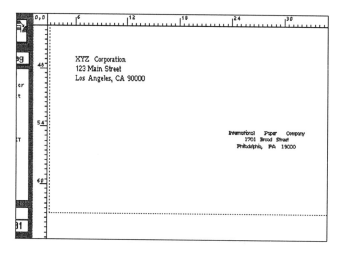

➡ *NOTE: If your screen shows tab and line break symbols, select Hide Tabs and Returns from the Options menu.*

Apply Tags to Page Two

■ Press PgDn to go to page two.

- Select the first headline "The Ventura Makeover" and tag it as Head1.

- Select the second headline "Take a great idea ... and make it greater" and tag it as Head2.

Leave the main body copy tagged as Body Text.

- Go to frame #9 and select the paragraph that begins "Contact your nearest..." and tag it as Body Center.

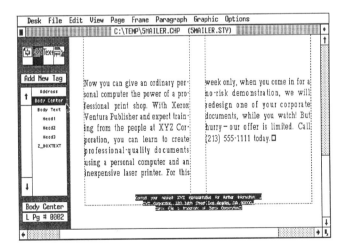

That was fast, wasn't it? The more you tag, the easier it becomes. Before you continue, let's examine the Head2 tag more closely. You may recall that you entered two tab characters as part of the Head2 text. The first tab setting is a center tab and the second tab setting is right-justified. To position the tabs correctly you should measure their locations from the edge of the frame (not the edge of the page). The location of the second tab forces the text past the visible column guides. We chose this tab location so the text would line up with the rightmost picture frame.

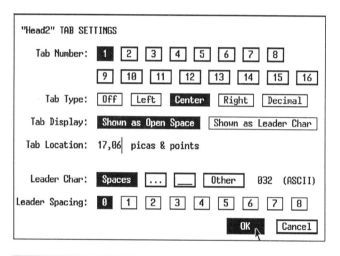

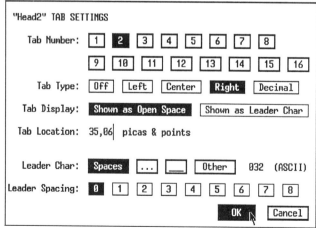

➡ *NOTE: Tab settings can push text outside the normal frame and column boundaries.*

Stopping Point

This is a good place to stop and save what you've done so far. Check your progress against the sample page below.

The Ventura Makeover

Take a great idea ... and make it greater

Now you can give an ordinary personal computer the power of a professional print shop. With Xerox Ventura Publisher and expert training from the people at XYZ Corporation, you can learn to create professional-quality documents using a personal computer and an inexpensive laser printer. For this week

only, when you come in for a no-risk demonstration, we will redesign one of your corporate documents, while you watch! But hurry—our offer is limited. Call (213) 555-1111 today.

Contact your nearest XYZ representative for further information.
XYZ Corporation, 123 Main Street Los Angeles, CA 90000
Xerox ®is a trademark of Xerox Corporation

If you wish, you can quit now and return to this project later. If you have the time, continue on now to the next section. In the pictures section you will learn some great new tricks and techniques.

Pictures

In this section you will add the final graphic touches to the advertisement. You will start by drawing fold lines with the line tool on page one. Then you will place three line-art pictures into frames on page two.

Add Fold Lines to Page One

Create the three tiny fold lines on the front page of the mailer using the line tool from graphics drawing.

■ Press Home to go to page one.

■ Enable frame setting mode. Select the top frame (frame #1). Then enable graphics mode.

➡ NOTE: *The lines are tied to a frame instead of the underlying page. If the graphics were tied to the underlying page, they would appear on every page of the document.*

Change the grid settings.

■ Grid Settings   Horizontal Spacing: 01,00 picas
                    Vertical Spacing: 01,00 picas

■ Select the line icon from the Sidebar and draw two lines, each one pica wide. Place the first at position 22 on the vertical ruler and 25 on the horizontal ruler. Draw the second starting at position 43,06 on the vertical ruler and 25 on the horizontal ruler. Use the following illustration as your guide:

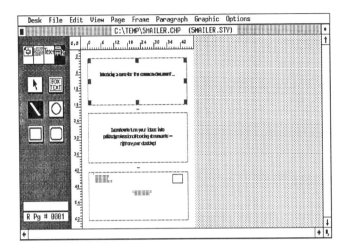

Place Pictures on Page Two

An advertisement relies heavily on visual imagery to create an impact and convey a message. For this example, you will place three pictures. Two of them are Encapsulated Postscript Files (which Ventura treats as line art) and the third is a standard line-art picture (in GEM format). If you do not have a Post-Script printer, leave the two EPS frames blank, or fill them with any picture of your choice. EPS files will not print on non-PostScript printers.

■ Enable frame mode.

■ Select the left frame (frame #6) and place the file 5COURIER.EPS.

■ Select the right frame (frame #7) and place the file 5AD.EPS.

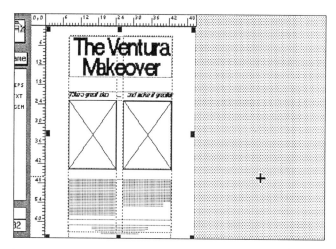

➠ TIP: If, as you try to place a picture in an empty frame, you see the message, "You're about to overwrite an existing caption. You won't be able to recover the caption text. Is that OK?," choose Yes. Ventura displays this message if you previously typed in text or added a caption to the frame.

When Ventura loads a PostScript file into a frame, it displays an "X" on the screen. You will not see the picture until you print the chapter.

➠ TIP: Since it is impossible to preview an EPS file on-screen for cropping, it is important to make the frame size the same aspect ratio as the EPS file.

Add Drop Shadows to the Frames

A drop shadow gives the illusion of depth to a two-dimensional object. One way to create a drop shadow is to lay one frame on top of another. The bottom frame, which is gray or black, is offset slightly so only the two edges show. However, this method may not work on all printers, and slows down some others. We recommend a second method: drawing two rectangle shapes with a gray screen pattern at right angles to each other.

Before you start drawing, choose a grid value that will make it easy to place your shapes on the page.

■ Enable frame mode and select the left picture frame (frame #6). Then enable graphics mode.

■ Grid Settings   Horizontal Spacing: 00,03 picas
Vertical Spacing: 00,03 picas

➥*IMPORTANT: Remember, graphics are tied to whatever frame is selected when you enable graphics drawing mode.*

Draw a Horizontal Shadow

■ Draw a rectangle along the bottom edge of the left frame. Stretch it to the right to create the bottom shadow.

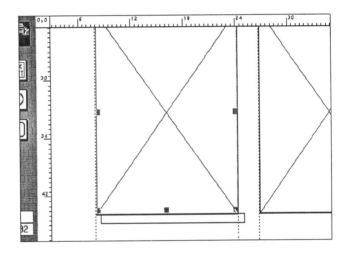

Change the Rectangle's Attributes

Now change the line and fill attributes of the rectangle.

■ Line   Thickness: None
Attributes   Defaults: Save to…

■ Fill   Color: Black
Attributes   Pattern: 4, Transparent
Defaults: Save to….

Draw a Vertical Shadow

■ Draw a second rectangle at a right angle to the first as shown in the following illustration.

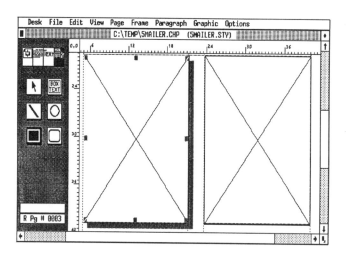

➡ *NOTE: Don't be discouraged if it takes some time to draw the two drop shadows. If you want, go on to the next section (placing and sizing an image) and complete the shadows later.*

When you are satisfied with the size and position of the drop shadow, use the Send to Back option, so the rectangles don't cover up the frame's ruling lines.

WARNING: If you omit this next step, the ruling line around at the bottom and side of the frame will not be visible when you print the page.

■ Select both rectangles. Select Send to Back from the Graphic menu.

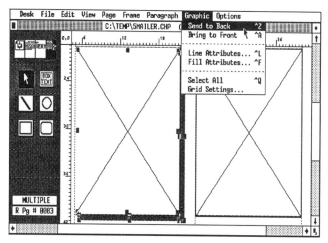

Shadow the Second Frame

Add another drop shadow to the picture frame on the right (frame #7) using the techniques explained above.

Since each frame has its own snap-to grid settings independent of one another, make sure you set the horizontal and vertical spacing to 00,03 picas before you draw the second set of rectangles.

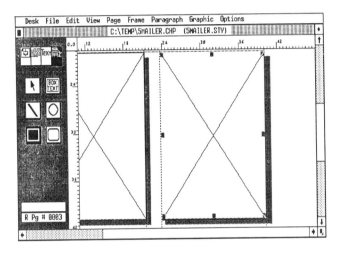

➡ *NOTE: You could also copy the two rectangles to the clipboard. Then you could switch to frame setting mode, select the second frame, switch to graphics mode and paste in the rectangles.*

Place and Size an Image

Now that you've completed the drop shadows, you will place a picture of a computer in the bottom frame (frame #8) which contains the body copy. First, however, add a smaller frame within the frame to contain the picture.

■ Enable frame mode. Add a frame using the dimensions shown in the following illustration. Position the center of the frame in the center of the gutter margin. Use Sizing & Scaling to verify its position and dimensions.

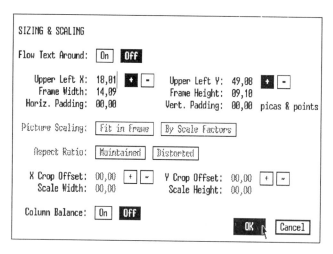

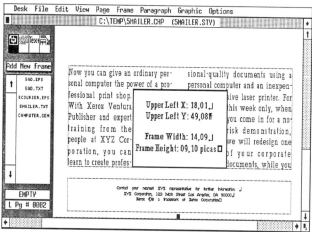

Ventura automatically flows the body text around the new frame. Now place the computer image inside.

■ With the new frame still highlighted, place the file COM-PUTER.GEM.

Scale the Image

After placing the picture, use the Sizing & Scaling dialog box to scale the picture in the frame and to make the text runaround.

■ Select Sizing & Scaling from the Frame menu. Choose Text Flow Around: Off, Picture Scaling: By Scale Factor, and

■ Aspect Ratio: Distorted. Enter X Crop Offset: 7,00, Y Crop Offset: 11,06. Scale Width : 30,00 and Scale Height: 30,00.

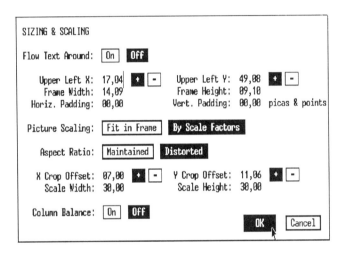

When you turn Flow Text Around Off, Ventura allows the text to flow over the frame and the picture inside it.

Create a Text Runaround

Now that you've turned text flow around off, you will place small frames over portions of computer to create an irregular text runaround. Place the frames in a pyramid arrangement to make the text run around in a stair step fashion.

Before you add your frames make sure that Line Snap is On and Column Snap is Off.

➡ *TIP: Turning Line Snap On guarantees that the new frames will be increments of the body text. You will be able to create frames exactly one or two lines deep.*

■ Add four small frames over the computer image as shown in the following illustration (Use your best judgment to gauge the size).

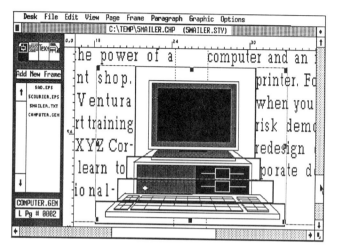

Kern the Headline

Before you complete this project, we'll show you how to make some adjustments to your headlines and body copy. Because of space limitations, we will not go through all the fine-tuning that would ordinarily occur for an advertisement. We will, however, introduce you to the methods. Once you grasp these techniques, you can use them to adjust this and other documents until all the details are perfect.

Kerning is a typographic technique that allows you to selectively reduce the amount of space between individual letter pairs and leave the rest of the word the same. Kerning (or the lack of it) is most noticeable in display type of 18 points or larger. Ventura has two ways to kern: automatically and manually. Automatic kerning occurs only if the fonts for your printer come with special files called kerning tables. Kerning tables contain information about special letter pairs that look better spaced more closely. Certain letter combinations are improved by kerning, such as AV, YO, Ve, LY, and Te. The following illustration shows how kerning alters the appearance of the word wave.

```
+-----------------------------------------+
|                                         |
|           WAVE                          |
|                                         |
|           WAVE                          |
|                                         |
+-----------------------------------------+
```

➥*NOTE: You will not do any damage if you specify automatic kerning for fonts that do not have kerning information. Ventura will simply ignore the command.*

In the example above, the kerning table contains information that told Ventura just what to do if it found a capital letter A followed by a capital letter V. More specifically, it told Ventura just how far to move the V to the left to improve the appearance of this letter pair. Although we used "AV" as an example, most kerning tables also include information on 200 or so other combinations.

To implement automatic kerning, you must take two steps: (1) turn it on globally for the entire document and (2) turn it on for each tag that you want kerned. You must take both steps. Turning kerning on globally has no effect if you haven't turned it on for the individual tags. Likewise, turning it on for an individual tag does nothing unless you also remember to turn it on globally.

Enable Automatic Kerning for the Headline

Let's begin by enabling automatic kerning for the headline. Later you will do some manual kerning as well. First verify that kerning is globally on.

■ Select Page Layout from the page menu. Choose Kerning: Globally On.

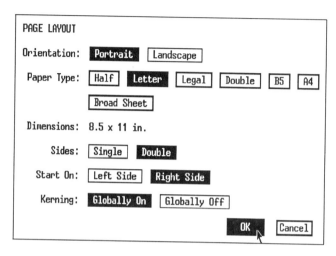

■ Enable paragraph tagging. Select the headline "The Ventura Makeover" in frame #4.

■ Select Typographic Controls from the Paragraph menu. Choose Automatic Kerning: On and Letter Spacing: Off. Make Tracking 0.040 Ems Tighter.

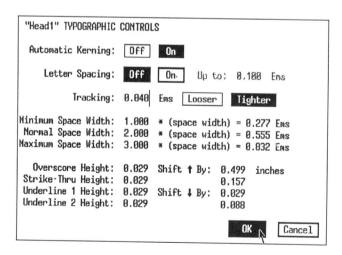

With Typographic Controls you also tightened the type with the tracking command. Refer to chapter three for a complete explanation of tracking.

Perform Manual Kerning on the Headline

If you don't like the results from the automatic kerning, or if your printer doesn't allow it, you can also kern manually. For example, here's how to move the "e" in the word "Ventura" close to the "V".

■ Enable text editing. Highlight the "e" in Ventura.

■ Select Set Font from the Sidebar. Move the cursor to Kern and type: **04.00**

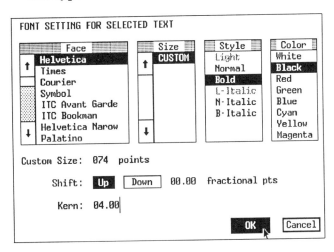

This moves the "e" 4 points closer to the V. The amount of kerning is a matter of personal taste. We suggest you experiment with different values until you come up with the best look.

About Screen Kerning

You may not notice much difference on the screen when you apply kerning. Check Set Preferences from the Options menu to see if On-Screen kerning is On for all display type 18 points or larger.

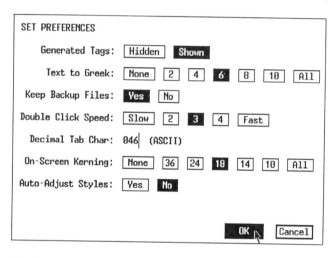

Ventura permits you to select the size at which to show kerning on the screen. In general it is best to show on-screen kerning only for large type sizes or not at all. Otherwise, on-screen kerning slows down the display. And because of the low resolution of computer screens, it is not effective or accurate at lower point sizes. Because Ventura uses generic screen fonts, on-screen kerning is an approximation at best.

➡ *TIP: The only way to accurately gauge the effects of typographic adjustments is to print out the page.*

About Letter Spacing

Besides tracking and kerning, Ventura has another typographic control called Letter Spacing. To understand letter spacing, it is first necessary to understand how Ventura justifies text. Although the explanation below is not intended to be technically thorough, it will help you understand the letterspacing option.

As it flows text onto the page, Ventura fits as many words as possible onto each line before moving to the next. If the words do not fit precisely, Ventura tries to add or subtract space between words, *but not between letters.* Ventura will not normally reduce the space beyond the minimum or maximum word spacing values. Ventura has default maximum and minimum space widths, but you can change them in the Typographic Controls dialog box.

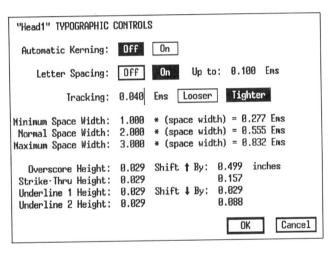

Quite often Ventura cannot fit the words onto the line without exceeding the maximum or minimum values. In that case, it searches for the discretionary hyphens that were placed in the text file when it was loaded. If it can find a hyphenation point, Ventura will split a word, so part goes on one line and part goes on another.

Even with the help of hyphenation, Ventura still encounters some lines that cannot be justified without exceeding the maximum space width. These lines, which have too much white space between the words, are known as loose lines. You can instruct Ventura to highlight these lines by selecting Show Loose Lines from the Options menu.

There are several ways to reduce the number of loose lines:

- Manually hyphenate words (sometimes Ventura's hyphenation algorithm misses opportunities)

- Edit your text

- Allow Ventura to use its letterspacing feature to adjust the space between individual letters as well as the space between words

➡ *NOTE: Even if you fix the loose lines with letterspacing, Ventura will still highlight them on screen.*

Enter Letter Spacing

Let's use the letter spacing technique to fine tune the body copy. You will tell Ventura that it is allowed to add a small amount of space between letters if necessary to justify a line.

■ Enable paragraph tagging mode and select the body text tag.

■ Typographic   Letter Spacing: On
  Controls   Up to: 0.100 Ems

Experiment with Fixing Loose Lines

As we mentioned above, letter spacing is just one of the ways you can avoid loose lines in body copy. If you are interested, you may want to take some time to experiment on your own to further reduce the number of loose lines in the ad copy. Try adding a discretionary hyphen or two, (place the text cursor where you want and press Ctrl-hyphen) edit the text, or stretch one of the small frames. If you want to continue practicing these fine-tune adjustments, refer to the following illustration for places to hyphenate text. Since this is for practice only, do not be concerned if your text is off a word or letter. The important thing is to understand that you have several powerful typographic tools at your command.

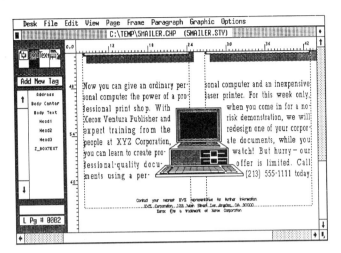

Now that you've completed the ad, let's see the results of your efforts and print the chapter.

Chapter

Take a moment to save your work (press ^S). Then use the Print option to print out the entire document.

➥ *NOTE: Because of the size of the Encapsulated Postscript files, allow extra time.*

■ Select To Print from the file menu. Choose All.

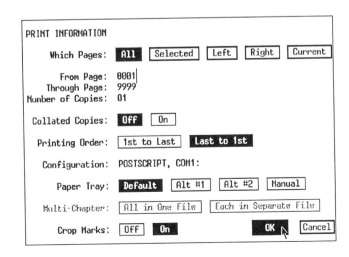

Print to File

As you see from the final printed version of the advertisement, an Encapsulated Postscript file allows you to take a "snap-shot" of a page and make it part of a document. You can make your own EPS file by using the print option Print To File. Before we conclude this chapter, we'd like to show you how you to make an EPS file from the second page of this document.

■ Go to the second page (the advertisement itself).

➡NOTE: You can only make an EPS file of one page at a time.

■ Select Set Printer Information in the Options menu.

In this dialog box you can select which printer port (LPT1, COM1) to print a file to, or you can choose to print to a filename.

■ Choose Filename.

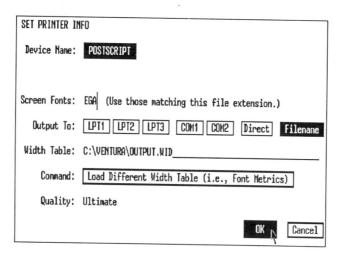

➡NOTE: You may want to review Chapter Three for an explanation of the other printer options in this dialog box.

WARNING: Remember to use Set Printer Info to return the settings to the right communications port after you are finished making the EPS file.

■ Select To Print from the file menu. Select Current and OK.

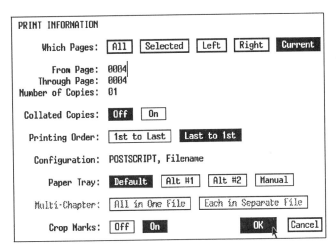

Ventura displays the Item Selector, which asks you for the name of the print file.

- Move the cursor to the Directory line and replace the filename extension C00 with EPS.

- Locate the C:\TEMP subdirectory and type in the file name, 5MAILER.EPS on the Selection line.

➥ *TIP: Always use the .EPS extension when printing to Encapsulated Postscript files.*

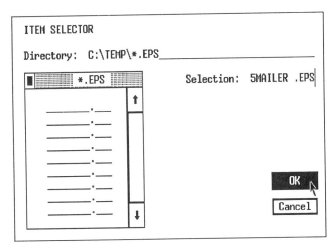

Ventura prints as normal, except the output goes to the file instead of to the printer. Once you create an EPS file, you can load it into a frame like any other picture.

Tips

Picture Tips

❏ Use a standalone graphics program for complex illustrations. Ventura's built-in graphics functions are most useful for annotating existing drawings or producing very simple illustrations such as organization charts.

❏ Ventura does not store or modify outside graphics files. It stores a pointer to the file.

❏ If you revise a picture with an outside program and give it the same name as the old version, Ventura will load the new picture the next time you open the chapter.

❏ When sizing pictures with By Scale Factors, remember that the numbers shown represent the original size of the picture. To change the picture, enter the new values you want.

❏ When using By Scale Factors together with Aspect Ratio: Maintain, Ventura lets you choose the width. Then it calculates the necessary height to avoid distorting the aspect ratio.

❏ Scanned images look better if you leave them at their original size. If you must enlarge or reduce, do so in integer amounts.

❏ A positive X offset moves the picture to the left. A positive Y offset moves the picture up.

❏ Reset the zero point of the ruler for more accurate positioning of graphics elements.

❏ To create a text runaround, turn Text Flow Around to Off in the original frame. Then use smaller overlapping frames to keep the text away from the object.

More Box Text Tips

❏ Use the snap-to grid for easy, precise sizing and placement of box text.

❏ Once the first box text looks correct, use the Save To buttons in the Line and Fill Attributes dialog boxes. These buttons store the settings. From then on, every box text you draw will have the same attributes.

❏ If you must position a box text with extreme accuracy, attach the upper left corner of the box text to the upper left corner of a small, invisible frame. Use Sizing & Scaling to position the frame. Since the box text is attached, it will move to the correct position too.

❏ If you must size a box text with extreme precision, first draw a frame of that size. Use Sizing & Scaling to verify the size. Then place the box text over the sizing frame. You can then delete the frame. Be careful to attach the box text where you really want it, and not to the sizing frame, which will be deleted.

❏ Use Send to Back and Bring to Front from the graphics menu to force graphics shapes to overlap in the order you want them to.

❏ See Chapter Four for more tips on Box Text.

Other Tips

❏ Always format the underlying page first, even when creating a freeform document. Use the underlying page as a guide to positioning page elements.

❏ Type non-keyboard characters by holding down the Alt key while typing the decimal code on the numeric keypad.

❏ To select a frame underneath another, click the mouse button on the frame you want while holding down the Ctrl key. Each time you press Ctrl-Click, Ventura selects the next layer down. Continue clicking until you see handles around the frame you want.

❏ To achieve automatic kerning, you must (1) turn it on globally using Page Layout from the Page menu and (2) turn it on for the individual tag using Typographic Controls from the Paragraph menu.

❏ Use the Set Preferences dialog box from the Options menu to set On-Screen Kerning to None. Screen kerning slows down the display and is generally not very accurate.

❏ Enter additional discretionary hyphens on-screen with Ctrl-Hyphen.

❏ To keep Ventura from hyphenating a word, enter a discretionary hyphen immediately after the word.

❏ Enter additional discretionary hyphens permanently by adding the word to the user hyphenation dictionary. This dictionary is called HYPHUSER.DIC and is found in the Venture subdirectory. Use the ASCII mode of your word processor.

❏ To permanently prevent Ventura from hyphenating a word (such as a product name), enter it into the user hyphenation dictionary without a hyphen.

❏ To create an EPS file, choose the PostScript printer and print the page to a file, using the Set Printer Info dialog box.

Chapter Six
Skills Checklist

Theory

✓ Using frames to design a complex page

Text

✓ Converting from different word processors

Style

✓ Creating a fold line

✓ Improving display type with tracking and kerning

✓ Professional-looking drop caps

✓ Using pull quotes for spacing and graphic effect

Pictures

✓ An easy way to build a calendar

Chapter

✓ Saving production time with chapter templates

A Three-Column Newsletter

Producing newsletters is one of the most popular desktop publishing applications. With Ventura and a laser printer, there is virtually no limit to what you can do. In Chapter Three you learned how to build a simple, two-column newsletter. In this chapter, you will tackle a second newsletter, a three-column format that shows off some of Ventura's advanced design capabilities. You will create this sophisticated layout using the skills and effects listed to the left. At the end of the chapter we will also explain two time-saving production tips that make newsletter production faster and easier.

Theory

The Grid System

It is easiest and most efficient to build newsletters by pouring text into frames. The format of the underlying page determines the size and placement of those frames. For example, a two-column page presents two alternatives: (1) frames that are one column wide or (2) frames that are two columns wide.

A three-column underlying page offers more alternatives. Frames can be one, two or three columns wide. As you can imagine, four- and five-column pages offer even more possibilities. However, more alternatives also means more decisions. In general, four- and five-column grids are best left to those with graphics arts experience.

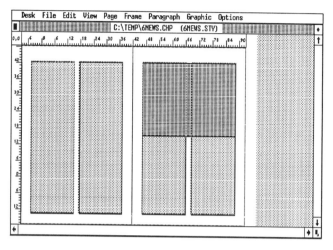

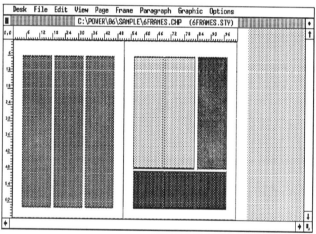

The three-column format, on the other hand, is a good com-
promise. It is simple enough that production doesn't become
too time-consuming. Yet it is also flexible enough to provide
the variety and visual excitement lacking in one- and two-
column formats. You can fit more text on the page with three
columns than with one or two. And you have many more ways
to present illustrations. In short, you can solve almost any
layout problem within the framework of a three-column grid.
For these reasons, it is the most popular newsletter style. You
will learn it in this chapter.

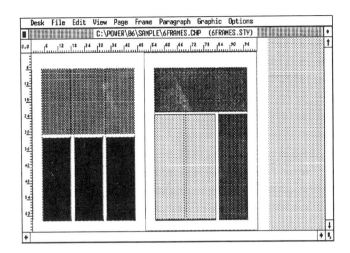

The Danger of Overdesign

As you venture into more complex layouts, beware of an affliction that strikes many first-time desktop publishers: Overdesignitis. This disease results in an overwhelming urge to cram as many fonts, rules, patterns and other effects onto one page as possible.

Good page design doesn't call attention to itself. For instance, when readers pick up a business-oriented newsletter, you do not want their first reaction to be surprise, amazement or shock. Rather, you want the design to pull them into the page and entice them to start reading. Overdesign shouts. It says "Stop! Look at me first! See what I can do!" Proper page design, by contrast, talks in a quiet voice: "Come on in, make yourself comfortable, here's something you'll enjoy...."

So don't let Ventura's power lure you into the trap of overdesign. Don't let your layouts become a barrier to communication. Yes, you want enough pizzazz so pages look pleasing and professional. But your main goal is to make it easier for busy readers to find information.

Before

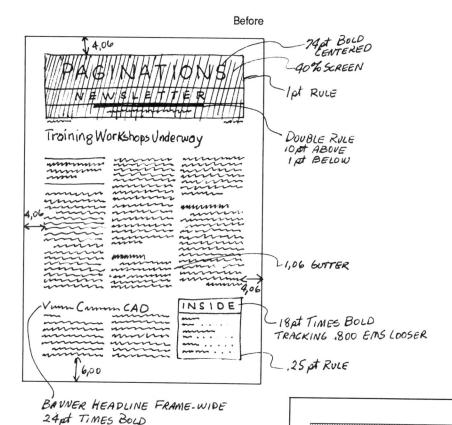

24pt BOLD CENTERED

40% SCREEN

1pt RULE

DOUBLE RULE
10pt ABOVE
1pt BELOW

1,06 GUTTER

18pt TIMES BOLD
TRACKING .800 EMS LOOSER

.25pt RULE

BANNER HEADLINE FRAME-WIDE
24pt TIMES BOLD

After

PAGINATIONS
N E W S L E T T E R
Design and Production News for Ventura Publishers

Volume 1, Number 1   Winter 1988

Training Workshops Underway

Ventura Publisher users may now enroll in training workshops

Ventura Publisher workshops in basic and advanced skills begin this month. Interested XYZ personnel may enroll by contacting Joan Bolden of Marketing Communications at ext. 325.

Ms. Bolden will conduct basic skills workshops three times this month. She has also scheduled two advanced seminars, one on newsletter production and the second on the production of long documents such as books and manuals.

"To allow for individual attention and practice, enrollment is limited to six students per session," said Ms. Bolden, who will initially conduct all the seminars herself. "The basic workshop begins with an overview of Ventura Publisher and its capabilities, plus an on-screen demonstration of the dozens of different documents that can be created with this software package." In the second half of the day-long workshop, attendees will practice individual workstations. They will learn the basic Ventura skills necessary to load and format their own documents using a style sheet from XYZ's growing library of preformatted designs. Ms. Bolden said that other members of the Marketing Communications Department would be trained to give the workshops and provide support to users on demand increases.

Basic Workshops

Attendees at the basic workshops will receive a training guide and a reference book. The training guide and its accompanying software disk are used as the basis for the hands-on exercises that make up the second half of the sessions. It can also be used for self-paced advanced self-study after the workshop. The reference book provides a more complete explanation of Ventura's features and offers insights into the best methods of operation.

Advanced Seminars

The advanced seminars will focus on specialized skills necessary for the creation of specific document types. In addition to learning advanced Ventura techniques, attendees will also be taught graphic arts skills. They will receive a mini-course in design, plus tips on production techniques, including the preparation of so-called camera-ready art — pages that are ready to be taken to an offset printer to be photographed. These photographs are made into printing plates, and the document can then be
See WORKSHOP next page

Ventura Complements CAD

by Joe Esposito

Xerox Ventura Publisher is proving to be a perfect complement to the computer-aided design and drafting programs already in use by the Engineering Department.

Since Ventura Publisher can accept graphic files in AutoCAD slide format, DXF file format and HPGL format, CAD users can now include electronic AutoCAD drawings in technical documents and manuals. The Engineering Department has been an enthusiastic user of AutoCAD, the leading CAD program, for more than two years. Its 2D and 3D capabilities make it the perfect
See CAD page 3

I N S I D E
Training Workshops Underway 1
Ventura Complements CAD 1
Newsline 2
Tip of the Month 3

Planning the Newsletter

The first thing you see on the front page of the sample newsletter is the logo. The logo draws attention to the page and identifies the publication. Most newsletters need a carefully thought-out logo design because it sets the tone for the rest of the publication. For instance, as you proceed through this chapter, you will see how several effects from the logo are repeated elsewhere. Newsletters benefit from a design theme that is repeated throughout. This consistency improves the look while helping readers identify different parts of the publication.

The headlines are sized in proportion to the logo and to each other. This hierarchy — the bigger the story the bigger the headline — helps the reader judge which information is most important.

Since this newsletter will be mailed, the back page includes space for a label and a stamp. Depending on the amount of editorial space you need, you can allocate a full, half or fraction of a page to mailing information.

As you create layouts of your own, you will discover that Ventura contains lots of built-in power you can put to work in your newsletters. Here are some of the effects you will learn to use to add character and punch to your newsletter designs.

- Three-column format
- Frame backgrounds
- Custom and double rules
- Big first character
- Boldface lead-ins
- Box text for a calendar

Even though this newsletter is more a complex layout than the one from Chapter Three, *the same basic principles apply*. First you will format the underlying page. Next you will add frames using the page as your guide. Then you will place text into the frames.

Ventura Prep

Verify that the options are set the way you want them. In particular, be sure that Column and Line Snap are on so frames automatically snap to the underlying page. Choosing Show Column Guides also makes it easier to position frames.

If You Have the Publishing Power Disk

Instead of building the newsletter chapter from scratch, you will use the sample newsletter chapter from the Publishing Power disk. The chapter file contains the newsletter style sheet and most of the frames for the newsletter text.

Open the Newsletter Chapter

- Open the chapter C:\POWER\6NEWSLET.CHP.

- Load the ASCII text files 6NEWSLT1.TXT, 6NEWSLT2.TXT, 6NEWSLT3.TXT, 6NEWSLT4.TXT, 6NEWSLT5.TXT, and 6NEWSTOC.TXT from the C:\POWER subdirectory.

- Use Save As New Style to save the style sheet as C:\TEMP\6NEWS.STY

- Load the image file, WPVP.IMG (GEM / HALO DPE) from the C:\POWER subdirectory.

  ➡ NOTE: If Ventura automatically places the image on the underlying page, use Remove Text/File to remove the image from the frame (do not remove it from the Assignment List).

Converting File Formats

If you publish a newsletter made up of different articles from different writers, you are likely to receive files in different formats. Ventura can convert from one file format to another. After loading a text file you can use File Type/Rename from the Edit menu to convert it to a different word processing format. Thanks to File Type/Rename you can standardize the text format of the newsletter without restricting writers to any one word processor.

For practice, convert the six ASCII text files you just loaded into your favorite word processing format (at the same time you rename them).

Change Formats

Follow these instructions for each of the six files in turn. First, place the file on the underlying page. Then call up the File Type/Rename dialog box. Type in the new name (and new location) and choose the new file format. As always, you will be placing the new file in the \TEMP subdirectory along with the projects from other chapters. Here's how it would look if you were changing 6NEWSLT1.TXT to Microsoft Word format:

```
┌─────────────────────────────────────────────────────────┐
│ FILE TYPE / RENAME                                        │
│                                                           │
│   Old Name:  C\POWER\6NEWSLT1.TXT_____      │
│                                                           │
│   New Name:  C:\TEMP\6NEWS-1.TXT|_____      │
│                                                           │
│ Text Format:  [Generated]  [ASCII]  [WordStar US]  [MultiMate] │
│                                                           │
│               [MS-Word]  [Writer]  [WordPerfect]          │
│                                                           │
│               [WordStar UK]  [XyWrite]  [DCA]             │
│                                                           │
│                                          [ OK ]  [Cancel] │
└─────────────────────────────────────────────────────────┘
```

If you were changing to MultiMate format, the dialog box would look identical except that the MultiMate button would be highlighted instead.

When you have finished, put the next file on the underlying page and repeat the process.

Here's a listing of the new file names (you can change the extension to your own word processing format if you prefer):

Load from C:\POWER	Save to C:\TEMP
6NEWSLT1.TXT	6NEWS-1.TXT
6NEWSLT2.TXT	6NEWS-2.TXT
6NEWSLT3.TXT	6NEWS-3.TXT
6NEWSLT4.TXT	6NEWS-4.TXT
6NEWSLT5.TXT	6NEWS-5.TXT
6NEWSTOC.TXT	6TOC.TXT

WARNING: Neither the format change or the name change-/relocation takes effect until you save the chapter.

Using File Type/Rename merely tells Ventura "Please make these changes the next time you save to the disk." If you abandon the chapter without saving you will lose the changes.

- After you rename all the text files, save the chapter as C:\TEMP\6NEWS.CHP

If You Do Not Have the Publishing Power Disk

- Using your favorite word processor, type the text files for Chapter Six from Appendix A. Save them under the C:\TEMP subdirectory using the names listed in the right column in the table above.

- Load the original Ventura style sheet &NEWS-P3.STY from the C:\TYPESET subdirectory. Change the margins and columns to match the nearby illustration. Save and rename the style sheet as C:\TEMP\6NEWS.STY.

- Load the sample image file, CHANEL.IMG from the C:\TYPESET subdirectory or substitute your own bit-mapped image in place of the one provided on the Power disk.

Style

Since the newsletter is composed of text files in frames, it is easier to add frames before placing text. Start by formatting

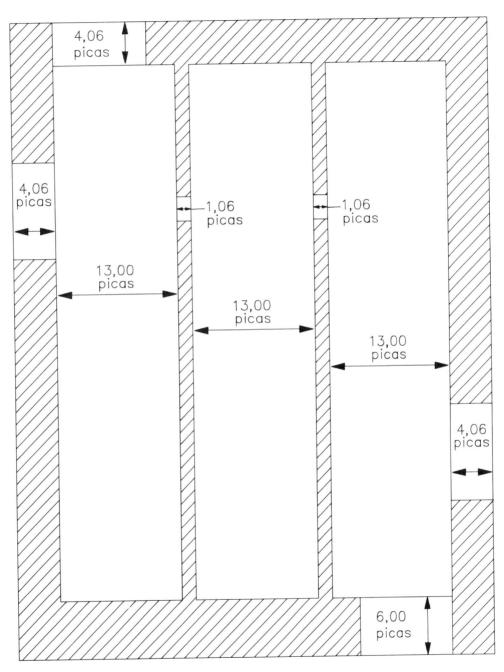

Trim size 51 x 66 picas
(8.5 x 11 inches)
Right Page

the underlying page, then use it as a guide for drawing the frames.

Verify the Page Layout

Although the 6NEWS.STY style sheet should have the correct values for page layout, margins, columns and global kerning, verify that the values match the figure above.

Add a Footer

Add a footer to complete the global formatting.

■ Select Headers & Footers. Choose Right Page Footer, Usage: On. Move to Left and type: **Fall/Winter 1988** then move to Right and type: **Page [P#]**

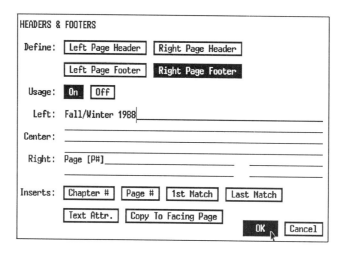

■ Choose Left Page Footer, Usage: On. Move to Left and type: **Page [P#]**, then move to Left and type: **Paginations**

■ Choose Turn Footer Off for the first page of the newsletter.

Add Frames to Page One

Place nine frames on page one using the following illustration as a guide for their size and position. Then use Sizing & Scaling to fine-tune frame size and placement. (Don't forget that you can create identical frames by copying the first one to temporary memory and then pasting copies onto the page.)

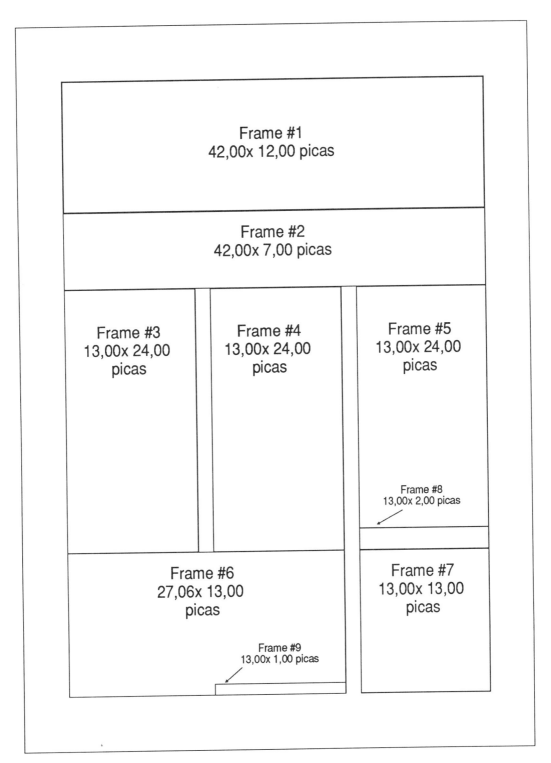

➦*NOTE: With Line Snap On, the frames (frames #6 and #7) at the bottom of the page will extend below the column margin guide. Nevertheless, the text in both columns will line up properly with the bottom of the column guide.*

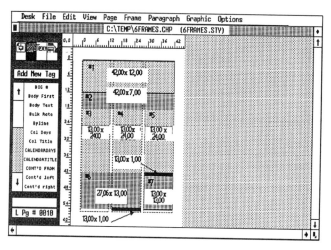

➦*NOTE: Place the two small "jump text" frames (frames #8 and #9) inside the column frames as shown in the next illustration.*

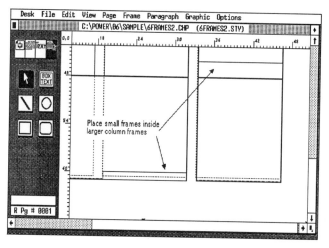

Add a Ruling Box Around

When you are finished adding the frames, make a ruling box around the frame reserved for the logo.

■ Select the topmost frame (frame #1).

- Ruling Box   Width: Frame
  Around   Height of Rule 1: 24.00 points

Add a Pattern

To add what is called *editorial color* to the page design, put a gray fill pattern inside the Logo frame (frame #1).

- Select Frame Background from the Frame menu. Choose Color: Black and Pattern: 1.

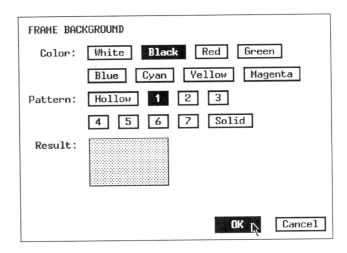

Change Columns

Use Margins & Columns to change the bottom left frame (frame #6) to a two-column format. The size of the columns inside this frame will exactly match the columns on the underlying page.

- Margins &   # of Columns: 2
  Columns   Column 1: 13,00 picas
                   Gutter: 01,06 picas
                   Column 2: 13,00 picas

Add a Ruling Box Around the TOC

- Select the frame that will contain the TOC (frame #7).

- Ruling Box   Width: Frame
  Around   Height of Rule 1: 00.24 points

Add Frames on Page Two

If you do not have the Power disk and the sample newsletter chapter file, use the following illustrations as a guide to lay out the remaining frames on pages two, three and four. When you are finished proceed on to the next section.

If you are using the Power disk, proceed directly onto the section entitled, "Add a Dashed Ruling Line Above" (page 6-17).

■ Insert/Remove   Insert New Page
   Page   After Current Page

Use the following illustration to guide the placement of frames on page two. Then check for accuracy with Sizing & Scaling.

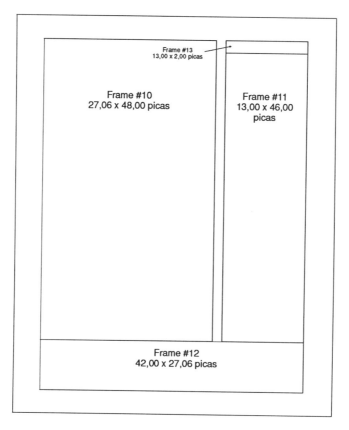

Add Margins and a Ruling Box Around

To finish page two, add margins and a ruling box around the

frame reserved for the staff box (frame #12). Start by adding margins to the frame. This keeps the text in the frame from touching the ruling box around it.

■ Select the frame for the staff box (frame #12).

■ Margins & Columns   Top: 02,00 picas
Bottom: 02,00 picas
Left: 01,00 pica
Right: 01,00 pica

■ Select Ruling Box Around. Choose Frame. Give Rule 1 a height of 00.24 points.

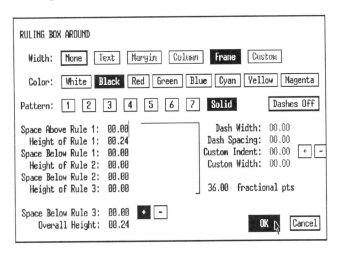

On to Page Three

Good work — you're halfway through placing the frames. Two more pages to go. Insert another page before drawing the frames on page three.

■ Insert/Remove Page   Insert a New Page After Current Page

Add Frames

Using the nearby illustration as a guide, draw the five frames on page three, then check your results with Sizing & Scaling. The upper right frame (frame #18) is reserved for a picture and a caption. You will add a caption to this frame in the picture section of this chapter. For now, simply leave enough space for the caption.

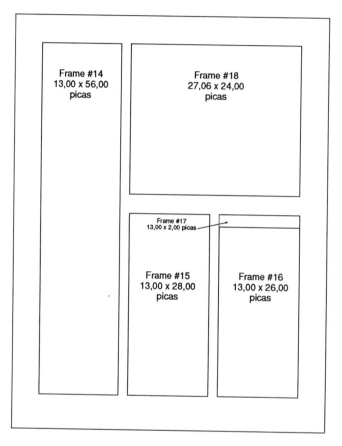

Add a Ruling Box Around the Picture Frame

To visually separate the picture from the rest of the text, add a ruling box around the frame that will contain it.

- Select the frame that will contain the picture (frame #18).

- Ruling Box   Height of Rule 1: 00.24 points
  Around

Insert Page Four

- Insert/Remove   Insert a New Page
  Page   After Current Page

Add Frames

Add the two frames shown below.

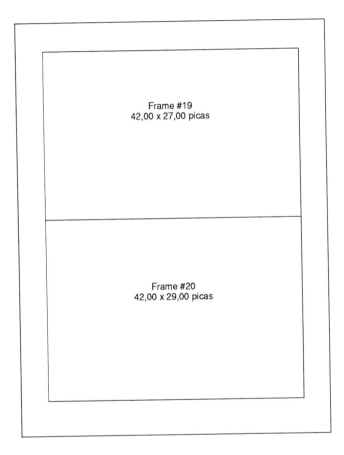

Frame #19
42,00 x 27,00 picas

Frame #20
42,00 x 29,00 picas

Add a Dashed Ruling Line Above

To create a fold line, add a dashed rule above the bottom frame on page four.

■ Go to page four.

■ Select the bottom frame (frame #20).

■ Select Ruling Line Above. Choose Dashes Off. Make the Dash Width: 02.16 points and the Dash Spacing: 02.16 points. Give Rule 1 a height of 00.48 points.

➡ *NOTE: When you click on the button labelled Dashes Off, Ventura turns on the dashed line feature .*

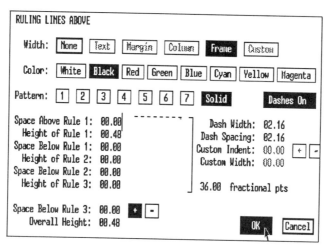

```
RULING LINES ABOVE

Width:  [None] [Text] [Margin] [Column] [Frame] [Custom]

Color:  [White] [Black] [Red] [Green] [Blue] [Cyan] [Yellow] [Magenta]

Pattern: [1] [2] [3] [4] [5] [6] [7]  [Solid]        [Dashes On]

Space Above Rule 1:  00.00  - - - - - - - -   Dash Width:    02.16
   Height of Rule 1:  00.48                    Dash Spacing:  02.16
Space Below Rule 1:  00.00                     Custom Indent: 00.00  [←] [→]
   Height of Rule 2:  00.00                    Custom Width:  00.00
Space Below Rule 2:  00.00
   Height of Rule 3:  00.00                  ⌋ 36.00  fractional pts

Space Below Rule 3:  00.00  [+] [-]
   Overall Height:   00.48                        [OK]  [Cancel]
```

Place Text Files

Now that the frames are completed, you are ready to place the text. Start with the two articles on page one.

■ Press Home to go to page one.

■ Select frame #3.

■ Select 6NEWS-1.TXT from the Assignment List.

Ventura pours as much of the text file it can fit in the frame and then stops.

➥NOTE: *Most of the sample text files have been pretagged. Ventura will automatically format these paragraphs as you place the text.*

Finish placing the first article.

■ Select frame #4 and select 6NEWS-1.TXT from the Assignment List.

■ Select frame #5 and select 6NEWS-1.TXT from the Assignment List.

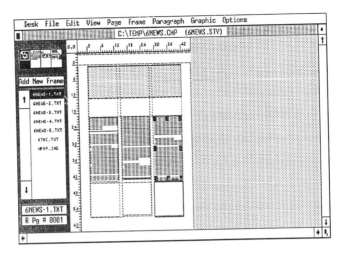

You will place the rest of 6NEWS-1.TXT when you get to page two. For now, continue working on page one. Place the article "Ventura Complements CAD" (6NEWS-2.TXT).

■ Select frame #6 and place the text file 6NEWS-2.TXT.

Ventura flows the text in the two columns and stops when it reaches the end of the second frame. You will place the remaining text when you get to page three.

■ Select frame #7 and place the text file 6TOC.TXT.

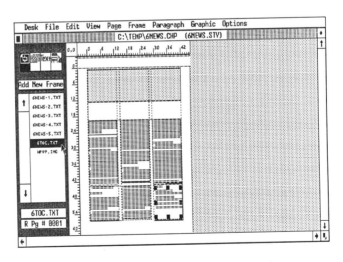

Your newsletter is starting to shape up!

➡ *TIP: You do not have to place all of a file at once. Ventura will "remember" where you left off when you get to the next page. Generally, the most efficient way to work is to do everything you can on one page before moving on to the next.*

Add Logo Text on Page One

To complete the text on page one, add the logo, headline, dateline, and jump text to the proper frames. Change to normal or enlarged view (your choice) so you can see the text as you type.

■ Enable text editing mode.

■ Click anywhere in the logo frame and type the following three paragraphs:

```
PAGINATIONS [Enter]
NEWSLETTER [Enter]
Design   and   Production   News   for   Ventura
Publishers
```

Add Dateline and Headline

■ Click anywhere in frame #2 and type the next two paragraphs:

```
Volume 1, Number 1 [Tab] Winter 1988 [Enter]
Training Workshops Underway
```

The text in the first two frames should look like the nearby sample screen.

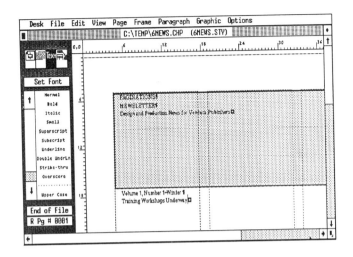

Add Jump Text

■ Click once inside the small frame (frame #8) above the Table of Contents and type:

See WORKSHOP next page

■ Click anywhere in the small frame at the bottom of the page (frame #9) and type:

See CAD page 3

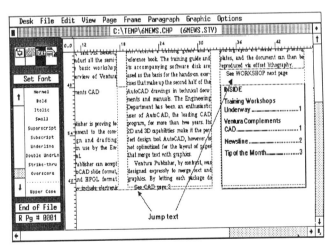

➡ *NOTE: The logo, headline and jump text will be stored as part of the chapter's caption file.*

If you wish to place this text into separate files, switch to frame setting mode. Select the frame containing the text you want to put in a separate file. Select File Type/Rename from the Edit menu. Ignore the name you see listed as Old Name. Type in the new name and location and click OK.

Place Text on Page Two

■ Press PgDn to go to page two.

■ Enable frame setting mode.

■ Select Frame #10 and place the text file 6NEWS-3.TXT.

Now continue the article from page one in frame #11 and put a new article into frame #12.

■ Select frame #11 and place the text file 6NEWS-1.TXT.

■ Select frame #12 and place the text file 6NEWS-4.TXT.

When you have finished, your page will look similar to the illustration below:

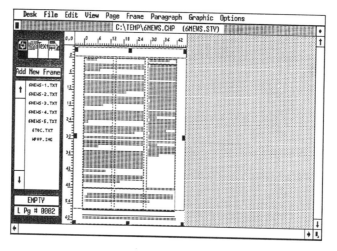

Notice that the text does not completely fill frame #11. How do you handle the empty space? You could type in additional text. Or you could add something to take up space, like an illustration or a *pull quote* (sometimes called a *lift out*).

Add a Pull Quote

A pull quote is a short quotation or extract that can be used as a graphic element to fill space and to attract attention to an article.

To create this pull quote, you will add a small frame inside the existing frame. To set it apart from the rest of the text add vertical padding and rules to the frame. The style of the rules is derived from the graphic look of the logo. After you add the frame, you will type in the pull quote text.

■ While still in frame setting mode, select Add New Frame.

■ Starting at position 20 picas on the vertical ruler, draw a frame 13 picas wide by 09 picas high inside frame #11.

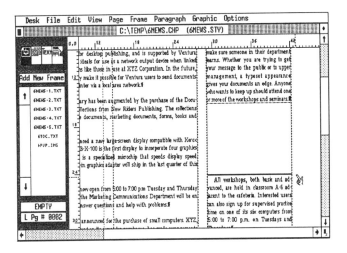

Add Padding

Add vertical padding to keep the text from butting up against the pull quote frame.

■ With the frame still highlighted, select Sizing & Scaling. Make the vertical padding 00,06 picas.

```
┌─────────────────────────────────────────────────────────────────┐
│ SIZING & SCALING                                                  │
│                                                                   │
│ Flow Text Around:  [On]  [Off]                                    │
│                                                                   │
│     Upper Left X:  33,06  [+] [-]    Upper Left Y:  20,06  [+] [-] │
│      Frame Width:  13,00             Frame Height:  09,00          │
│   Horiz. Padding:  00,00            Vert. Padding:  00,06  picas & points│
│                                                                   │
│  Picture Scaling:  [Fit in Frame]  [By Scale Factors]             │
│                                                                   │
│    Aspect Ratio:   [Maintained]  [Distorted]                      │
│                                                                   │
│   X Crop Offset:  00,00  [+] [-]    Y Crop Offset:  00,00  [+] [-] │
│     Scale Width:  00,00             Scale Height:   00,00          │
│                                                                   │
│  Column Balance:  [On]  [Off]                                     │
│                                              [OK]   [Cancel]      │
└─────────────────────────────────────────────────────────────────┘
```

You have just added padding of 6 points above (00,06 picas) and 6 points below the frame — a total of 12 points which is equal to the line spacing of the body text. By making the padding an integer of the body text line spacing, you maintain even spacing throughout the document.

Add Ruling Lines to the Pull Quote Frame

- Ruling Line   Width: Frame
  Above   Height of Rule 1: 00.24 points

- Ruling Line   Width: Frame
  Below   Height of Rule 1: 00.24 points

Add the Pull Quote Text

- Enable text editing mode. Click anywhere inside the pull quote frame. Type the pull quote text using non-keyboard characters to create the quote marks. (For example, [Alt-169] means "type 169 on the numeric keypad while holding down the Alt key." This procedure creates an open quote mark when you release the Alt key.)

  [Alt-169]Anyone who wants to make an impression on paper should attend a Ventura Training Workshop[Alt-170]

  ➡ TIP: you can also enter open and close quotes with Ventura's built-in keyboard shortcuts, Ctrl-Shift -[and Ctrl-Shift -] .

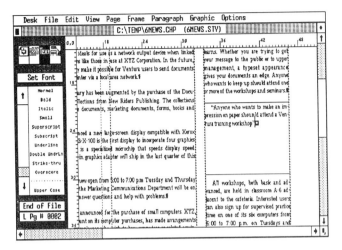

Add Jump Text

Next type in the jump text and change its attributes.

- While still in text editing mode, click anywhere inside the small frame at the top of the right-hand column (frame #13) and type: **WORKSHOP from page 1**

- Highlight the word "WORKSHOP." First choose Bold, then choose Italic from the Assignment List.

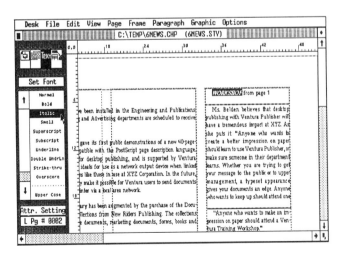

Create Run-In Heads

In addition to using headings on a separate line, you can also draw the reader's attention with run-in heads. Run-in heads use boldface, italic or small capitals for the first few words of a paragraph. To create the boldface run-in heads in frame #10, highlight the text (by dragging or the shift-click method), then choose Bold from the the Assignment List.

- Enable text editing mode.

- Select the two following phrases in the first two paragraphs in frame #10 and make them bold:

"Ventura Workstations..."

"Digital Laser Corporation..."

The rest of the run-in heads have been completed for you. When you are finished your page should look like this:

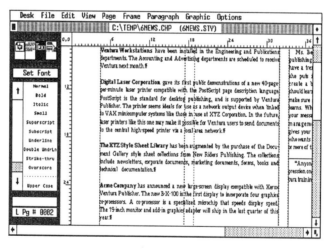

Place Text on Page Three

- Press PgDn to go to page three.

Place the article "Preformatting Ventura Documents" in frame #14 and frame #15 and the rest of the article "Ventura Complements CAD" in frame #16 as explained below.

- Enable frame setting mode.

- Select frame #14 and place 6NEWS-5.TXT.

- Select frame #15 and place the rest of 6NEWS-5.TXT.

■ Select frame #16 and place the rest of 6NEWS-2.TXT.

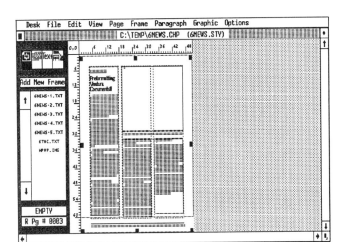

Add Jump Text

■ Enable text editing mode. Click anywhere inside the small frame above the right-hand column (frame #17). Then type:

CAD from page 1

■ Highlight the word "CAD." Choose Bold and Italic from the Assignment List.

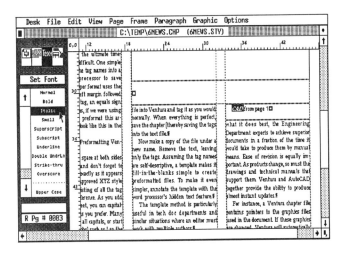

Add Text to Page Four

One more lap to the finish line. Use text editing mode to create the return address and the postage information on page four and you will be finished with the text.

- Press PgDn or End to go to page four.

- Click anywhere in the bottom frame on page four (frame #20) and type the following address (using Ctrl-Enter to create a line break):

```
New Riders Publishing [Ctrl-Enter]
31125 Via Colinas, Unit 902 [Ctrl-Enter]
West Lake Village, CA 91362 [Enter]
```

- Start a new paragraph for the postage text and type:

```
Bulk Rate [Ctrl-Enter]
US Postage [Ctrl-Enter]
PAID [Ctrl-Enter]
LOS ANGELES, CA [Ctrl-Enter]
PERMIT # 1111
```

- Highlight the text "PAID, LOS ANGELES, CA, PERMIT #1111" and select Bold from the Assignment List.

- Highlight the text "LOS ANGELES, CA PERMIT # 11111" and select Small from Assignment List.

When you are finished, check that your page looks similar to the illustration below:

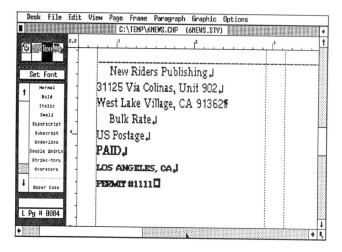

Stopping Point

This is a good point to stop, take a break and save your work (press Ctrl-S). You've already done a lot of work, so we should probably remind you the first time through is always the hardest when working with Ventura. Make no mistake — it takes a substantial effort to produce a newsletter the first time around. But don't become discouraged. Once you've set up your pages and finished the first issue, the production gets easier each time, particularly if you use the techniques we show you at the end of this chapter.

If you want to rest now, and start again later, save the changes to the document and quit Ventura. When you have more time, load Ventura, open the chapter C:\TEMP\6NEWS.CHP and start from where you left off.

If you want to continue, proceed directly to the next section: Tagging the Newsletter.

Tagging the Newsletter

With the text in place, you can format the rest of the newsletter with tags. As always, start with the body text tag. Then proceed from the first frame to the last until all the text is tagged.

■ Go to page one.

■ Enable paragraph tagging mode.

■ Select the second paragraph in frame #3, which starts "Ms. Belden will conduct basic skills workshops ...."

Confirm that body text matches the following attributes:

■ Font

Face: Times
Style: Normal
Size: 010 points

■ Alignment

Justified
Overall Width: Column-Wide
First Line: Indent
In/Outdent Width: 01,00 pica

- Spacing   Inter-Line: 12.00 points
                        Add in Above: When Not At Column Top

When you're finished with body text, go to frame #1 and add a new tag called Logo.

Add the Logo Tag

The logo is the most important element on the front page. It distinguishes a newsletter from others, projects the overall tone and lends consistency from issue to issue. The logo's size should relate to the other elements on the page. It should be easy to read without conflicting with the headlines.

- Select the paragraph "PAGINATIONS."

- Add New Tag   Tag Name to Add: Logo

- Font   Face: Times
                        Style: Bold
                        Size: 072 points

WARNING: If you are using a non-Postscript printer, you may not be able to print fonts as large as 72.00 points. Use the largest size available to you instead.

- Alignment   Center
                        In/Outdent Width: 00,00 picas

➡*NOTE: Tags are copied from body text, which has a first-line indent of 01,00 picas. Therefore, you must cancel this indent for the tags that follow.*

- Spacing   Inter-Line: 80.00 points
                        Add in Above: Always

Now use kerning and tracking to reduce the space between the individual letters and improve the appearance of the type.

- Select Typographic Controls from the Paragraph menu. Choose Automatic Kerning: On, Letter Spacing: Off. Make Tracking 0.050 Ems Tighter.

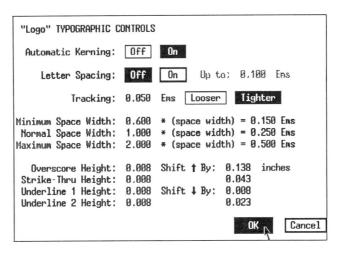

Add LogoSub Tag

Now add a tag named "LogoSub."

■ Highlight the paragraph "NEWSLETTER" in frame #1.

■ Add New Tag   Tag Name to Add: LogoSub

■ Font   Face: Times
          Style: Bold
          Size: 030 points

■ Alignment   Center
               In/Outdent Width: 00,00 picas

■ Spacing   Above: 02.00 points
             Inter-Line 34.00 points
             Add in Above: Always

As you saw earlier, you can use tracking to reduce the individual space between characters and make a headline more legible. However, you can also use tracking to *add space* between characters for a special effect. You will now add extra space between letters in the LogoSub tag.

■ Select Typographic Controls. Choose Automatic Kerning: On, Letter Spacing: Off. Make Tracking 0.750 Ems Looser.

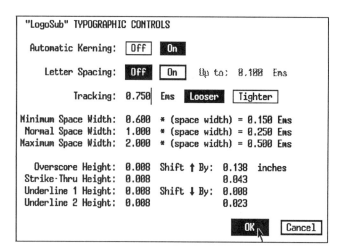

```
"LogoSub" TYPOGRAPHIC CONTROLS

   Automatic Kerning:  [Off]  [On]

     Letter Spacing:  [Off]  [On]    Up to:  0.100  Ems

          Tracking:  0.750|  Ems  [Looser]  [Tighter]
Minimum Space Width:  0.600  * (space width) = 0.150 Ems
 Normal Space Width:  1.000  * (space width) = 0.250 Ems
Maximum Space Width:  2.000  * (space width) = 0.500 Ems

   Overscore Height:  0.008  Shift ↑ By:  0.138  inches
 Strike-Thru Height:  0.008               0.043
 Underline 1 Height:  0.008  Shift ↓ By:  0.008
 Underline 2 Height:  0.008               0.023

                                    [OK]  [Cancel]
```

Add a Ruling Line Above and Below the LogoSub Tag

With the paragraph still highlighted, add ruling lines above and below.

- Ruling Line   Width: Frame
  Above   Height of Rule 1: 01.00 point

- Ruling Line   Width: Frame
  Below   Height of Rule 1: 01.00 point

Add Motto Tag

- Select the paragraph "Design and Production News for Ventura Publishers."

- Add New Tag   Tag Name to Add: LogoMotto

- Font   Face: Times
                      Size: 012 points

- Alignment   Center
                      Overall Width: Frame-Wide
                      In/Outdent Width: 00,00 picas

- Spacing   Inter-Line: 12.00 points
                      Add in Above: Always

Now use tracking to tighten the spacing between letters.

- Typographic   Letter Spacing: Off
  Controls   Tracking: 0.030 Ems Tighter

Add a Custom Rule to the LogoMotto Tag

To create the effect of a double line — one thick and one thin — you will add a custom rule above the LogoMotto tag. Even though these two lines look like one unit, they are not. The top, thinner rule is part of the LogoSub tag above. The bottom, thicker rule will be attached to the LogoMotto tag.

■ With the motto paragraph still highlighted, select Ruling Line Above. Choose Custom. Make the Space Above Rule 1 00,01 picas. Give Rule 1 a height of 00,10 picas. Enter a Custom Indent of 06,00 (+) picas and a Custom Width of 30,00 picas.

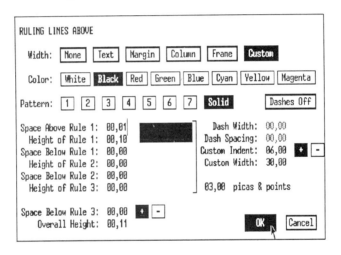

Add a Dateline Tag

Now move to the next frame to create the Dateline and Headline tags. In Chapter Three, you learned how to create a dateline by placing two different tags on the same line. Now we will show you another way to achieve the same effect, but this time using tabs.

■ Select the paragraph "Volume 1, Number 1...."

■ Add New Tag   Tag Name to Add: Dateline

■ Font   Face: Times
                               Style: N-Italic
                               Size: 010 points

■ Alignment   Left
                     In/Outdent Width: 00,00 picas

■ With the paragraph still highlighted, select Tab Settings from the Paragraph menu. Choose Tab #1, Tab type: Right, Tab Display: Shown as Open Space. Make the Tab Location: 42,00 picas.

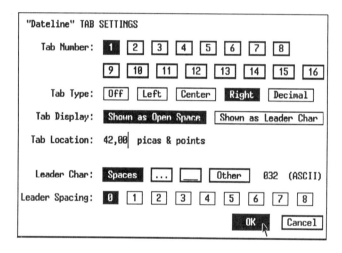

Since tab settings are always measured from the left margin, setting a right tab at 42,00 picas (the width of the frame) positions the words "Winter 1988" next to the right margin.

Tag the Headline

Since most of the text on this page has already been preformatted for you, there are only a few more paragraphs to tag.

■ Tag the paragraph "Training Workshops Underway" as Head1.

- Select both jump text paragraphs and tag them as Cont'd Right.

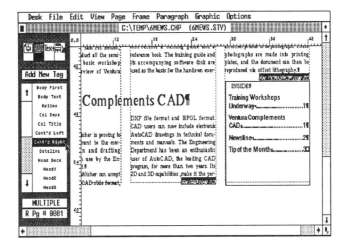

- Select the paragraph "Ventura Complements CAD" and tag it as Head2.

To create the banner headline ("Ventura Complements CAD") we gave the tag a frame-wide alignment. Ventura stretches the text across the full width of the frame. If you are unclear about the difference between frame- and column-wide alignment, open the Alignment dialog box for Head2 and switch back and forth a few times.

➼ *TIP: You can also create a banner headline by placing text in a separate frame that spans more than one column. You used this second technique to create the Head1 headline above the first article.*

Tag the TOC

The last format changes on this page are in the Table of Contents (TOC) in the bottom right frame (frame #7). Add a new tag called Dept. Title.

- Enable paragraph tagging mode.

- Select the word "Inside" in the bottom right frame.

- Add New Tag   Tag Name to Add: Dept. Title

- Font   Face: Times
  Style: Bold
  Size: 018 points

- Alignment   Center
  In/Outdent Width: 00,00 picas

- Spacing   Below: 06.00 points
  Inter-Line: 24.00 points

Add Tracking to the Dept. Title Tag

Use tracking to add more space between the letters and mimic the graphic effect used in the logo.

- Typographic   Letter Spacing: Off
  Controls   Tracking 0.800 Ems Looser

Add Ruling Lines

A ruling line above and below the Dept. title tag separates it from the TOC entries.

- Ruling Line   Width: Frame
  Above   Height of Rule 1: 01.00 point
  Space Below Rule 1: 06.00 points

- Ruling Line   Width: Frame
  Below   Height of Rule 1: 01.00 point

Check the Page

Page one is now complete. Take a moment to look carefully for changes that might improve the design. For instance, examine the TOC title ("INSIDE"). If it does not appear properly centered you might want to add an em space (Ctrl-Shift-M) or an en space (Ctrl-Shift-N) in front of the word. Likewise, check that the jump text lines up with the text in the adjacent column. If it does not, adjust the size or position of its frame (turn Line Snap Off temporarily).

Finally, shorten the middle frame (frame #4) by one line space. This will straighten the text in the adjacent columns.

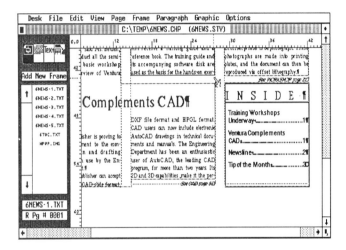

➡ *TIP: If you come across alignment problems in a frame-intensive document, try adjusting your frames so they do not touch. Sometimes, when frames butt up against each other, Ventura pushes the text in the upper frame up a line.*

Apply Dept. Title Tag

■ Press PgDn to move to the next page.

■ Enable paragraph tagging mode. Select the paragraph "Newsline" at the top of frame #10 and tag it as Dept. Title.

■ Select the jump text "WORKSHOP from page 1" and tag it as Cont'd Left.

Add a Pull Quote Tag

Earlier, you created a special frame that separated the pull quote from the main text. Now you will enhance its appearance by enlarging the size of the text and adding a second ruling line above. This second line echoes the double line effect from the logo.

■ Select the paragraph that begins "Anyone who wants ...."

■ Add New Tag   Tag Name to Add: Pull Quote

■ Font   Face: Times
                  Style: B-Italic
                  Size: 14.00 points

■ Alignment   Left
                  In/Outdent Width: 00,00 picas

■ Spacing: Inter-Line: 14.00 points
                  In From Left: 06.00 points
                  In From Right: 06.00 points

■ Select Ruling Lines Above. Make the Width: Custom. Give Rule 1 a height of 00,08 picas and Space Below Rule 1: 01,01 picas. Make the Custom Indent: 00,09 picas and the Custom Width: 10,00 picas.

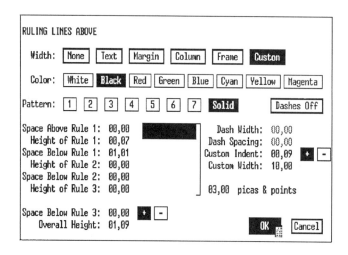

Add a Big First Character to the Staff Box

Now let's change the text in the staff box frame at the bottom of page two. To set it apart from the surrounding text, change the text to italics and add a big first character.

- Select the paragraph from the staff box "Paginations is published...."

- Font   Face: Times
                          Style: N-Italic
                          Size: 010 points

- Alignment   In/Outdent Width: 00,00 picas

- Select Special Effects from the Paragraph menu. Choose Big First Character. Choose Set Font Properties and Face: Times Roman, Style: B-Italics, and Size: 024 points. Click OK to return to the first dialog box. Now choose Space for Big First: Custom and make the custom lines 001. Click OK to close the dialog box.

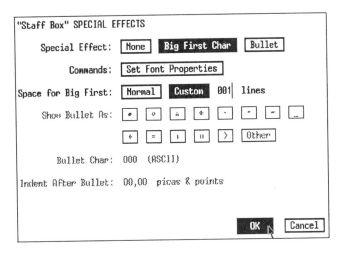

If you had chosen Space for Big First: Normal, Ventura would have made its own best decision where to place the big first character. In this particular case — a 24-point big first character on 12-point lines — it would have chosen two lines. It would have set the first character on the baseline of the *second* line, creating a two-line indent.

When you choose Custom instead, you get to decide which baseline to use. By entering 1, for example, you tell Ventura to place the big first character on the baseline of the *first* line. To make a big first character start below the first line, enter a number greater than one.

Apply Cont'd Left Tag

- Press PgDn to move to page three.

- Select the jump text "CAD from page 1" and tag it as Cont'd Left.

Add an End of Article Symbol on Page Three

To distinguish the beginnings and ends of articles in a newsletter, it is common to place a special editorial symbol, like a hollow or solid filled square at the end of the article. In a text-intensive, multi-column format, this symbol is easy to spot and guides the reader from the end of one story to the beginning of another. We will show you how to create a special end of article symbol using a special font made up entirely of small symbols called *dingbats*.

➡ *NOTE: The Dingbats described here are a special font available for PostScript printers. If you do not have a PostScript printer, the dingbats will not print.*

➡ *NOTE: If you do not have a PostScript printer, substitute a character from the international character set. You might, for instance, use ASCII 158. Enter this character by typing Alt-158 with the numeric keypad. Since this is an international character, you do not have to switch to the Dingbat font.*

- Enable text editing. Place your cursor in front of the end of file marker at the end of the middle frame on page three (frame #15).

Now enter the dingbat symbol ❑ using its decimal equivalent. Unless you have PostScript screen fonts, you will not see the dingbat on the screen. Rather, you will see the letter "q." However, the dingbat will take its correct appearance when you print.

- Type:

ALT-113

■ While still in text editing, highlight the "q" and select Set Font from the SideBar. Choose Zapf Dingbats.

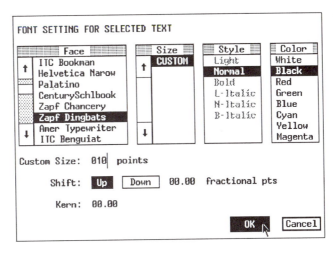

The other articles already have this character in at the end of the file. If you do not have a PostScript printer (and cannot, therefore, print the Dingbat font), you may want to substitute a different symbol from the international character set.

The Final Page

Since the rest of page three is already preformatted, go to the last page of the newsletter.

■ Press End.

Add ReturnAddress Tag

To complete the style section, you will add two tags that reside on the same line: a ReturnAddress tag and a Bulk Rate tag.

The ReturnAddress Tag

■ Enable paragraph tagging mode.

■ Select the paragraph that begins "New Riders Publishing...."

■ Add New Tag   Tag Name to Add: ReturnAddress

■ Font   Face: Helvetica
                         Size: 010 points

■ Alignment   Left
                     In/Outdent Width: 00,00

■ Spacing   Above: 24.00 points
                     Inter-Line: 24.00 points
                     Add in Above: Always
                     In From Right: 02,00 picas

As you learned earlier, you can use Breaks to place two tags on
the same line. The first tag — in this case the ReturnAddress
tag — uses a line break before.

■ Breaks   Line Break: Before
                     Allow Within: Yes
                     Keep With Next: No

The Bulk Rate Tag

Now create the Bulk Rate tag and change Line Break to After
so it appears on the same line with ReturnAddress.

■ Select the paragraph that begins "Bulk Rate..."

■ Add New Tag   Tag Name to Add: Bulk Rate

■ Font   Face: Helvetica
                     Size: 010 points

■ Alignment   Center
                     In/Outdent Width: 00,00 picas

■ Spacing   Above: 24.00 points
                     Add in Above: Always
                     In From Left: 30,00 picas
                     In From Right: 02,00 picas

Using In From Left and In From Right pushes the Bulk Rate
tag to the right margin. This prevents it from overlapping the
ReturnAddress tag when the two reside on the same line.

Now place Bulk Rate on the same line as the Return Address.

■ Breaks   Line Break: After

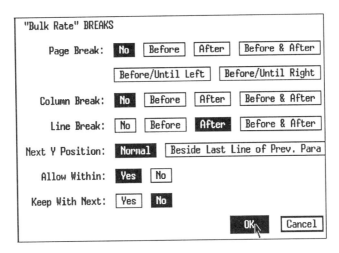

Add Ruling Lines to the Bulk Rate Tag

Add the finishing touches by adding ruling lines above and below the margins of the BulkRate tag.

■ Ruling Rule   Margin
   Above   Height of Rule 1: 04.00 points
                   Space Below Rule 1: 06.00 points

■ Ruling Line   Margin
   Below   Space Above Rule 1: 06.00 points
                   Height of Rule 1: 04.00 points

Pictures

Illustrations are an important part of many newsletters. In this section, you will import and scale an image file and use box text shapes to draw a monthly calendar. Let's start by adding an illustration and caption to the article on page three.

Place the Picture

■ Press PgUp to move back to page three.

■ Enable frame setting mode.

■ Select Frame #18 and place the image file WPVP.IMG.

Scale the Picture

■ Sizing &   Picture Scaling: Fit in Frame
   Scaling   Aspect Ratio: Distorted

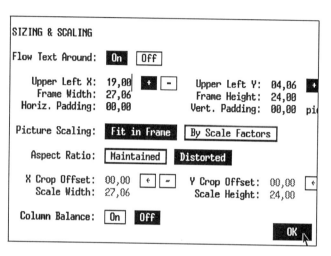

By choosing Distorted, you allow Ventura to stretch the dimensions of the picture as much as needed to fit it exactly inside the frame.

Add a Caption

■ Anchors &   Caption: Below
   Captions

Ventura places an empty caption frame on the page. Now add the caption text inside this frame.

■ Enable text editing mode. Place the cursor in front of the end of file marker inside the caption frame. Type:

Insert tag names into word processing files to preformat Ventura documents

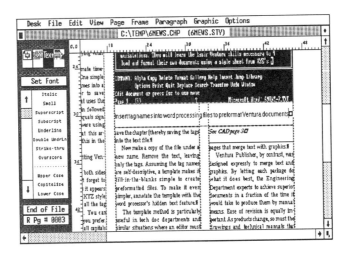

Draw a Calendar

Many readers consider the calendar the most useful part of a newsletter. It lists current and future events in an eye-catching, visual format. By placing the calendar on the back page you make it easy for someone to find and refer to throughout the month.

■ Go to page four.

Before you begin to draw, select the parent frame for the graphics and set up a snap-to grid.

■ Enable frame setting mode.

■ Select the top frame on page four (frame #19), then enable graphics drawing mode.

■ Grid Settings   Grid Snap: On
Horizontal Spacing: 06,00 picas
Vertical Spacing: 02,00 picas

Draw the Title Box

Start by drawing the box text frames to contain the Calendar title and the days of the week.

■ Select the box text icon from the Sidebar. Starting at the upper left column margin, draw a box text 42,00 picas wide (the width of the frame) by 2,00 picas high (one snap unit).

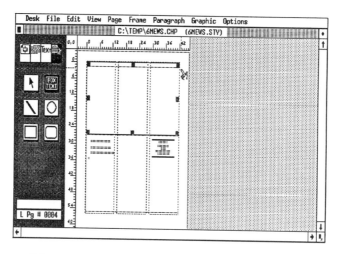

- ■ Line
  Attributes

None

- ■ Fill
  Attributes

Color: White
Pattern: Hollow, Transparent
Default: Save To

Draw the Days of the Week

Draw one box text for the first day. Then use copy and paste to duplicate the shape across the frame.

- ■ Switch to normal or enlarged view to draw the next shape. Starting at 2 picas on the vertical ruler, draw a box text 6 picas wide by 2 picas high.

- ■ Line
  Attributes

Thickness: Thin
End Styles: Square
Default: Save To

- ■ Fill
  Attributes

Color: Black
Pattern: 2, Transparent

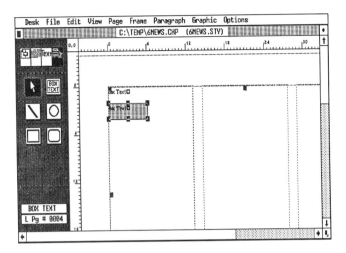

Copy the Shape

■ Press Shift-Del to copy the last shape you drew into temporary memory. Press Ins to paste a copy on the page.

Remember, Ventura pastes the copy on top of the original. Use the mouse to move the shape to the right. Thanks to the grid, it will snap into position.

Complete the Remaining Boxes

Use the steps explained above to copy and move five more box shapes. Spread them across the page in a single line:

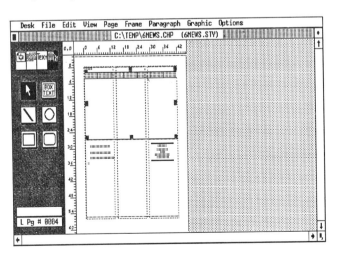

Finish the Calendar

To add the days of the week, you will make make one box text shape, then copy it six times across the width of the frame. Then you will copy the entire row four times, using Shift-Click to select the entire row at once.

➡ *TIP: Be careful when trying to move an entire row of boxes. You must avoid accidentally resizing the boxes, or selecting just one and leaving all the others behind.*

When moving an entire row, place the cursor in the center of one box. Do not place it near any of the handles. After pressing the mouse button, *do not move the mouse until the four-way arrow appears*. If the pointing finger appears instead, release the button immediately without moving the mouse. Then reposition the cursor and try again.

With these precautions in mind, complete the steps outlined below.

Draw the First Box

Change the vertical grid settings to make it easier to create the right size box.

- Grid Settings   Grid Snap: On
                   Horizontal Spacing: 06,00 picas
                   Vertical Spacing: 04,00 picas

- Starting from position 4 on the vertical ruler draw a box text 6 picas wide by 4 picas high.

Copy the Box

- Press Shift-Del to copy the first box to temporary memory.

- Paste a copy of the box back onto the page.

- Use the mouse to move the copy to the right until it snaps into place.

- Paste five more copies and move them into position to complete one row of the calendar.

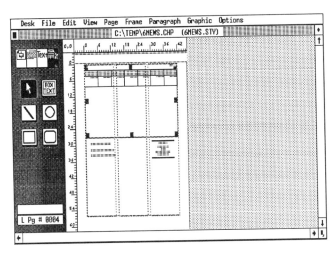

Copy the Row

Now copy the entire row of boxes into the clipboard.

■ Select the first box. Shift-Click to select the remaining boxes. Then press Shift-Del to copy the entire row into temporary memory.

■ Press Ins to paste a copy of the row onto the page.

■ Place the cursor in the middle of one box shape. Drag the entire row of shapes down one grid unit.

■ Paste three more copies and move them into position to complete the calendar.

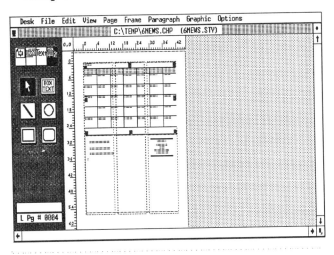

➡️NOTE: If you have trouble moving the shapes as a group, move them one at a time.

Add Text to the Calendar

Now that all the box text shapes are in place, use text editing mode to replace the words "Box Text" with the correct calendar text. Use the illustration below as a guide.

➡️NOTE: Use a line break Ctrl-Enter to separate lines within a box text.

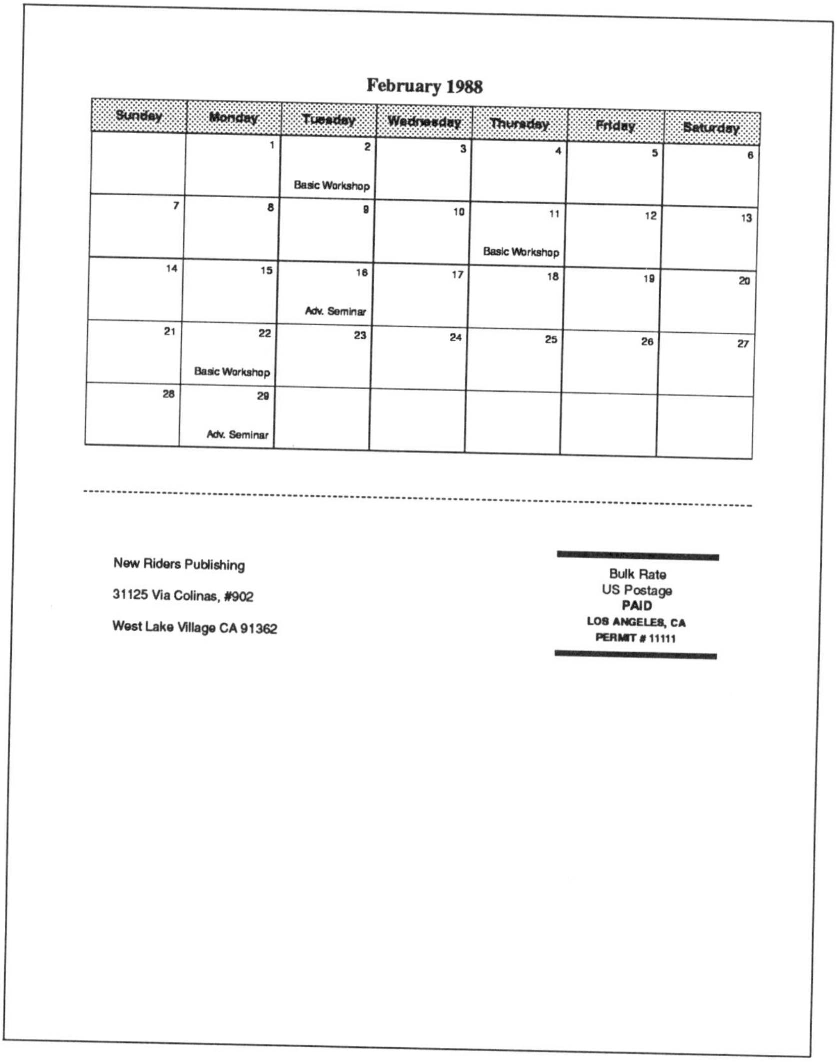

February 1988

Sunday	Monday	Tuesday	Wednesday	Thursday	Friday	Saturday
		1	2	3	4	5
		Basic Workshop				
7	8	9	10	11	12	13
				Basic Workshop		
14	15	16	17	18	19	20
		Adv. Seminar				
21	22	23	24	25	26	27
	Basic Workshop					
28	29					
	Adv. Seminar					

New Riders Publishing

31125 Via Colinas, #902

West Lake Village CA 91362

Bulk Rate
US Postage
PAID
LOS ANGELES, CA
PERMIT # 11111

Apply Tags to the Calendar

Use the predefined tags in the Assignment List to format the calendar.

■ Select the paragraph "February 1988" and tag it as Cal Title.

■ Tag all the days of the week as Cal Days.

Chapter

Nice work. After completing this project, you're ready to take on any type of newsletter, whether simple or complex. Let's take a look at the finished product.

■ To Print   Which Pages: All
Printing Order: Last to 1st

Once you have the final copy in your hands, inspect each page, looking for small changes that will improve its appearance. Remember, no matter how good it might appear on the screen, the true test of your talents show up after printing.

Creating a Chapter Template

As promised, we're going to finish this chapter with tips that speed newsletter production. Once you establish a successful format, the hard part has been done. You can reuse your newsletter chapter over and over again for future issues.

Here's how it works. Open the newsletter and save it under a new name — TEMPLATE.CHP, for example, or BLANK.CHP. Now remove all the text files and graphics files with Remove Text/File from the Edit menu.

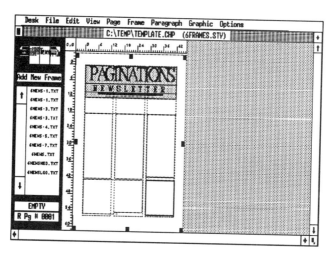

➡️ *NOTE: You do not have to remove the logo text, unless you are using the same template for different newsletters with different names.*

Now save TEMPLATE.CHP again. From now on, you will use this chapter full of blank frames as your starting point. Start by renaming the template so you preserve it intact. Then load and place text files into the empty frames. Change the headers and footers if necessary to reflect the new dates. Adjust frame sizes, add frames, edit copy and make any other minor changes as necessary to make the new text and pictures fit. Newsletters that vary quite a bit from month to month may require more extensive adjustments. Even so, you will still be finished with the newsletter in a fraction of the time it takes to build one from scratch.

Another Time-Saving Trick

If you want to save a step, simply use the same file names for each issue's text and pictures. This technique is most useful if the newsletter format is nearly the same each month. Make a copy of the first issue under a new name, but *do not remove the text and graphics files*. Keep this new version in a subdirectory of its own, together with all the files that make up the chapter. For example, you might call the copy FINAL.CHP and store it in a directory called \FINAL because this is the chapter you will use to print the final version of the newsletter each month.

Collect the text and graphics for each new issue in a separate subdirectory (for instance, \JANUARY, \FEBRUARY, \MARCH, etc.). When everything's ready to go, copy the files to the \FINAL directory, but *rename the files so they match the names used in the first issue.* Once you've updated the files in \FINAL directory, you can load FINAL.CHP. Since the file names are the same, Ventura will immediately flow the new text and graphics into the old layout. You won't even need to place the files. You will, however, need to make some minor adjustments before printing.

Tips

Text Tips

❑ After you convert a text file format, or rename it to a new location, the changes do not take effect until you save the chapter. If you abandon the chapter without saving, you will lose the changes.

❑ To create a dashed line effect, choose Ruling Line Above, Below or Ruling Box Around from either the frame or paragraph and select Dashes Off. You can adjust the width of the dashes and the space between them.

❑ The text you type directly into a frame or caption is stored in Ventura's caption file. If you wish to save the text as a separate file use File Type/Rename from the Edit menu. Ignore the name you see listed in Old Name. Type in the new name and location and click OK.

Style Tips

❑ A pull quote is a short quotation that can be used as a graphic element to fill space or add emphasis to an article. To make a pull quote, place and size a separate frame within a column. Then type the pull quote text directly into the frame. Add a new tag called Pull Quote and change the text attributes to create the desired effect.

❏ Use tracking to reduce or increase the space between individual letters in a word.

❏ To create a banner headline, tag the text as frame-wide, or place text in a separate frame that spans more than one column.

❏ If you choose Space for Big First: Normal, Ventura makes its best guess where to place the big first character. When you choose Custom instead, you decide which baseline to use. By entering 1, for example, you tell Ventura to place the big first character on the baseline of the first line. To make a big first character start below the first line, enter a number greater than one.

Picture and Frame Tips

❏ It is easiest and most efficient to build newsletters by pouring text into frames.

❏ Frames can have fill patterns and up to three ruling lines around.

❏ Frames that reside on top of the underlying page can have the same or different margins and columns as the underlying page.

❏ Make the vertical padding of frames equal to the current inter-line spacing of the body text tag.

❏ If you come across text alignment problems in frame-intensive layouts, try adjusting the frames so they do not touch each other. Sometimes when frames butt up against each other, Ventura pushes the text in the upper frame up one line.

❏ Be careful when you move a group (a row or a column) of graphic shapes together. To avoid accidentally re-sizing them, or selecting one by itself, be sure to select them by placing the cursor in the center of one of the boxes. Do not place the cursor anywhere near the handles. After you press the mouse button, do not move the shapes until the four-way arrow appears.

Chapter Tip

❑ You can re-use a standard chapter format over and over again by converting it into a chapter template. Take the original chapter and save it as a new chapter. Then remove all the text and picture files. Once they are removed, save the new chapter with a name like BLANK.CHP. From now on, you will use this chapter, including its frames, headers and footers, and so forth, to begin your new projects.

Chapter Seven
Skills Checklist

Theory

✓ Creating a directory from a database file

Text

✓ More timesaving tips on pre-tagging

Style

✓ Live headers and footers that change from page to page

✓ How to make crop marks

✓ Advanced typographic techniques: Reverse text

Pictures

✓ Creating thumb tabs with repeating frames

✓ Dressing up frames with fill patterns

Chapter

✓ Printing multiple chapters in a publication

✓ Speeding production with chapter templates

A Directory

Combining the power of a database program with Ventura's batch formatting allows you to publish professional-quality directories quickly and easily. In this chapter, you will create a sample directory using the skills and techniques listed on the facing page.

In Chapter Two you learned the basics of preparing text in advance, including how to use bracket codes to enter attributes directly into word processing files. In this chapter, you will also learn how to enter tag names directly. In addition, we will pass along a few ideas on how to use a database program to generate pretagged files for Ventura.

Theory

Because of time and space limitations, you will not actually use a database to build the sample document in this chapter. However, the text file you will load into the sample document resembles a file you would get from a database. If you expect to use a database in your real-life applications, you will benefit from understanding the theory of using a database to generate pretagged files.

The Power of Pretagging

The fastest way to format text from a database is to include tag names in the text file. As soon as the file is loaded into Ventura, the style sheet definitions are automatically applied. Pretagging virtually eliminates the need to tag inside Ventura and reduces layout time and formatting errors. You can, of course, produce sophisticated documents without pretagging.

In the long run, however, this pretagging shortcut saves time and increases productivity.

Rules for Pretagging

Ventura treats all untagged paragraphs as body text. For this reason, you do not need to pretag body text. All other paragraphs, however, can be pretagged using the format @**TAGNAME** = . The at sign (@) comes first followed by the tag name (e.g. HEAD1, HEAD2, etc.), a space, an equals sign, and a second space. Leaving out any character or space cancels the tagging instruction. Likewise, the tag will not take effect unless it is the first thing in the paragraph and flush against the left margin. In addition, the tag name in the text file must match the name in the style sheet *exactly*. Ventura doesn't care whether you capitalize or not, but it does care that you spell both versions the same.

In the files you will load for this chapter, the *@Head Section =* is the tag name for the title of each directory section. *@Head1 =* is the tag for the first-level heading which in this case are single letters that precede each alphabetical section; *@Head2 =* is the tag for the second level heading, and so on. Reverse-L arrows (↵) at the end of lines indicate line breaks. Paragraph symbols (¶) indicate paragraph returns.

At first glance, it seems like extra trouble to type in tag names at the beginning of each paragraph. Once you settle on a standard set of names, however, you can store them as keyboard macros (with your word processor or a separate program like Smartkey). Then you can enter tags in a split second by pressing a single macro key. Or, as suggested below, you can have a database program do the work for you.

You'll find more tips on pretagging text at the end of the chapter.

Using a Database with Ventura

Database programs are more practical than word processors for generating lists and directories. Businesses use database programs to maintain client lists, mailing lists, inventory lists, and so forth. You can transform such a list into a Ventura document by using the database to generate an ASCII file, which can be loaded into Ventura. Creating an ASCII file is usually as simple as printing a report to disk.

However, a "raw" ASCII file needs lots of formatting once inside Ventura. You can make things even easier by using the database to pretag the file. Here's the strategy:

- Prepare a thumbnail sketch of the directory. Choose names for the tags (for instance, Head1, Head2, Company Name, Phone #, etc.).

- Use Ventura to create a style sheet with matching tag names. Format it to match the thumbnail sketch.

- Sort the database to pull out the specific information you need.

- Specify a database report with the fields in correct order.

So far you've done nothing out of the ordinary with Ventura or with the database. To pretag, however, you must take two additional steps:

- Use the database report generator to insert the tag names in front of the fields.

- Print the report (which now includes the tag names) to disk.

Once you've generated the pretagged ASCII file, you can load it into Ventura. The text will be formatted as soon as you place it.

Linebreaks Versus Paragraphs

The sample text file you will use in this chapter contains line breaks as well as paragraph returns. For long documents such as directories, you should get in the habit of using line breaks to create new lines whenever both lines have the same tag name. Line breaks consume less memory than returns. Memory considerations do not come into play for short documents, but they can become a concern with long documents, especially those with many lines of small type and memory-intensive effects such as leader dots.

A database can enter line breaks by inserting the bracket code <R> in place of a carriage return.

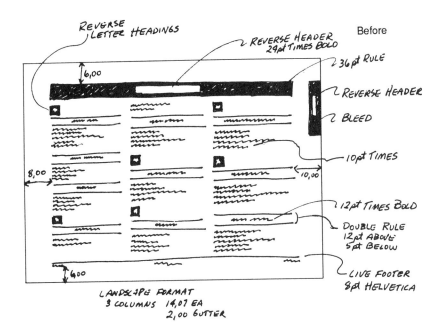

Before

REVERSE LETTER HEADINGS

REVERSE HEADER 29pt TIMES BOLD

36pt RULE

REVERSE HEADER

BLEED

10pt TIMES

12pt TIMES BOLD

DOUBLE RULE 12pt ABOVE 5pt BELOW

LIVE FOOTER 8pt HELVETICA

6,00

8,00

10,00

6,00

LANDSCAPE FORMAT
3 COLUMNS 14,07 EA
2,00 GUTTER

After

Manufacturers

Mfgs

A

Adobe, Inc

1870 Embarcadero Rd.
Palo Alto, CA 94303
Product: *PostScript, Illustrator, Adobe Type Library*
Phone: *(415) 852-0271*

Allied Linotype Co.

425 Oser Ave.
Hauppauge, NY 11788
Product: *Linotronic 100 and 300*
Phone: *(516) 434-2016*

Autodesk, Inc.

2320 Marinship Way
Sausalito, CA 94965
Product: *AutoCAD, AutoSketch*
Phone: *(415) 332-2344*

D

Datacopy Corp.

1215 Terra Bella Ave.
Mountain View, CA 94043

Product: *Model 730 Scanner*
Phone: *(415) 965-7900*

Digital Research Inc.

60 Garden Court
Monterey, CA 93942
Product: *GEM Desktop, GEM Draw Plus, GEM Paint*
Phone: *(408) 649-3896*

H

Hewlett-Packard

P.O. Box 15
Boise, ID 83707
Product: *Laserjet Plus, Laserjet II, Scan-jet*
Phone: *(208) 323-3869*

I

Imagen

2650 San Tomas Expressway
Santa Clara, CA 95051
Product: *DDL Language*
Phone: *(408) 986-9400*

L

Lotus Development Corp.

55 Cambridge Parkway
Cambridge, MA 02142
Product: *Lotus 1-2-3, Symphony, Freelance,Graphwriter*
Phone: *(617) 577-8500*

M

Media Cybernetics

8484 Georgia Ave., Ste. 200
Silver Spring, MD 20910
Product: *Halo Desktop Publishing Editor*
Phone: *(301) 495-3305*

MicroPublishing

21150 Hawthorne Blvd., Ste. 104
Torrance, CA 90503
Product: *microPublishing Report Newsletter, Ventura Style Sheets*
Phone: *(213) 376-5724*

1988 Edition   Manufacturers A–M   Page 1

Planning the Directory

Directories are text-intensive documents with detailed listings of people, products, organizations, etc. Most directories are quick reference guides. They are scanned and skimmed to pinpoint information. As such, they should be designed to help the reader find facts quickly and efficiently. Since most directories maintain the same format from page to page they are fast to format, especially if you pretag the files.

The landscape format of this chapter's sample directory provides a spacious three-column style. Graphic techniques such as reverse type, ruling lines, and thumb tabs help the reader spot different sections, headings and entries. For instance, the thumb tabs bleed to the edge. Even with the book closed, the reader can tell where one section begins and the other ends by glancing at the edge of the page. The reverse type, used to identify each heading, provides contrast between major headings and lesser entries and helps establish the hierarchy of information.

Here are some of the effects and techniques you'll learn in the directory:

- Live headers
- Thumb tabs
- Landscape layout
- Reverse (or shaded) type
- Crop marks

This chapter's sample contains two partial sections of a three-section directory. The first section is arranged alphabetically by manufacturer, the second by category. You will create each section as a separate chapter. At print time, you will use Ventura's multi-chapter operation to combine them into a single publication. In actual practice, you may find it practical to create directories of up to 30-40 pages as a single chapter. For longer directories, we recommend breaking the individual sections into separate chapters.

Ventura Prep

If You Have the Power Disk

Load and rename/relocate the files for this chapter.

■ Load text file 7LIST.TXT from C:\POWER. Use File Type/Rename to save it as C:\TEMP\7DIRECT.TXT.

■ Load the style sheet 7LIST.STY from the C:\POWER subdirectory. Save it as C:\TEMP\7DIRECT.STY.

■ Save the chapter as C:\TEMP\7DIRECT.CHP.

If You Do Not Have the Power Disk

If you don't own the Power disk, type in 7DIRECT.TXT from Appendix A. Save it as C:\TEMP\7DIRECT.TXT. Load &TBL2-L1.STY from C:\TYPESET. Modify it to match the nearby illustration. Save it as C:\TEMP\7DIRECT.STY.

WARNING: When you type in the directory file listings in ASCII format, remember to place two carriage returns between each paragraph. This warning applies to database files you create on your own.

Text

For this project, you will act as if you have already used a database program to generate and preformat the ASCII file 7LIST.TXT (which you loaded in the Ventura Prep section above). Although the text file contains tag names, those tags have not yet been defined in the style sheet, so all the text is displayed as body text. When you get to the Style section, you will build the tags while learning some new graphic effects.

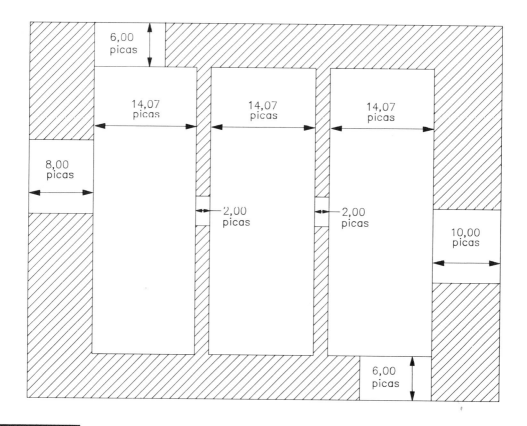

Style

In the style section you will learn a variety of useful techniques, including crop marks, advanced header and footer capabilities, leader dots and more.

Global Page Layout

If you loaded the preformatted style sheet from the Power disk, all the page settings should be in tact. To be on the safe side, confirm that the page layout is set to landscape and verify the margins and columns.

■ Page Layout   Orientation: Landscape
                     Sides: Double
                     Start On: Right

- Margins & Columns

  # of Columns: 3
  Column margins: 14,07 picas
  Gutter margins: 02,00 picas
  Top margin: 06,00 picas
  Bottom margin: 06,00 picas
  Left: 08,00 picas
  Right: 10,00 picas

Draw Crop Marks

Although the size of the paper is 11 x 8.5 inches, the paper will be trimmed by 1/2 inch on all four sides to create a page size of 10 x 7.5. Crop marks (also called *trim marks*) show the "live area" of the paper.

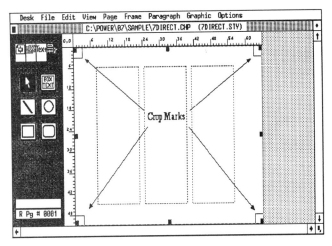

The crop marks in the illustration were created on the underlying page with the Ventura's line drawing tool mode. Marks on the underlying page repeat on every page of the document. Before you draw the lines, plan the grid settings. Since you are trimming the paper 1/2 inch (3,00 picas) on each side, make the grid settings 03,00 picas. The grid setting guarantees that the crop marks will be exactly 3 picas from the edge of the paper.

- Select the underlying page then enable graphics drawing mode.

- Grid Settings   Grid Snap: On
  Horizontal Spacing: 03,00 picas
  Vertical Spacing: 03,00 picas.

- Change to normal or enlarged view to draw the crop marks.

- Select the line icon from the Sidebar. Starting on position 3 on the horizontal ruler, draw a 3,00 pica vertical line.

- Line   Thickness: Thin
  Attributes   End Styles: (Beginning and End) Square
  Defaults: Save To

- Now draw a 3,00 pica horizontal line starting at position 3 on the vertical ruler.

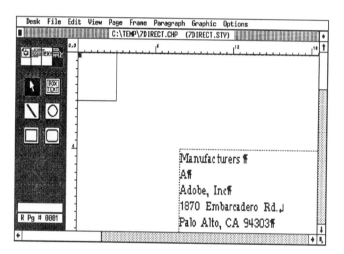

The grid settings force your lines into position.

➡ *NOTE: You may have to experiment a few times before you get the hang of drawing lines with a mouse. Keep trying until you master this new skill.*

Repeat the above steps to place crop marks at the other three corners. Your finished page should look like this:

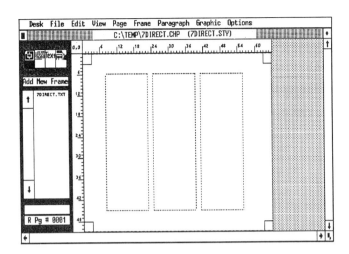

Desk File Edit View Page Frame Paragraph Graphic Options

C:\TEMP\7DIRECT.CHP (7DIRECT.STY)

Add New Frame

7DIRECT.TXT

R Pg # 0001

➥*NOTE: You can also use Ventura's built-in crop mark feature
from the To Print dialog box instead of drawing marks on the
page.*

Although Ventura has a crop mark feature, we taught you to
draw your own crop marks as an alternate technique.
Ventura's crop marks are visible only on the printed page.
They cannot be seen on the screen, since they are not selected
until print time. By contrast, if you draw the crop marks you
can see them on the screen, which helps when you visualize
the page design. To get Ventura generated crop marks for this
size directory you would have *to reduce the size of the underlying page* to 10 x 7.5. But reducing the size of the underlying
page makes it harder to accomplish bleed effects like the
thumb tabs in this chapter.

In general, Ventura's built-in crop marks are most useful
when working with the Paper Type: Half option from the Page
Layout dialog box, or for those who have a printer that creates
pages larger than 8.5 x 11. In most other cases, we recommend
drawing the marks yourself.

Build the Footer

Headers and footers are vital to the usefulness of a reference
document. They help readers zero in on the facts they need.
For instance, a phone book's header shows the first and last
names on the page. A dictionary's header tells the first and last

word on the page. Headers and footers that change from page to page are called *live headers and footers*.

For this exercise, you will build a footer that shows the first and last entries on each page. The commands to accomplish this effect are shown in the following dialog box:

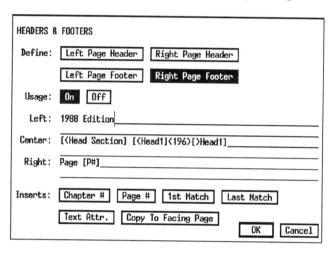

Let's step through the creation of this powerful technique:

■ Select Headers & Footers. Select Define: Right Page Footer, Usage: On.

■ Move to Left and type: **1988 Edition**

■ Move to Center and select 1st Match. Delete the words "tag name" and replace them with: **Head Section**

Next, use the right arrow key to move past the right bracket. Press the space bar to enter a space following the right bracket.

You have just given the 1st Match instructions. Ventura will look on every page and find the first paragraph tagged as Head Section. It will display this paragraph in the footer. If it doesn't find a new Head Section, it will use one from a previous page.

■ Select 1st Match again. Delete the words "tag name" and replace them with: **Head1**

Because of this command Ventura will also display the first occurrence of Head1 in the center of the footer.

■ Move past the right bracket and select Text Attr. Delete the letter "D" and replace it with: **196**

You just told Ventura to print an en dash. The decimal code for en dash is 196.

■ Move past the right bracket and select Last Match. Delete the words "tag name" and replace them with: **Head1**.

This copies the last occurrence of Head1 to the center footer.

■ Move to Right and type: **Page** followed by a space.

■ Choose Page #.

Now copy these settings to the left page and modify them slightly.

■ Choose Copy to Facing Page to copy the footer settings to the left page.

■ Select Define: Left Page Footer, Usage On. Move to Right, press Esc to clear the line and type: **Desktop Publishing Directory**

Click OK to close the dialog box.

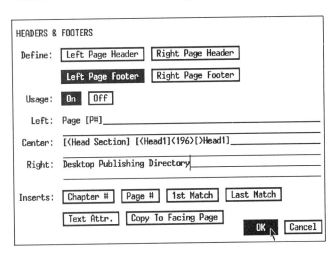

Change the Footer Frame Margins

When the paper is trimmed, it will lose 1/2 inch from each side.

If you trimmed the page as it is, the footer text might be clipped off.

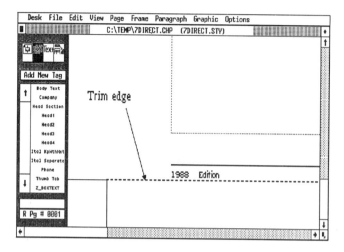

To raise the footer into the live area, change the top margin of the footer frame.

■ Margins &   Top: 01,00 pica
  Columns

Notice that the right and left margins of the footer are equal to the page margins. You raised the footer text on the page by reducing the top margin from 2,00 to 1,00 pica.

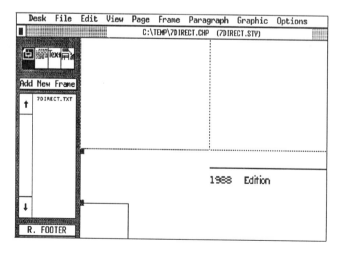

➡️ *TIP: You can also change the position of headers and footers*

using Spacing from the Paragraph menu. Spacing attributes are stored with the style sheet and can be reused if it is easier. Document attributes, such as footer margins, are stored with the chapter. They cannot be reused unless you construct a chapter template (as described in Chapter Six). Sometimes, however, you cannot achieve the effect you want without changing the header or footer margins, especially if you have large trim margins.

Building New Tags

Now that you've completed the changes to the underlying page, you are ready to build tag definitions. Start with the body text tag, then proceed through the document paragraph by paragraph.

Body Text

■ Select the paragraph, "1870 Embarcadero Rd." and check that the body text tag matches these settings:

■ Font   Face: Times
Style: Normal
Color: Black
Size: 010 points

■ Alignment   Justified
Overall Width: Column-Wide

■ Spacing   Inter-Line: 12.00 points
Add in Above: When Not At Column Top

Build the Head Section Tag

The Head Section tag uses Ruling Line Above to create reverse type. Later, in the picture section, we will show you how to achieve the same effect using white text and a solid black frame.

➡*NOTE: Certain printers may not be able to print out white text on a black background. You can, however, achieve a similar effect using black text with a gray patterned rule (or frame). We will show you how to create both effects.*

■ Enable paragraph tagging mode. Select the first paragraph, "Manufacturers."

The tag name, Head Section, appears in the Current Selection box.

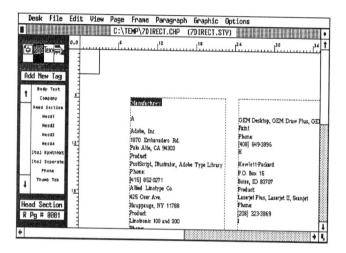

■ Font   Style: Bold
                          Color: White
                          Size: 024 points

Because you just made the text white, it is invisible against the white screen. However, as soon as you drop a black background behind it, the text will become visible again.

■ Alignment   Center
                          Overall Width: Frame-Wide

Frame-wide alignment forces the text across the three column width.

■ Spacing   Below: 24.00 points
                          Inter-Line: 24.00 points
                          Add in Above: Always

■ Breaks   Page Break: Before/Until Right

This Page Break selection places a page break before every Head Section tag. As a result, every section starts on a separate right-hand page.

➥NOTE: *If you want the Head Section tag to start on either a new right or a new left page, choose Page Break: Before instead of Before/Until Right.*

Create Reverse Type

Now create the reverse type effect with Ruling Line Above. The strategy behind this effect is simple: You make the type white and drop a black ruling line on top of it.

➥NOTE: *If your printer is incapable of reverse type, follow the substitute procedures explained below.*

Start by giving Rule 1 a height larger than the type. In this example, Head Section is 24 points and Rule 1 is 36 points. If you did nothing else, the rule would appear above the white type. However, you can shift the rule downwards, by entering a negative amount of Space Below Rule 3. If you enter a positive value, Ventura *adds* space below the rule. If you enter a negative value, Ventura *subtracts* space so the rule shifts downwards.

➥TIP: *Although it is called Space Below Rule 3, this measurement refers to the space below the last rule, whether that last rule is the first, second or third.*

To figure out how much to shift the rule downwards, use the following formula, which centers the type within the ruling line:

• Add the ruling line height and the font size

• Divide by two

For instance, here's how to determine the Space below Rule 3 for the example above:

• 36 + 24 = 60

• 60 ÷ 2 = 30.

You would, therefore, make the space Below Rule 3 equal to negative 30 points if you wanted to center the type exactly in the middle of the rule. However, the formula is only a starting point. In many cases, you may want to adjust the value to create a more pleasing visual balance. For instance, in this example, we will use 34 points (instead of 30) to move the rule four points further down and set the text slightly above the center of the rule.

■ Select Ruling Line Above. Choose Width: Frame. Give Rule 1 a height of 36.00 points. Make the Space Below Rule 3: 34.00 points. Choose the minus sign.

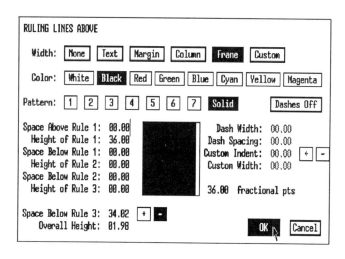

If You Cannot Print Reverse Type

If your printer is incapable of reverse type, create black text on a gray rule instead. Use the same steps as above, but change the font color to Black and make the Ruling Line Above a gray pattern. For instance you would select:

■ Font   Style: Bold
              Size: 024 points

■ Select Ruling Line Above. Choose Width: Column, Color: Black, Pattern: 3. Make the height of Rule 1: 36.00 points and the Space Below Rule 3: (minus) 34.00 points:

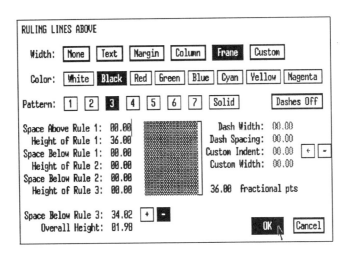

Change the Head1 Tag

The next tag is Head1. You will use the method described above to create the reverse type. Since the file was pretagged, the changes you make to the first tag will ripple through the document and change all the other Head1 paragraphs.

■ Select the paragraph "A."

■ Font   Style: Bold
                Color: White
                Size: 018. points

■ Alignment   Left
                In/Outdent Width: 06.00 points

■ Spacing   Above: 18.00 points
                Inter-Line: 18.00 points
                Add in Above: When Not At Column Top

To prevent Ventura from isolating the Head1 tag at the top or bottom of a page or column, select the Keep With Next option from the Breaks dialog box.

■ Select Breaks. Choose Keep With Next: Yes.

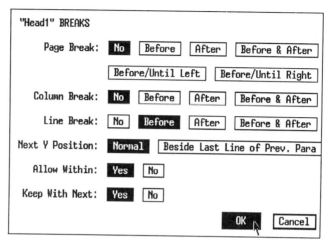

Create the Ruling Line Above

Now create a ruling line above and move it down over the white type. This time, however, you will use a custom width to limit the size of the rule.

■ Select Ruling Line Above. Choose Width: Custom. Give Rule 1 a height of 24.00 points. Make the Space Below Rule 3 (minus) 24.00 points. Then make the Custom Width 24.00 points.

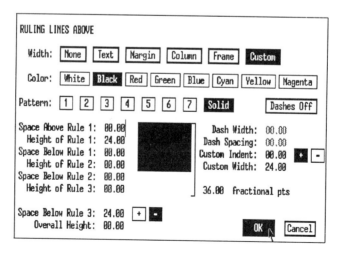

➡ *NOTE: The centering formula would indicate a negative space of 21 points (18 + 24 = 42. 42 ÷ 2 = 21). We have increased this by 3 points to raise the type slightly above the centerline.*

If You Cannot Print Reverse Type

To make black text on a gray rule, change the font color to Black and the rule Pattern to 3.

Change the Head2 Tag

Now change the Head2 tag.

■ Select the paragraph "Adobe, Inc."

■ Font   Style: Bold

■ Alignment   Center

■ Spacing   Above: 12.00 points
                Below 12.00 points
                Inter- Line: 14.00 points

The space below separates the title from the entries below.

■ Breaks   Keep With Next: Yes.

Keep With Next prevents the title from being isolated at the top or bottom of a column or page.

■ Select Ruling Line Above. Choose Width: Column. Give Rule 1 a height of 02.00 points. Set Space Below Rule 1 to 02.00 points.

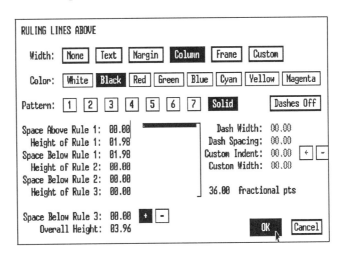

■ Select Ruling Line Below. Choose Width: Column. Set Space

Above Rule 1 to 02.00 points and give Rule 1 a height of 00.50 points.

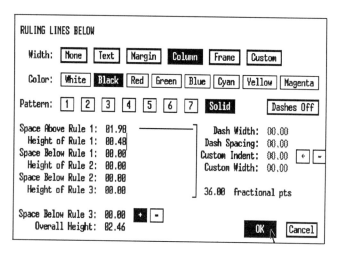

Change Head3

■ Select the paragraph "Product."

■ Font   Style: Bold

■ Alignment   Left

■ Breaks   Keep With Next: Yes

The Breaks dialog box accomplishes two things. Line Break Before allows another tag on the same line. Keep With Next: Yes keeps the listing from being isolated from the next tag.

Change the ItalKpWthNxt Tag

■ Select the paragraph "PostScript, Illustrator, Adobe Type Library."

The tag name Ital KpWthNxt (short for Italics Keep With Next) appears in the Item Selection Box.

■ Font   Style: N-Italics

■ Select Alignment. Choose Left. Make the In/Outdent Width: 00,06 picas. Choose Relative Indent: Length of Previous Line.

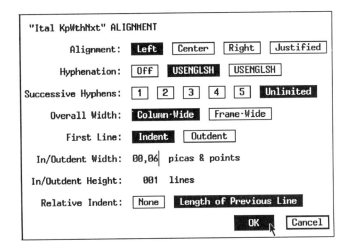

■ Breaks   Line Break: After
                   Keep With Next: Yes

Line Break: After allows the Ital KpWthNxt tag to reside on the same line as the previous one.

Change the Ital Separate Tag

The next tag encountered is Ital Separate. It is identical to the Ital KpWthNxt tag, except that Keep with Next is set to No. The No setting permits Ventura to break the text to a new column after this tag.

■ Select the paragraph "(415) 852-0271"

■ Font   Style: N-Italic

■ Alignment   Left
                   In/Outdent Width: 00,06 picas

                   Relative Indent: Length of Previous Line

■ Breaks   Line Break: After
                   Keep With Next: No

Stopping Point

Here's the stopping point for the chapter. So take a moment to save your work and relax. You should also congratulate yourself, since you've learned a variety of powerful techniques. Check to make sure your document matches the following illustration:

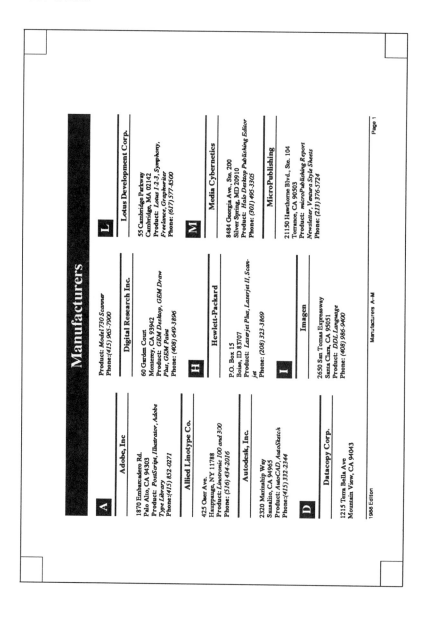

If you don't have time to continue, quit Ventura and come back later. Simply open the chapter C:\TEMP\POWER \7DIRECT.CHP and jump right into the pictures section.

You are ready to proceed with the pictures section. If you plan to continue without a break, proceed directly to the next section.

Pictures

Now that you have finished the style section, you are ready to make thumb tabs. As explained earlier, thumb tabs make it easier to find different sections of a directory. To create them, you make repeating frames. As the name implies, a repeating frame shows up on every page of the document. First you must plan ahead:

• Determine how high the thumb tab should be.

For the three-section directory, the height of each thumb tab will be 1/3 of the total column height, or 13,00 picas.

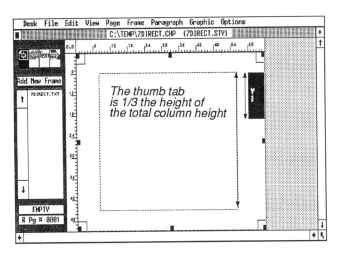

• Calculate how wide the thumb tab should be.

You will make the thumb tab wider than necessary, so it will bleed off the edge of the paper. Since the margin from the live area to the trim edge is 3,00 picas, you could make the thumb tab 4,00 or 5,00 picas — anything larger than 3,00 picas will extend past the trim area. However, we recommend a six-pica box because it is easier to position. You can butt it up against the column guide and the edge of the paper for perfect alignment.

Create the Thumb Tab Frame

■ Enable frame mode. Select Add New Frame.

■ Starting at position 60,00 on the horizontal ruler and 6,00 on the vertical ruler, draw a thumb tab frame 6,00 picas wide by 13,00 picas high.

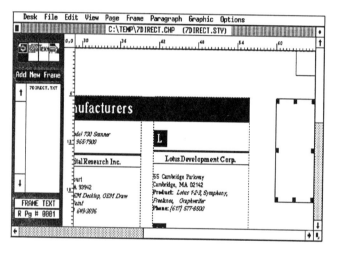

Verify the position and size of the frame with the Sizing & Scaling dialog box.

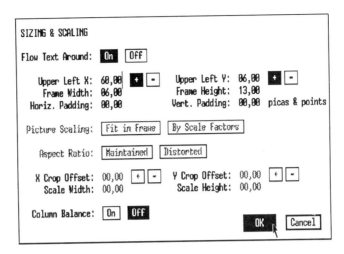

Add a Frame Margin

By adding a right margin inside the thumb tab frame, you guarantee that the text inside the frame will be centered inside the three-pica area that remains *after trimming*. Without the right margin, the text would be centered inside the full six-pica width — and part of it would get trimmed off by the printer.

■ With the thumb tab frame still highlighted, select Margins & Columns. Make the right margin 03,00 picas.

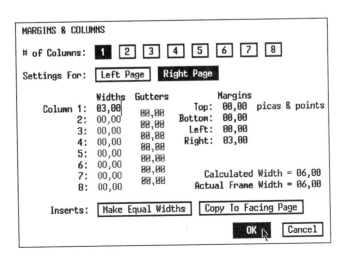

Add Text to the Thumb Tab Frame

To make the vertical text within the frame, use line breaks as spacers after each letter in the word.

■ Enable text editing and type:

```
[Ctrl-Enter] [Ctrl-Enter] [Ctrl- Enter]
M [Ctrl-Enter]
f [Ctrl-Enter]
g [Ctrl-Enter]
s [Ctrl-Enter]
```

Now tag the paragraph to make it white text.

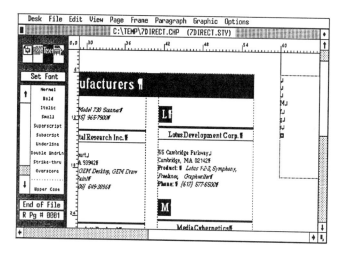

■ Enable paragraph tagging mode. Select the letters "Mfgs" and tag them as Thumb Tab.

The white text is invisible against the screen.

Change the Frame Pattern

Change the frame pattern to solid black.

■ Enable frame mode and highlight the thumb tab frame.

■ Select Frame Background from the Frame menu. Choose Black and Solid.

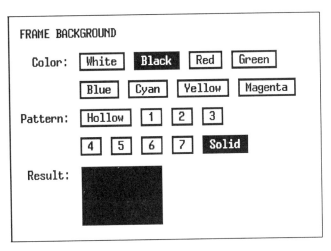

The thumb tab should look like this:

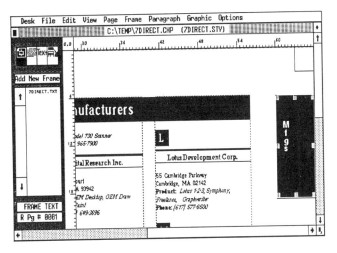

Copy the Thumb Tab Frame

Make a copy of the frame to place on the second page of the directory.

■ With the thumb tab frame still selected, copy it into temporary memory (press Shift-Del).

Be sure to make this copy before taking the next step. You will need to paste in this frame on page two.

Change the Thumb Tab Frame to a Repeating Frame

To make the thumb tab repeat on every right page, turn it into a repeating frame.

■ Select Repeating Frame from the Frame menu. Choose For All Pages: Right, On Current Page: Show This Repeating Frame.

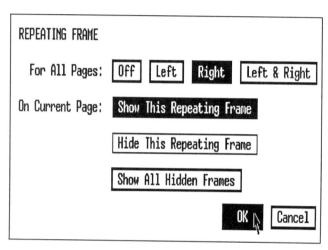

➡️ *NOTE: You cannot copy, delete or change a repeating frame. To make changes to a repeating frame, first change it back to normal, then make the changes, then make it a repeating frame again.*

Create a Thumb Tab for the Left Page

Thumb tabs gain part of their effectiveness because they sit back-to-back on both sides of a page. This creates a black area that can easily be seen along the edge of the document. To mirror the thumb tab from the first page, you will paste the copy onto page two, then move it into its new position.

■ Press PgDn to go to page two.

■ Press the Ins key or select Paste from the Edit menu.

The thumb tab frame will appear in the same position it had on the first page. Now move it to the left page margin, as shown below.

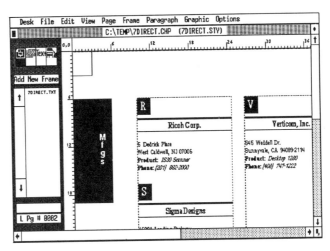

Use Sizing & Scaling to position the frame accurately. Otherwise, the two frames may not line up back-to-back.

■ Select Sizing & Scaling. Make the Upper Left X: 00,00 picas and the Upper Left Y: 06,00 picas.

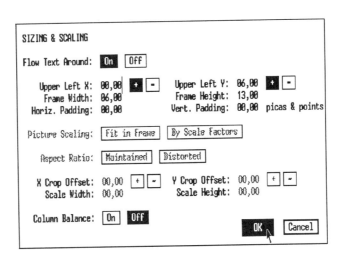

Verify Frame Margins

Check the frame margins so the text is properly centered within the tab. (The margins should be the mirror opposites of the margins for the right page.)

■ Margins &
Columns

Left: 03,00 picas
Right: 00,00 picas

Make the Thumb Tab a Repeating Frame

As you did on page one, make the thumb tab a repeating frame.

■ Repeating   For All Pages: Left
  Frames   On Current Page: Show this Repeating
               Frame

Create a Template Chapter

Now that you've formatted the first section of the directory, you can use it to create a blank template. Normally we would teach this technique in the chapter section. However, we want you to practice starting with a template. As you will see, a template speeds production. For instance, it saves the time of recreating headers and footers.

Before you continue, make a note of the last page number in the chapter. When you open the next chapter, you will renumber it starting with the next page in the sequence

■ Press End to move to the last page. Note the last page number (page two).

Noting the page number probably seems trivial in the case of this sample exercise. Because this is a teaching example, not a true directory, there are only two pages. In real life, directory sections will have many more pages. It will be important to take this step before moving to the next section.

Save your chapter with its existing name before turning it into a template.

■ Press ^S.

Now save the chapter under a new name to make a copy, which you will turn into a template.

■ Select Save As from the File menu. Save the chapter as C:\TEMP\DIRPLATE.CHP.

Remove the Files

The next step in creating a template chapter is to remove the files.

■ Enable frame mode. Select the underlying page.

■ Select Remove Text/File from the Edit menu. Choose Remove from: List of Files.

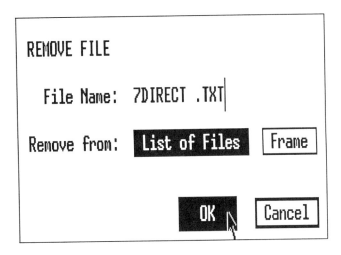

Ventura removes the text file 7DIRECT.TXT from the Assignment List.

Save the C:\TEMP\DIRPLATE.CHP again in its new "empty" state.

■ Press ^S.

You just made a template — an "empty" chapter. Now you are ready to use it for the next section of the directory.

Load Text into the Template

Load the text for the second section. Since the text is pretagged and all the tag definitions are present in the style sheet, the document is formatted as soon as you bring it in.

■ Load and place the text file 7CATGORY.TXT from the C:\POWER subdirectory.

The text flows onto the underlying page.

Rename the Text

■ Select the underlying page.

- Select File Type/Rename from the Edit menu. Rename the text file as C:\TEMP\7DIRECT2.TXT.

- Save the new chapter as C:\TEMP\7DIRECT2.CHP.

By saving under a new name, you preserve the template in its original form. This template could be used over and over again to create different directory sections.

Change the Thumb Tab

The thumb tab for the second section of the directory will be shifted down so it aligns with the bottom edge of the first tab.

To make a copy of the original thumb tab, select the frame and change it from a repeating frame to a normal frame (remember, you cannot copy a repeating frame).

- Select the thumb tab frame. Select Repeating Frame from the Frame menu. Choose For All Pages: Off.

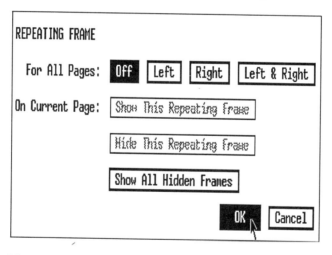

Now you are ready to copy the frame.

WARNING: Do not delete the original frame until you place the copy. You will use the original as a guide to line up the second thumb tab.

- Press Shift-Del or select Copy from the Edit menu.

Now paste a copy on top of the original.

■ Press the Ins key or select Paste Frame from the Edit menu.

Move the frame into place below the first thumb tab, so the top edge aligns with the bottom edge of the original.

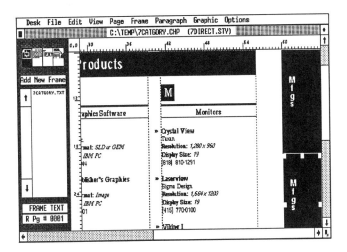

Once the frame is properly placed, delete the original.

■ Select the top frame and press Del.

Change the text in the frame to read "Products."

■ Enable text mode. Delete the text from the frame.

■ Now type:

```
[Ctrl-Enter]
 P [Ctrl-Enter]
 r [Ctrl- Enter]
 o [Ctrl-Enter]
 d [Ctrl-Enter]
 u [Ctrl-Enter]
 c [Ctrl-Enter]
 t [Ctrl-Enter]
 s [Ctrl-Enter]
```

Make a Second Thumb Tab on Page Two

Go to the next page and repeat the above instructions to create a second thumb tab.

- Select the left thumb tab frame.
- Make it a non-repeating frame.
- Copy it to temporary memory.
- Paste a copy on top of the original.
- Move the new frame into place below the first thumb tab, so the top edge aligns with the bottom edge of the original.
- Delete the original once the frame is properly placed.
- Change the text in the frame to read "Products."

When you are finished your screen should look like this for page two:

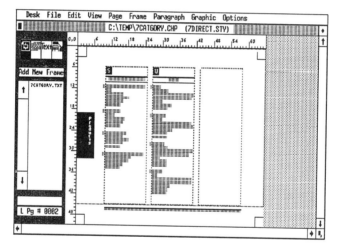

Because of space limitations, we will not show you how to complete the third section of the directory. You would, however, use the identical steps and methods.

Chapter

In this section, you will renumber the chapters, place both sections into a publication and print the publication.

Renumber the Chapter

Renumber the second section to start on page three. (In this teaching example, the first chapter was only two pages long. Normally, it would be much longer. Nevertheless, the principles are the same.) When you print the chapters, the second section will then be numbered sequentially from the previous chapter.

■ Press Home to go to page one of the chapter 7DIRECT2.CHP.

■ Select Page Counter from the Page menu. Choose Restart Counting: Yes, With Number: 0003, and Number Format: 1,2.

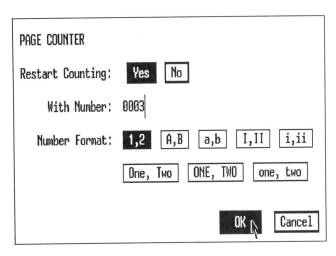

Since the directory is composed of two chapters, you can use Ventura's Multi-Chapter function to print both at once. First put both chapters into a publication. Then use the Print option from the Multi-Chapter dialog box to print both chapters with a single command. Although you are using only two chapters in our example, you can use this same technique to print many chapters at once.

■ Select Multi-Chapter from the Options menu.

➡*NOTE: If you have made any changes, Ventura asks if you want to Save or Abandon. Choose Save.*

Create a New Publication

■ Select New from the Multi-Chapter dialog box.

Add the two directory chapter names to the publication.

■ Select Add Chapter. Select C:\TEMP\7DIRECT.CHP from the Item Selector.

The chapter appears at the top of the Multi-Chapter dialog box.

Now add the next chapter.

■ Select Add Chapter again. Select C:\TEMP\7DIRECT2.CHP from the Item Selector.

Ventura returns you to the dialog box and displays the two chapter names.

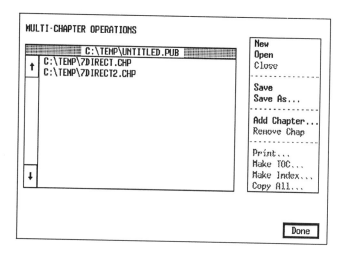

Now you are ready to save the chapters as a publication.

■ Select Save As from the File menu and save the publication as C:\TEMP\DIRECTOR.PUB.

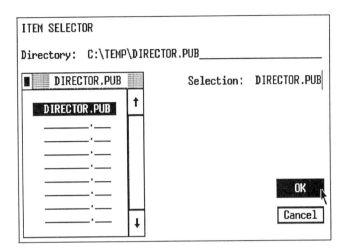

The publication name appears in the menu bar. Once the publication is created you can print it.

■ Select Print. Choose All, Last to 1st.

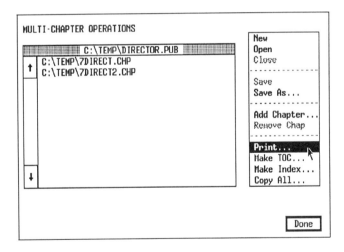

Ventura prints out both chapters, one after another.

Tips

Pretagging Tips

❏ Always use the format @TAGNAME = . Make sure the tag name is the first thing in the paragraph.

❏ Ventura assumes that any paragraph without a tag name is body text.

❏ The tag name must precede the rest of the paragraph. Ventura applies the tag name until it encounters a hard carriage return (¶). Then it switches back to body text, or to the next tag name.

❏ Put the @ sign in the left margin. If the @ sign is any other place in the text file, it will not be recognized as part of the tag code.

❏ Tag names are not case-sensitive. Ventura doesn't recognize any difference between upper and lower case.

❏ Always match the tag name in the text file with the tag name in the current style sheet. Ventura recognizes *any* minor mismatch between tag names, including spaces. For instance, CHAP # and CHAP# would be listed as two separate tags in the Assignment List.

❏ When Ventura finds tag names in the text file that are not part of the current style sheet, it lists them in the Assignment List in uppercase and displays them on the screen with body text attributes.

❏ Use the @PARAFILTR = tag to strip out double carriage returns in a document. This allows you to retain normal spacing (two carriage returns between paragraphs) for readability in the text file, but strips out the extra returns when you bring the file into Ventura.

❏ Tags added in Ventura with paragraph tagging mode will be saved back to the original text file when the chapter is saved.

❏ When producing files in ASCII format, make sure to enter two carriage returns between each paragraph.

❏ The fastest way to format a text generated from a database is to include the tag names in the text file.

Miscellaneous Tips

❏ You can create crop marks manually by drawing line shapes on the underlying page. They will repeat on every page of the document. You can also use Ventura's built-in crop marks in the print option. Use the automatic crop marks when you are creating half-size pages, or if you have a printer that can print larger than 8.5 x 11 format.

❏ You can create live headers and footers that change from page to page throughout the document in the Headers & Footers dialog box. If you select 1st Match, Ventura places the first occurrence of the tag in the header (or footer). If you select Last Match, Ventura places the last occurrence of the tag into the header (or footer). If Ventura doesn't find the tag on a page, it uses one from a previous page.

❏ Initially, the frame margins of headers and footers are set to vertically center the header. However, you can raise or lower the header or footer by changing the frame margins (in Margins & Columns) or by changing the space above or below (in Spacing). The spacing attributes are stored with the style sheet and therefore can be reused. The header and footer frame margins are stored with the chapter and can only be reused by creating a chapter template.

❏ A reverse type effect can be created by placing white text in a black frame, or by dropping a solid black rule down over white text. If you want to use reverse text as a predominant effect in your style sheet, it's best to make it as a tag using the rule above technique.

❏ Some PostScript printers cannot print white type on a black background. Substitute black type on a gray background.

❏ Space Below Rule 3 refers to the space below the last rule in the tag (or frame), whether that last rule is the first, second or third. If you enter a positive value the Ventura adds space below the rule and the rule shifts upwards. If you enter a negative space, Ventura subtracts space below the rule, so it shifts downwards.

❏ The Breaks option Keep With Next can be used to keep tags from being isolated at the top or bottom of a column or page.

❏ A relative indent set to the Length of the Previous Line adds a first line indent equal to the length of the last line in the paragraph. When this is used in combination with the Breaks option, you can make two tags reside on the same line side-by-side.

❏ To make a thumb tab that repeats on every page of the document, use a repeating frame.

❏ Once you make a frame into a repeating frame you cannot cut or delete it. Change it back to a normal frame with the Repeating Frame dialog box if you need to make changes.

❏ Multi-Chapter allows you to combine a list of chapters together into a publication. Once the publication is created, you can print all the chapters at once.

Chapter Eight
Skills Checklist

Theory

✓ The parts of a book

Text

✓ Working with footnotes

✓ Inserting index entries into
text

Style

✓ How to use the page and
chapter counters

✓ Creating a drop cap for
starting text

Chapter

✓ Creating a
professional-quality table
of contents

✓ Creating an electronic
index

✓ Printing crop marks

A Book

For book publishers large and small, Ventura can mean faster production and lower costs. In this chapter you will learn the special Ventura skills that apply to long documents. You may need to make a few changes to your current production practices to accommodate the realities of working with Ventura.

Theory

There are three parts to a traditional book: the front matter, the main text, and the back matter. Each section has its own format and style, but all three work together to complement the overall design.

It is tempting to put a book into one large chapter file. For easier production, however, we recommend a separate Ventura chapter for each book chapter.

As for page numbering, you may find it simplest to begin with the first page of the first chapter. The front matter can then be handled separately. Traditionally, page numbers in the front matter are displayed in lower case Roman numerals or omitted entirely.

Preformatting text files in advance can help reduce the bottlenecks that typically occur in the book production cycle. By establishing standard tag names and using bracket codes, authors and editors can format as they write.

Before

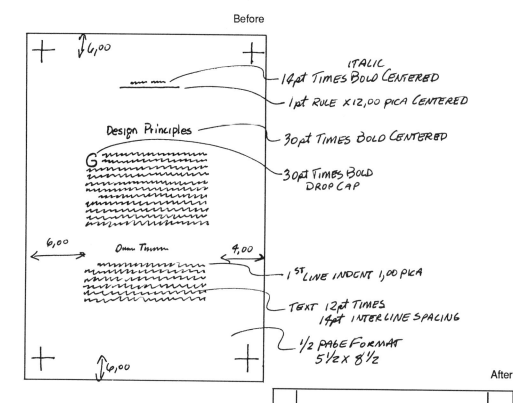

↓6,00

ITALIC
← 14pt TIMES BOLD CENTERED

← 1pt RULE ×12,00 PICA CENTERED

Design Principles

← 30pt TIMES BOLD CENTERED

G

← 30pt TIMES BOLD
  DROP CAP

6,00 →   4,00

← 1ST LINE INDENT 1,00 PICA

TEXT 12pt TIMES
14pt INTERLINE SPACING

½ PAGE FORMAT
5½ × 8½

↓6,00

After

Chapter Six

Design Principles

Getting top-quality books from a desktop publishing system requires special know-how in two areas: design and printing. This chapter discusses the theory of design. The following chapter, Chapter Seven, outlines the steps to take before going to a commercial printer.

This chapter offers comments on the principles of book design *as they apply to desktop publishing*. In some cases, the realities of desktop publishing force changes from traditional methods.

Design Terminology

If you're new to page design and typography, you'll need to learn a few words. You'll encounter this vocabulary over and over again in software manuals and in conversations with graphic designers and commercial printers. This specialized terminology applies to three

Planning the Book

For the example in this chapter, you will use the 5.5 x 8.5 *half-size* format. This size lends itself to text-intensive books with only a few illustrations. It is easy and economical to produce; it is easy to bind (either perfect, sewn or saddle-stitched); it fits nicely in your hand. In the corporate environment, it is especially useful for in-house booklets and software documentation.

The page design taught in this chapter is quiet and understated. White space is used to convey an open feeling and make the page more readable. There are large right and left margins with a generous amount of space separating the chapter title and subheads from the body text. Single horizontal rules separate the header and index title from the rest of the body text.

In this project, you will use several special Ventura long-document features:

- Generating a table of contents
- Generating an index
- Inserting footnotes
- Automatic figure numbering
- Changing chapter and page counters
- Printing crop marks

To learn these multi-chapter techniques, you will work with four chapters in all: one for a table of contents, two main text chapters, and one for an index.

Ventura Prep

If You Have the Publishing Power Disk

■ Load the text file 8DESIGN.TXT from the C:\POWER subdirectory then place it on the underlying page. Using File Type/Rename from the Edit menu, save and rename it as C:\TEMP\8BOOK.TXT.

Since there are no pictures to place in this document, load the proper style sheet.

■ Load the style sheet 8DESIGN.STY from the C:\POWER subdirectory and save it under the name C:\TEMP\8BOOK.STY.

■ Save the chapter as C:\TEMP\8BOOK.CHP.

If You Do Not Have the Publishing Power Disk

■ In your word processor, rename any two existing text files as 8BOOK.TXT and 8PRINT.TXT. Copy them to the C:\TEMP subdirectory. Choose files of more than five pages if possible.

■ Load the &BOOK-P1.STY style sheet from the C:\TYPESET subdirectory and save it as C:\TEMP\8BOOK.STY.

■ Format the style sheet to match the next illustration.

■ Select Save As from the File menu to save the chapter under the name and location C:\TEMP\8BOOK.CHP.

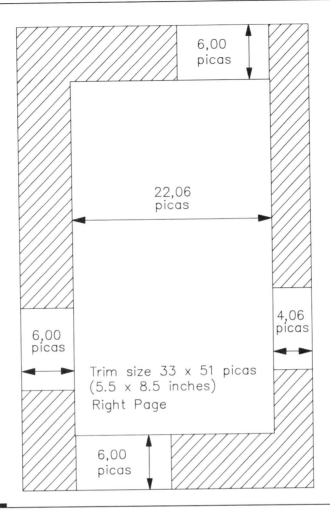

6,00
picas

22,06
picas

4,06
picas

6,00
picas

Trim size 33 x 51 picas
(5.5 x 8.5 inches)
Right Page

6,00
picas

Text

In this section, you will learn a variety of powerful text functions. You will create footnotes and learn to enter index references. If you do not expect to use either of these two features, you may skip ahead to the style section.

The sample text file for this chapter (8BOOK.TXT) has already been pretagged and precoded (with the exception of tag definitions that are intentionally omitted for instructional purposes).

Insert a Footnote

Before inserting footnotes in Ventura, you must first set the format using Footnote Settings from the Page menu. Once you have the format set, creating a footnote is a two-step process: (1) insert the reference into the text file and (2) type in the footnote text at the bottom of the page.

Set the Footnote Format

Confirm that the text file 8BOOK.TXT has been loaded and placed on the underlying page. Then set the footnote format. Your first task is to design how the footnotes will appear on the page. You only have to do this once for the entire document.

- Footnote Settings   Usage & Format: # From Start of Page (User Defined)
Position of Number: Superscript

Now create a separator line to visually separate the footnote from the main body text.

- Make the Separator Line Width 12,00 picas, the Space Above Line: 01,01 picas. Switch from picas & points to fractional points and make the Height of Line: 00.24 points.

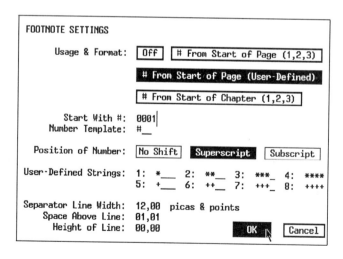

→ NOTE: Be careful to make the height of the line 00.24 fractional points, not picas. If you switch back to picas & points, the height will show as 00,00 picas. Do not be concerned. Your *measurements have not disappeared. They are simply too small to show up in picas & points mode.*

The separator line is measured from the left edge of the page, not from the margin. The portion of the line in the margin does not print. The left margin is 6,00 picas, and the separator line is 12,00 picas. The portion of the separator line in the margin (the first 6,00 picas) will not print. The portion on the line area (the second 6,00 picas) will print.

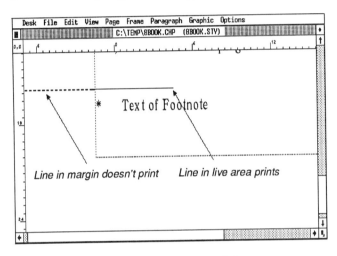

The separator line is not yet visible on your screen. It will appear after you insert the footnote reference in the following step.

Insert the Footnote Reference

After setting the format, you're ready to insert footnote references in the text file.

■ Go to page seven and change to normal view.

■ Enable text editing mode.

■ Place your cursor after the period at the end of the sentence as shown in the following illustration.

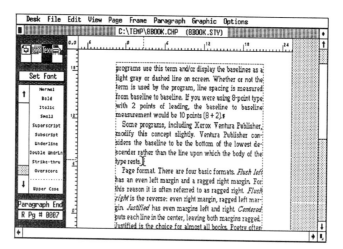

➡ *NOTE: Do not be concerned if there are minor discrepancies between the text on your screen and the text shown here.*

■ Select Insert Footnote from the Edit menu.

A small degree symbol marker (°) shows the location of the footnote reference in the text. Ventura also displays the separator line, the footnote symbol (the asterisk), and the words "Text of the Footnote" at the bottom of the page.

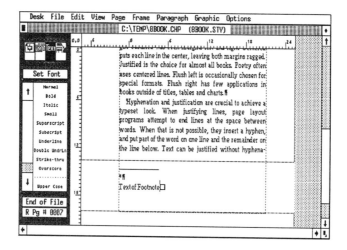

➡ *NOTE: If the degree marker (°) does not appear, select Show Tabs & Returns from the Options menu.*

Add Footnote Text

After you insert the footnote reference into the text, replace the words "Text of the Footnote" at the bottom of the page with the sample footnote text below.

■ With the text cursor, delete the words "Text of Footnote." Then type:

```
For more information on this program, see In-
side Xerox Ventura Publisher by James Cavuoto
and   Jesse   Berst   (MicroPublishing   and   New
Riders, Westlake Village, CA, 1987)
```

When you are finished the footnote should look like this:

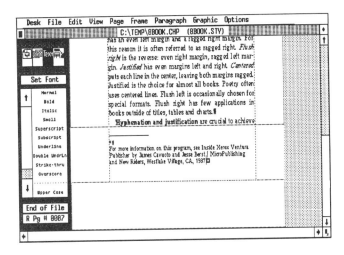

The footnote text is a generated tag named Z_FNOT ENTRY. For now, do not be concerned with its appearance. When you get to the Style section of the chapter, you will change the tag.

➡ *NOTE: Like headers and footers, footnotes occupy their own frames. You can raise or lower the footnote on the page by changing the inside margins of this frame. You cannot resize the frame.*

To delete a footnote and its reference delete the footnote symbol (°). When the footnote symbol and its corresponding footnote text are deleted, Ventura automatically renumbers the other footnotes in the chapter.

Indexing with Ventura

Indexing is a difficult concept to teach and to learn. The best way to master the process is simply to go through it a time or two. It is a three-step process: (1) insert index references into the text file; (2) generate the index file; (3) format the generated index file. For the moment, you will insert sample index entries into the text file. Later, in the Chapter section, you will generate the index and format it.

Before you insert your first index reference, take a moment to review the different levels of an index as shown in the following illustration.

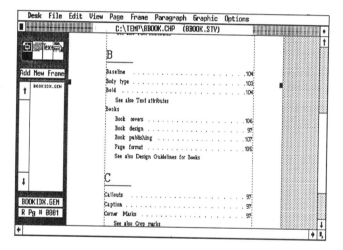

In the figure above, each major index section is preceded by a letter heading — A, B, C , and so forth. The first entry below the letter is the Primary Entry (for example, Books in the illustration above). The indented words are Secondary Entries (for example, Book covers, Book design, and Book publishing). See and See Also references can also be secondary entries. For instance, "See Also Design Guidelines for Books" is a secondary entry in the illustration above. Instead of listing a page number, the See and See Also references direct the reader to another entry in the index.

Insert an Index Entry

To learn how to insert references, you will place a Primary Entry and a See Also Entry. The Primary Entry will appear on two pages. Ventura will list both page numbers when it generates the index as shown below.

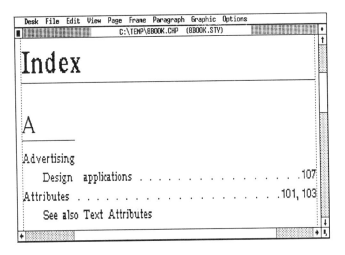

- Go to page five.

- Place the cursor immediately in front of the "A" in the word "Attributes" in the third paragraph. (The word Attribute is underlined in the next illustration to help you place the text cursor on the page.)

- Select Insert/Edit Index Entry from the Edit menu.

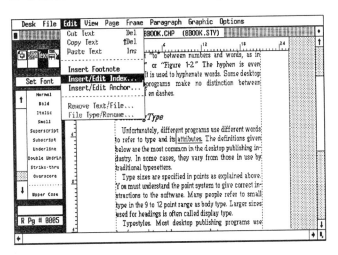

■ Select Type of Entry: Index. Place the text cursor on the Primary Entry line and type: **Attributes**

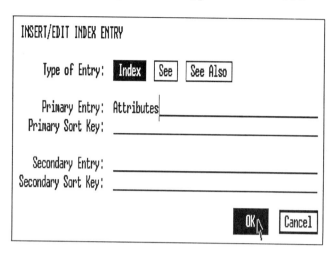

Now add the identical entry on another page.

■ Go to page six.

■ Place the text cursor in front of the "a" in the word "attributes" in the third paragraph.

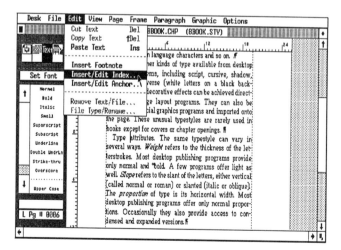

■ Select Insert/Edit Index Entry.

■ Select Type of Entry: Index. Place the text cursor on the Primary Entry line and type: **Attributes**

➡ *TIP: When you insert multiple entries be careful to use identical spellings.*

For instance, if you were to enter the word Attributes as one Primary Entry and the word Attribute as the other Primary entry, Ventura would create two different entries in the index instead of one entry with multiple page numbers.

Add a See Also Entry

Ventura permits you to go back to a reference to make changes or additions. Let's return to the previous index reference and add a secondary entry.

■ Go to page five.

■ Place the cursor immediately in front of the degree symbol (°) that precedes the word "attributes."

■ Move the cursor back and forth with the arrow keys until the words "Index Entry" appear in the current Selection box.

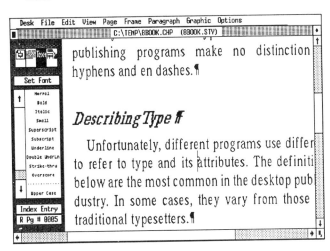

■ Select Insert/Edit Index Entry. Select Type of Entry: See Also. Place the cursor next to Secondary and type: **Text Attributes**

```
┌─────────────────────────────────────────────────┐
│  INSERT/EDIT INDEX ENTRY                          │
│                                                   │
│      Type of Entry:  [Index]  [See]  [See Also]   │
│                                                   │
│     Primary Entry:  Attributes|                   │
│  Primary Sort Key:  _____      │
│                                                   │
│   Secondary Entry:  Text Attributes_____       │
│ Secondary Sort Key: _____      │
│                                                   │
│                              [ OK ]  [Cancel]     │
│                                                   │
└─────────────────────────────────────────────────┘
```

Because of space limitations, we will not ask you to insert additional index entries. Instead, we have done this for you in the files you loaded from the Power disk. We have inserted additional entries into the text file so you will have enough entries to generate a sample index later. If you look closely, you will see the degree symbols marking these entries on the screen.

Stopping Point

You've learned two of Ventura's most complex features, footnoting and indexing. This is a good place to save your work and take a break. When you're ready to continue, return to the style section.

Style

If you are returning to this project after shutting down your computer, open the chapter C:\TEMP\8BOOK.CHP to resume where you left off. In this next section, you will learn about page and chapter counters, and widows and orphans.

Verify the Page Layout

Verify the settings for Page Layout and Margins & Columns.

■ Page   Orientation: Portrait
Page Type: Half
Sides: Double
Start On: Right
Kerning: Globally On

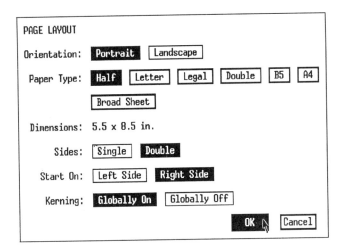

■ Margins &   # of Columns: 1
    Columns   Settings For: Right Page
Margins: Top, Bottom and Left: 06,00 picas
Right: 04,06 picas

➡ *NOTE: The above settings are for the right page. The left and right margins are reversed for the left page.*

Build the Header

- Select Headers & Footers from the Page menu.

- Choose Define: Right Page Header, Usage On. Type: **Design Principles** on the Left line and **[P#]** on the Right line.

- Choose Define: Left Page Header, Usage On. Type: **[P#]** on the Left line and **Chapter [C#]** on the Right line.

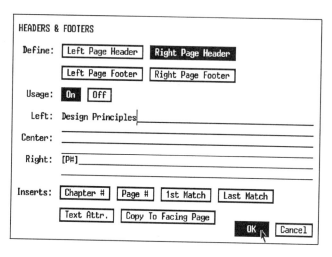

- Turn off the header on the first page.

Reset the Chapter Counter

In the header you just made, the chapter number is displayed as part of the header text. For each consecutive book chapter you must update the Chapter Counter so this number is correct. If you do not update the counter, the header will read "Chapter 1" for every chapter. The Chapter Counter controls both the number and the numbering style.

■ Select Chapter Counter from the Page menu.

■ Choose Restart Counting: Yes, With Number: 0006. Choose the Number Format: 1,2.

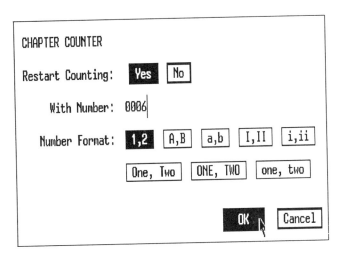

You have restarted the chapter counter at six. The header will now read "Chapter 6." If you had chosen, for example, the One, Two button, it would read "Chapter Six". If you had chosen I, II, it would read Chapter VI.

Change the Page Counter

The Page Counter function is similar to the chapter counter. It allows you to maintain consecutive page numbering from one chapter to the next. In the example below, assume that the previous five chapters of this book have taken 96 pages. You will, therefore, reset the starting page number of Chapter Six to 97.

■ Go to the first page of the document.

■ Select Page Counter from the Page menu.

■ Choose Restart Counting: Yes, With Number: 0097.Choose the Number Format 1,2.

■ Press Page Down to go to page 2.

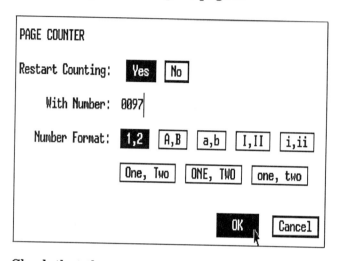

Check that the number in the header is 98.

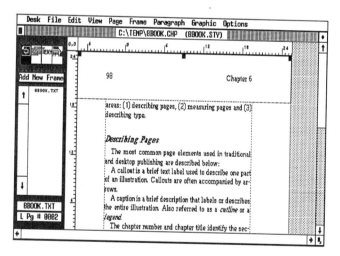

➡ *NOTE: The page numbers you see at the bottom of the Sidebar are not affected by the Page Counter dialog box. The new page numbers appear only when you print the chapter.*

Widows and Orphans

A widow is a single line of text at the top of the page. An orphan is a single line at the bottom. The Widows & Orphans dialog box determines the minimum number of lines Ventura can leave at the top or bottom of a page or column. For this book chapter, set the widow control to two and the orphan control to one.

■ Select Widows & Orphans from the Page menu. Choose At Top (Widow): 2 and At Bottom (Orphan): 1.

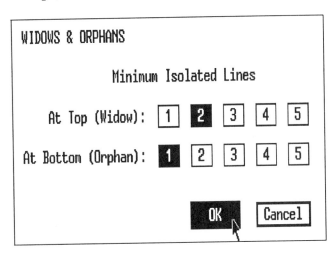

Tag the First Paragraph

Now that you've completed the overall page format, fine tune the appearance of the document by changing two tags.

Change the starting text of the chapter by making a big first character. Earlier in this book (in Chapter Six), you learned to make a big first character rise above the first line. This time, you will create a big first character that drops below the baseline. This effect is often called a Drop Cap.

■ Go to page one.

■ Enable paragraph tagging mode.

■ Select the first paragraph of the chapter, which was pretagged as Body First.

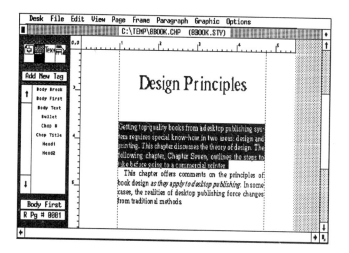

- **Special Effect**   Big First Char
                       Space for Big First: Normal

Selecting normal lets Ventura choose the number of lines the character will take up based on the point size of the big first character. You will set that point size next.

- Without leaving the Special Effects dialog box, choose Set Font. When the Font dialog box appears, choose Style: Bold and Size: 30.00 points.

Before you exit the Font dialog box, use the Shift option to shift the first big character down a few points. This adjustment will ensure that the first big character lines up properly with the first line of the paragraph.

- Select Shift: Down. Enter 01.00 point.

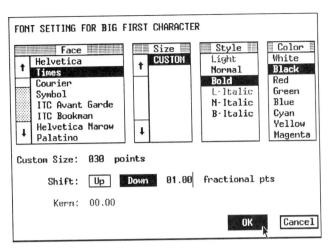

Click OK to return to the Special Effects dialog box. Click OK again to return to the workspace.

Change the Footnote Tag

Once you change the attributes of the footnote tag, you will be ready to move on to the Pictures Section.

■ Go to page seven and select the footnote text.

■ Font   Face: Times
                 Style: N-Italics
                 Size: 10.00 points

■ Alignment: Left
                 Overall Width: Column-Wide.

■ Spacing   Inter-Line: 10.00 points
                 Add in Above: Always
                 In From Left: 01,06 picas

For now, these are the only two tags you need to change. Later, you will apply tags to the generated table of contents and index files.

Pictures

Since you will not be placing any pictures in this sample project, proceed directly to the Chapter section.

Chapter

So far you have formatted the text and inserted index entries. You are now ready to advance to the Chapter section, where you will generate a table of contents (TOC) and an index. To do either function, you must first make a publication. The publication would normally include all the chapters in the book. For this example, you will include Chapter Six, which you completed above, and Chapter Seven, a fully-formatted sample chapter from the Publishing Power disk (or typed in from the Appendix).

Preparing for the Publication

Before you generate a TOC or index, you must reset the page and chapter counters for every chapter in the publication. If you were to omit this step, the page numbers in the TOC and index would be incorrect.

Renumber Chapter Seven

Go to the end of the sample Chapter Six (8BOOK.CHP) to find the last page number in the chapter.

➡ *TIP: When renumbering chapters, use the number in the header or footer, not the number in the sidebar.*

■ Press the End key to go to the last page in the chapter.

Note that the page number is 107 and the page is right-handed. Traditionally, book chapters start on a right-hand page. Therefore, to maintain this format, insert a blank left page at the end of the chapter.

■ Insert/Remove   Insert Page After Current Page
    Page

Now, the last page is 108. Count the new empty page as the last page in the chapter. Chapter Seven will start on the right-hand page number 109.

Save the chapter.

■ Press Ctrl-S.

Open Chapter Seven

Now change the starting page number of Chapter Seven.

■ Select Open Chapter from the File menu and open the C:\POWER\8PRINT.CHP chapter.

■ Save the chapter as C:\TEMP\8PRINT.CHP.

Reset the Chapter Counter.

■ Select Chapter Counter from the Page menu.

■ Select Restart counting: Yes, With Number: 0007. Keep the Number Format: 1,2.

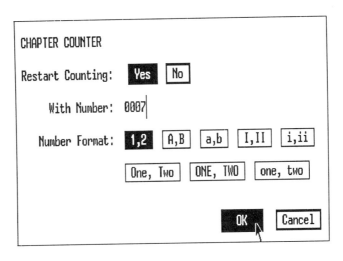

Reset the Page Counter.

■ Select Page Counter from the Page menu.

■ Select Restart counting: Yes, With Number: 0109. Keep the Number Format: 1,2.

The header changes to reflect the new page and chapter numbers.

Once you renumber the chapter, save Chapter Seven, then continue on to make the publication.

■ Press Ctrl-S.

Create a Publication

To create the publication use the Multi-Chapter dialog box in the Options menu.

➡*NOTE: You can create a publication from within any chapter. You do not need to select Multi-Chapter from the first chapter in the publication.*

■ Select Multi-Chapter from the Options menu.

The current chapter name, C:\TEMP\8PRINT.CHP appears in the Multi-Chapter dialog box.

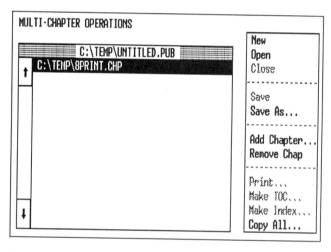

Now add the second chapter to the list.

■ Select Add Chapter.

■ Select the chapter, 8BOOK.CHP, from the C:\TEMP sub-directory.

The chapter name 8BOOK.CHP is listed in the dialog box below 8PRINT.CHP.

Rearrange the Chapter List

Before saving the publication, rearrange the chapters in the list so that 8BOOK.CHP (chapter six) comes before 8PRINT.CHP (chapter seven).

■ Press and hold the mouse button over 8BOOK.CHP. When

the hand cursor appears, drag the file to the top of the list, then release the button.

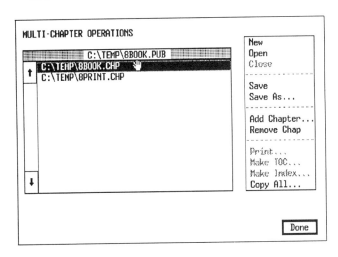

Save the list of chapters as a publication.

■ Select Save As from the dialog box.

■ Use the Backup button to locate the C:\TEMP subdirectory. Then type in the publication name: 8BOOK.PUB.

Generate Table of Contents

After you make the the publication, you are ready to generate the TOC. A table of contents provides an outline of a book's major topics and sub-topics, along with their page numbers. Ventura generates a TOC in two steps. First it searches the publication for the tag names you specify. Then it generates a text file that shows each instance of those tags and the page on which they appear.

The generated TOC text file can be loaded and formatted like any other text file. Ventura assigns each level of the TOC a generated tag. For example, Level One is tagged as Z_TOC Lvl 1, level two is Z_TOC Lvl 2, etc. As with other generated tags, you can change the attributes of the tags to achieve the desired effect.

■ While still in the Multi-Chapter dialog box, select Make TOC.

➡️*TIP: You cannot select the Make TOC option if a chapter is highlighted.*

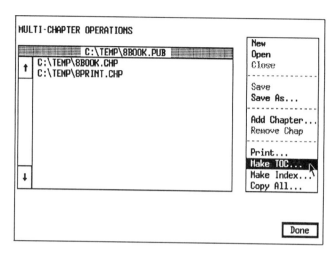

The Generate Table of Contents dialog box appears. Notice that the name of the current publication is displayed next to TOC File except that the last three letters have been changed to TOC and the file extension to GEN. This is the default name that Ventura assigns to a generated TOC file.

```
GENERATE TABLE OF CONTENTS

    TOC File:  C:\TEMP\8BOOKTOC.GEN
Title String:  Table of Contents
    Level 1:  _____
    Level 2:  _____
    Level 3:  _____
    Level 4:  _____
    Level 5:  _____
    Level 6:  _____
    Level 7:  _____
    Level 8:  _____
    Level 9:  _____
    Level 10: _____

    Inserts:  [ Tag Text ]  [ Tab ]  [ Chapter # ]  [ Page # ]

              [ Text Attr. ]
                                        [ OK ]  [ Cancel ]
```

➡️*NOTE: You can change the name of this file, but we recommend that you do not change the three letter extension GEN.*

You will not change the Title String that tells Ventura to display the words "Table of Contents" at the top of the page. You will, however, make additions to the other levels of the TOC.

■ Place the text cursor next to Level 1: and select the Text Attr. button at the bottom of the dialog box.

The bracket code <D> appears on the line.

■ Delete the D and replace it with the letter B.

The bracket code <B> turns on the Bold text attribute.

■ Move the cursor past the right bracket and choose [C#].

[C#] tells Ventura to display the number of the chapter.

■ Choose the Tab button from the bottom of the dialog box.

The Tab symbol appears on the line. The Tab separates the chapter # from the next tag name.

■ Select Tag Text. The code [*tag name] appears on the line. Delete the words "tag name." Type in: `Chap title`.

[*Chap title] tells Ventura to scan for all occurrences of the tag Chap title and list them as level 1 in the TOC.

■ Move the cursor past the right bracket and select the Tab button.

The Tab separates the entry from the page number that follows. Later in this chapter you will use this tab setting to add leader dots between the entries and the page numbers.

■ Choose the [Page #] button.

[P#] tells Ventura to display the page number on which it found this occurrence of the tag.

■ Choose the Text Attr. button.

The bracket code <D> appears on the line. <D> turns off the Bold text attribute.

When the TOC is generated and formatted the first level will look something like this:

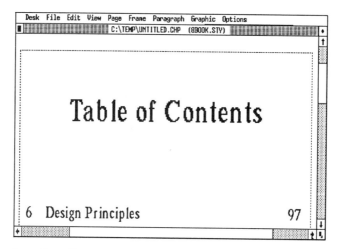

Insert the Codes for Second and Third Levels

Place the text cursor on the Level 2 line and type in the codes shown below. Use the buttons as shortcuts.

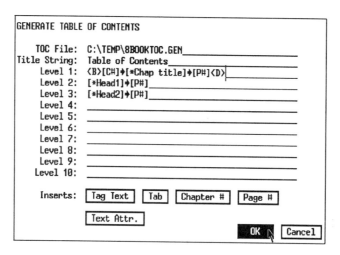

■ Generate the TOC by clicking the OK button.

Ventura displays a message that it is generating the TOC text file and shows which chapter files it is scanning. When the TOC is finished, you return to the Multi-Chapter dialog box. Later you will format this file. For the moment, continue on in the Multi-Chapter dialog box.

Generate an Index

Do you remember the index entries you inserted into the text file? Ventura will generate its index based on those references (plus some extras we inserted for you in advance). Once the index is complete, you will load and format both the index and the TOC generated files.

■ With the Multi-Chapter dialog box still open, select Make Index from the Multi-Chapter sidebar.

The Generate Index dialog box appears on the screen. On the Index File line Ventura displays the current publication name with the last three letters changed to IDX and the extension changed to GEN. Do not change this file name.

Leave the Title String as "Index" which tells Ventura to display the word "Index" as the title.

■ Select Letter Headings: On.

Selecting Letter Headings On tells Ventura to place an A before the entries starting with A, a B before the B index entries, and so forth.

■ Move the cursor to the For Each # Line and delete both occurrences of the [C#] code. This tells Ventura to display only the page numbers in the completed index, not the chapter numbers.

■ Choose OK to generate the index.

```
GENERATE INDEX

    Index File:  C:\TEMP\8BOOKIDX.GEN_____

   Title String:  Index_____

 Letter Headings:  [On]  [Off]

       Before #s:  _____
      For Each #:  [P#] - [P#]_____
     Between #s:  ,_____
        After #s:  _____
        "See ":  See _____
    "See Also":  See also _____

        Inserts:  [Tab]  [Chapter #]  [Page #]  [Text Attr.]

                                        [OK]  [Cancel]
```

During generation, Ventura locates the index references, and builds them into a sorted list with corresponding page numbers. After each entry Ventura inserts a line break and a horizontal tab character. After the last entry of a letter heading, Ventura inserts a paragraph return.

The index contains three generated tags: Z_Index Title, X_Index LTR, and Z_INDEX Main. Later in this chapter you will change the attributes of these generated tags.

After generating the index, Ventura returns you to the Multi-Chapter dialog box.

■ Choose Done to exit the Multi-Chapter dialog box.

■ Choose Save to save the changes you made to the publication.

Formatting the TOC and the Index

This is a good place to pause and remind ourselves where we've been and where we are headed. At this point, you have used Ventura to generate "raw" text files. By searching the chapter, Ventura was able to find and insert the page numbers where each entry can be found.

With that work out of the way, you can load and format the TOC and the Index text files. You will create them as two separate chapters using the same style sheet (8BOOK.STY). Begin with the TOC.

➡*NOTE: If you are in a hurry, you can skip over this formatting section, since it does not introduce any new skills. However, we suggest you read over it, if you plan to do TOCs and indices of your own. For instance, because of the way Ventura outputs the index file, you must use Tab Settings to create the proper indents.*

Start a New Chapter

Since you are using the same style sheet, you can simply "empty out" the workspace by choosing New from the File menu.

■ Select New from the File menu.

The screen is emptied of text and graphics, but Ventura retains the current 8BOOK.STY style sheet.

■ Enable frame mode and select the underlying page.

■ Select Load Text/Picture from the File menu. Select Type of File: Text, Text Format: Generated # of Files: One.

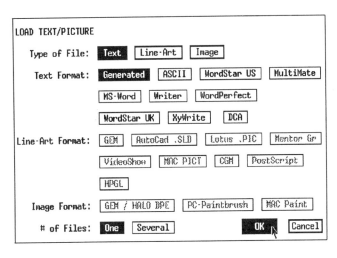

WARNING: Be sure to select Text Format: Generated rather than ASCII.

■ Load the text file 8BOOKTOC.GEN from the C:\TEMP subdirectory and place it on the page.

■ Select Save As to save the chapter location as C:\TEMP\BOOKTOC.CHP.

Change the Z_TOC Title Tag

Change the text attributes of the generated tags in the TOC. Start with the title.

■ Enable paragraph tagging mode.

■ Select the paragraph "Table of Contents" (Notice the tag name Z_TOC TITLE in the Current Selection Box).

■ Font   Style: Bold
                  Size: 024 points

■ Alignment   Center
                   Overall Width: Column-Wide
                   In/Outdent Width: 00,00 picas

■ Spacing   Above: 30.00 points
                   Below: 60.00 points

                   Inter-Line: 24.00 points
                   Add in Above: Always

■ Breaks   Page Break: Before/Until Right

Selecting Before/Until Right forces the TOC to start on a right-hand page, the traditional placement in books.

Change the Z_TOC Lvl 1 Tag

■ Select the paragraph "6 Design Principles 97."

■ Font   Size: 012. points

■ Alignment   Left
                   Overall Width: Column-Wide
                   In/Outdent Width: 00,06 picas

■ Spacing   Above: 30.00 points
                   Below: 08.00 points
                   Inter-Line: 12.00 points
                   Add in Above: When Not at Column Top

You will now use tab settings to position the text across the page.

■ Tab Settings   Tab Number: 1
                   Tab Type: Left
                   Tab Display: Shown as Open Space
                   Tab Location: 02,00 picas

                   Tab Number: 2
                   Tab Type: Right
                   Tab Display: Shown as Open Space
                   Tab location: 21,09 picas

Change Z_TOC Lvl 2 Tag

■ Select the paragraph "Design Terminology 97."

■ Alignment   Left
                   Overall Width: Column-Wide
                   In/Outdent Width: 02,00 picas

■ Spacing   Inter-Line: 14.00 points
                   Add in Above: When Not at Column Top

■ Tab Settings   Tab Number: 1
                   Tab Type: Right
                   Tab Display: Shown as Leader Character
                   Tab Location: 21,09 picas
                   Leader Char: (...)
                   Leader Spacing: 3

Change Z_TOC Lvl 3 Tag

■ Select the paragraph "Describing Pages 98."

■ Alignment   Left
                   Overall Width: Column-Wide
                   First Line: Indent
                   In/Outdent Width: 04,00 picas

■ Spacing   Inter-Line: 14.00 points
                   Add in Above: When Not At Column Top

■ Tab Settings   Tab Number: 1
                   Tab Type: Right
                   Tab Display: Shown as leader
                   CharacterTab Location: 21,09Leader
                   Char: (...)
                   Leader Spacing: 3

Apply the Tags

When you are finished the table of contents should look like this:

Table of Contents

Congratulations on completing your first table of contents. Now save your work.

- Press Ctrl-S

- Create a New chapter for the index. Remove the BOOK-TOC.GEN file from the list of files with Rename Text/File from the Edit menu. Load the generated file 8BOOKIDX.GEN from the C:\TEMP subdirectory and place it on the underlying page. Save the chapter as C:\TEMP\BOOKIDX.CHP. With the text file loaded, you're ready to change the tags.

Change the Z_Index Title Tag

- Enable paragraph tagging mode. Select the title "Index" at the top of the page.

- Font   Style: Bold
                 Size: 024 points

- Alignment   Left
                 Overall Width: Column-Wide

■ Spacing

Above: 30.00 points
Below: 24.00 points

Inter-Line: 24.00 points
Add in Above: Always

■ Ruling Line
  Below

Width: Column
Color: Black
Pattern: Solid
Space Above Rule 1: 02.00 points
Height of Rule 1: 00.24 points

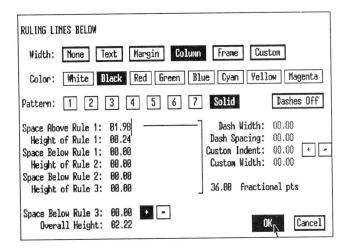

Change the Z_Index Ltr Tag

■ Select the letter "A" at the top of the page.

■ Font

Style: Bold
Size: 018 points

■ Alignment

Left
Overall Width: Column-Wide

In/Outdent Width: 00,00 picas

■ Spacing:

Above: 14.00 points
Below: 14.00 points

Inter-Line: 14.00 points
Add in Above: When Not at Column Top

■ Breaks

Keep With Next: Yes

The Keep With Next option makes sure the letter heading is not isolated from the index entries that follow it.

■ Ruling Line Below

Width: Custom
Space Above Rule 1: 02.00 points
Height of rule 1: 00.24 points
Custom Width: 48.00 points

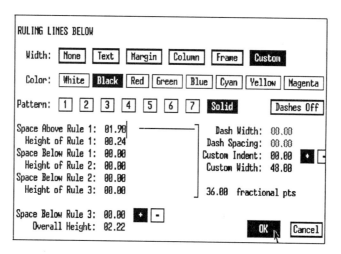

```
RULING LINES BELOW

Width:   [None]  [Text]  [Margin]  [Column]  [Frame]  [Custom]

Color:   [White] [Black] [Red] [Green] [Blue] [Cyan] [Yellow] [Magenta]

Pattern: [1] [2] [3] [4] [5] [6] [7] [Solid]         [Dashes Off]

Space Above Rule 1: 01.98  ⌐─────────⌐  Dash Width:    00.00
 Height of Rule 1: 00.24              │  Dash Spacing:  00.00
Space Below Rule 1: 00.00            │  Custom Indent:  00.00  [+] [-]
 Height of Rule 2: 00.00             │  Custom Width:   48.00
Space Below Rule 2: 00.00            │
 Height of Rule 3: 00.00             ⌐  36.00  fractional pts

Space Below Rule 3: 00.00  [+] [-]
 Overall Height: 02.22                          [OK]  [Cancel]
```

Change the Z_INDEX Main Tag

The rest of text in the index file is the Z_INDEX Main tag. The Primary and Secondary index entries are positioned with horizontal tab characters.

■ Select the first index entry.

■ Font

Size: 10.00 points

■ Alignment

Left
Overall Width: Column-Wide
In/Outdent Width: 00,00 picas

■ Spacing

Inter-Line: 14.00 points
Add in Above: When Not at Column Top

■ Tab Settings

Tab Number: 1
Tab Type: Left
Tab Display: Shown as Open Space
Tab Location: 00,00

Tab Number: 2
Tab Type: Left
Tab Display: Shows as Open Space
Tab Location: 01,06 picas

Tab Number: 3
Tab Type: Right
Tab Display: Shown as Leader Character
Tab Location: 22,06 picas
Leader Char: (...)
Leader Spacing: 3

The screen should look like this:

When you have completed the changes to the index tags, save the chapter.

■ Press ^S.

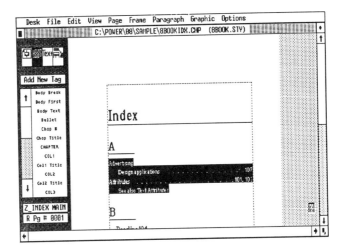

Print the Publication

Now that you've created the TOC, the index and two sample chapters, you are ready to print them. First, add the TOC and the index to the C:\TEMP\8BOOK.PUB publication.

■ While still in BOOKIDX.CHP, select Multi-Chapter from the Options menu.

■ Open the C:\TEMP\8BOOK.PUB publication if it is not already open. Select Add Chapter and choose 8BOOK-TOC.CHP.

■ Select Add Chapter and choose 8BOOKIDX.CHP.

Move the TOC chapter to the top of the list.

■ Drag C:\TEMP\8BOOKTOC.CHP to the top of the publication list.

■ Select Save to save the publication.

When Ventura asks you if you want to overwrite the existing publication, select Yes.

Print Crop Marks

Now print out all the chapters listed in the publication. This time you will tell Ventura to print crop marks. Ventura is able to print crop marks as long as they reside within the live area of the printer (the area of the page on which the printer can actually produce marks). Almost all laser printers can show crop marks that fall inside a 7 x 10 area.

➥ *TIP: To find out the exact live area of your printer, print out the sample chapter CAPABILI.CHP in the C:\TYPESET subdirectory.*

■ Print   Which Pages: All
                    Crop Marks: On

Ventura prints out each chapter of the publication in order.

➡ *NOTE: This project contains more than 30 pages. It will take longer to print than others, shorter sample chapters in this book.*

Tips

Book Tips

❏ The last thing you must do before generating an index and TOC, is to check the last page of each chapter in order and jot down the last page number. Then open the next chapter and use Page Counter from the Page menu to restart the numbering in correct sequence.

❏ If you want each chapter to start on a right-hand page (as is traditional), check that the preceding chapter ends on a left-hand page. If not, insert a blank left-hand page at the end of the preceding chapter.

❏ Changing page numbers with Page Counter does not affect the page numbers shown at the bottom of the sidebar.

❏ Some publishers use a single style sheet for the whole book. Others create a separate style sheet for each section. Because Version 1.1 of Ventura does not automatically number sequentially across chapters, it may be tempting to put the entire book in one large chapter file. In practice, very large chapters can lead to crashes or other problems, especially, if there are many pictures involved.

❏ Putting the entire book into one chapter file also makes it difficult to work in groups. When one person is busy with the one and only file, no one else can work on it. For easier access and manageability, most books should have separate Ventura chapters for every book chapter.

Footnote and Index Tips

❏ The footnote separator line is measured from the left edge of the page, not from the margin. Only the portion *inside* the margin actually prints. Suppose, for example, that you have a five-pica margin. If you wanted a three-pica separator

line, you would enter a Separator Line Width of eight picas
(5 + 3 = 8). Only the three-pica portion that is inside the
margin would print.

❑ If you cannot see the degree symbol which marks footnotes,
anchors and index entries, choose Show Tabs & Returns
from the Options menu.

❑ Footnotes occupy a special frame created by Ventura. You
can change the margins inside this frame, but you cannot
change the size of the frame.

❑ You can insert footnotes, anchors and index entries directly
into word processing files using the following bracket codes:
Footnote: <$Ftext>
Anchor (same page): <$&anchor name>
Anchor (below): <&anchor name>[^]
Anchor (above): <&anchor name[^]>
<$Iprimary; secondary>

❑ Indexes and tables of contents are created with Multi-
Chapter from the Options menu.

Chapter Nine
Skills Checklist

Theory

✔ Merging CAD with Desktop Publishing

Text

✔ Preparing text files for tables (vertical tabs)

Style

✔ How to format numbered lists

✔ How to use spacing and breaks to create multiple columns

✔ A special note tag with ruling box around

✔ Adding space with a tag

Pictures

✔ Attaching callouts to illustrations

✔ Anchoring frames to text references

Chapter

✔ Why and how to print to disk

A Technical Manual

Modern industry has produced a new generation of publishers, writers and designers, dedicated to creating "user-friendly" technical manuals. These manuals are instrumental in selling and maintaining high-tech equipment, from microwaves to machinery to personal computers. In this chapter, you will learn some special techniques for producing technical documentation with Ventura. The checklist on the left gives you an overview of the skills you will learn.

Theory

Technical documentation is one of the most complex, demanding applications for Ventura. Consequently, this chapter is a bit longer than some others. It may also require more than one attempt to create some of the effects. If you can stick with it, however, you will be rewarded with hands-on knowledge of some of Ventura's most powerful capabilities. Before starting with the project, let's take a moment to examine how Ventura deals with technical illustrations.

Technical Illustrations

Skip this section if you do not use illustrations from line-art programs, such as AutoCAD.

As a general rule, line-art is used for technical drawings and illustrations because of its higher quality (see Chapter Five for more details on the difference between line-art and images). AutoCAD is one of the most popular line-art programs. AutoCAD drawings can be imported into Ventura in three different formats (SLD, GEM and HPGL), two of which produce line-art.

AutoCAD Slide Files (SLD) are image files (bit-mapped graphics) produced by taking a "snap shot" of an AutoCAD screen. Their quality is only as good as the resolution of the screen. Consider using slide files if you have access to a monitor with at least a 1,024 x 960 resolution, or if you do not require high-quality images. Otherwise, you'll get better results from line-art.

You can import AutoCAD line drawings in two ways: in GEM format (via Ventura's DXFTOGEM utility) or in HPGL format (Hewlett Packard Graphics Language).

DXFTOGEM Conversion

Ventura's conversion utility takes AutoCAD DXF files (which it cannot read directly) and transforms them into GEM files (which it can use in documents). Before using the DXFTOGEM conversion, you must produce a DXF drawing file in AutoCAD (or any other CAD program that supports the DXF drawing interchange format). After the DXF file is created, use the DOS copy command to copy the file to the C:\VENTURA subdirectory.

Move to the C:\Ventura subdirectory. At the DOS prompt, type:

`DXFTOGEM Filename Filename`

First type the command name, followed by the AutoCAD DXF file name, a space, and the GEM file name, leaving off the three-letter extension. The DXF and the GEM file names can be the same or different. For example, here's the command for converting a DXF file named SAMPLE.DXF to a GEM file named CADTEST.GEM:

`DXFTOGEM SAMPLE CADTEST`

After creating the GEM file, copy it to the subdirectory of your choice.

➥ *TIP: The DXFTOGEM utility is normally located in the C:Ventura subdirectory. If you cannot find it there, load it from the Ventura Utilities disk (#11).*

You may find that certain AutoCAD shapes are lost during the DXFTOGEM conversion. For a complete listing of shapes that are converted, see the Xerox Ventura Publisher Reference Manual.

HPGL Format

HPGL is an alternative to DXF. To create a HPGL file in AutoCAD, first configure your plotter as any Hewlett Packard plotter (e.g. HP 7475). Then plot the drawing to a file instead of to the plotter. The resulting file has an .PLT extension. You can load this file directly into Ventura, by selecting Line-Art Format: HPGL in the Load Text/Picture dialog box. Simply change the .HPG extension to .PLT on the Directory line of the Item Selector before selecting a file.

Before

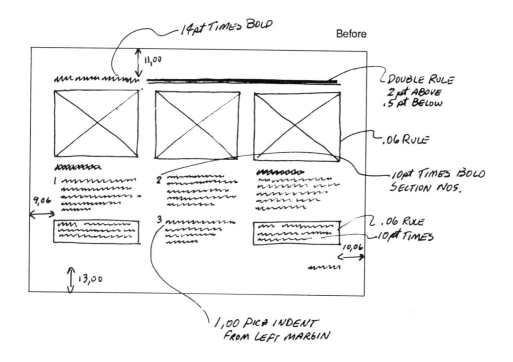

14pt TIMES BOLD

11,00

DOUBLE RULE
2 pt ABOVE
.5 pt BELOW

.06 RULE

10pt TIMES BOLD
SECTION NOS.

.06 RULE
10pt TIMES

10,06

9,06

13,00

1,00 PICA INDENT
FROM LEFT MARGIN

After

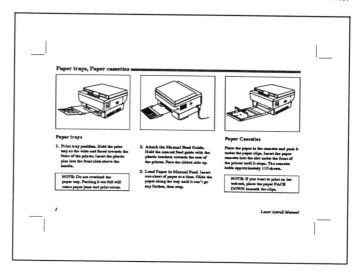

Paper trays, Paper cassettes

Paper trays

1. Print tray position. Hold the print tray so the wide end faced towards the front of the printer. Insert the plastic pins into the front slots above the handle.

   NOTE: Do not overload the paper tray. Packing it too full will cause paper jams and print errors.

2. Attach the Manual Feed Guide. Hold the manual feed guide with the plastic brackets towards the rear of the printer. Face the ribbed side up.

3. Load Paper in Manual Feed. Insert one sheet of paper at a time. Glide the paper along the tray until it can't go any further, then stop.

Paper Cassettes

Place the paper in the cassette and push it under the paper clips. Insert the paper cassette into the slot under the front of the printer until it stops. The cassette holds approximately 110 sheets.

   NOTE: If you want to print on letterhead, place the paper FACE DOWN beneath the clips.

3

Laser AstroZ Manual

Planning the Manual

Whether it deals with a microwave or a microcomputer, the primary responsibility of a technical manual is to teach the user to operate and benefit from the system. It must include the technical specifications. It must also help the user get started, discover features and learn both elementary and advanced operations. Finally, it must help people know what to do when things go wrong.

The manual you will create in this chapter includes instructions for assembling and using a laser printer. Its landscape format provides space for three columns without crowding the text. The three-column format also provides flexibility for varying picture sizes and column combinations. On some pages, the left column is used for the major heading and nothing else. The resulting white space serves to give the page an open, spacious, non-intimidating feeling.

Throughout the manual, lists are identified with bullets, and step-by-step instructions are distinguished with boldface section numbers. The instructional steps are indented from the numbers to make them easy to read and easy to see on the page. The box around the warnings is a device that draws the reader's attention to important material not included within the main body of text.

The manual has two standard sizes for illustrations. Smaller pictures fit three across. Because they are positioned directly above explanatory text, they do not require captions or callouts. The large, standalone illustrations, however, have no explanatory text except a headline and therefore require captions and callouts.

The nearby illustration shows the manual in the planning and final stages. In addition to many of the skills you already have learned, you will use the effects below to create the technical manual:

• Column breaks

• Section numbers

- Tables (vertical tabs)
- Rules around table entries
- Callouts for illustrations

Ventura Prep

If You Have the Publishing Power Disk

■ Load the files 9TABLE.TXT and 9TECHDOC.TXT from the C:\POWER subdirectory. They are in ASCII format. Use File Type/Rename to save them respectively as C:\TEMP\9TBL.TXT and C:\TEMP\9TECH.TXT. Leave the file 9TECH.TXT on the underlying page.

■ Load the style sheet, 9TECHDOC.STY from the C:\POWER subdirectory and save it as C:\TEMP\9TECH.STY.

■ Load the Line-Art format files 9-LASER1.GEM, 9LASER-2.GEM, 9LASER-3.GEM and 9LASER-4.GEM.

■ Save the chapter as C:\TEMP\9TECHDOC.CHP.

If You Do Not Have the Power Disk

■ Use your word processor to type in the text files 9TECH-DOC.TXT and 9TABLE.TXT from Appendix A. Save each file in turn as C:\TEMP\9TECH.TXT and C:\TEMP\9TBL.TXT.

■ Load the &TBL2-L1.STY style sheet from the C:\TYPESET subdirectory. Change the margins and columns to match the illustration below. Then save the revised style sheet as C:\TEMP\9TECH.STY.

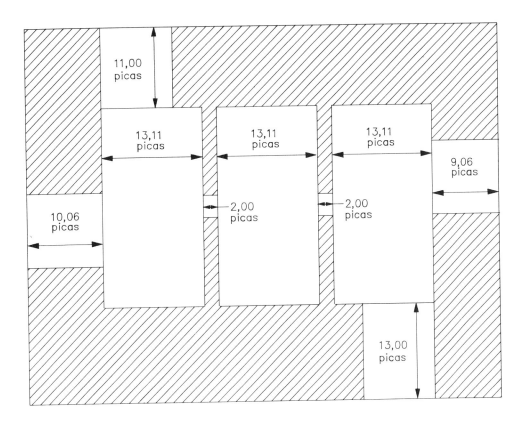

■ Since you do not have access to the AutoCAD drawings included on the Power Disk, load any four pictures to use as substitutes in the picture section of this chapter.

■ Save the chapter as C:\TEMP\9TECHDOC.CHP.

Style

You will learn several powerful new functions in the style section of this chapter. You will start by learning a fast way to draw crop marks. Then you will learn about new tagging effects using column breaks, page breaks and ruling lines. You will continue with an example of auto-numbering, a useful technique for technical documentation.

Add Crop Marks

Crop marks designate the live area of the paper. For this document, you will draw the crop marks at each corner of the underlying page so they appear on every page of the document.

➥ *TIP:It is easier to draw crop marks if you temporarily change the margin settings to equal the trim size. Then you can use the (temporary) column guides to help you position the lines.*

- Enable frame setting mode and select the underlying page. Select Margins & Columns from the Frame menu.

- Choose # of Columns: 1. Make the Top and Bottom margins 09,00 picas, and the Left and Right margins 07,06 picas.

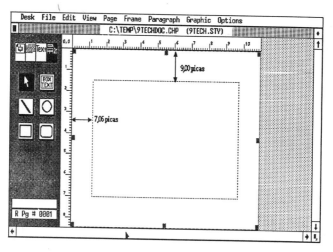

Choose Grid Settings

- With the underlying page selected, enable graphics drawing mode.

By making the grid settings an integer relation to the margins, the lines automatically snap to the margin.

- Grid Settings Grid Snap: On
  Horizontal Spacing: 01,06 picas
  Vertical Spacing: 01,06 picas

- Select the line icon. Starting from the upper left corner of

the column margin draw a upwards line perpendicular to
the column guide.

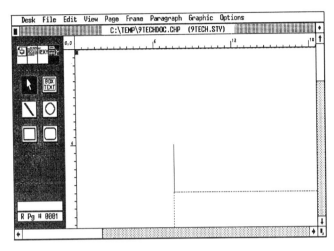

Make sure the line attributes match the following values:

■ Line   Thickness: Thin
  Attributes   End Styles: (Beginning and End) Square
                  Defaults: Save To

➠ *TIP: If you hold down the Shift key after selecting the line
shape, you can continue to draw lines without re-selecting the
line icon.*

■ Select the line icon. Starting the upper left corner of the
  column guide draw a right-to-left line perpendicular to the
  column guide.

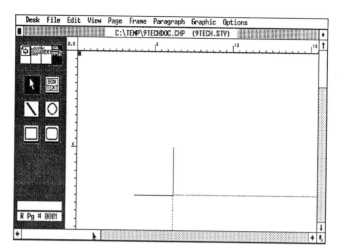

Repeat the steps above to create crop marks on the remaining three corners. When you are finished, reset the margins and columns to their original values. Refer to the following illustration for proper sizes.

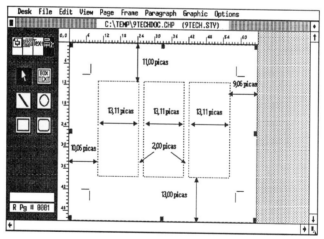

Build the Footer

Complete the overall format by building the footer.

- Select Headers & Footers from the Page menu.

- Choose Right Page Footer, Usage On. Move to the Left line and choose First Match. Delete the words "tag name" and type: **Head1**

- Move to Right line and choose the Page # button.

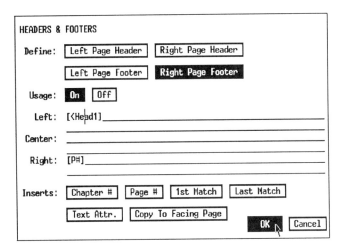

- Choose Left Page Footer, Usage On. Move to the Left line and choose the Page # button.

Move to the Right line and type: **Laser AstroZ Manual**

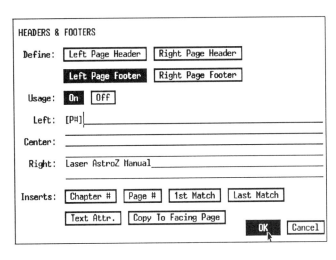

The footer text is automatically formatted as soon as you close the dialog box.

Raise the Footer

To prevent the footer from being cropped off at print time, you must raise it upwards on the page.

■ Enable frame setting mode. Select the footer frame and change its margins.

■ Margins &   Top: 02,00 picas
  Columns

Verify the Body Text Settings

■ Select the paragraph on page one, "Thank you for choosing the Laser AstroZ...."

■ Enable paragraph tagging mode.

■ Font   Face: Times Roman
                     Style: Normal
                     Color: Black
                     Size: 010 points

■ Alignment   Left
                     Overall Width: Column-Wide

■ Spacing   Above: 12.00 points
                     Inter-Line: 12.00 points
                     Add in Above: When Not At Column Top

Use the Body Break Tag

To isolate the title page text from the rest of the document, tag an empty paragraph with the Body Break tag. Since the body break tag (which has already been defined in the style sheet) includes a Page Break After, the following text will be forced to the next page.

■ Enable text editing. Place the text cursor at the end of the paragraph "Guide to Operations — Model XYZ-11" and press Enter.

■ Enable paragraph tagging mode.

■ Select the empty paragraph and tag it as Body Break.

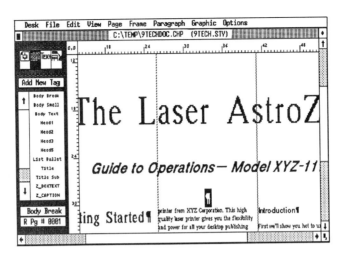

When the title page is complete, go to page two to continue tagging.

■ Press PgDn to go to the second page.

Change the Head1 Tag

To isolate the Head1 tag in the far left column, include a column break before and after. The Column Break Before keeps the text from slipping back to a previous page. The Column Break After forces the following text to start at the top of the next column.

■ Select the paragraph "Getting Started."

■ Select Breaks. Choose Column Break: Before and After.

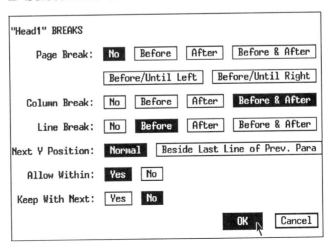

Use the Body Break Tag

Put a page break after the Body Small paragraph at the end of page one.

■ Enable text editing mode. Place the text cursor after the word "CA," and press Enter.

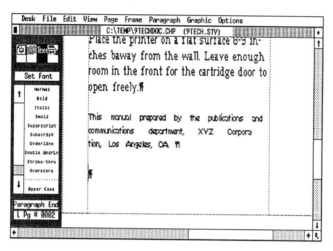

■ Without moving the cursor from its current position, press ^K to bring up the Assign Func. Keys dialog box.

■ Assign the Body Break tag as F1. Press Enter to close the dialog box.

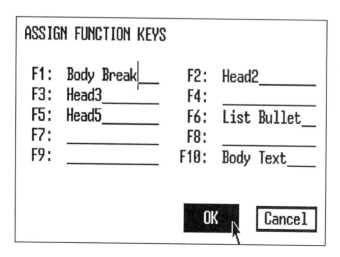

■ Press F1 to cause the paragraph return you just typed to be tagged as Body Break.

The remaining text is pushed to the next page.

➡ *TIP: If you accidentaly hit the wrong function key while tagging, you can usually recover by pressing the correct key immediatly, before you do anything else.*

About Auto-Numbering

For the first two pages of the manual, you formatted the manual using predefined tags from the style sheet. In the next section, you'll create some advanced effects by adding several tags.

Many technical documents include section numbers, outlines, or numbered lists. Ventura's automatic numbering can handle these chores for you. It can create anything from simple lists to multi-level outlines. Rearrange part of the list, and Ventura will renumber it for you — automatically.

Automatic numbering includes two basic steps: First, you choose which tags to number and what style of numbering to use; second, you format the numbers Ventura has generated.

For the first step, use the Auto-Numbering dialog box from the Page menu to choose which tags to number and what style to use. For example, here is an example that would number each instance of a Head1 tag with a roman numeral (I, II, III, IV, etc.)

```
┌──────────────────────────────────────────────────────┐
│ AUTO-NUMBERING                                         │
│                                                        │
│    Usage:  [ On ] [ Off ]                              │
│                                                        │
│  Level 1:  [*Head1,I].|_____        │
│  Level 2:  _____        │
│  Level 3:  _____        │
│  Level 4:  _____        │
│  Level 5:  _____        │
│  Level 6:  _____        │
│  Level 7:  _____        │
│  Level 8:  _____        │
│  Level 9:  _____        │
│ Level 10:  _____        │
│                                                        │
│  Inserts:  [ Chapter # ] [ 1,2 ] [ A,B ] [ a,b ] [ I,II ] [ i,ii ] │
│            [ Suppress Previous Level ] [ Text Attr. ]  │
│                                     [ OK ] [ Cancel ]  │
└──────────────────────────────────────────────────────┘
```

When Ventura creates the numbers, it assigns generated tags at the same time. The name of the tag depends on the level of the numbers. Numbers created at Level 1 are tagged as Z_SEC1. Level 2 numbers are tagged as Z_SEC2, and so on. Once Ventura has generated and tagged the numbers, you can format them as you like.

The theory of auto-numbering will become more clear after you perform the sample project in this chapter.

To create the numbered list of instructions you will add a new tag named List #. The tag is indented from the margin to make room for the section numbers (which you will add below using Ventura's auto-numbering feature).

■ Press PgDn to go to page three.

■ Enable paragraph tagging mode.

■ Use Shift-Click to select the paragraph beginning "Lift the release lever...."

■ Add New Tag   Tag Name to Add: List #

■ Spacing   In From Left: 01,00 pica

Select the other two paragraphs shown below and tag them as List #.

Next, we will show you how to use Ventura's autonumbering to generate the section numbers.

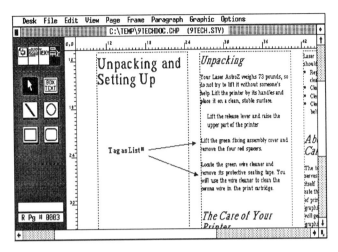

Auto-Numbering

To create a numbered list of instructions, use the auto-numbering dialog box. By placing the List # tag on Level 1, you instruct Ventura to place numbers before each paragraph tagged as List #. After Ventura generates the number, you can format the list to make the numbers and paragraphs reside on the same line.

➡ NOTE: *Although we are teaching a single-level list, you can use these same basic principles to create multi-level numbered lists such as outlines.*

■ Select Auto-Numbering from the Page menu.

■ Choose Usage On. Move to the Level 1 line and choose the Inserts button: 1,2. This button determines the number format for the list.

■ Delete the words "tag name." Type **List #**. Move the cursor past the right bracket and type a period (.). This period will appear after the automatically generated numbers to separate them from the text that follows. Click OK to complete the dialog box.

```
AUTO-NUMBERING

   Usage:  [On]  [Off]

   Level 1:  [*List #,1].|_____
   Level 2:  _____
   Level 3:  _____
   Level 4:  _____
   Level 5:  _____
   Level 6:  _____
   Level 7:  _____
   Level 8:  _____
   Level 9:  _____
   Level 10: _____

   Inserts:  [Chapter #]  [1,2]  [A,B]  [a,b]  [I,II]  [i,ii]

             [Suppress Previous Level]  [Text Attr.]

                                        [OK]  [Cancel]
```

Notice that the numbers (which are tagged as Z_SEC1) and the text paragraphs (tagged as List #) appear on separate lines. To place both number and paragraph text on the same line, change the attributes of the Z_SEC1 tag and the List # tag.

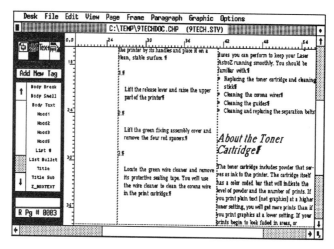

Change the Z_SEC1 Tag

■ Select the number 1 (the Z_SEC1 tag).

■ Font   Style: Bold

■ Spacing   Above: 12.00 points
                     Add in Above: Always.

■ Breaks   Line Break: Before
                    Keep With Next: Yes

Change the List # Tag

■ Select the first List # paragraph, "Lift the release lever and raise the upper part of the printer."

Now change the tag to include a Line Break *After*. This allows the List # and Z_SEC1 tag to reside on the same line.

■ Breaks   Line Break: After

Earlier, you used the Alignment dialog box to create the indent that prevents List # paragraphs from butting up flush against the numbers when they reside on the same line. When you are finished the list should look like this:

Add a Page Break

To complete the page, place a page break after the paragraph that begins "The toner cartridge includes powder..." The text after the page break will move to the next page.

■ Enable text editing mode.

■ Place the text cursor after the last paragraph and press Enter.

■ Press F1 to tag the new paragraph as Body Break.

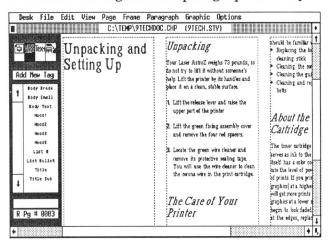

Stopping Point

Let's pause here to summarize where we've been and what lies ahead. You certainly have reason to be pleased with yourself. In the last few pages, you have been working with two of Ventura's most powerful and sophisticated functions, Breaks and Auto-Numbering. The ability to associate breaks and numbers with tags sets Ventura apart from ordinary programs. When you can manipulate these two dialog boxes with ease, you will stand out from the crowd.

Before you break, check your progress with the following illustrations.

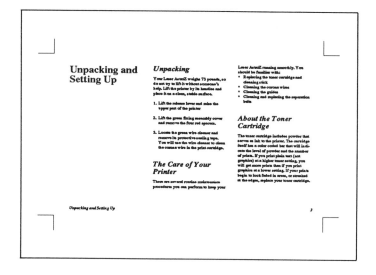

If you're planning a pit stop now, save the document and exit from Ventura. When you're ready to resume working, load Ventura and open the chapter C:\TEMP\9TECHDOC.CHP to start up where you left off.

If you're continuing, go to the next section where you will learn a well kept secret about auto-numbering. You will also produce some advanced effects with ruling lines.

Add Head4 and Rule Tags

■ Press PgDn to go to the next page.

At this point you will create a heading called Head4 and a double rule. The double rule is set up so that it always stretches from the end of Head4 to the edge of the page, no matter how long or how short the Head4 paragraph turns out to be. This advanced effect uses two different tags side by side on the same line. Here's a preview of what you will accomplish.

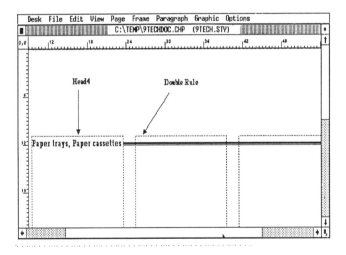

Save the chapter (press Ctrl-S) before you proceed).

Add the Head4 tag.

■ Enable paragraph tagging mode.

■ Select the paragraph "Paper trays, Paper cassettes"

■ Add New Tag   Tag Name to Add: Head4

■ Font   Style: Bold
                  Size: 014 points

■ Alignment   Left
                  Overall Width: Frame-Wide

■ Spacing: Above: 00.00 points
                  Inter-Line: 18.00 points

■ Breaks   Page Break: Before
                  Keep With Next: No

```
┌─────────────────────────────────────────────────────────────┐
│ "Head4" BREAKS                                                │
│                                                               │
│   Page Break:  [No] [Before] [After] [Before & After]         │
│                [Before/Until Left] [Before/Until Right]       │
│                                                               │
│ Column Break:  [No] [Before] [After] [Before & After]         │
│                                                               │
│   Line Break:  [No] [Before] [After] [Before & After]         │
│                                                               │
│ Next Y Position: [Normal] [Beside Last Line of Prev. Para]    │
│                                                               │
│  Allow Within:  [Yes] [No]                                    │
│                                                               │
│ Keep With Next: [Yes] [No]                                    │
│                                                               │
│                                     [OK]   [Cancel]           │
└─────────────────────────────────────────────────────────────┘
```

The Page Break Before guarantees that Head4 will always start on a new page.

Next add the Rule tag. The pragraph tagged as Rule will include two characters: a horizontal tab and a paragraph return. You will set the tab so it extends to the right margin. Then you will put a ruling line above the text. In this case, however, the text is nothing but the (invisible) tab setting. Ventura therefore extends the rule to the end of the "text" — that is, to the end of the tab setting at the right margin.

WARNING: The effect you are learning is a complex one. Do not be concerned if text temporarily overlaps as you proceed. Once you complete all the steps, the text will realign properly.

If you cannot achieve this effect the first time through, choose Abandon from the File menu. Ventura will return you to the point you were at the last time you saved. Then you can try this technique again from the beginning.

■ Enable text editing mode.

■ Place the text cursor before the "P" in the word "Paper trays" on the the second line. Press Enter to create an empty paragraph.

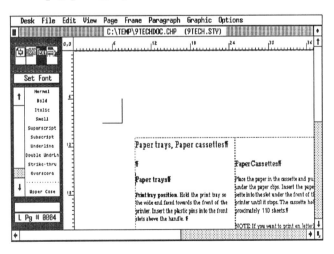

Now enter the tab character.

- Place the text cursor in front of the paragraph symbol (¶) and press the tab key once.

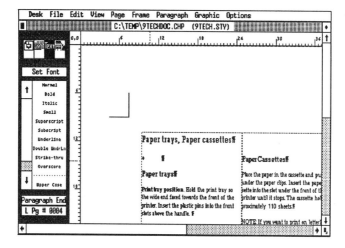

Now change the tab location with Tab Settings in the Paragraph menu.

- Enable paragraph tagging mode.

- Select the paragraph that includes only the tab character and a return.

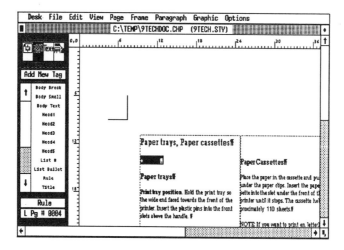

- Add New Tag   Tag Name to Add: Rule

■ Alignment   Left
                   Width: Fame-Wide
                   First Line: Indent
                   In/Outdent Width: 00,04 picas
                   Relative Indent: Length of Previous line

The relative indent means that this tag will align itself immediately after the end of the previous line, no matter how long or how short that line may be. Since we don't want the rule to butt up flush against the text, you also specify an additional 4 points (00,04 picas) to provide a small amount of space.

■ Tab Settings   Tab Number: 1
                   Tab Type: Right
                   Tab Display: Shown as Open Space
                   Tab Location: 46,00 picas

The 46,00 pica tab setting moves the paragraph symbol to the right margin.

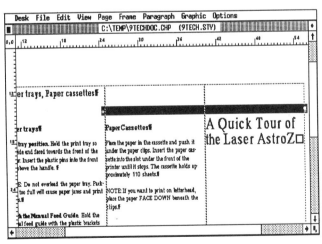

At this point the tags still reside on separate lines. Use the Breaks dialog box to put them on the same line.

■ Breaks Line
 Breaks: After

Add a Ruling Line Above

You've placed the Rule tag on the same line, but it doesn't make much difference yet because there is nothing showing in the Rule paragraph. Now you will make it visible by specifying two ruling lines above.

In the next step you are going to create a double rule that is the width of the text. You do not, however, want any text to show, so you will use a tab stop (which is invisible) instead of actual text. You will place this tab stop at the right margin. As a result, the text-wide double rule stretches to the right margin as well.

■ With the empty paragraph still highlighted, select Ruling Line Above. Choose Width: Text. Give Rule 1 a height of 02.00 points and the Space below it 02.00 points. Give Rule 2 a height of 00.50 points. Make the Space Below Rule 3 a negative (-) 09.00 points.

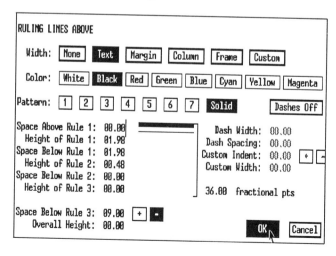

The minus value shifts the rule down from its original location and aligns it with the Head4 paragraph.

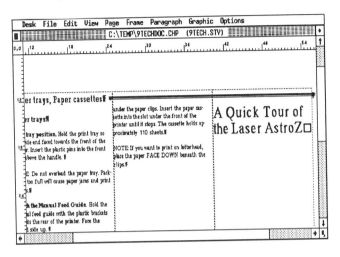

■ Breaks   Line Break: After

By removing the break before and changing to a break after, you permit the double rule to move up next to the Head4 tag.

Add the Note Tag

The Note tag isolates special warnings and procedures inside a box. To create the box around the Note tag, use the Ruling Line Around dialog box. As is often the case with Ventura, there is more than one way to create the effect we will show you below. You could also achieve a similar effect with frames or with box text. Each method has its advantages and disadvantages. The method below relies on tag attributes. It has the advantage of allowing you to change the look throughout the entire document by changing a single tag.

■ Select the paragraph that begins "NOTE: Do not overload the paper tray ..." in the first column of the page.

- Add New Tag   Tag Name to Add: Note
- Spacing   Above: 12.00 points
                  Below: 12.00 points
                  In From Left: 01,00 pica
                  In From Right: 01,00 pica
- Select Ruling Box Around. Choose Width: Column. Give Rule 1 a height of 00.06 points and make the Space Below Rule 1: 03.00 points.

The Space Below Rule 1 adds extra space between the text and the ruling box.

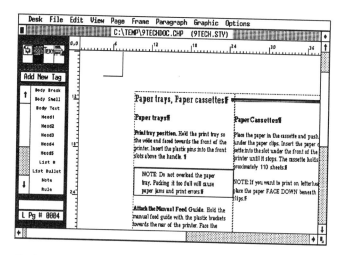

Once the Note tag is defined, apply it to the next Note paragraph.

- Select the paragraph that begins "NOTE: If you want to print on letterhead ..." in the second column and tag it as Note.

Warning: Use ruling box around with caution. When a paragraph with a ruling box around crosses a page or column boundary, the paragraph continues but the ruling box does not.

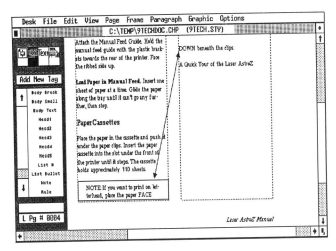

forced over a column boundary when you add or delete text from other paragraphs nearby. To create the same box effect without the danger of crossing a boundary, place text inside a frame or a box text.

➡ *NOTE: You can force Ventura to keep all of the paragraph together by choosing Allow Within:No from the Breaks dialog box. Ventura will not allow line breaks within the paragraph. Instead it will move the entire paragraph to the next column or page. However, this method has the disadvantage of leaving large gaps of white space at the bottom of the previous column.*

Create a Second List

You will now create a second numbered list by tagging three paragraphs as List #.

WARNING: Because the List # tag has a Line Break After, the three paragraphs you tag will shift on top of preceding paragraphs. This temporary confusion will be eliminated as soon as you renumber the chapter.

■ Select the following paragraphs and tag them with the List # tag.

"Print tray position..."

"Attach the Manual Feed Guide..."

"Load Paper in Manual Feed..."

To generate numbers for the newly tagged List # paragraphs, use Ventura's Renumber Chapter function.

■ Select Renumber Chapter from the Page menu or press ^B.

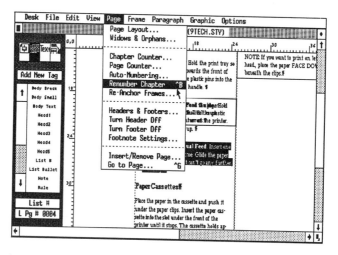

➡ *TIP: Despite the name, Renumber Chapter does not affect chapter numbering. It applies only to autonumbering.*

Create Multiple Lists

After renumbering, the instructions are numbered sequentially, but they start with the number four.

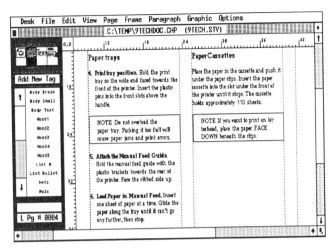

Ventura starts with the number four because it assumes that sequence continues from the list on the previous page.

In some cases, you may want a list that is numbered sequentially throughout the chapter. In other cases, however, you want to start the numbering over again at one. We will show you a quick way to restart the numbering.

Whenever Ventura encounters a Level 1 tag, it resets the numbering for all the lower levels. By putting ordinary body text at Level 1, you trick Ventura into restarting the numbering for Levels 2 and below. In this case, then, you will use body text for Level 1 and List # for Level 2.

■ Select Auto-Numbering from the Page menu.

■ Place the text cursor next to Level 1 line and press ESC to delete the current entry. Choose Inserts: 1,2. Delete the 1, the comma, and the words "tag name." Then type: **Body text**

By deleting the 1, you tell Ventura to number body text *but not to show the numbers*. In effect, then, you have "invisible" numbers.

■ Move the text cursor next to the Level 2 line. Select Inserts: 1,2. Remove the words "tag name" and type: **List #**

■ Add a period after the right bracket. Click OK to clsoe the dialog box.

```
AUTO-NUMBERING

   Usage:  [On]  [Off]

  Level 1:  [*Body text]_____
  Level 2:  [*List #,1].|_____
  Level 3:  _____
  Level 4:  _____
  Level 5:  _____
  Level 6:  _____
  Level 7:  _____
  Level 8:  _____
  Level 9:  _____
  Level 10: _____

  Inserts:  [Chapter #]  [1,2]  [A,B]  [a,b]  [I,II]  [i,ii]

            [Suppress Previous Level]  [Text Attr.]
                                              [OK]  [Cancel]
```

■ Select Renumber Chapter to display the new section numbers.

The list now starts over at one.

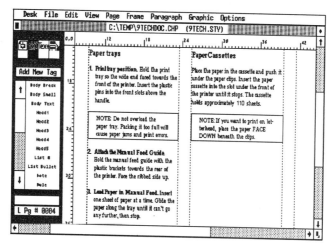

➡ *NOTE: The numbers are now tagged as Z_SEC2, since they are now on Level 2 in the Auto-Numbering dialog box. If you are using the style sheet from the Power disk, this tag has already been defined for you. If not, copy the attributes set forth for Z_SEC1 earlier in this chapter.*

Add a Page Break

When you're finished with auto-numbering, enter a page break after the last Note paragraph to push the rest of the text to the next page. Then leave the page as is. Later, when you get to the picture section, you will add frames and pictures to this page.

- Enable text editing mode.

- Place the text cursor at the end of the paragraph "NOTE: If you want to print on letterhead ...." Press Enter.

- Press F1 to tag the new paragraph as Body Break.

Place the 9TBL.TXT File

You have formatted the final paragraph in the 9TECH.TXT file. Now you are ready to place and tag the second text file, 9TBL.TXT. Before you place the text, insert a new page to contain it.

➡ *NOTE: Later in the picture section, you will add a frame and an illustration on page five.*

Before we continue, let's take stock once again. You've already dealt with breaks and auto-numbering. Now you are ready to tackle what the Ventura manual calls *vertical tabs*. It's a complicated procedure but extremely powerful. Even if it seems a bit confusing, try to stick it out to the end of the exercise.

➡ *NOTE: If you do not use tables in your documents, skip this section and go directly to the pictures section. However, if you use tables of any kind, we recommend that you learn vertical tabs.*

- Press End to go to page four.

- Insert/Remove   Insert Page After
  Page   Current Page

Ventura inserts a new blank page and takes you to it.

The second text file will be placed in a separate frame.

- Enable frame setting mode. Add a new frame that starts at the upper left corner of the left column and extends across the three columns all the way to the lower right corner of the column guide.

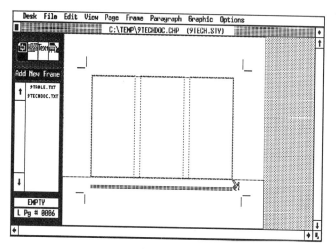

With the frame still selected, place the text file.

- Select the file name, 9TBL.TXT from the Assignment List.

Creating a Table

There are several ways to create tables in Ventura. You can use tab settings; you can use box text; or you can use the technique referred to as *vertical tabs* in the Ventura Reference Manual.

In this chapter you will learn the vertical tabs method. In addition, you will use Ruling Box Around from the Paragraph menu to separate each listing with a line.

We will start by reviewing the process and showing examples. Then we will give you a chance to try it yourself.

To use vertical tabs, you must do two things. First you must properly format the text file. Second, you must give each column a separate tag.

➡*NOTE: As a general rule, use tab settings when each table entry is only a single line. For tables with multi-line entries, it is easier to use vertical tabs, which allow each column to have more than one line.*

Preparing Text for Vertical Tabs

The text file you loaded (9TBL.TXT) is already in the proper format. To prepare text vertical tabs, *type each column entry as a separate paragraph.* Do not enter a tab stop at the end of an entry. The following illustration shows what the sample file looks like before loading it into Ventura.

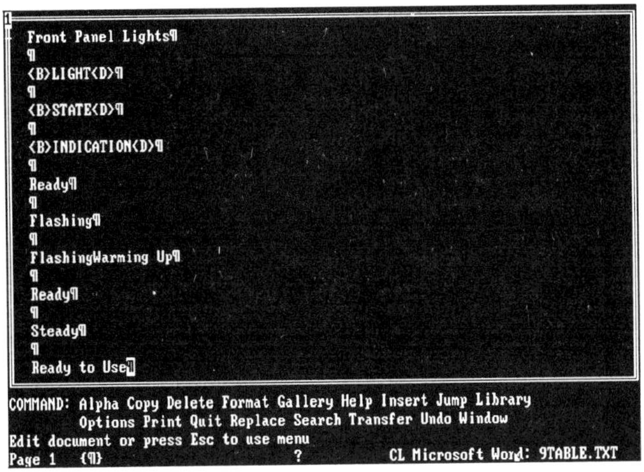

Once you create, load, and place the text you are ready to create the tags for each column.

Using Spacing with Vertical Tabs

Spacing and Breaks are the two keys to building columns with vertical tabs. With In From Left and In from Right Spacing you restrict the text to individual columns.

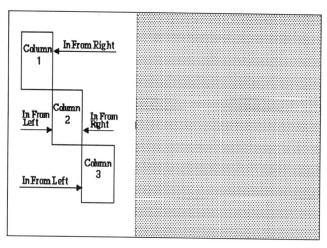

The hard part is calculating the settings. Start by deciding the width of the columns and gutters. In the example you will build below, we divided the space into three equal columns of 15,04 picas. Once you know these widths, you must translate them into settings for In From Left and In From Right. To figure these settings, subtract the cumulative column widths from the margins.

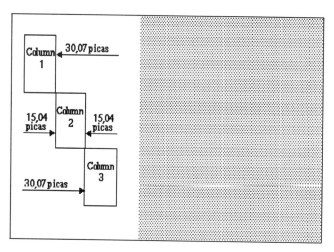

Using Breaks with Vertical Tabs

After using the Spacing to confine the text to columns, move to Breaks. Change the line breaks to allow the tags to coexist on the same line. In the example below, the left column has a line break before; the center column has no line breaks; and the right column has a line break after. After making these changes, the table will look like this:

```
 Desk  File  Edit  View  Page  Frame  Paragraph  Graphic  Options
█ ▓▓▓▓▓▓▓▓▓▓▓    C:\TEMP\9TECHDOC.CHP  (9TECH.STY)    ▓▓▓▓▓▓▓▓▓▓▓  ◆
0,0       6        12       18       24       30       34       42    ↑
18


                          Front Panel Lights


12         LIGHT              STATE            INDICATION
           Ready              Flashing         Flashing Warming Up
           Ready              Steady           Ready to Use
           Ready              Dark             Power Off
           Active/paper Out   Flashing         Processing Data
6          Active/Paper Out   Dark             Idle
           Active/Paper Out   Steady           Paper Out
           Paper Jam          Steady           Paper Jam
                                               See Troubleshooting

0
                                                                    ↓
←                                                                  ◆ ▯
```

The example above shows the text centered within each column. It could just as easily have been flush right or justified.

Using Box Around with Vertical Tabs

For most applications, the steps explained above will suffice. In some cases, however, you may want to enclose each entry within lines. For instance:

```
 Desk  File  Edit  View  Page  Frame  Paragraph  Graphic  Options
█ ▓▓▓▓▓▓▓▓▓▓▓    C:\TEMP\9TECHDOC.CHP  (9TECH.STY)    ▓▓▓▓▓▓▓▓▓▓▓  ◆
0,0       6        12       18       24       30       36       42    ↑
18
 ┌──────────────────┬──────────────┬──────────────────────┐
 │                   Front Panel Lights                     │
 ├──────────────────┼──────────────┼──────────────────────┤
12│       LIGHT       │    STATE     │     INDICATION        │
 ├──────────────────┼──────────────┼──────────────────────┤
 │      Ready        │   Flashing   │ Flashing Warming Up   │
 ├──────────────────┼──────────────┼──────────────────────┤
 │      Ready        │   Steady     │   Ready to Use        │
 ├──────────────────┼──────────────┼──────────────────────┤
 │      Ready        │   Dark       │   Power Off           │
 ├──────────────────┼──────────────┼──────────────────────┤
 │   Active/paper Out│   Flashing   │   Processing Data     │
 ├──────────────────┼──────────────┼──────────────────────┤
6 │   Active/Paper Out│   Dark       │      Idle             │
 ├──────────────────┼──────────────┼──────────────────────┤
 │   Active/Paper Out│   Steady     │   Paper Out           │
 ├──────────────────┼──────────────┼──────────────────────┤
 │   Paper Jam       │   Steady     │   Paper Jam           │
 │                   │              │ See Troubleshooting   │
 └──────────────────┴──────────────┴──────────────────────┘
0
                                                                    ↓
←                                                                  ◆ ▯
```

You will have a chance to add lines around in this sample project. Now that we've reviewed the key concepts, go ahead and create the table.

Add Tbl3 Title Tag

Start by creating a tag for the table title.

■ Enable paragraph tagging mode.

■ Select the paragraph "Front Panel Lights."

■ Add New Tag   Tag Name to Add: Tbl3 Title

■ Font   Style: Bold
                  Size: 014 points

■ Alignment   Center
                  Overall Width: Frame-Wide

■ Spacing   Above: 00.00
                  Inter-Line: 14.00 points
                  Add in Above: When Not at Column Top

■ Ruling Box   Width: Frame
  Around   Height of Rule 1: 00.24 points

Add the Tag for the First Column

At this point, you will create the tags for all three columns. To make the tags self-descriptive, we use names such as Tbl3 Col1, which represent the first column in a three-column table.

■ Select the paragraph "LIGHT."

■ Add New Tag   Tag Name to Add: Tbl3 Col1

■ Font   Size: 012 points

■ Alignment   Center
                  Overall Width: Column-Wide

■ Spacing   Inter-Line: 14.00 points
                  Add in Above: When Not at Column Top.

Now create a temporary right margin with In From Right Spacing.

■ Make the In From Left Spacing 00,00 picas and the In From Right Spacing 30,07 picas.

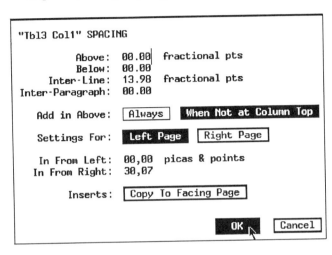

Next add a Ruling Box Around this paragraph.

■ Select Ruling Box Around. Choose Width: Margin. Give Rule 1 a height of 00.24 points.

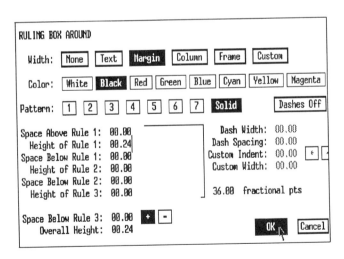

You selected margin because you want the ruling box to surround the "temporary margin" created by the In From Right spacing.

Add the Tbl3 Col2 Tag

You built the first column. Now create a tag for the second column.

■ Select the paragraph "STATE."

■ Add New Tag   Tag Name to Add: Tbl3 Col2

■ Font   Size: 012 points

■ Alignment   Center
                Overall Width: Column-Wide

■ Spacing   Inter-Line 14.00 points
                Add in Above: When Not at Column Top
                In From Left: 15,04 picas
                In From Right: 15,04 picas

The In From Left Spacing and the In From Right Spacing create a temporary left and right margin to restrict the text to the center of the page.

■ Breaks   Line Break: No

■ Ruling Box   Width: Margin
   Around   Height of Rule 1: 00.24 points

Add the Tbl3 Col3 Tag

Finally, create the tag for the third column.

■ Select the paragraph "INDICATION."

■ Add New Tag   Tag Name to Add: Tbl3 Col3

■ Font   Size: 012 points

■ Alignment   Center
                Overall Width: Column-Wide

■ Spacing   Above: 00.00
                Inter-Line: 14.00 points
                Add in Above: When Not at Column Top

Now create a temporary left margin.

■ Make In From Left Spacing 30,07 picas and In From Right Spacing 00,00 picas.

■ Breaks   Line Break: After

```
"Tbl3 Col3" SPACING

          Above:  00.00  fractional pts
          Below:  00.00
     Inter-Line:  14.00  fractional pts
Inter-Paragraph:  00.00

Add in Above:    │ Always │   ▌When Not at Column Top▐

Settings For:    │ Left Page │   ▌Right Page▐

In From Left:    30,07│  picas & points
In From Right:   00,00│

Inserts:     │ Copy To Facing Page │

                              ▌  OK  ▐   │ Cancel │
```

■ Ruling Box   Width: Margin
  Around   Height of rule 1: 00.24 points

Good work. Now that you've created all three column tags, apply them to the text file in the frame. Use the following illustration to match the proper paragraph with the proper tag.

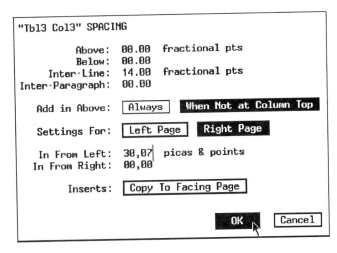

After the table is complete, use a line break to add a blank line to selected boxes in the table.

■ Enable text editing mode.

■ Place the text cursor in front of "F" in "FRONT PANEL LIGHTS" and press Ctrl-Enter.

■ Place the text cursor after the "s" in "FRONT PANEL LIGHTS" and press Ctrl-Enter.

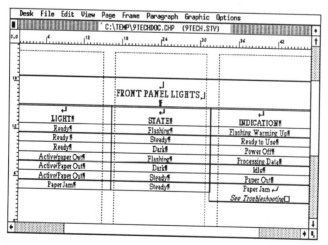

Now add line breaks before the words "LIGHT," "STATE," and "INDICATION."

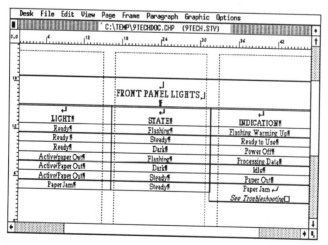

➡ *TIP: Sometimes the screen fails to redraw after entering a line break, and one line appears to be on top of another. To force the screen to redraw, press Esc.*

Create three blank boxes that separate the first text line from the rest of the entries.

■ Place the text cursor after the "N" in the word "INDICA-TION." Press Enter three times.

Three empty boxes appear beneath the column entry INDICA-TION.

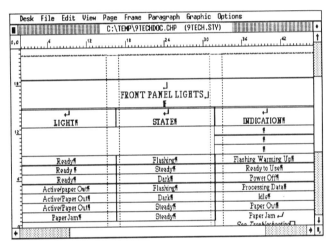

Tag each empty box to reposition them in the proper column.

■ Enable paragraph tagging mode.

■ Select the paragraph symbol (¶) inside the first empty box and tag it as Tbl3 Col1.

■ Select the second paragraph symbol and tag it as Tbl3 Col2.

■ Leave the last empty box as is.

```
 Desk  File  Edit  View  Page  Frame  Paragraph  Graphic  Options
███▓▓▓▓▓▓▓▓▓▓▓▓▓▓▓▓▓    C:\TEMP\9TECHDOC.CHP  (9TECH.STV)  ▓▓▓▓▓▓▓▓▓▓▓▓▓
0,0 ...6........12.......18.......24.......30.......36.......42


                        FRONT PANEL LIGHTS↵
                              ¶
              LIGHT¶             STATE¶            INDICATION¶
                ¶                  ¶
             Ready¶            Flashing¶        Flashing Warning Up¶
             Ready ¶           Steady¶          Ready to Use¶
             Ready¶            Dark¶            Power Off¶
          Active/paper Out¶    Flashing¶        Processing Data¶
          Active/Paper Out¶    Dark¶            Idle¶
          Active/Paper Out¶    Steady¶          Paper Out¶
          Paper Jam¶          Steady¶           Paper Jam ↵
                                                See Troubleshooting□
```

Add line breaks in the first two columns of the last line (after "Paper Jam" and "Steady") to complete the table.

```
 Desk  File  Edit  View  Page  Frame  Paragraph  Graphic  Options
███▓▓▓▓▓▓▓▓▓▓▓▓▓▓▓▓▓    C:\TEMP\9TECHDOC.CHP  (9TECH.STV)  ▓▓▓▓▓▓▓▓▓▓▓▓▓
0,0 ...6........12.......18.......24.......30.......36.......42


                        FRONT PANEL LIGHTS↵
                              ¶
              LIGHT¶             STATE¶            INDICATION¶
                ¶                  ¶
             Ready¶            Flashing¶        Flashing Warming Up¶
             Ready ¶           Steady¶          Ready to Use¶
             Ready¶            Dark¶            Power Off¶
          Active/paper Out¶    Flashing¶        Processing Data¶
          Active/Paper Out¶    Dark¶            Idle¶
          Active/Paper Out¶    Steady¶          Paper Out¶
          Paper Jam↵          Steady↵           Paper Jam ↵
             ¶                  ¶                See Troubleshooting□
```

Now that you've completed the Style section continue with pictures.

Pictures

In this section, you will incorporate illustrations by adding new frames and importing AutoCAD pictures. You will also learn to anchor frames to text. As with the rest of this chapter, you will be learning advanced techniques that may take extra time and effort to master completely.

Add Three Frames

Before you place the pictures, add the frames to contain them.

■ Go to page four.

■ Enable frame setting mode. Select Add New Frame.

■ Add a frame, starting from position 15 on the vertical ruler and stretch it downwards 14,00 picas wide and 11,01 picas.

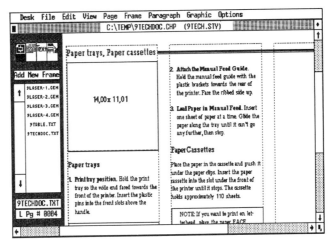

To visually separate the frame from the underlying page, add a ruling box around.

■ Ruling Box   Width: Frame
  Around   Height of Rule 1: 00.06 points

Copy the frame and paste it twice.

■ With the frame still selected, press Shift-Del.

■ Press the Ins key to paste a copy on top of the original.

■ Press Ins again to insert another copy of the frame.

■ Move the two copies into position. Make sure the top edges line up with the top edge of the first frame.

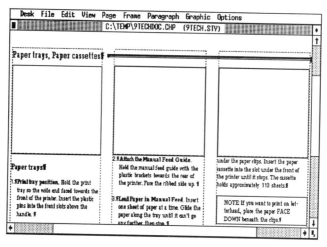

Place Pictures Inside the Frames

- Select the left-most frame and place the file 9LASER-1.GEM inside.

- Select the middle frame and place the file 9LASER-2.GEM inside.

- Select the right frame and place the file 9LASER-3.GEM inside.

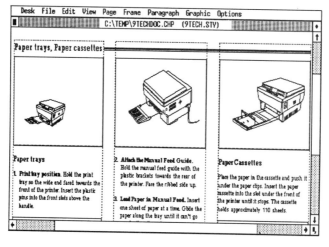

➡ *NOTE: If you do not have these three pictures from the Power Disk, substitute others of your own choosing.*

Size and Scale the Pictures

Use Sizing & Scaling to scale the pictures in the frames. Use the following illustration to gauge the scale and aspect ratio for the three frames.

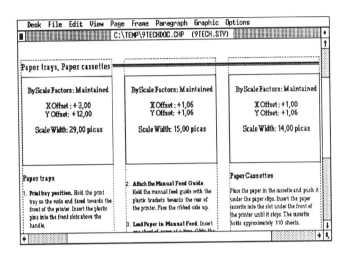

Add a Spacer Paragraph

When you placed the frames, the text automatically reflowed on the page. Now finish the formatting with one adjustment. Add a spacer tag to an empty paragraph in the second column to keep the spacing of the numbered items even.

■ Enable text editing mode.

■ Place the text cursor after the last period in the first Note paragraph in column 1. Press Enter. Then press F10 to make the empty paragraph body text.

■ Enable paragraph tagging mode.

■ Select the empty paragraph you just created (which was tagged as Note).

■ Add New Tag   Tag Name to Add: Spacer

■ Spacing   Above: 12.00 points
Inter-Line: 12.00
Add in Above: Always

The extra space created by the spacer paragraph shifts the text down.

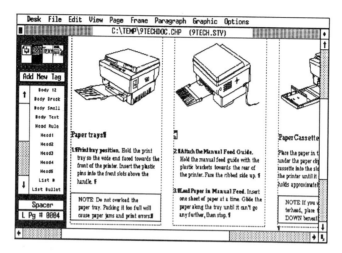

➡ NOTE: You did not use body text as the spacer because body text would cause the auto-numbering to reset to one.

Add the Final Illustration

Go to page five and add the frame for the final illustration.

■ Go to page five

■ Enable frame mode.

■ Select Add New Frame. Start the frame at the upper left corner of the second column and stretch it 30,00 picas wide and 24,00 picas high.

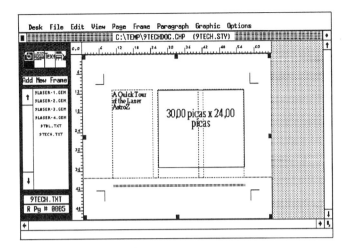

- With the frame still selected, choose the file 9LASER-4.GEM from the Assignment List.

- Sizing &   Picture Scaling: Scale Factors
  Scaling   Aspect Ratio: Maintained
                    X Crop Offset: +08,00 picas
                    Y Crop Offset: +20,00 picas
                    Scale Width: 63,00 picas

➡ *NOTE: If you do not have this picture from the Power Disk, substitute one of your own.*

Add a Caption Label

You're almost finished with the manual. Let's make just a few more enhancements to the page, include automatic figure numbering.

- With the frame still selected, choose Anchors & Captions from the Frame menu.

- Choose Caption: Below. Move to the Label line and type: **Figure** followed by a space.

- Choose the Chapter # button, type: **<196>** (the code for an en dash), and click on the Figure # button.

```
┌─────────────────────────────────────────────────┐
│  ANCHORS & CAPTIONS                               │
│                                                   │
│   Anchor:  _____                            │
│                                                   │
│   Caption:  [Off] [Above] [Below] [Left] [Right]  │
│                                                   │
│     Label:  Figure [CH]<196>[FH]|                 │
│                                                   │
│   Inserts:  [Table #] [Figure #] [Chapter #] [Text Attr.] │
│                                                   │
│                                    [OK]  [Cancel] │
└─────────────────────────────────────────────────┘
```

Add Caption Text

■ Enable text editing.

■ Place the text cursor in front of the end of paragraph mark and type:

The front view of the Laser AstroZ, showing the display panel, the toner cartridge door, the release lever, the paper cassette, and the print tray.

Add a Frame Anchor

We promised to show you some advanced picture techniques, and frame anchoring is one of the most useful. Anchoring keeps frames on the same page as the text they refer to. It is a two-step process: (1) insert an anchor reference into the text file and (2) attach an identical reference to the frame. Once a frame has been anchored, you can make large additions or deletions to the text without the fear that you will move the frames. The Re-Anchor Frames function searches the text file for anchor references and then moves frames to the correct pages again.

As is so often the case, the best way to understand this advanced function is to try it out. Start by placing an anchor reference into the text on page four.

■ Enable text editing mode.

- Place the text cursor after the "Z" in the phrase "A Quick Tour of the LaserAstroZ."

- Select Insert/Edit Anchor from the Edit menu.

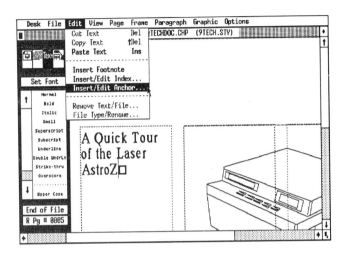

- Move the text cursor to the Frame's Anchor Name and type:
  1-1

- Choose Frame's New Location: Fixed, On Same Page As Anchor.

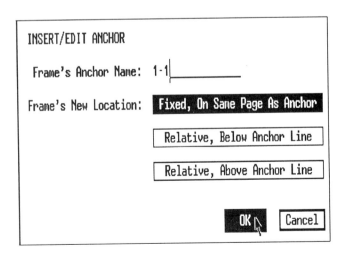

If Show Tabs & Returns is selected, you will see the degree symbol (°) in the text to indicate the anchor reference.

➥ *TIP: Like footnotes and index entries, anchor references can be typed directly into text files using a bracket code. See the tips at the end of Chapter Eight for details.*

After placing the anchor reference in the text, attach it to the frame with Anchors & Captions.

■ Enable frame mode. Select the frame.

■ Select Anchors & Captions from the Frame menu.

■ Move the text cursor to the Anchor line and type: **1-1**

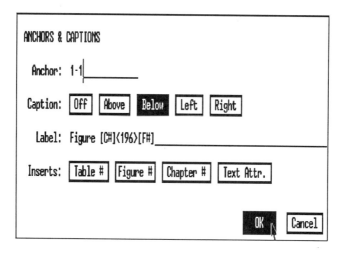

WARNING: *Type the anchor reference exactly the same in both dialog boxes. Otherwise, Ventura cannot match the two references.*

Re-Anchoring Frames

There is no need to use anchoring until a frame is separated from the text reference. Just to see the feature in operation, try deleting the frame you just anchored. Move to any other page of the document and paste it there. Now reanchor.

■ Select Re-Anchor Frames from the Page menu (or Press Ctrl-B).

The frame returns on the page containing the anchor reference in the text. You may need to re-position it slightly.

Adding Callouts

Ventura's graphics tools are perfect for adding callouts to pictures. Using box text and lines, you can create annotations and arrows. Since graphic shapes stay tied to the parent frame, when you move the frame, the callouts move with it.

Draw Box Text

To create callouts, start by creating box text. Then you will type in the actual words, and draw arrows pointing to specific features in the picture.

First set the horizontal and vertical grid settings.

■ With the frame on page four still selected, select graphics drawing mode.

Since the frame was selected when you entered graphics drawing mode, it will be the parent to the shapes you draw.

■ Grid Settings   Grid Snap: On
                   Horizontal Spacing: 00,06 picas
                   Vertical. Spacing: 00,06 picas

■ Select the box text icon. Draw a box text shape 06,00 picas wide and 03,00 picas high. Position it approximately as shown below.

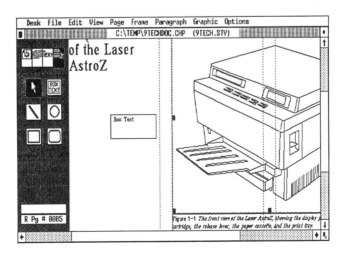

- **Line Attributes**   Thickness: None
                               Defaults: Save To

- **Fill Attributes**   Color: White
                               Pattern: Hollow, Transparent
                               Defaults: Save To

Now add the text of the callout.

- Enable text editing.

- Delete the words "Box Text" and type: `Display Panel`

➡ *NOTE: Although you could have drawn the arrow before typing the words, you would have been forced to guess at the precise location. Placing the arrow after typing the callout makes placement easier.*

- Enable graphics drawing and select the line icon. Starting from the end of the word "Panel," draw a line from the text to the picture as shown below:

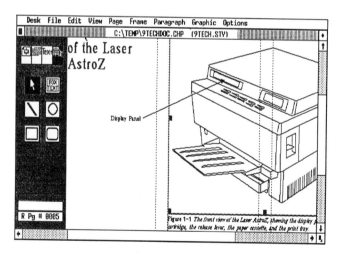

➡ *TIP: Make sure the frame is selected when you enter graphics drawing mode or the line may be attached to the underlying page by mistake.*

■ Line
  Attributes

Thickness: Thin
End Styles: (Beginning) Arrow
Defaults: Save To

Repeat the steps above to add two more callouts as shown below:

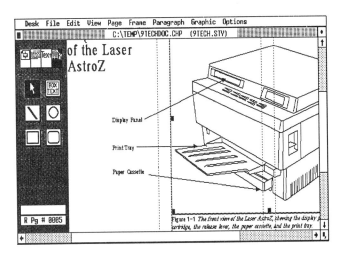

When you are finished, save the chapter and move on to the Chapter section.

Chapter

With long documents such as technical manuals, printing is a time-consuming task that takes control of the printer and the computer. If you write, edit and print from the same workstation, printing becomes a major bottleneck. Fortunately, Ventura provides a workaround that can save time and expense.

As you saw earlier in chapter eight, the Multi-Chapter dialog box includes its own Print operation. When you select the print option, you can send the publication to a file instead of a printer. Once the print files are created on disk, you can use a print spooler to print in the background while you continue to work in Ventura. Or you can print the file at a separate workstation, via a network, or at an outside service bureau.

In this section, you will create a publication that includes all the sample chapters in the C:\TEMP subdirectory. Then you will print the publication to a disk file.

Set the Printer Info

- Select Set Printer Info from the Options menu.

- Choose Output To: Filename

Create a Publication

- Select Multi-Chapter from the Options menu. Choose Save to save the changes you made to the chapter.

- Select New to create a new publication.

- Select Add Chapter. Select 1REPORT.CHP from the C:\TEMP subdirectory.

Repeat the step above to add all the chapters to the publication list. Arrange them in order as shown in the following illustration.

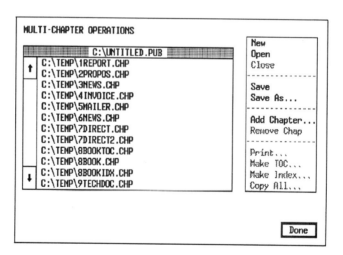

- Select Save As. Save the new publication as POWER.PUB in the C:\TEMP subdirectory.

After creating the publication, you are ready to print.

- Select Print from the Multi-Chapter dialog box.

■ Choose Which Pages: All, and Multi-Chapter: All in One.

Notice that in this Print dialog box, the Multi-Chapter option offers two ways to output the file. In separate (chapter) files or in one file. If you print in separate files, Ventura automatically assigns the extension C00, C01, C02, and so forth to each consecutive chapter. If you select All in One, Ventura saves the publication as one single file with the extension C00.

■ Choose: Multi-Chapter: All in One.

■ In the Item Selector, type the print file name, POWER.C00.

WARNING: Skip this last step if your time is limited or if you have insufficient disk space to hold this all-in-one print file.

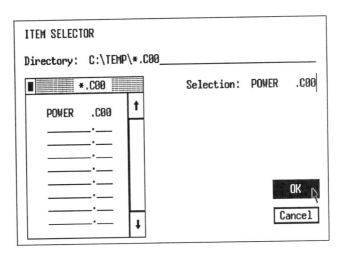

Ventura prints the entire publication to a single disk file.

Tips

Text Tips

❏ You can create a special "page break" (body break) tag that includes a Page Break: After. To force a page break within the text file, tag an empty paragraph with the page break tag. All the text following the tag will be forced to the next page.

❏ Autonumbering includes two basic steps: first you choose which tags to number and what style of numbering to use. Second, you format the numbers that Ventura generates.

❏ Initially the generated section number tags have the same attributes as body text. You can format them like any paragraph.

❏ You can create a traditional outline format (uppercase Roman numerals, uppercase letters, lower case Roman, and so forth) with the Auto-Numbering dialog box. Insert the Suppress Previous Level symbol ([-]) as the first item on the Level line. This selection instructs Ventura to suppress printing of the higher level numbers.

❏ Whenever Ventura encounters a Level 1 tag, it resets the numbering for all the lower levels.

❏ Using body text to reset numbering will not work properly if you want to intersperse body text between consecutive numbers in the same list. In these cases, you can create a special "Reset" tag. Here's how you do it:

First, go to the Auto-Numbering dialog box and place the tag name Reset on the Level 1 line. Now select an empty paragraph and add a tag called Reset. Align the new tag flush right. Set the line spacing to a very small amount. Use the Breaks dialog to set the Line Breaks to No. In essence, you will create an invisible tag that resides on the same line with other paragraphs. Its only function is to signal Ventura when to start renumbering from one.

❏ When a tag with a ruling box around crosses a page or column boundary, the paragraph text continues but the ruling line does not. To avoid this problem, try creating the same effect with box text or text inside a frame.

❑ Generally, it's best to use tab settings when creating a table with single line entries. For tables with multiple-line entries, it is easier to use vertical tabs which allow each column to have more than one line.

❑ To prepare text for vertical tabs, make sure you enter each table entry as a single line. Enter a carriage return instead of a tab at the end of each line.

❑ Spacing and Breaks are the key to creating a table. Use In From left and In From Right Spacing to restrict text to individual columns. Use Breaks to allow multiple tags to reside on the same line.

Picture Tips

❑ You can create a special "spacer" to insert extra spaces between paragraphs. Simply tag an empty paragraph with the above, below, or inter-line spacing desired.

❑ Frame anchoring allow you to tie frames to the text reference they refer to. Once a frame has been anchored you can make large additions and deletions to a text file without worry that the frame will be displaced from its text reference.

❑ Like text references and footnotes, frame anchors can be typed directly into the text file in advance using a bracket code. The anchor codes are as follows:
Place Picture frame on same page: <$&anchor name>
where anchor name is the frame reference name specified in Anchors & Captions.
Picture frame below: <$&anchor name[v]>
Picture frame above: <$&anchor name[^]>

❑ Make sure you type the anchor name exactly the same in the Insert/Edit Anchor dialog box and the Anchors & Caption dialog box. Otherwise Ventura cannot match the two references.

❑ When drawing callouts, make sure you select the desired picture frame before you select graphics drawing mode.

Otherwise, the graphics and box text you draw will be tied to the underlying page.

Miscellaneous Tips

❑ Using the Multi-Chapter Print option, you can send an entire publication to a file instead of to the printer. Once the file is created on the disk, you can send it to the printer with a print file.

❑ If you will be sending a print file that is different from your default printer, be sure to match the printer width table to the destination printer in the Set Printer Info dialog box.

❑ It is easier to draw crop marks manually if you temporarily reset the page margins to equal the trim size of the paper. Then you can use the column guides to help you position the marks.

Text Files

If you have the Power disk, you do not need to type in any text files. If you do not own the disk, you can do the projects by typing the text files shown below. Although you can substitute other files, you may experience difficulties following along, since your screens and printouts will not match those in the book.

The name of each file includes the location where you should store it. These locations match those in the book. Thus, C:\POWER\1RPRT.TXT means that you should create an ASCII file called 1RPRT.TXT and store it in the C:\POWER subdirectory. Type the files exactly as shown. Every bracket, code and carriage return has a purpose. Store the files in ASCII format. Most word processors have an ASCII option. If yours does not, you can accomplish the conversion by printing to a disk file.

To purchase the Power disk, turn to the order card at the back of the book. Rush delivery is available.

Chapter One

ASCII File to create: C:\POWER\1RPRT.TXT

Report on Installation and Implementation of Ventura Publisher

Executive Summary

XYZ Corporation has embarked on a program to implement Ventura Publisher software on existing IBM AT-compatible computers as needed throughout the company. The Marketing Communications department will oversee and supervise this project. Marketing Communications makes the following recommendations:

Use of Ventura in every department for all publishing/communications tasks

Designation of an in-house desktop publishing specialist with responsibility for training, maintenance and standards

A company-wide training program to teach basic Ventura skills

Advanced workshops as needed to teach specialized skills

Use of Ventura Company-Wide

The three-month pilot program undertaken by Marketing Communications has determined that Ventura Publisher can be used for every type of document currently produced by the company. Company-wide use of Ventura will reduce publishing/printing costs by 35% over the next two years (see chart next page). It will reduce the confusion and duplication of effort now in evidence, whereby every department had developed different (and often incompatible) solutions to publishing problems. It will also permit the company to establish and enforce appearance and image standards. Since Ventura Publisher uses style sheets to store formatting information, the company can create a library of approved designs and code them into style sheets. Every document produced with these style sheets will automatically meet minimum standards for graphic design and quality; and all documents seen by the public will reinforce the same image.

We have identified potential uses in five departments; more will be developed as users become more proficient with Ventura and discover new applications.

Accounting Department:

Creation and maintenance of electronic forms, including purchase orders, invoices, collection notices, plus formatting of financial statements and reports.

Advertising Department:

In-house creation of direct mail flyers, brochures and, resulting in improved turnaround time and reduced fees from outside agencies and service bureaus.

Marketing Communications:

Company newsletters, both internal and those intended for customers, plus brochures and product specification sheets.

Internal Publications Department:

Directories, price lists, catalogs and other long documents for customer use generated in support of marketing, plus book-length instruction manuals and product manuals.

Engineering:

Technical manuals, repair manuals, spec sheets and other documentation of the company's products.

In-House Desktop Publishing Specialist

The Marketing Communications Department has conducted extensive interviews at other companies that have implemented desktop publishing. We have learned that designation of an in-house specialist is virtually a requirement for success, regardless of the type of hardware and software in use. A top-notch desktop publisher must be proficient both in the use of the software, and in graphic design. We cannot expect most employees to spend the time and effort to acquire this special mix of skills on top of their existing duties.

Fortunately, Ventura Publisher makes it easy to implement the centralized approach. The major complexity lies in building the style sheets so they accomplish the three-fold purpose of (1) taking advantage of Ventura's power features, (2) meeting the standards of good graphic design and (3) staying consistent with the company image. The desktop publishing specialist will be responsible for maintaining a library of style sheets.

Once these style sheets have been built, they can be distributed to other departments. The software is very easy to use once documents have been designed. Other employees will be able to use these style sheets on their departmental Ventura workstations after a minimum of training.

Marketing Communications has discovered a third-party source for advanced style sheets. The purchase of low-cost style sheet collections will give the desktop publishing specialist a running start. He or she will begin with a large library of documents which can be modified as needed.

Company-Wide Basic Training for Ventura

Marketing Communications recommends that the company's in-house desktop publishing specialist develop a day-long seminar on Ventura Publisher. This seminar will accomplish two purposes:

It will explain and demonstrate the wide range of documents that can be created with Ventura. This will permit users to make better use of this new tool and increase Ventura's value to them

It will teach the basic skills needed to implement the style sheets designed by the desktop publishing specialist. He or she will show attendees the rudimentary skills of loading and printing a document.

The teaching portion of the seminar will be accomplished by completing the first three chapters of POWER PUBLISHING WITH VENTURA, a self-paced teaching guide with accompanying software disk. Each attendee will receive a copy of this book for further self-study as desired. Marketing Communications also recommends that every Ventura workstation be provided with one copy of the book INSIDE XEROX VENTURA PUBLISHER as a reference tool and guide to supplement the user's manual.

Advanced Workshops

Marketing Communications recommends that the in-house desktop publishing specialist develop advanced workshops for those departments expected to become heavy users of Ventura. These may include the Publishing Subsidiary and the Engineering Department. The advanced workshops will focus on specialized skills and advanced techniques. This extra training will permit these departments to become more self-sufficient and to use Ventura for more complex documents. In addition to teaching software skills, the workshops should also spend time on graphic design. Once again, the illustrated exercises from the book POWER PUBLISHING WITH VENTURA will be used as the basis for the workshops. We estimate that each workshop will total about 12 hours, spread over two or three days.

Chapter Two

ASCII File to create: C:\TEMP\PROPOSAL.TXT

Consulting Proposal to ABC Company

XYZ Corporation

September 1, 1988

Consulting Proposal to ABC Company

Project Description

XYZ Corporation proposes to advise ABC Company on all aspects of desktop publishing systems, including needs analysis, product and market surveys, specifications and purchase, and system implementation.

The initial short-term goal is to computerize the production of ABC's internal and external publications using personal computers and desktop publishing software. This short-term goal must be substantially completed before the end of ABC's fiscal year six months from now. The long-range objective is to integrate all of ABC's publications into a company-wide system with common procedures, databases and shared output devices.

Statement of Work

XYZ proposes to accomplish and complete this project in five phases, as described in more detail:

Phase One

Market Research. XYZ will analyze commercially available products for suitability. Phase One will culminate in an in-depth report outlining alternatives and recommendations.

Phase Two

Evaluate Needs. XYZ will gain an in-depth knowledge of ABC's computerization needs through on-site and telephone interviews. We will consider such areas as:

Word processing and editorial requirements

Graphics requirements

Laser printer requirements

Ease of learning and use

Speed and throughput requirements

Phase Three

Installation. Once ABC makes it purchase decision, XYZ will oversee installation, setup and conversion. This will include integration of hardware, software and peripherals, plus the initial setup. Setup will include the creation of electronic formats, style sheets and document templates for reuse by ABC personnel.

Phase Four

Data Conversion. Once the system is installed, XYZ will supervise the conversion of current databases and publications to an electronic form. This will include the use of optical character recognition whenever possible to minimize the time and cost of data entry. Where it is not possible to optically read existing information, XYZ will supervise data entry personnel who will rekey the data into the computers. XYZ will design and implement custom keyboard macro programs to facilitate data entry.

Phase Five

Training and Implementation. With the system up and running and data converted to electronic form, XYZ will train ABC personnel in proper computer procedures, use of the software and interfacing to typesetters, databases and other existing systems. This will include training ABC personnel in all aspects of the word processing/page layout interface, including computer basics, word processing basics, desktop publishing basics, and backup procedures.

XYZ will be available to support the system as needed, whether to (1) troubleshoot problems, (2) explore ways to gain further value from existing hardware and software, (3) more fully integrate the system with other hardware and software or (4) expand the system.

Project Costs

The spreadsheet below illustrates XYZ's best estimate of the costs required to complete the project within a three month period.

ASCII File to create: C:\TEMP\LOTUS.TXT

→JANUARY→FEBRUARY→MARCH
Phase One→5000.00→2750.00→1225.00
Phase Two→2500.00→1175.00→895.00
Phase Three→1600.00→1600.00→0.0
Phase Four→1500.00→1500.00→3750.00
Phase Five→2500.00→2500.00→2500.00
TOTALS→$13100.00→$9525.00→370.00

Chapter Three

ASCII File to create: C:\TEMP\3HEAD.TXT

Cost savings predicted
@HEADLINE = President Approves Desktop Publishing Company-Wide

ASCII File to create: C:\TEMP\3LOGO.TXT

@MASTHEAD = The Newsletter
@CREDO = News and Information for Employees of the XYZ Corporation
@DATE = Fall/Winter 1988
@VOLUME = Vol. 1 No. 4

ASCII File to create: C:\TEMP\3NEWS-1.TXT

President Xavier Y. Zygniewski announced today his approval of a
12-month plan to install desktop publishing workstations in key
departments throughout XYZ Corporation. The announcement follows a
three-month pilot study conducted by the Marketing Communications
Department.

<169>We initially thought that desktop publishing would only have
advantages for one or two departments,<170> said President Zygniewski,
<169>but our study revealed that it could save time and money throughout
the company while improving the appearance and effectiveness of our
documents.<170>

Several technological advances make the company-wide strategy feasible.
First, XYZ was able to standardize on a single software program for all
applications. This standardization will reduce startup, training and
support costs. Second, the selected software, Xerox Ventura Publisher,
will run on the IBM XT- and AT-compatible computers already in place at
XYZ. Many of the other software packages would have required the
purchase of new or incompatible computers. Mr. Zygniewski confirmed that
the new software will be phased in over a 12-month period on a
department-by-department basis, beginning with Marketing Communications.

<169>We are delighted to be pioneering the move to desktop publishing
for XYZ,<170> said John Depthorne, Manager of Marketing Communications.
<169>We will be passing on what we learn in the form of workshops and
seminars for employees in other departments.<170> The Marketing
Communications Department has hired a desktop publishing specialist to
oversee installation, training and support (see related story page 2).

Mr. Depthorne said the pilot program demonstrated that XYZ can expect
cost savings in the area of 35% over the manual means now used to
produce many company documents. In addition, turnaround time can usually
be cut by 50% as well, since the documents no longer need to be sent to
an outside company or department for typesetting and pasteup. These
tasks can now be accomplished electronically on the screen of a
microcomputer.

These time and cost savings provided the initial spur to adoption of
desktop publishing, but they are not the only benefits. <169>We are
firmly convinced that the new desktop publishing program will
substantially improve the look and the impact of XYZ's documents,<170>
said Mr. Depthorne. <169>If you want a document treated with importance,
it must look important. Ventura Publisher will give every department the
ability to create great-looking pages.<170>

The new desktop publishing specialist will be making a library of
professional-quality style sheets, XYZ employees can obtain the benefits
of graphic design and typesetting even if they have no special training.
All they will need to do is select an appropriate style sheet and use it
to process their document.

<169>The average consumer is becoming increasingly attuned to
high-quality graphic design,<170> said President Zygniewski. <169>They
have come to expect it. In the future, companies that do not produce
attractive documents will be at a disadvantage. We are determined that
the documents we produce at XYZ, both internal and external, will
demonstrate the same commitment to quality that has always set this
company apart from the crowd.<170>

ASCII File to create: C:\TEMP\3-NEWS2.TXT

XYZ Hires DTP Specialist

@DECKHEAD = Joan Belden Joins Marketing Communications Team

By Joe Smith

The Marketing Communications Department has hired an experienced desktop
publishing (DTP) specialist to help XYZ make the transition to the new
technology. Ms. Belden, formerly the president of her own consulting
firm, is a noted authority on electronic publishing in general, and
Ventura Publisher software in particular.

<169>The selection of Ventura Publisher as the company-wide standard
will greatly simplify the transition to desktop publishing,<170> said
Ms. Belden. <169>It is easy enough for anyone to use while offering the
most powerful formatting capabilities available on a microcomputer.<170>

Ventura Publisher allows users to merge text and graphics to create
publishing-quality doc<->uments, such as newsletters, technical manuals,
books, and proposals, that might otherwise be sent to a print shop or
typesetter. The package runs on the IBM PC/XT, IBM PC/AT, and other PC
compatibles. It supports popular laser printers, including the Xerox
4045, the Apple LaserWriter and the HP LaserJet.

Previous desktop publishing programs took a hand-intensive approach that
attempted to mimic what graphic artists and typesetters had done by hand
for centuries. The personal computer screen was an electronic paste-up
board. While this approach was easy for artists to pick up, it did not
result in much time-saving because the user was still faced with the
drudgery of hand-adjusting each piece of text on each page. In addition,
only users with design talent and training could expect to achieve
good-looking results.

<169>Ventura does away with the need for every user to be a graphic
designer,<170> explained Ms. Belden. <169>The design ideas of a
professional can be encoded in a style sheet, and then that style sheet
can be used by anyone else.<170> Ms. Belden has already embarked on the
task of building a library of preformatted designs for XYZ. Users from
any department will be able to choose from this library to create
documents of their own by pouring text and graphics files into the
precoded formats.

<169>A style sheet defines the rules for a complex layout,<170>

continued Belden. <169>Once these rules are defined, non-typesetters can quickly achieve typesetter-quality results simply by tagging the paragraphs of their own document as a Headline, Sub-Head, etc. Style sheets let even beginners achieve a typeset look, and let professionals get results that previously required typesetting and paste-up by high-priced professionals.<170>

Ms. Belden will be instituting several programs to help XYZ personnel get up to speed in Ventura. She will be completing approximately four new style sheets per week from a list compiled by XYZ departmental managers. Once completed and approved, these formats will be available for reuse.

Belden will also be leading workshops, including a basic workshop for beginners and advanced seminars for power users. In addition, she will produce a quarterly <169>newsletter<170> of tips, tricks, techniques, shortcuts and news of interest to XYZ's Ventura users. Belden will be distributing the first edition of this newsletter next month.

Chapter Four

ASCII File to create: No text files

Chapter Five

ASCII File to create: C:\TEMP\5MAILER.TXT

Now you can give an ordinary personal computer the power of a pro-fessional print shop. With Xerox Ventura Publisher and expert training from the people at XYZ Corporation, you can learn to create professional-quality documents using a personal computer and an inexpensive laser printer. For this week only, when you come in for a no-risk demonstration, we will redesign one of your corporate documents, while you watch! But hurry<197>our offer is limited. Call (213) 555-1111 today.

Chapter Six

ASCII File to create: C:\TEMP\6NEWS-1.TXT

@HEAD DECK = Ventura Publisher users may now enroll in training workshops

@BODY FIRST = Ventura Publisher workshops in basic and advanced skills begin this month. Interested XYZ personnel may enroll by contacting Joan Belden of Marketing Communications at ext. 323.

Ms. Belden will conduct basic skills workshops three times this month. She has also scheduled two advanced seminars, one on newsletter production and the second on the production of long documents such as books and manuals..

<169>To allow for individual attention and practice, enrollment is limited to six attendees per session,<170> said Ms. Belden, who will initially conduct all the seminars herself. <169>The basic workshop begins with an overview of Ventura Publisher and its capabilities, plus an on-screen demonstration of the dozens of different documents that can be created with this software package.<170> In the second half of the day-long workshop, attendees will practice on individual workstations. They will learn the basic Ventura skills necessary to load and format their own documents using a style sheet from XYZ's growing library of preformatted designs. Ms. Belden said that other members of the Marketing Communications Department would be trained to give the workshops and provide support to users as demand increases.

@HEAD3 = Basic Workshops

Attendees at the basic workshops will receive a training guide and a reference book. The training guide and its accompanying software disk are used as the basis for the hands-on exercises that make up the second half of the seminar. It can also be used for self-paced advanced self-study after the workshop. The reference book provides a more complete explanation of Ventura's features and offers insights into the best methods of operation.

@HEAD3 = Advanced Seminars

The advanced seminars will focus on specialized skills necessary for the creation of specific document types. In addition to learning advanced Ventura techniques, attendees will also be taught graphic arts skills. They will receive a mini-course in design, plus tips on production techniques, including the preparation of so-called camera-ready art <197> pages that are ready to be taken to an offset printer to be photograph. These photographs are made into printing plates, and the document can then be reproduced via offset lithography.

Ms. Belden believes that desktop publishing with Ventura Publisher will have a tremendous impact at XYZ. As she puts it: <169>Anyone who wants to create a better impression on paper should learn to use Ventura Publisher, or make sure someone in their department learns. Whether you are trying to get your message to the public or to upper management, a typeset appearance gives your documents an edge. Anyone who wants to keep up should attend one or more of the workshops and seminars.

All workshops, both basic and advanced, are held in classroom A-6 adjacent to the cafeteria. Interested users can also sign up for supervised practice time on one of its six computers from 5:00 to 7:00 p.m. on Tuesdays and Thursdays.

The classroom features state-of-the-art equipment: including high resolution monitors and network cards. All workstations can access the classroom's Postscript laser printer.

Although employees are free to practice Ventura skills on their own workstations, the practice sessions provide the opportunity to work with a skilled Ventura trainer.

XYZ personnel can also use the classroom to preview the different documents available in XYZ's library style sheets.<F129M> q<F255D>

ASCII File to create: C:\TEMP\6NEWS-2.TXT

Ventura Complements CAD

@BYLINE = by Joe Esposito

@BODY FIRST = Xerox Ventura Publisher is proving to be a perfect complement to the computer-aided design and drafting programs already in use by the Engineering Department.

Since Ventura Publisher can accept graphics files in AutoCAD slide format, DXF file format and HPGL format. CAD users can now include electronic AutoCAD drawings in technical documents and manuals. The Engineering Department has been an enthusiastic user of AutoCAD, the leading CAD program, for more than two years. Its 2D and 3D capabilities make it the perfect design tool. AutoCAD, however, is not optimized for the layout of pages that merge text with graphics.

Ventura Publisher, by contrast, was designed expressly to merge text and graphics. By letting each package do what it does best, the Engineering Department expects to achieve superior documents in a fraction of the time it would take to produce them by manual means. Ease of revision is equally important. As products change, so must the drawings and technical manuals that support them. Ventura and AutoCAD together provide the ability to produce almost instant updates.

For instance, a Ventura chapter file contains pointers to the graphics files used in the document. If these graphics are changed, Ventura will automatically include the new drawings the next time the document is loaded, as long as the new files have the same name as the old. Keeping the document up-to-date is as simple as replacing old files with new ones. <F129M>q<F255D>

ASCII File to create: C:\TEMP\6NEWS-3.TXT

NEWSLINE

@BODY FIRST = Ventura Workstations have been installed in the Engineering and Publications departments. The Accounting and Advertising departments are scheduled to receive Ventura next month.

@BODY FIRST = Digital Laser Corporation gave its first public demonstrations of a new 40-page-per-minute laser printer compatible with the PostScript page description language. PostScript is the standard for desktop publishing, and is supported by Ventura Publisher. The printer seems ideals for use as a network output device when linked to VAX minicomputer systems like those in use at XYZ Corporation. In the future, laser printers like this one may make it possible for Ventura users to send documents to the central high-speed printer via a local area network.

<B>@BODY FIRST = The XYZ Style Sheet Library<D> has been augmented by the purchase of the Document Gallery style sheet collections from New Riders Publishing. The collections include newsletters, corporate documents, marketing documents, forms, books and technical documentation.

<B>@BODY FIRST = Acme Company <D>has announced a new large-screen display compatible with Xerox Ventura Publisher. The new B-X-100 is the first display to incorporate four graphics co-processors. A co-processor is a specialized microchip that speeds display speed. The 19-inch monitor and add-in graphics adapter will ship in the last quarter of this year.

<B>@BODY FIRST = The Ventura Classroom<D> is now open from 5:00 to 7:00 p.m Tuesday and Thursday of every week. A member of the Marketing Communications Department will be on hand during those hours to answer questions and help with problems.

<B>@BODY FIRST = An employee discount<D> was announced for the purchase of small computers. XYZ, which receives a volume discount on its computer purchases, has made arrangements to pass this discount on to employees who wish to buy computers or related equipment for home use.

<B>@BODY FIRST = A new desktop publishing-related job position<D> has been created in the Engineering Department, which recently announced its intention to convert its entire library of technical documentation to electronic form. The department's technical drawings were moved to electronic form two years ago. Now the production of technical manuals and other technical documentation will be automated as well. In accordance with company policy, the new position will be filled from within XYZ if possible. If no suitable internal candidates present themselves within two weeks, the job will be advertised in local papers.

<B>@BODY FIRST = ABC Company<D> has released a low-cost document scanner capable of sensing and transmitting 16 levels of gray. Priced under $3,000, the scanner permits desktop publishers to convert halftones to electronic form.

ASCII File to create: C:\TEMP\6NEWS-4.TXT

@STAFF BOX = Paginations is published quarterly for the employees of XYZ Corporation, Los Angeles, CA. Copyright 1988 by XYZ Corporation, all rights reserved. Reproduction in whole or in part without written permission is strictly forbidden. The editors welcome submissions, but cannot be responsible for manuscripts or their return.

ASCII File to create: C:\TEMP\6NEWS-5.TXT

@KICKER = Tip of the Month

@HEAD2 = Preformatting Ventura Documents

Ventura Publisher allows you to preformat text files by inserting tags names into the original word processing file. By inserting these tags in advance, you save the time of paging through the document and tagging each text paragraph in Ventura. This is also a handy way to divide responsibilities, so writers can tag documents without worrying what the format will look like.

Preformatting is the ultimate time-saver and it's not difficult. One simple trick is to program the tag names into a keyboard macro processor to save typing time. The proper format uses the at sign (@) at the left margin followed by the name of the tag, an equals sign (=) and the text. Thus, if we were using a word processor to preformat this article, the title might look like this in the file:

@HEADLINE = Preformatting Ventura Documents

Don't forget the space at both sides of the equals sign and don't forget to spell the tag name exactly as it appears in the style sheet. Approved XYZ style sheets come with a listing of all the tag names for handy reference. As you add tags to the style sheet, you can capitalize the name or not as you prefer. Many people choose to use all capitals, or start the name with a symbol such as ! so the tags stand out from the text.

@HEAD3 = Choosing Tag Names

By choosing <169>generic<170> tag names, you will find that you can reuse them over and over again. For instance, tags like <169>Title,<170> <169>List,<170> and <169>Subhead<170> will apply to most documents. Then by changing style sheets, you can change the entire format of the document.

If you don't like the keyboard macro idea, try building word processor template files. Load an unformatted text file into Ventura and tag it as you would normally. When everything is perfect, save the chapter (thereby saving the tags into the text file.

Now make a copy of the file under a new name. Remove the text, leaving only the tags. Assuming the tag names are self-descriptive, a template makes it fill-in-the-blanks simple to create preformatted files. To make it even simpler, annotate the template with the word processor's hidden text feature.

The template method is particularly useful when an editor must work with multiple authors.

Authors can also assist in the layout process by inserting tags that create space for illustrations. If you uses visuals in standard sizes, create a tag that leaves the correct amount of space on the page. The authors can type in the name of the illustration or even its caption. This tagged paragraph creates space where the layout editor will want to place the actual frame. The editor can delete the tag and insert the frame that will contain the illustration.

ASCII File to create: C:\TEMP\6TOC.TXT

```
INSIDE
@TOC ENTRY = Training Workshops Underway→1
@TOC ENTRY = Ventura Complements CAD2→
@TOC ENTRY = Newsline→2
@TOC ENTRY = Tip of the Month→3
```

Chapter Seven

ASCII File to create: C:\TEMP\7DIRECT.TXT

```
@HEAD SECTION = Manufacturers
@HEAD1 = A
@HEAD2 = Adobe, Inc
1870 Embarcadero Rd.<R>Palo Alto, CA 94303
@HEAD3 = Product:
@ITAL KPWTHNXT = PostScript, Illustrator, Adobe Type Library
@HEAD3 = Phone:
@ITAL SEPARATE = (415) 852-0271
@HEAD2 = Allied Linotype Co.
425 Oser Ave.<R> auppauge, NY 11788
@HEAD3 = Product:
@ITAL SEPARATE = Linotronic 100 and 300
@HEAD3 = Phone:
@ITAL SEPARATE = (516) 434-2016
@HEAD2 = Autodesk, Inc.
2320 Marinship Way<R>Sausalito, CA 94965
@HEAD3 = Product:
@ITAL KPWTHNXT = AutoCAD, AutoSketch
@HEAD3 = Phone:
@ITAL SEPARATE = (415) 332-2344
```

```
@HEAD1 = D
@HEAD2 = Datacopy Corp.
1215 Terra Bella Ave<R>Mountain View, CA 94043
@HEAD3 = Product:
@ITAL KPWTHNXT = Model 730 Scanner
@HEAD3 = Phone:
@ITAL SEPARATE = (415) 965-7900
@HEAD2 = Digital Research Inc.
60 Garden Court<R>Monterey, CA 93942
@HEAD3 = Product:
@ITAL KPWTHNXT = GEM Desktop, GEM Draw Plus, GEM Paint
@HEAD3 = Phone:
@ITAL SEPARATE = (408) 649-3896
@HEAD1 = H
@HEAD2 = Hewlett-Packard
P.O. Box 15<R>Boise, ID 83707
@HEAD3 = Product:
@ITAL KPWTHNXT = Laserjet Plus, Laserjet II, Scanjet
@HEAD3 = Phone:
@ITAL SEPARATE = (208) 323-3869
@HEAD1 = I
@HEAD2 = Imagen
2650 San Tomas Expressway<R>Santa Clara, CA 95051
@HEAD3 = Product:
@ITAL KPWTHNXT = DDL Language
@HEAD3 = Phone:
@ITAL SEPARATE = (408) 986-9400
@HEAD1 = L
@HEAD2 = Lotus Development Corp.
55 Cambridge Parkway<R>Cambridge, MA 02142
@HEAD3 = Product:
@ITAL KPWTHNXT = Lotus 1-2-3, Symphony, Freelance, Graphwriter
@HEAD3 = Phone:
@ITAL SEPARATE = (617) 577-8500
@HEAD1 = M
@HEAD2 = Media Cybernetics
8484 Georgia Ave., Ste. 200<R>Silver Spring, MD 20910
@HEAD3 = Product:
@ITAL KPWTHNXT = Halo Desktop Publishing Editor
@HEAD3 = Phone:
@ITAL SEPARATE = (301) 495-3305
@HEAD2 = MicroPublishing
21150 Hawthorne Blvd., Ste. 104<R>Torrance, CA 90503
```

```
@HEAD3 = Product:
@ITAL KPWTHNXT = microPublishing Report Newsletter, Ventura Style Sheets
@HEAD3 = Phone:
@ITAL SEPARATE = (213) 376-5724
@HEAD1 = R
@HEAD2 = Ricoh Corp.
5 Dedrick Place<R>West Caldwell, NJ 07006
@HEAD3 = Product:
@ITAL KPWTHNXT = IS30 Scanner
@HEAD3 = Phone:
@ITAL SEPARATE = (201) 882-2000
@HEAD1 = S
@HEAD2 = Sigma Designs
46901 Landing Parkway<R>Fremont, CA 94538
@HEAD3 = Product:
@ITAL KPWTHNXT = LaserView Display System
@HEAD3 = Phone:
@ITAL SEPARATE = (415) 770-0100
@HEAD2 = Symsoft
P.O. Box 477<R>Mountain View, CA 94040
@HEAD3 = Product:
@ITAL KPWTHNXT = HotShot
@HEAD3 = Phone:
@ITAL SEPARATE = (415) 941-1552
@HEAD1 = T
@HEAD2 = Tall Tree Systems
1120 San Antonio Rd.<R>Palo Alto, CA 94303
@HEAD3 = Product:
@ITAL KPWTHNXT = JLaser Plus
@HEAD3 = Phone:
@ITAL SEPARATE = (415) 964-1980
@HEAD1 = V
@HEAD2 = Verticom, Inc.
545 Weddell Dr.<R>Sunnyvale, CA 94089-2114
@HEAD3 = Product:
@ITAL KPWTHNXT = Desktop 1280
@HEAD3 = Phone:
@ITAL SEPARATE = (408) 747-1222
```

ASCII File to create: C:\TEMP\7DIRECT2.TXT

```
@HEAD SECTION = Products
@HEAD1 = F
```

```
@HEAD2 = Fonts and Font Software
@HEAD4 = Adobe Typeface Library
@COMPANY = Adobe Systems Inc.
@HEAD3 = PostScript:
@ITAL KPWTHNXT = Yes
@HEAD3 = Computers:
@ITAL KPWTHNXT = Macintosh, IBM PC
@PHONE = (415) 852-0271
@HEAD4 = Conofonts
@COMPANY = Conographics
@HEAD3 = PostScript:
@ITAL KPWTHNXT = No
@HEAD3 = Computers:
@ITAL KPWTHNXT = IBM PC
@PHONE = (714) 474 -1188
@HEAD4 = Fluent Fonts
@COMPANY = Genny Software Research and Development
@HEAD3 = PostScript:
@ITAL KPWTHNXT = Yes
@HEAD3 = Computers:
@ITAL KPWTHNXT = Macintosh
@PHONE = (409) 860-5817
@HEAD4 = Hewlett Packard Soft Fonts
@COMPANY = Hewlett Packard
@HEAD3 = PostScript:
@ITAL KPWTHNXT = No
@HEAD3 = Computers:
@ITAL KPWTHNXT = IBM PC
@PHONE = (800) 538-8787
@HEAD4 = PC Fontware
@COMPANY = Bitstream
@HEAD3 = PostScript:
@ITAL KPWTHNXT = No
@HEAD3 = Computers:
@ITAL KPWTHNXT = IBM PC
@PHONE = (617) 497-6222
@HEAD1 = G
@HEAD2 = Graphics Software
@HEAD4 = AutoCAD
@COMPANY = Autodesk,Inc.
@HEAD3 = Ventura Format:
@ITAL KPWTHNXT = SLD or GEM
@HEAD3 = Computers:
```

```
@ITAL KPWTHNXT = IBM PC
@PHONE = (415) 332-2344
@HEAD4 = Desktop Publisher's Graphics
@COMPANY = IMSI
@HEAD3 = Ventura Format:
@ITAL KPWTHNXT = Image
@HEAD3 = Computers:
@ITAL KPWTHNXT = IBM PC
@PHONE = (415) 454-7101
@HEAD4 = Halo DPE
@COMPANY = Media Cybernetics
@HEAD3 = Ventura Format:
@ITAL KPWTHNXT = Halo DPE
@HEAD3 = Computers:
@ITAL KPWTHNXT = IBM PC
@PHONE = (301) 495-3305
@HEAD4 = PC Paintbrush Plus
@COMPANY = ZSoft
@HEAD3 = Ventura Format:
@ITAL KPWTHNXT = PC Paintbrush
@HEAD3 = Computers:
@ITAL KPWTHNXT = IBM PC
@PHONE = (404) 980-1950
@HEAD1 = M
@HEAD2 = Monitors
@HEAD4 = Crystal View
@COMPANY = Taxan
@HEAD3 = Resolution:
@ITAL KPWTHNXT = 1,280 x 960
@HEAD3 = Display Size:
@ITAL KPWTHNXT = 19
@PHONE = (818) 810-1291
@HEAD4 = Laserview
@COMPANY = Sigma Design
@HEAD3 = Resolution:
@ITAL KPWTHNXT = 1,664 x 1200
@HEAD3 = Display Size:
@ITAL KPWTHNXT = 19
@PHONE = (415) 770-0100
@HEAD4 = Viking I
@COMPANY = Moniterm
@HEAD3 = Resolution:
@ITAL KPWTHNXT = 1,280 x 960
```

```
@HEAD3 = Display Size:
@ITAL KPWTHNXT = 19.6
@PHONE = (612) 935-4151
@HEAD4 = Wy-700
@COMPANY = Wyse Technology
@HEAD3 = Resolution:
@ITAL KPWTHNXT = 1,280 x 800
@HEAD3 = Display Size:
@ITAL KPWTHNXT = 15
@PHONE = (408) 433-1000
@HEAD1 = S
@HEAD2 = Scanners - Graphics and OCR
@HEAD4 = Crystal Scan Image Scanner Model 3001
@COMPANY = Taxan Corporation
@HEAD3 = Scan Area:
@ITAL KPWTHNXT = Platen Feed
@HEAD3 = List Price:
@ITAL KPWTHNXT = $1,695
@PHONE = (818) 810-1291
@HEAD4 = Datacopy 730
@COMPANY = Datacopy
@HEAD3 = Scan Area:
@ITAL KPWTHNXT = Flatbed
@HEAD3 = List Price:
@ITAL KPWTHNXT = $1,800
@PHONE = (800) 821-2898
@HEAD4 = Microtek MS-300C
@COMPANY = Microtek Lab, Inc.
@HEAD3 = Scan Area:
@ITAL KPWTHNXT = Platen Feed
@HEAD3 = List Price:
@ITAL KPWTHNXT = $1,795
@PHONE = (213) 321-2121
@HEAD4 = The Laser Scanner, Model KS-300
@COMPANY = Princeton Graphics Systems
@HEAD3 = Scan Area:
@ITAL KPWTHNXT = Platen Feed
@HEAD3 = List Price:
@ITAL KPWTHNXT = $1,095
@PHONE = (609) 683-1660
@HEAD1 = U
@HEAD2 = Utilities
@HEAD4 = PubSet
```

```
@COMPANY = EDCO Services
@HEAD3 = Description:
@ITAL KPWTHNXT = Software typesetter driver to send Ventura documents
directly to your typesetter
@HEAD3 = List Price:
@ITAL KPWTHNXT = $2,500
@PHONE = (813) 962-7800
@HEAD4 = VPToolbox
@COMPANY = SNA, Inc.
@HEAD3 = Description:
@ITAL KPWTHNXT = File management program that lets you review the
contents of related files and style sheets
@HEAD3 = List Price:
@ITAL KPWTHNXT = $99
@PHONE = (609) 683-1237
@HEAD4 = VP/Saddle
@COMPANY = The Laser Edge
@HEAD3 = Description:
@ITAL KPWTHNXT = Enhanced features for printing books and booklets with
PostScript Printers
@HEAD3 = List Price:
@ITAL KPWTHNXT = $79
@PHONE = (415) 835-1581
@HEAD4 = Headline
@COMPANY = Corel
@HEAD3 = Description:
@ITAL KPWTHNXT = Application program which gives access to the powerful
graphics features of PostScript
@HEAD3 = List Price:
@ITAL KPWTHNXT = $89
@PHONE = (613) 728-8200
```

Chapter Eight

ASCII File to create: C:\TEMP\8BOOK.TXT

```
@CHAP # = Chapter Six

@CHAP TITLE = <$IDesign;Design Principles>Design Principles

@BODY FIRST = Getting top-quality books from a desktop publishing system
requires special know-how in two areas: design and printing. his chapter
discusses the theory of design. The following chapter, Chapter Seven,
outlines the steps to take before going to a commercial printer.

This chapter offers comments on the principles of <$IBooks;Book
```

design>book design <MI>as they apply to desktop publishing<D>. In some cases, the realities of desktop publishing force changes from traditional methods.

@HEAD1 = Design Terminology

If you're new to page design and typography, you'll need to learn a few words. You'll encounter this vocabulary over and over again in software manuals and in conversations with graphic designers and commercial printers. This specialized terminology applies to three areas: (1) describing pages, (2) measuring pages and (3) describing type.

@HEAD2 = <$IDescribing pages>Describing Pages

The most common page elements used in traditional and desktop publishing are described below:

A <$ICallouts>callout is a brief text label used to describe one part

of an illustration. Callouts are often accompanied by arrows.

A <$ICaption>caption is a brief description that labels or describes the entire illustration. Also referred to as a <$ACutline;Caption><MI>cutline<D> or a <MI>legend<D>.

The chapter number and chapter title identify the section of the book. Often one or both are repeated in the header.

<$ICrop marks><$SCrop marks;Describing Pages>Crop marks are small lines, usually at the corner of the live area, that show the offset printer where to cut the pages after printing. They are also used by the printer to align each page correctly. Also called <$ICorner Marks><$ACorner marks;Crop marks>corner marks, or trim marks.

The <$IFolio>folio is the page number.

A <$IFooter>footer is a line or two of text that appears at the bottom of every page (or almost every page). A footer may include the folio (page number) or other information.

A <$IGutter>gutter is the white space between two areas of text. Gutters appear between columns on a page. The word also refers to the margin between facing pages.

A <$IHeader> header is a line or two of text that appears at the top of every page (or almost every page). A header often includes the title of the book, the title of the chapter and/or the folio. Alternating <$IHeader;Alternating headers and footers>headers and footers put different information on left and right pages. Quite often the header is omitted from the first page of a chapter.

A <$IHeading>heading is a few words set off from the rest of the text to describe a major section of the chapter. Also called a main heading.

A keyline is a thin rule that shows the printer where to position a halftone or other illustration.

The live area is the area of the page that receives ink when printed. The margins are the white borders that surround the live area. Margins must be carefully considered to take into account the look of the book, the binding method and the limitations of laser printers. A subhead is a few words set off from the rest of the text to describe a minor section of the chapter. Also called a <MI>minor heading<D>.

@HEAD2 = Measuring Pages

Most Americans are comfortable with inches. But for desktop publishing, the method called <MI>printer's measure<D> or <MI>the point system<D> is superior. Since type sizes are always specified in points, it makes sense to use printer's measure for everything on the page so you don't waste time converting back and forth. In addition, the point system has units that are much smaller than inches, so it is rarely necessary to complicate things with fractional units. By contrast, using inches requires you to make many fractional computations.

For these reasons, printer's measure is the easiest way to talk to a page layout program. (Most programs let the user choose between inches, centimeters or printer's measure.) The two most important units in printer's measure are <MI>points<D> and <MI>picas<D>.

Points are a very small unit, about 1/72 inch. They are used to measure type sizes and rules. The point size of a typeface is is roughly the measurement from the highest ascender (the top of a <169>b<170> for instance) to the lowest descender (the bottom of a <169>g<170>). This is only an approximation, since point sizes originate from the metal body used to carry type in the days before phototypesetting. The best way to get familiar with point sizes is by example. You'll soon develop an eye for the most common sizes.

Picas are a larger unit. Don't confuse them with the typewriter style of the same name. They are equal to 12 points (about 1/6 inch). Printers and typographers use picas to measure lines, margins and columns.

Figure 6-2 shows a page from this book with the measurements expressed in picas and points. (The measurements refer to the full-sized page.)

<$IEm Dash>Ems and <$IEn Dash>ens are less important but you'll hear them mentioned. Ems and ens vary according to the size of the type. In 12-point type, an em is 12 points. In 18-point type it is 18 points, and so on. An en is 1/2 the em. In 12-point type, then, the en is 6 points; in 18-point type it is 9 points, and so on.<MS>

The em is the basis for spacing. An <MI>em indent<D>, also called an em square, is an indent from the left margin equal to the em size <197> 12 points in 12-point type, 18 points in 18-point type, and so on. It is the standard indent for books.

The most common use for the em is to describe the <MI>em dash<D>. The em dash is, obviously, the length of one em. Em dashes are used to separate sentences <197> like this. The most common convention is to use the em dash without any space between the dash and the word<197>like this. It is also acceptable to use the em dash with a space on both sides, as has been done in this book.

En dashes are half the length of the em. They are used to represent <169>to<170> between numbers and words, as in <169>1950<196>1955<170> or <169>Figure 1-2.<170> The hyphen is even shorter yet. It is used to <$IHyphenation;Use of en dash>hyphenate words. Some desktop publishing programs make no distinction between hyphens and en dashes.

@HEAD2 = Describing Type

Unfortunately, different programs use different words to refer to ype and its attributes. The definitions given below are the most common in the desktop publishing industry. In some cases, they vary from those in use by traditional typesetters.

Type sizes are specified in points as explained above. You must understand the point system to give correct instructions to the software. Many people refer to small type in the 9 to 12 point range as <$IBody type>body type. Larger sizes used for headings is often called <$IDisplay Type><$ADisplay Type;Headings>display type.<MI>Typestyles. Most desktop publishing programs use typeface and typestyle synonymously to mean one particular type design. Each design has a name. Helvetica is one typestyle; Century Schoolbook is another; and so on. To choose a different design from the page layout program, the user specifies it by name or picks its name from a menu.

A font is one particular variety of a typestyle. Thus, most software manuals would refer to Dutch as a typestyle and 12-point Dutch bold italic as a font. Most publishing programs have a <$IFonts>Font menu item where the user can specify all the attributes of the typestyle.

Kinds of type. Different people divide type in different groups. Book publishers are most likely to use three different kinds: serif, sans serif and symbol. Serifs are curlicues that decorate the ends of letters, so serif type is distinguished by these tiny lines. This book uses a serif typestyle. Sans is the French word for without, so sans serif is type without the curlicues. And symbol fonts, sometimes called <$IFonts;Pi fonts>pi fonts, contain special characters, symbols, foreign language characters and so on.<MI>

There are other kinds of type available from desktop publishing systems, including script, cursive, shadow, outline and reverse (white letters on a black background). These decorative effects can be achieved directly in some page layout programs. They can also be created in a special graphics programs and imported onto the page. These unusual typestyles are rarely used in books except for covers or chapter openings.

Type attributes. The same typestyle can vary in several ways. <MI>Weight<D> refers to the thickness of the letterstrokes. Most desktop publishing programs provide only normal and <$IBold><$ABold;Text

Attributes>bold. A few programs offer light as well. <MI>Slope<D> refers
to the slant of the letters, either vertical (called normal or roman) or
slanted (italic or oblique). The <MI>proportion<D> of type is its
horizontal width. Most desktop publishing programs offer only normal
proportions. Occasionally they also provide access to condensed and
expanded versions.

@HEAD2 = Other Important Terms

Understanding printer's measure is the most important part of becoming a
good desktop designer. But you'll also encounter a few other phrases:The
<$IBaseline>baseline is the invisible line the type sits on. Some
programs use this term and/or display the baselines as a light gray or
dashed line on screen. Whether or not the term is used by the program,
line spacing is measured from baseline to baseline. If you were using
8-point type with 2 points of leading, the baseline to baseline
measurement would be 10 points (8 + 2).<MS>

Some programs, including Xerox Ventura Publisher, modify this concept
slightly. Ventura Publisher considers the baseline to be the bottom of
the lowest descender rather than the line upon which the body of the
type rests.

Page format. There are four basic formats. <MI>Flush left<D> has an even
left margin and a ragged right margin. For this reason it is often
referred to as ragged right. <MI>Flush right<D> is the reverse: even
right margin, ragged left margin. <MI>Justified<D> has even margins left
and right. <MI>Centered<D> puts each line in the center, leaving both
margins ragged. Justified is the choice for almost all books.

Poetry often uses centered lines. Flush left is occasionally chosen for
special formats. Flush right has few applications in <$IBooks;Page
format>books outside of titles, tables and charts.

<$IHyphenation;Hyphenation and justification>Hyphenation and
justification are crucial to achieve a typeset look. When justifying
lines, page layout programs attempt to end lines at the space between
words. When that is not possible, they insert a hyphen, and put part of
the word on one line and the remainder on the line below. Text can be
justified without hyphenation, but this forces the program to stretch
the words too far apart. The computer program needs to know where it is
allowed to insert hyphens when needed. Good page layout programs insert
invisible <$IHyphenation;Discretionary hyphens>discretionary hyphens
into text files when they are loaded. These discretionary hyphens tell
the program where to divide a word if necessary. By hyphenating a word,
the program can fit a few extra characters on the line, improving the
spacing and appearance.

@HEAD1 = <$ABooks;Design Guidelines for Books><$IDesign;Design
Guidelines for Books>Design Guidelines for Books

Good page design is inconspicuous <197> it calls attention to the
message, not to itself. But just because good design isn't loud and
flashy doesn't mean there isn't a lot going on behind the scenes.

Definite rules, skills and aesthetic choices go into the creation of book pages. Until now, this knowledge was the province of specialists. Desktop publishing, however, forces untrained users to grapple with the same decisions.

Fortunately, there is a way to harness the power of desktop publishing <197> <MI>design<D>. Design is a business tool, a way to make words more effective. It is often regarded as an innate ability <197> you're born with it or you're not. In reality, you <MI>can<D> learn the fundamentals of good design. Creating straightforward, professional pages just takes a little know-how. You can get such pages by consistently applying a few safe and sane rules.

@HEAD2 = <$IDesign;Purpose of>The Purpose of Page Design

Page design has five goals:

@BULLET = Attract attention

@BULLET = Please the eye

@BULLET = Provide guideposts

@BULLET = Improve legibility

@BULLET = Make production easier and more efficient

Attracting the eye. The attention-grabbing power of design does not play a large role in <$IBooks;Book covers>books, except on covers. Covers are such a crucial part of marketing that they are best left to design professionals. It is valuable to understand, however, that cover design can set a book apart on the shelves and entice browsers.

Pleasing the eye. Once again, this aspect of design does not have the same crucial role in <$IBooks;Book publishing>book publishing as in magazine publishing and <$IAdvertising;Design applications>advertising. Nevertheless, a book's physical format can add (or detract) from its sales appeal. To compete in the marketplace, books must meet certain minimum standards of design and attractiveness. What's more, the book must project the right image for the target market, whether business, educational, scientific or mass market.

This chapter does not go into the more esoteric aspects of pleasing the eye. But it is valuable to realize that top-quality books utilize balance, symmetry and proportion for aesthetic effect. Novice desktop publishers are well-advised not to stray too far from time-tested formats.

Guiding the eye. A page can be a structuring device, a way to organize information. The eye needs guideposts or it becomes lost in a sea of type. Readers need signals so they don't miss key information. Good page design makes documents easier to use by providing these visual cues. There are three keys to guiding the eye: contrast, separation and consistency.

Light against dark, small against large, slanted against upright, one typestyle against another <197> these are all examples of contrast. The eye picks up these differences, which provide signals and separation. Visual separation tells the eye that something new is coming along. You can achieve it with contrast, with barriers or with formatting. Barriers are page elements that stop the eye. The most common barrier <197> and generally the best one <197> is white space. This book, for example, contains extra white space above <$IHeadings>headings and subheadings. Rules (lines across the page) are another effective barrier. Format can also provide visual separation. The way text is spaced and indented give clues to the reader. The more complex the document, the more important it is to use formatting to guide the reader <197> one reason technical documentation often has several levels of indents. Headings, subheadings, lists and quotes are often good candidates for special formatting.

But contrast and separation won't accomplish their purpose without consistency. Once a rule has been established, it should be used throughout the book. Every heading, for example, should use the same format.

<$IDesign;Design Guidelines for Books>Improving legibility is the fourth goal of page design. The way text is laid out on the page affects how easy it is to read.You must be careful to avoid designs that look good on the screen but are difficult to read for long stretches.

Making production easier and more efficient is the final goal of page design and certainly one of the most important. Page designs must take into account the realities of today's desktop publishing programs to minimize their weaknesses and play up their strengths. Often a few small changes can make a format much faster and easier to work and/or improve the final printed result. At the same time, a page design should be cost-efficient <197> for example, by using trim sizes that correspond to standard offset press dimensions.

ASCII File to create: C:\TEMP\8PRINT.TXT

@CHAP # = Chapter Seven

@CHAP TITLE = Offset Printing From Laser Mechanicals

@BODY FIRST = This is not a report on printing or production. Nevertheless, it will be valuable to briefly review the traditional production process. We can then examine how that process changes for desktop publishing. Our discussion centers around laser printers, but much of the advice also applies when electronic pages are sent to phototypesetting machines. The workflow is the same. The difference is that phototypeset pages don't need the extra precautions necessary with low-resolution laser type.

@HEAD1 = Traditional Book Printing

Traditionally, book publishers delivered camera-ready copy to the

lithographer (the commercial printer). This material was in the form of
<169>mechanicals.<170> Mechanicals were made by pasting type and line
art onto stiff mounting boards. These mechanicals were then photographed
to produce printing plates. Photographs were not pasted on the boards.
Original photographs have continuous tone <197> a full range of shades
ranging from dark to light. Printing is an all or nothing, black or
white process <197> either there's ink on the page or there's not. To
simulate continuous tone, a photograph must be <MI>screened<D>. This
process converts the photo into a <MI>halftone<D>. A halftone breaks the
photograph into tiny dots. Since the human eye perceives closely spaced
black dots as gray, a halftone permits a printing press to simulate the
shades of a continuous tone photograph.

Black and white line art can be treated like text <197> it does not
require a halftone. But continuous tone drawings <197> those with
shadings and gray tones <197> must be converted into halftones before
printing. Black and white pictures need one halftone. Color photographs
need four, one for each of the three primary colors and one for black.
These four halftones are called <MI>color separations<D>.

The more dots per inch, the better the quality of a halftone. Newspapers
typically use a screen of 65 to 85 dpi. Inexpensive books sometimes use
100-line screens (100 dpi), which give quality that's good but not
great. Modern photocopiers can reproduce screens up to 100 dpi. Most
books, however, are printed using the superior resolution of 133- to
150-line screens. After the halftoning process, the converted photograph
can be recombined with the text to form the complete page. How the
photographs are combined with the text depends on the type of printing.
<MI>Getting It Printed<D>, an outstanding book for anyone who buys
printing services, divides the industry into two categories: commercial
printers and quick printers. Commercial printers typically produce
longer jobs. They produce metal printing plates by combining line
negatives (negatives of the text and the line art) with halftone or
separation negatives (negatives of photographs). Quick printers are
sometimes used for short-run books. They produce plates directly without
an intervening negative stage. For this reason, photographs must be
pasted onto the page in the correct position before they are given to a
quick printer. Those photographs must first be converted to a printable
form through halftoning.

@HEAD1 = The Desktop Workflow

Desktop publishers do most of their paste-up electronically. Then they
substitute laser-printed pages for mounting boards. Typically, the text
is laid out first. Then line art is placed on the page, since line art
can be imported directly into page layout programs.

@HEAD2 = Preparing Photographs

Photographs, on the other hand, must still be handled the old-fashioned
way. Although page layout programs can accept scanned photos, the end
result is generally not up to the standards of book publishers. So a
space, or <MI>window<D> is created for each photo. What you do with the

window depends on whether you are using a commercial printer or a quick printer.

If you are going to a commercial printer, the windows are left blank. The photographs are given to him separately. He makes separate negatives of the text (including the windows) and the photos. At this time the photographs are screened (converted to a halftone) and scaled (re-sized) if necessary. Then the two negatives are combined in a process called <MI>stripping.<D> This method produces the best results. It is mandatory for color photographs.

There is a second, less expensive alternative for black and white photos. If you are using a quick printer, you must paste the photos onto the page directly. However, normal photos won't reproduce, so they must first be screened. Rather than creating a halftone negative, as you would for a commercial printer, you obtain a halftone <MI>positive<D>. hile it is being screened, the photo is also re-sized if necessary. This converted version of the photograph is pasted directly onto the laser-printed page, in the window. The combined page is given to the lithographer. This method is less expensive, because the lithographer no longer has to strip the two negatives together. He can take a single shot of the combined page and use it to create a printing plate. There is, however, some loss of image quality (reproducing a photo of a photo). There is also the risk that cut lines will show.

Positive halftones go by several different names, including <MI>PMTs<D>, <MI>veloxes<D> and <MI>stats.<D> Although there are slight differences, they all work in the same basic fashion. Many books and references state that 100 dpi is the best you can expect using the PMT method. In fact, knowledgeable printers can obtain results up to 120 dpi. The loss in quality, therefore, does not have to be great. On the other hand, this second alternative does require the desktop publisher to do some paste-up.

There are two easy ways to obtain a positive halftone. The best is to take the photo to a commercial printer or a trade camera shop. (To locate trade camera services, look in the yellow pages under <169>lithographic negative and plate makers.<170>) These services turn photos into positive halftones for $5 to $15 each. At the same time they can resize the photo if necessary. Ask them to use fixer during development. Otherwise the prints will yellow and fade in a few months.

When you get the screened PMTs back, check to make sure they are printed on pure white paper with no chemical stains. If quality is not a concern and the photo is the right size already, you can also buy special plastic screens. The plastic is pasted on top of the photograph on the page. Cost is $3 to $4 per sheet from most graphic arts supply houses. You can achieve up to 85 dpi or so with this method <197> somewhat less than the 100 dpi most experts consider the minimum for a professional-quality book. You can also use a 85 dpi or 100 dpi photocopier screen for "homemade" veloxes. Run the photo through the copier with the screen on top. Use the copier's facilities to enlarge or reduce. Paste the resulting image directly onto the page. <MI>Warning<D>: quality suffers with this method.

Use rubber cement to paste photos down. Pay extra attention to the edges
<197> if they lift up they will cause a shadow line on the printed page.
Use extra glue, then rub off any excess that shows after it's dry with a
special rubber cement lifter available at art supply stores. You can
also paste line art directly onto the page if you prefer to use existing
hand drawings rather than creating the art with the computer.

@HEAD2 = Positioning Photographs

Whether you strip photos or paste them on the page you must create a
window. Decide which photographs you plan to use, what size they will be
and where they belong in the text. Using the tools of the page layout
program, create a box for each picture. Make it the exact size you want
the final photo. Place a thin rule around the box. This rule is called
the keyline, and it's vital. The lithographer uses it to properly size
and position the halftone. So will you if you decide to paste positive
halftones directly onto the page. Normally the lithographer will drop
out the keyline so it does not show on the printed page. If you want the
rule to show, specify "Keyline prints" in your instructions.

Both the photos and the windows must be carefully labeled. Desktop
publishers have an advantage here. They can use the text editing
capabilities of the page layout software to insert labels in the center
of the blank window as they go along.

Here's another possibility for creating windows: draw a box as before.
Now use the page layout program to fill the box with black. This solid
black box is the equivalent of the Rubylith window some layout artists
use to key photographs to mechanicals. When the page is photographed by
the lithographer, the black box leaves a transparent window on the film
negative. The separately prepared halftone negative is positioned behind
this window.

With the keyline method, the lithographer actually cuts the negative
long the line before stripping in the halftone. This provides the
ultimate in quality, since there's no intervening layer of film. Ask the
printing company which method it prefers. If you are using the PMT or
velox method, keylines are the way to go. Why waste toner and print time
creating black boxes? All you need is something to indicate where to
paste down the velox.

@HEAD2 = Scanning and Digitizing

If the job requires special care, consider using a scanner to provide
position stats. In traditional publishing, a position stat is a
photocopy that's pasted on the page in the window. It's only function is
to show the printer what goes where. If you have a scanner, you can
accomplish the same thing electronically. Digitize the photograph and
place it in the window using the desktop publishing software. Scanned
images from today's technology are not good enough for reproduction. At
best they produce the equivalent of a 50 to 70-line screen. But scanned
images are the ultimate in convenience and safety. It's virtually
impossible to put the wrong picture on the page when you can look at a
sample. But they may be too much trouble for all but the most demanding

projects. Most scanners still cost over $1000. Creating scanned images requires extra time and effort. And storing the results demands lots of space on the hard disk.

If there's one thing a commercial printer wants it's consistency <197> consistent density and consistent placement. Density refers to the type. Placement refers to the position of folios, rules, column tops and bottoms, captions, key lines and other repeating page elements. They must be in the same place from page to page. Consider a rule at the top of the page. If the desktop publisher places it inconsistently, the lithographer will be unable to use it to align pages. The rule will <169>jump<170> up and down as the reader pages through the book. And it may not match up across the top of facing pages.

@HEAD1 = Crop Marks

While using the page layout program, you can take several steps to make life easier for the lithographer. One is to add keylines for photos, as discussed above. Another is to place crop marks on each page. Crop marks are also known as <169>register<170> or <169>corner<170> marks. These tiny lines help the lithographer position the page. Lithographers can work without crop marks. In such cases, they try to line up each page by using the folio or a rule as the <169>anchor.<170>

Some lithographers also suggest avoiding ragged right margins. Ragged right is a good effect for certain brochures and newsletters, but it's generally inappropriate for books. If margins are even and consistent, the lithographer can use them to help position the pages. But commercial printers are happier when they can work from crop marks. Most prefer hairline rules placed just outside the live area. However, some lithographers like register marks placed inside the trim area. Ask in advance, then use your page layout program to produce the marks.

The specifics of creating crop marks depends on the software. In Ventura Publisher, for example, lines placed on the Underlying Page appear on every page of the document. Ventura also has a built-in crop marks feature. Most software packages have a similar "Master Page," "Repeating Page" or "Underlying Page" feature to place crop marks throughout the manuscript.

@HEAD1 = Screen Tints

Most page layout programs provide screen tints. A screen is a pattern of tiny dots. With black ink, the dots make an area look gray. With colored ink they give a light tint. Lithographers use percentages to describe the amount of ink laid down. A 10% screen is very light; a 90% screen is very dark. Screen tints are used to highlight an area, to set text apart and to accent charts and graphs. Often type is <MI>overprinted<D> <197> laid down on top of the tint.

Short-run publishers who use quick printers must supply complete mechanicals. They must, therefore, put the screen tint on the page themselves. One alternative is to use the page layout program. Trouble is, the dots produced by laser printers are too large for top-quality screens. There's no problem if the screen if simply used as a pattern to fill in a pie chart or a graph. But if type is difficult to read when placed on top of a coarse screen. The smaller the type, the harder it is to read. To minimize problems, use screens of 20% or less (if the program doesn't specify percentages, use one of the two lightest shades). eep the type as large as possible <197> 14 points or bigger if possible.

An alternative is to buy tint material from an art supply store and paste it over the area to be screened. Use this option if you must put small type inside a large screened area. Buy tint material with the highest resolution you can find.

Publishers who use commercial printers should ask the printer do the screen. Indicate the area to be screened. Use a non-reproducing blue pencil, a stick-on Post-It note or write the instructions on top of a see-through tissue overlay.

@HEAD1 = Color printing

Multicolored documents are created in several passes through the printing press. Each time another color is added to a page, it must be sent through the press again. The lithographer must have a separate plate for each color. Normally, the commercial printer makes these color separations. It costs extra, of course. But desktop publishers can easily create their own separations, thereby saving money and time.

The process described here works for spot color. Continuous tone color photographs must still be handled using traditional methods. The method relies on the ability of some software to specify the color of different text elements. It is most effective with programs such as Xerox Ventura Publisher that use style sheets <197> document formatting guidelines that can be prepared once and used over and over again.

This paragraph describes a method for Ventura Publisher, but it can be adapted to other programs as well.

Let's use a two-color example. The same principles would apply for more than two colors. Consider, for instance, black text with blue headings. Start by creating the document as normal. The style sheet for this step will have all text elements specified as black. Now create another style sheet for each color. These style sheets will be identical to the first except for the color of the text elements.

To create a color separation for the black text, specify that all the headings (all the blue text) should print in white. By changing the color to white, the text disappears <197> white text on white paper is invisible. The beauty of this method is that the invisible headings are still on the page. Consequently, the position of the page elements does not change. The overlay for each color will match up with the others.

The third and final style sheet reverses the process. All the headings print in black. Everything else is set to print in white. When you print this version out on the laser printer, it shows only the text that is to be printed in blue ink. The lithographer will match the two separations to create a composite page with the black and the blue text in perfect registration.

The beauty of the system described here is its speed and ease-of-use. The only real investment in time is to create the two extra style sheets. Once these have been prepared, the user can create color separations in moments just by calling up the different style sheets and printing out the separate versions. If your page layout program does not have these capabilities, you can simulate the effect by manually deleting text, as long as you do so without changing the position of anything on the page. Naturally, you can also use the traditional method. Specify which elements are to be what color and let the printer prepare the separations.

@HEAD1 = Covers

Some publishers may be tempted to produce covers using laser mechanicals. It is not recommended. Most covers use display type on slick stock. That's simply too demanding for the 300 dpi resolution of laser printers. The imperfections stand out. The design of the cover is also an issue. Most publishers are unlikely to do as good a job as a professional designer. Buyers judge books by their covers, especially wholesalers, distributors and retailers. If those individuals aren't impressed, your books will never get on the shelves for readers to find. The most common failing of small independent publishers is to put a good book inside a shoddy, amateurish cover. If you insist on producing camera ready art for the cover, send the file to a phototypesetter for high resolution output. And be sure to calculate carefully for the spine. You must know the number of pages and the bulk of the paper (the pages per inch) to figure the correct width. Printers say it is very difficult to correct for an improperly-sized spine.

@HEAD1 = Adjusting Page Count

Desktop publishing differs from traditional publishing in another key aspect <197> the ability to make last minute changes. That capability can be put to good use to make the books you publish mesh properly with the work customs of commercial printers.

The final page count is vitally important to a book printing job, and desktop publishers are ideally suited to adapt to the constraints of the printing industry. Lithographers print in signatures of 16 and 32 pages. You can save money by working within these limitations. Poor planning can force the lithographer to add a "bastard eight" (an undersized, eight-page signature). This extra work can add a surprising amount to the total print bill.

And it's unnecessary, since desktop publishing gives you the control to tailor books to the right size. If the final page count is not a multiple of 16, make changes until it fits. Often a small change creates a substantial difference by the time it ripples through the entire manuscript. To shorten a book, try removing words and lines. Add hyphens to shorten paragraphs. Expand margins slightly. Reduce the size of illustrations. Go down a point size or two. Or try a different typestyle <197> some take more space than others, even when set at the same size and line spacing.

In other cases, you might want to up the page count. For instance, you might be able to increase 156 pages to 160 by removing a single line from each page. An added bonus would be more white space and a more readable manuscript. Or you could add illustrations, or make existing illustrations slightly larger. As long as you need extra pages to fill up the signature anyway, consider adding some order cards at the back, or a page or two of sales copy and testimonials at the front.

@HEAD1 = Improving the Look of Laser-printed Pages

Several advanced techniques can boost the quality of pages printed from laser mechanicals. Although desktop laser printers can create impressive documents, the density and resolution of the type simply isn't up to the standards of traditional phototypesetters. Nowhere is this more apparent than when laser output is used as mechanicals for offset printing. Three problems occur most often:

@BULLET = Washed out areas <197> sections or even entire pages that have a pale gray, washed-out appearance

@BULLET = Broken letters <197> characters where small sections have dropped out

@BULLET = The jaggies <197> rough, uneven edges and diagonals caused by the low resolution of laser printers

Fortunately, there are tricks and techniques that improve the quality of pages printed from laser mechanicals.

@HEAD2 = Improving Mechanicals

SELECTING THE RIGHT TYPEFACE is the first step. Some typefaces are more suitable than others for offset reproduction. If you produce more than one or two books each year, experiment with different typefaces. It may be cost effective to purchase additional fonts, either from the original supplier or from an outside company. As a bonus, your documents will not have the all-to-familiar "Times-Roman body, Helvetica headlines" look that is common to 90% of all desktop publishing documents.

Getting dark, dense type is the next challenge. Laser printers, unfortunately, are plagued by drop outs and washed out, gray areas. Sometimes, the problem lies with the toner or the toner cartridge. It also has to do with the way printers work. Some laser printer engines are better than others at creating solid black areas. The Canon CX engine at the heart of most first- generation laser printers was notorious for weak, gray letters. If your printer has a front panel control of any kind, put it on the darkest setting. Many pros also suggest removing the toner cartridge and rotating it. This may overcome clumping and clotting and help achieve a uniform print quality across the page. And some cartridges work better than others. When you find one that creates dense, dark type, set it aside and save it for special print jobs.

It's best to have type as dark and dense as possible. Nevertheless, if all the pages are slightly pale, most lithographers can compensate. What they hate is type that fluctuates from page to page or, worst of all, within each page. Check each page before the job goes to the lithographer. Reprint any pages that aren't consistent.

SPRAYING WITH A MATTE FIXATIVE usually causes laser-printed pages to <169>darken up.<170> Not only does the fixative make black areas appear darker, it also protects the pages. Fixative helps prevent smears, fingerprints and flaking. The aerosol cans are sold at art supply stores. Any fixative suitable for charcoal drawings will also work with laser-printed pages.

SPECIAL LASER PRINTER PAPER is sometimes recommended for laser mechanicals. The theory is that this paper has whiter whites and blacker blacks. It also has a smoother even coating that makes it easier for the camera operator to produce a good negative. Warning: Some desktop publishers complain that certain coated laser papers jam repeatedly in laser printers. Buy a small sample and test first.

Special paper may be an especially good idea for publishers who create galleys with the laser printer and paste them up using traditional methods. Some special papers contain wax holdout that minimizes problems from waxing and paste-up. Be aware, however, that coated papers must be treated with care. The laser-printer type tends to crack and fall off if coated pages are bent, folded or stacked.

PHOTOREDUCTION is a difficult technique, but it also has great potential for improving pages from laser mechanicals. Reducing an image makes flaws less apparent. (Conversely, enlarging magnifies flaws. That's why you should never enlarge laser type). By reducing laser type, you increase its apparent resolution. Most laser printers create type at 300 dpi. Researchers think the human eye loses its ability to distinguish dots at about 450 dpi. Most phototypesetters produce at 900 dpi or higher.

It would seem an obvious step, then, to create pages at a larger size and reduce them down. In practice, this method creates problems. You can, for example, start with 18 point type and photoreduce it to 10 points. Unfortunately, the letterspacing and line spacing will be incorrect. Although subtle, these spacing problems begin to be noticeable when type is reduced more than 10 percent or so. In addition, fine lines or dot patterns may end up too thin to print, or disappear altogether. You may not want to make a small face even smaller or decrease the margins too much.

Careful planning is essential to make sure everything fits properly on the page after the photoreduction. As anyone who has sized photos already knows, its easy to make mistakes. Basically, it's just another step and one that many publishers don't want to bother with.

THERE IS A SIMPLER METHOD for pages where the live area is 5 x 7 or
smaller. Start by laying out the page exactly as you would otherwise.
Use normal linespacing, letterspacing and type sizes. At print time,
however, use the Print dialog box to enlarge. The laser printer will
increase by the percentage you specify. (Note: Some programs cannot
perform this enlargement function. Others require a separate, add-on
program.)

Now take the enlarged page to the lithographer and instruct him to
reduce back down to the original size. Since these are the dimensions
you originally worked with, everything will be exactly as you saw it on
the screen. The letterspacing, margins, and so on will be correct, but
the type will be at a higher apparent resolution.

Why doesn't this technique work for pages larger than 5 x 7? Today's
laser printers accept 8 1/2 x 11 paper, but they can only print to
within an inch or so of the margin, for an effective live area of only 7
1/2 x 10. You can enlarge a 5 x 7 page up to about 150% before you run
out of room. When you bring this 150% enlargement back down to the
original 5 X 7, you will have achieved an effective resolution of 450
dpi.

This photoreduction technique can distinctly improve the look of a page.
One Southern California publishing company, for example, wanted to
produce a final live area of 3 3/4 x 6. Through trial and error, they
discovered they could enlarge by 165% before coming up against the laser
printer's "dead zone." By bringing this enlargement back down to the
original size, they achieved an apparent resolution approaching 500 dpi.

What if you must produce pages larger than 5 x 7? Access to an 11 x 17
printer is one answer. The Dataproducts LZR-2665 is a PostScript
compatible laser printer that produces 11 x 17 pages at 26 ppm. At
$17,900, it's too high-priced for most desktop publishers, but you may
be able to find a service bureau or print center to output final copy
for a page charge.

@HEAD2 = The Lithographer Can Help

So far we've covered how the publisher should prepare laser mechanicals.
In addition, the lithographer can take steps to improve the final output.

ALTERING THE EXPOSURE is one relatively simple technique. The kind of
alteration depends on whether the lithographer creates a positive or a
negative. In either case, the idea is the same: to alter the exposure so
the type looks darker. For the traditional, high-quality method
involving a film negative, a 10 percent underexposure is generally
enough to help "fill in" the type.

Discuss this concept with the lithographer. Most of them are more
familiar with the same procedure done in reverse. For example, when
creating negatives, camera operators will often <MI>over<D>expose. This
causes tiny specks and dots to disappear and become white. Sometimes
operators refer to a "dropout" halftone, since the overexposure causes
imperfections and small details to drop out. If the operator knows how

to alter exposure for dropouts, ask if he can do the same thing in reverse to make the type denser. One warning: When you darken the type, you also darken dirt, dust and other imperfections that would normally disappear. Both the publisher and the lithographer must take exceptional care to make sure the mechanicals are spotless.

THE PAPER STOCK can also make a difference. Work with the lithographer to select the paper that gives the best look for the money. There may not be much point in going to expensive coated stock. Slick paper only brings out the shortcomings of laser type by making jagged edges and drop outs more visible. On the other hand, cheap newsprint will cause the ink to spread, making characters even fuzzier. A good grade of uncoated book stock is probably the best bet. Ask the lithographer to run some tests and give his suggestions.

Chapter NINE

ASCII File to create: C:\TEMP\9TECH.TXT

```
@TITLE = The Laser AstroZ
@TITLE SUB = Guide to Operations<197> Model XYZ-11
@HEAD1 = Getting Started
@HEAD2 = A Word to Owners
```

Thank you for choosing the Laser AstroZ printer from XYZ Corporation. This high quality laser printer gives you the flexibility and power for all your desktop publishing needs. The Laser AstroZ comes standard with PostScript, as well as Hewlett-Packard PCL and HPGL for programs you still use that are non-PostScript compatible.

```
@HEAD3 = Introduction
```

First we'll show you hot to unpack and install your Laser AstroZ printer. You should carefully check to make sure you have the following items:
```
@LIST BULLET = ONE IBM PC DISKETTE in 5-1/4" format
@LIST BULLET = A PRINT TRAY and manual feed guide
@LIST BULLET = A PAPER CASSETTE and toner cartridge
@HEAD2 = You and Your Printer
```

Before you install your printer, make sure it is located in a well-ventilated area away from direct sunlight. Check to make sure that your office's electrical wiring is adequate. The line voltage should not vary from the factory warrantied voltage marked on the back of the printer. Avoid placing the printer in an office with abrupt changes in temperature. Do not place the printer near open faucets, heaters, air conditioners, humidifiers, or radiators.

Place the printer on a flat surface 8-9 inches away from the wall. Leave enough room in the front for the cartridge door to open freely.

@BODY SMALL = This manual prepared by the publications and communications department, XYZ Corporation, Los Angeles, CA.

@HEAD1 = Unpacking and Setting Up

@HEAD2 = Unpacking

Your Laser AstroZ weighs 73 pounds, so do not try to lift it without someone's help. Lift the printer by its handles and place it on a clean, stable surface.

Lift the release lever and raise the upper part of the printer

Lift the green fixing assembly cover and remove the four red spacers.

Locate the green wire cleaner and remove its protective sealing tape. You will use the wire cleaner to clean the corona wire in the print cartridge.

@HEAD2 = The Care of Your Printer

There are several routine maintenance procedures you can perform to keep your Laser AstroZ running smoothly. You should be familiar with:
@LIST BULLET = Replacing the toner cartridge and cleaning stick
@LIST BULLET = Cleaning the corona wires
@LIST BULLET = Cleaning the guides
@LIST BULLET = Cleaning and replacing the separation belts

@HEAD2 = About the Toner Cartridge

The toner cartridge includes powder that serves as ink to the printer. The cartridge itself has a color coded bar that will indicate the level of powder and the number of prints. If you print plain text (not graphics) at a higher toner setting, you will get more prints than if you print graphics at a lower setting. If your prints begin to look faded in areas, or streaked at the edges, replace your toner cartridge.

Paper trays, Paper cassettes

@HEAD5 = Paper trays

<B>Print tray position<D>. Hold the print tray so the wide end faced towards the front of the printer. Insert the plastic pins into the front slots above the handle.

NOTE: Do not overload the paper tray. Packing it too full will cause paper jams and print errors.

<B>Attach the Manual Feed Guide<D>. Hold the manual feed guide with the

plastic brackets towards the rear of the printer. Face the ribbed side up.

<B>Load Paper in Manual Feed.<D> Insert one sheet of paper at a time. Glide the paper along the tray until it can't go any further, then stop.

@HEAD5 = Paper Cassettes

Place the paper in the cassette and push it under the paper clips. Insert the paper cassette into the slot under the front of the printer until it stops. The cassette holds approximately 110 sheets.

NOTE: If you want to print on letterhead, place the paper FACE DOWN beneath the clips.

@HEAD1 = A Quick Tour of the Laser AstroZ

ASCII File to create: C:\TEMP\9TBL.TXT

FRONT PANEL LIGHTS
<B>LIGHT<D>
<B>STATE<D>
<B>INDICATION<D>
Ready
Flashing
Flashing Warming Up
Ready
Steady
Ready to Use
Ready
Dark
Power Off
Active/Paper Out
Flashing
Processing Data
Active/Paper Out
Dark
Idle
Active/Paper Out
Steady
Paper Out
Paper Jam<R>
Steady<R>
Paper Jam<R> <MI>See Troubleshooting<D>

Colophon

Desktop publishing is in its infancy. Users are still learning how to integrate this new technology into their business operations. Our experiences at New Riders Publishing may help others who are making the transition to electronic page layout, especially those in a workgroup environment.

We learned a number of valuable lessons while putting *Publishing Power* together. The most difficult issue is not the technology, but how to manage it:

- How to name files to distinguish different sections, authors, versions, etc.

- How to archive

- How to notate and handle revisions

- How to get the right files to the right people

Project management becomes crucial, especially in workgroups where people work in parallel. Putting documents into electronic form makes it essential to carefully track each job. The more pages and pictures, the harder it is to keep everything organized.

We haven't found all the answers yet at New Riders, but at least we are beginning to ask ourselves the right questions. Hard disk organization was the starting point. All four workstations had identically-named subdirectories, so we could use DOS copy to move files back and forth. We started with a \POWER subdirectory, where we stored the style sheet. Below that was a subdirectory for each chapter. These chapter subdirectories were further subdivided for the chapter and text, pictures, and sample documents.

\Power

   \01
     \Chapter
     \Pictures
     \Sample

   \02
     \Chapter
     \Pictures
     \Sample

and so on for the rest of the book.

File names identified the book, the revision and the chapter. For instance, PV1-03 represented *Publishing Power with Ventura* (PV), the first revision (1), Chapter Three (-03). File extensions identified the type of file (word processing format, graphics format, etc.). Thus, PV1-03.CHP was the chapter file and PV1-03.WS was its WordStar text file. The system date and time (attached to files by DOS) were used as a last check against accidentally writing old versions on top of new ones. Each chapter had its own separate floppy disk backup (labeled and dated to avoid confusion with previous versions).

Because this book has so many pages and so many pictures, we experienced a few software glitches. Our magic number was 50. We seemed to be free of problems as long as the total of pages and frames was less than 50 — 30 pages of text with 20 frames; or 40 pages with 10 frames; etc.

We learned some other lessons, too (most of them the hard way). Here's our advice:

• Create a style guide for authors, so they can (1) put text files in the right form and (2) pretag the files.

• Perfect the style sheet before starting layout, even if it means running out a few test chapters.

• Work from a single chapter template for the entire book to guarantee that crop marks, headers, footers, frame sizes, margins and other repeating elements are identical from chapter to chapter.

- Check pages from the laser printer against a template (we use a light table). Otherwise, variations in laser printer output may create problems (for example, crop marks or headers that are slightly out of position).

Here are the production details:

Type style: Century Schoolbook (11-point body text), Helvetica (display, captions, headers)
Offset masters produced from 300 dpi laser output
Trim size: 7 x 9 inches, perfect bound.
Printing: Web offset, Griffin Printing Company, Glendale, CA
Paper stock: Hammermill Accent Opaque, 60#, white vellum
Cover: 12pt Frankote C1s

And here are the products we used to create this book.

File Management

Xtree
Executive Systems, Inc.
15300 Ventura Blvd. #305
Sherman Oaks, CA 91403

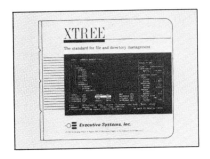

Graphics

AutoCAD
Autodesk, Inc.
2320 Marinship Way
Sausalito, CA 94965

Gem Draw Plus
Digital Research
Box DRI
Monterey, CA 93942

PC Paintbrush Plus
ZSoft Corporation
1950 Spectrum Circle #A-495
Marietta, GA 30067

Page Layout

Xerox Ventura Publisher
Xerox Corporation
Xerox Square
Rochester, NY 14644

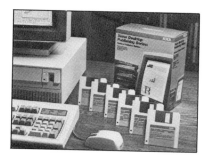

Screen Capture

HotShot
Symsoft
PO Box 4477
Mountain View, CA 94040

Word Processing

Microsoft Word
Microsoft Corporation
10611 NE 36th St.
Redmond, WA 98073

WordStar Professional 4.0
MicroPro International Corp.
33 San Pablo Ave.
San Rafael, CA 94903

Personal Computers

AST Premium/286
AST Research, Inc.
2121 Alton Ave.
Irvine, CA 92714

Monitors

Verticom 2Page Display
Verticom
545 Weddell Drive
Sunnyvale, CA 94089-2114

Sigma LaserView Plus
Sigma Designs, Inc.
4650 Landing Parkway
Fremont, CA 94538

Wyse W700
Wyse Technology
3571 N. First
San Jose, CA 95134

Mouse

Logitech Serial Mouse
Logitech U.S.A.
6505 Kaiser Drive
Fremont, CA 94555

Printer

Apple LaserWriter Plus
Apple Computer
20525 Mariani Ave.
Cupertino, CA 95014

The Power Disk

The Power Disk contains text files, style sheets and chapter files for use with the sample projects in *Publishing Power With Ventura*. You may obtain as many original copies of the Power Disk as you need by using the order form at the back of this book, or by phoning the number shown on the form.

The Power Disk requires Xerox Ventura Publisher Version 1.1 and PC-DOS/MS-DOS 2.0 or higher.

Benefits

The Power Disk saves time. It allows you to get right to the heart of the sample projects by copying text files, style sheets and chapter files to your hard disk. It contains many pages of text that you would otherwise need to type on your own. In addition, it includes style sheets with predefined tags, margins, columns and other basics. Because the style sheets are partially encoded, you can focus on the specific topics at hand, without the need to recreate basic parameters before startings.

Disclaimer

The Power Disk is provided on an as-is basis, as a convenience. New Riders Publishing is not liable or responsible to any person or entity with respect to any loss or damage in connection with or arising from the use of the disk. The disk is subject to change at any time without notice.

Copying the Disk

Before starting, make a backup copy of the disk using DISKCOPY. Store the original in a safe place, and use the copy as the working disk. The Power Disk is copyrighted. It is intended for your personal use. It may not be sold or transferred for profit.

After making a backup copy, you are ready to install the files onto the hard disk for use with the book.

- Put the working Power Disk in drive A:.

- Change to the A: drive.

- To read the documentation (a duplicate of this appendix) on screen, type HELP at the A: prompt. (Or enter the command TYPE README.1ST.)

- To stop the screen from scrolling, type Ctrl-S. Type Ctrl-S again to start the scrolling again.

- To produce a separate hard copy, turn your printer on and type COPY README.1ST PRN.

Installing on Hard Disk C:

You may install the Power Disk with a simple DOS COPY procedure provided (1) that your hard disk is designated as C: and (2) that you are able to set up a separate C:\POWER subdirectory. If you do not meet *both* conditions, you must also perform the additional procedure below titled "If Your Hard Disk Is Designated Other Than C:."

WARNING: If you use DOS COPY to move the files from the Power Disk to any place other than C:\POWER without following the additional procedures explained below, we cannot guarantee that it will work properly.

To use the Power Disk with the book, you will perform two steps: (1) create a C:\POWER subdirectory and (2) copy all the files from the floppy to that new subdirectory. Here are the steps to take:

- Move to the C: disk.

- At the C:> prompt type:

```
MD \POWER
CD \POWER
```

■ Put the working Power Disk in drive A:.

■ Type:

```
COPY A:*.*
```

The installation is complete. Remove the working Power disk from the A: drive and store it in a safe place. You may proceed to Chapter One and begin work.

If Your Hard Disk Is Designated Other Than C:

If your hard disk is named other than C:, you must perform an additional Multi-Chapter function before you can begin work. For instance, your hard disk may be designated as D:. Or, you may already have a C:\POWER subdirectory to which you do not wish to add any additional files. In either case, you can use the Power Disk, but only if you use the Multi-Chapter procedures explained below.

Ventura's chapters contain pointers that tell the program where to find the files it needs. The sample chapters on the Power disk point to the C:\POWER subdirectory. If you place them anywhere else, you must change their pointers before they will work properly. DOS COPY does not change the pointers. To do that you must use Multi-Chapter from the Options Menu.

First, decide where you want to place the Power files. For illustration, we will assume that you wish to place them in a subdirectory called D:\SAMPLE. In the instructions below, substitute the actual disk drive and subdirectory you wish to use whenever you see D:\SAMPLE.

WARNING: You must follow the installation instructions in the order shown. Otherwise, we cannot guarantee that it will work correctly.

■ Move to the D: disk.

■ At the D:> prompt type:

```
MD \SAMPLE
CD \SAMPLE
```

- Put the working Power Disk in drive A:. Do not remove it until the end of this procedure.

- Type:

  `COPY A:*.*`

- Load Ventura Publisher. Once it is on the screen, select Multi-Chapter from the Options menu. You do not need to open a chapter first.

- If there is a chapter showing in the Item Selector, make sure that it is NOT highlighted by clicking elsewhere inside the dialog box to deselect it.

- Select Open from the list at the side of the Multi-Chapter dialog box. The Item Selector will appear.

- Move the cursor to the Directory line. Press Esc to clear the line. Type:

  `A:\CHAPTERS\*.PUB`

- Press Enter

Ventura will look on your A: drive for publications. An Item Selector will appear. It will show only one publication, called POWER.PUB.

- Click on POWER.PUB to select it. Click OK.

The Multi-Chapter dialog box will now show a list of the chapters, A:6\CHAPTERS\NEWSLET.CHP and A:\CHAPTERS\8PRINT.CHP, that make up the POWER publication.

- Select Copy All from the list at the right side of the dialog box.

The Copy All dialog box will appear. At the top is a Source section that shows the publication A:\CHAPTERS\POWER.PUB.

- Move to the Destination section. Put the cursor on the line labeled PUB & CHPs. Press Esc to clear the line. Type in the name of your destination subdirectory. For example:

D:\SAMPLE

- Click once on the button titled Make All Directories the Same As the First.

All the directories will now read D:\SAMPLE.

➡ *NOTE: Before you click OK to start the archive process read the following warning.*

WARNING: As Ventura copies the chapter files onto your hard disk, you will see one or more of the following messages. You should respond by choosing the uppermost button as explained below.

■ Click OK.

Ventura will display several messages like the one below:

```
D:\SAMPLE\6NEWSLET.CHP already exists on the tar-
get drive. Do you wish to overwrite the old ver-
sion, keep the old file, or cancel the archive
process?
```

■ Choose Overwrite (the uppermost button).

You may also see a message similar to this one:

```
This file could not be found: C:\VENTURA\OUT-
PUT.WID. Do you wish to skip over it or retry with
a new disk, or cancel the archive process?
```

■ Choose Skip (the uppermost button).

When Ventura has finished copying, it will return you to the Multi-Chapter dialog box. You are ready to exit.

■ Choose Done

Remove the Power disk from drive A:. You are ready to begin work.

➡ *NOTE: See Chapter One for more information about Ventura files and pointers. See Chapters Three and Seven for hands-on practice with Multi-Chapter.*

Index

The Desktop Power Series

Market-leading how-to books, reference guides, companion disks and training materials for corporate and technical publishing from the desktop.

Inside Xerox Ventura Publisher

A Guide to Professional-Quality
Desktop Publishing on the IBM PC
James Cavuoto and Jesse Berst
328 pages, 130 illustrations
ISBN 0-934035-13-X, $19.95

The all-time bestselling Ventura book, newly revised and up-dated. Written by two of the industry's leading experts, this comprehensive reference takes readers from beginning commands through advanced concepts in one easy-to-understand guide. *Inside Xerox Ventura Publisher* includes inside information unavailable from any other source — dozens of undocumented short-cuts, advanced functions and tips.

"A remarkably clear guide..."
    Dr. C.J. Wallia, Editor, *Technical Communications*

"...a must for getting the most from Ventura..."
    Amy Wohl, *The Wohl Report on End-User Computing*

Publishing Power With Ventura

The Complete Teaching Guide to Xerox Ventura Publisher
Martha Lubow and Jesse Berst
576 pages, 230 illustrations
ISBN 0-934035-19-9, $24.95

Learn by doing! The first and only book that covers ALL of Ventura's commands and functions with simple, step-by-step tutorials. A top trainer and a noted Ventura expert lead you through the creation of real-life business documents. Hundreds of sample screens make it simple to follow along. The ideal book to help both the beginner and the advanced user tap the full potential and power of Ventura Publisher.

Publishing Power Disk

IBM-compatible floppy disk, $14.95

This companion disk to Publishing Power With Ventura contains every text file and style sheet used in the book. Beginners save time and effort because they don't have to type in text files to follow along with the book's examples. Advanced users also save time because the style sheets contain dozens of preformatted tags. Users are spared the effort of redefining basic tags, margins, columns, etc., so they can concentrate on advanced skills and techniques.

Publishing Power Book/Disk Combination

576-page book and IBM-compatible floppy disk
ISBN 0-934035-25-3, $39.90

And Just For Fun...

Cookies!

Low-Cost Software
IBM-compatible floppy disk and instruction booklet, $6.95

Tired and listless in the morning when you boot your computer? Cookies will put the fun back into computing. This IBM-compatible program displays a fortune every time it is run. Install it and get a cookie every day before you start work. Cookies can also tell you one-liners, helpful tips or whatever you decide. Comes with a batch of cookies ready-to-run. If they get stale, mix up a batch of your own!

Order Form

Yes, please send me the productivity-boosting books and disks checked below:

☐ **Check enclosed, payable to New Riders Publishing**

☐ **Charge to my credit card:**　　**Phone Orders: Call (818) 991-5392**

　　☐ **VISA**

　　☐ **MasterCharge**

Card #: _____

Expiration: _____

Signature: _____

Name: _____
(please print or type)

Company: _____

Address: _____

City: _____

State: _____ Zip: _____

Quantity	Description	Unit Cost	Total Cost
	Inside Xerox Ventura Publisher	$19.95	
	Publishing Power With Ventura (book only)	$24.95	
	Publishing Power Disk (disk only)	$14.95	
	Publishing Power With Ventura (book/disk)	$39.90	
	Cookies	$ 6.95	

New Riders Publishing
PO Box 4846
Thousand Oaks, CA 91360
(818) 991-5392

Shipping and Handling: See below	
Sales Tax: Californians please add 6.5%	
Total	

Shipping and handling: $3.50 for the first book and $1.00 for each additional book. Floppy disks $1.50. Add $15.00 for overseas delivery. Rush: $5.00 additional plus actual air freight charge.

To order: Fill in the reverse side, fold, and mail

NO POSTAGE
NECESSARY IF
MAILED IN THE
UNITED STATES

BUSINESS REPLY MAIL
FIRST CLASS PERMIT NO. 53   THOUSAND OAKS, CA

POSTAGE WILL BE PAID BY ADDRESSEE

NEW RIDERS PUBLISHING
P.O. Box 4846-P
Thousand Oaks, CA 91360